THE CONSERVATIVE ASCENDANCY

The
Conservative
Ascendancy

HOW THE GOP RIGHT
MADE POLITICAL HISTORY

Donald T. Critchlow

HARVARD UNIVERSITY PRESS
Cambridge, Massachusetts
London, England
2007

Publication of this book has been supported through the generous
provisions of the Maurice and Lula Bradley Smith Memorial Fund.

Library of Congress Cataloging-in-Publication Data
Critchlow, Donald T., 1948–
The conservative ascendancy : how the GOP right made political history / Donald T.
Critchlow.
p. cm.
Includes bibliographical references and index.
ISBN-13: 978-0-674-02620-9 (alk. paper)
ISBN-10: 0-674-02620-9 (alk. paper)
1. Republican Party (U.S. : 1845–)   2. Conservatism--United States--History.   3. United
States--Politics and government--1945–   I. Title.
JK2356.C73   2007
324.273409'045--dc22   2007023730

Contents

THE CONSERVATIVE ASCENDANCY

Introduction

In 2004 President George W. Bush, running as an avowed conservative, won reelection to the White House. His victory marked a fifty-year struggle by the GOP Right against the liberal political order. Conservative Republicans had built a well-disciplined, highly structured, well-financed, and soundly organized political machine able to mobilize partisan support at the grassroots level. Through this mobilization of supporters, Bush had introduced a level of partisanship into American politics unseen since the nineteenth century.

The Republican electoral triumph in 2004 was the culmination of a half-century of struggle by the Right to achieve political power in the United States. In the immediate aftermath of the Second World War, a small band of intellectuals launched a movement to stop what they saw as the advance of the collectivist state embodied in modern liberalism and the New Deal political order. They were joined by anti-Communist activists across grassroots America. These two forces, intellectual and popular, laid the foundations for the GOP Right. In their struggle against the dominant liberal state, conservatives gained control of the Republican party by defeating its liberal eastern wing. Their advance against liberalism and the Democratic party proved less steady, however. Indeed, at many points in the ensuing struggle, the GOP Right appeared headed for defeat and even political obscurity. Yet it held the course and pressed forward.

Modern liberalism proved to be a formidable opponent, politically and institutionally. The administrative state established in the New Deal and later expanded in the 1960s by Lyndon Johnson's Great Society institutionalized a liberal regime that was not easily overturned by conservative opponents. For years the GOP Right had proclaimed the principles of small government, individual responsibility, and free enterprise as an alternative to modern liberalism. After winning the White House and Congress, however, Republicans discovered firsthand that the modern welfare state was not so easily dismantled. The great majority of Americans had come to accept that through such programs as Social Security and Medicare, the federal government played an essential role in their lives. Even before winning election to the White House in 2000, presidential candidate George W. Bush appeared to have acknowledged this fact of political life by identifying himself as a "compassionate conservative." He promised to reform Social Security and Medicare without dismantling the welfare state. This led some conservative pundits to claim that Bush was not one of them, a true conservative. Their disapproval intensified following the Republicans' loss of Congress in 2006. Such criticism reveals the inevitable stress between purity of principle and political practice, intellectuals and politicians, and ideology and power.

The conservative ascendancy manifested an even deeper dilemma: The Right's ideology was vehemently antistatist in an age of mass democracy and Cold War hostilities. The quandary of modern conservatism was eloquently captured by the longtime anti–New Dealer journalist John T. Flynn, who observed that *civilized life is not possible without adequate government, but . . . government itself can be the greatest of social evils.*.[1] Flynn understood a central paradox of postwar conservatism: To dismantle power, you must first gain power. Support of the Cold War entailed the expansion of government through increased military expenditures, an arms race, and an interventionist foreign policy. By accepting the Cold War and America's responsibility to confront Soviet Communism, postwar conservatives accepted an expanded role for government and the erection of a huge military-industrial complex. They saw no alternative when confronted by the dangers that Soviet Communism posed to American national security. A libertarian tendency within the American Right accused conservatives of abandoning a central tenet of the Right—the belief that centralized government should be feared as an enemy to individual liberty—but this criticism remained confined to a small circle of ideological purists. Nonetheless, it struck at the core of the conservative dilemma in postwar America.

This book explores the ideological contradictions and political tensions that arose as the New Deal political coalition, based on urban voters in the North, labor unions, ethnic and racial minorities, and southern whites, fell apart and as a new conservative coalition sought to replace it. New Deal politics was premised on an industrial order composed of a unionized workforce earning high wages and benefits in a regulated corporate economy based on mass-production manufacturing. A welfare system was designed to take care of those citizens unable to work—widows, the disabled, the injured, the unemployed, and the aged. Farmers were to be provided with subsidies and price supports. In constructing the New Deal order, liberals had been constrained by the southern wing of the Democratic party and by Republican opponents. As a consequence, liberals failed to enact national health insurance or guarantee voting rights for African Americans in the segregated South.

In the second half of the twentieth century, the movement to a postindustrial economy undermined the New Deal liberal vision of the good society. The economy that emerged competed in a globalized marketplace. The workforce became more white collar and less unionized. As the focus on mass production shifted to high tech, companies left the large cities in the East for more favorable business environments in the Sunbelt. Deteriorating conditions in the cities, racial tensions, and opportunities for a better life led people to the suburbs. In this postindustrial society, traditional family structure was transformed. More women went to college and developed professional careers. Marriage ages increased, family size decreased, and the divorce rate went up. Middle-class affluence allowed Americans to devote more time to lifestyle and spiritual issues. Secular values challenged traditional religious values, while many Christian denominations emphasized self-fulfillment instead of sin, punishment, and eternal redemption. In this changing cultural environment, social issues such as gender equality, abortion, and gay rights took on new urgency and political salience for conservatives.

The globalized economy intensified acute social and racial tensions within American society. In the first half of the twentieth century, northern industrial cities had swelled with southern whites and African Americans. This situation had led to racial conflict. In the postwar period, large numbers of whites and African-American professionals deserted the older cities, leaving behind squalid, deteriorating urban cores marked by sharp rises in unemployment, out-of-wedlock births, illiteracy, and crime. Demands for racial, social, and political integration met with varying degrees of resistance in both the South and the North.

Postindustrial society also challenged ideas of nationalism and patriotism, in the face of a new global order of supranationalism, international trade, the free flow of capital, and a migratory workforce. Newly created international organizations, including the United Nations (UN), the World Bank, and the World Trade Organization (WTO), called for national interests to be subsumed into a vision of international cooperation. Yet even as American political leaders proclaimed international cooperation, many espoused the need to preserve those values closely identified with America—individualism, self-reliance, love of freedom, and patriotism.

The postindustrial economy and the society it fostered framed the context of the conservative revival. A greatly expanded middle class focused on domestic concerns. Workers were displaced from older industrial sectors, and neighborhoods in inner-city areas faced destruction and renewal. The search for better jobs encouraged regional migration out of the industrial Northeast and Midwest, creating an increasingly mobile society that strained traditional ties to family and church. Neither political party, Republican or Democrat, realized the full extent of the economic and social changes that were occurring in this economic revolution. Both parties, however, responded to constituents' anxieties and interests in their own ways. Whereas Democrats held fast to their New Deal liberal and internationalist vision, Republicans represented the fears of white middle-class and religious voters through a political platform of low taxes, national defense, preservation of family values, regulation of social morality, and opposition to policies that affirmed racial, gender, or sexual preferences in the public sphere. The Republican Right, in particular, embraced these positions, after a series of fits and starts, and proclaimed them in the electoral arena. This strategy greatly aided its fortunes.

At no time was the political outcome certain in the takeover of the Republican party by its conservative right wing. At different times the GOP Right tottered on complete defeat, only to be revived through political miscalculation on the part of its opponents or through good luck. The GOP might have remained a party of moderation and not a party of the

Right; and the Left might have vanquished the GOP Right. Yet neither happened. Although the course of the conservative movement was neither preordained nor inevitable, it did ultimately triumph over its foes. Contingency imparted an uneven development to the history of postwar conservatism as Republicans battled Republicans for control of their party, and conservatives battled liberals for control of government. But ultimately, the Right did ascend to political power against all odds.

Against this background of dramatic social and economic change within the nation and the international community, the Republican Right was invigorated and began its movement from the periphery of American politics to its center. The innumerable twists and turns of the GOP Right over the last sixty years tell us a great deal about the American political process in times of social, economic, and cultural change. It is the story of a moral and political vision and its malleability over time. The tensions and contradictions of modern American conservatism have a parallel in the limitations of liberalism in the postwar period. Time and again, liberals failed to take advantage of political opportunities to defeat the GOP Right at critical moments when the Right was in disarray. As a result, the Right was able to rebound from defeat and move forward with its political program. As it did so, partisanship intensified and ideological division between the parties and within the electorate widened, making compromise more difficult.

Although this increasing polarization created political discord, its effects were not necessarily deleterious for American democracy. Within the American political tradition, the health of the democracy is reflected in acrimonious debate and partisan vituperation. Party loyalty, ideological commitment, and political self-interest are essential to a functioning democracy, however distressing it is to those who prefer reason over passion, altruism over selfish concern, and their own views over those of others. The story of the GOP Right tells of ideological contradiction, political opportunism, and electoral triumph, as well as of deeply held beliefs about the nature of the individual and the good society. This is not a cautionary tale of how principle is betrayed by practice; nor is it a celebration of light over darkness. Instead, it is the story of how conservative beliefs were translated into political power, and how, through ideological and political compromise, the GOP Right made history in its ascent to power.

1

European Intellectuals and Conservative Firebrands

At the end of the Second World War, as the United States and its allies stood victorious over fascism, a small, unorganized band of intellectuals, joined by a large and equally unorganized collection of grassroots anti-Communists, launched a counteroffensive against the liberal New Deal economic and political order. The confluence of an intellectual movement and a popular grassroots anti-Communist movement produced a powerful force that reshaped the political landscape over the next four decades. The movements arose separately from each other, and their union was largely an accident of history. Without grassroots anti-Communism, right-wing intellectuals would most likely have been confined to academic circles, even with the popularity of such writers as the best-selling novelist Ayn Rand and the economist Friedrich Hayek, author of the widely read book *The Road to Serfdom* (1944). Without the infusion of ideas, grassroots anti-Communism would not have been sustained. The movements each emerged at a unique point in American history, the start of the Cold War between the United States and the Soviet Union.

The Cold War occurred under the liberal administration of President Harry S Truman, who assumed the presidency after the death of Franklin D. Roosevelt in April 1945. Truman shifted American foreign policy to a strategy of containing Soviet expansionism. He called for the rebuilding of postwar Europe through the Marshall Plan, which gave massive amounts of foreign aid to the countries of Western Europe to prevent their economic collapse. Under the leadership of the United States, the regional defense of Western Europe was organized through the North Atlantic Treaty Organization (NATO). Conservative Republicans led by Senator Robert Taft (R-Ohio) supported this strategy with reluctance. Yet it was within the context of the Cold War that the American Right was revived. Indeed, postwar conservatives turned the Communist issue against the liberals and the Democratic party, even as Democrats pursued and supported Cold War policies.

Before the Second World War, the American Right manifested a peculiar crankiness and eccentricity that prevented it from developing a sustainable political movement. The prewar period showed that intellectual criticism and a popular anti-Communism were not in themselves enough to establish a coherent opposition to New Deal liberalism. A disparate group of writers inveighed against New Deal collectivism, but their attacks were characterized by polemical invective.[1] Right-wing opposition to Roosevelt's interventionist policies to aid Britain in its war against Nazi Germany found some influence among members of the public opposed to U.S. entry into the war in Europe, but expressions of anti-Semitism by some leaders of the isolationist movement hurt the cause, even before the Japanese attack on Pearl Harbor in December 1941.[2] Postwar conservatives quickly distanced themselves from isolationist foreign policy and anti-Semitic cranks.

In the postwar period, serious intellectual thought imparted a depth to New Deal opposition that had been lacking before the Second World War. At the same time, a popular anti-Communist movement gained a wider political influence than it might otherwise have enjoyed without the Cold War. The postwar intellectuals who led the attack on what they saw as New Deal collectivism gave the American Right a new philosophical critique of modern liberalism generally absent from the prewar complaints against Franklin Roosevelt's New Deal. These intellectuals—Friedrich Hayek, Ayn Rand, Leo Strauss, Richard Weaver, Russell Kirk, and William F. Buckley, Jr., many of them European émigrés who had fled the Nazis—provided the Right with a systematic defense of individual rights, the free market, and personal liberty. Ideological tensions within the intellectual Right became apparent only as the movement took shape in the 1950s.

Whatever their differences, these intellectuals agreed that America was marching toward socialism. This collectivist advance, they maintained, began in the early twentieth century and accelerated during the economic depression of the 1930s under the administration of Franklin D. Roosevelt. For conservatives, the twentieth century had not been a century of progress, as liberals proclaimed, but a century run amok.

Though conservatism as a political movement had begun to form in the 1950s in opposition to the dominant New Deal liberal order, conservatives had not coalesced into a coherent, well-organized political faction within the Republican party. Indeed, as Ronald Reagan later said, the world of conservatives in the 1950s was "diffuse and scattered, without a unifying voice."[3]

The Howl of the Prewar Right

The American Right's impetus for revival came from these European intellectuals who fled to America to escape the brutalities of Soviet Communism and German fascism. In America they were joined by a younger generation of conservatives eager to battle the collectivist state. As a result, this conservative intellectual challenge came from cultural outsiders—Austrian economist Friedrich Hayek, Nazi refugees Eric Voegelin and Leo Strauss, Russian émigré Ayn Rand, Catholic, English-educated William F. Buckley, Jr., southerner Richard Weaver, Jewish economist Milton Friedman, and Oklahoma-born Willmoore Kendall. These intellectuals and writers infused the traditional American ideology of liberty with new philosophical insight into the importance of individual and property rights in preserving republican government. They gave coherence to the antistatist and anti–New Deal collectivist impulse that found expression in the 1920s and 1930s.

A deep sectarianism, fostered under the guise of upholding high, nearly pristine principles, prevailed in the American Right before the Second World War. Writers advocating individualism against what they saw as an emergent centralized government expressed opposition to mass democracy and industrial society. They believed that industrialism and mass democracy created conformity, radical egalitarianism, and a passive citizenry. These passive citizens were willing to relinquish their liberties for economic security as they looked to government to protect them from the vicissitudes of life. Such sentiment found expression in various forms in the American Right throughout the 1920s and intensified in the

1930s with the advent of Roosevelt's New Deal and the creation of the welfare state.

Deprecation of mass democracy and mass culture was prevalent in right-wing intellectual circles in the 1920s. H. L. Mencken, whose politics were too convoluted to be labeled conservative, though he became a vehement opponent of the New Deal in the 1930s, personified this loathing of common opinion.[4] Irving Babbitt, a Harvard University literature professor with whom Mencken corresponded, developed a more thorough, albeit less witty, critique of the denigration of high culture within a mass democracy. Babbitt disdained what he considered the decline of humanistic values in democratic culture, chiding one student, "I don't like this talk of democracy."[5] Distrustful of human nature, Babbitt joined with the New Humanists Paul Elmer More, Norman Foerster, and Seward Collins to deride mass democracy. These literary critics respected tradition and ordered liberty, which they believed were under attack by Marxist, Freudian, pragmatist, and naturalist schools of opinion.[6] The New Humanists criticized the excesses of democracy and egalitarian schemes of social salvation. Their attacks on the French Enlightenment philosopher Jean-Jacques Rousseau, author of *Emile* and *The Social Contract,* and their espousal of the "moral imagination" of Edmund Burke, an eighteenth-century English Whig and author of *Reflections on the Revolution in France* (1790), exerted a dwindling influence in the 1930s.

Similar criticisms of mass democracy were expressed in the prewar years by Albert Jay Nock, the editor of the short-lived magazine *The Freeman.* Nock wrote about the ills of mass democracy, the decline of individualism, and the degeneration of aesthetic values produced by mass culture.[7] He believed that the social ills of the industrial revolution had produced an ethos of egalitarianism and a centralized state. Ordained as an Episcopal priest in 1897, Nock experienced a crisis of faith and left the church. He initially was a supporter of liberal capitalism and a friend of William Jennings Bryan. By the 1920s, however, he had become an opponent of government regulation, the income tax, and mandatory education. From 1920 to 1925, he edited *The Freeman,* whose contributors included historian Charles Beard, social critic Thorstein Veblen, journalist William Henry Chamberlin, and conservative Suzanne La Follette, a cousin of U.S. Senator Robert La Follette from Wisconsin. When *The Freeman* failed, Nock turned to freelance journalism and teaching, becoming for a short while a visiting professor at Bard College.

In 1935 Nock published *Our Enemy, the State,* in which he lamented the rise of mass democracy, which upheld mediocrity in art, vulgarity in social life, and contumelious politics. *Our Enemy, the State* showed that Nock had become completely disillusioned with the possibilities of reform in American politics. He called for the formation of what he termed "the Remnant," a concept he drew from his friend Ralph Adams Cram, a leading architect of his day and a fellow reactionary.[8] The Remnant, Nock argued, was a small minority of individuals who understood the parasitic nature of the state and who would gain influence only after modern liberalism had become untenable. He believed that modern liberalism would ultimately fail because it was founded on a parasitical government that drained the productive forces from society. He feared what he called oriental despotism, the ancient enemy of the Western tradition. In 1941 he published a two-part essay titled "The Jewish Problem in America," which appeared in the *Atlantic Monthly* and led to charges of anti-Semitism. Nock's complaint was not against Jews per se, but against what he felt was their drift toward oriental despotism. While he was a fervent opponent of fascism and Nazism—as well as Communism—the essay betrayed an excruciating resistance to recognizing the virulent anti-Semitism of the Nazi regime and the religious bigotry of the United States in the 1930s. Nock's argument was an abstract attack on what he saw as a despotic tendency in modern culture, but it also reflected his elitism and his implicit intolerance of Orthodox Judaism.

In 1943 Nock published *Memoirs of a Superfluous Man,* which became a classic in postwar libertarian circles. The autobiography revealed Nock's complete alienation from modern society. After publication he became a friend of William F. Buckley, Sr., who shared Nock's isolationist views. Nock, like Buckley, was a fervent opponent of the New Deal and America's entry into the Second World War.

Nock was not alone among anti-New Dealers, many of whom complained about the corrosive effects of industrial capitalism and its natural consequence, mediocrity. Mass democratic culture and its insistence on social egalitarianism also drew criticism from conservatives. For example, the Southern Agrarians, a group of writers, poets, and literary critics associated with Vanderbilt University in Nashville, Tennessee, counterposed southern rural culture to industrialism and modern democracy. They upheld social hierarchy as the natural order of society.[9] These Southern Agrarians, who included Donald Davidson, Allen Tate, John Crowe Ransom, and Robert Penn Warren, called for an organic society that integrated religion and art. They decried the commercialism of agriculture, which had led to absentee ownership, tenant farming, and concentrated land holding. John Crowe Ransom went so far as to advocate a return to subsistence farming, and he urged farmers to reject the use of tractors for "literal horse-power, mule power."[10] Much of this conservative criticism was aimed at the fashionable progressive thought of the day and expressed a distrust of mass democracy.[11]

During the depression of the 1930s, authors like Henry Hazlitt, an editor of *The Nation,* John T. Flynn, a columnist for *The New Republic,* and the journalist John Chamberlain had developed a polemical critique of the New Deal that influenced later generations of conservatives.[12] Arguably, the sharpest critique of mass democracy appeared in 1932, with the translation of *The Revolt of the Masses,* by the Spanish philosopher José Ortega y Gasset. The book opened, "As the masses, by definition, neither should nor can direct their own personal existence, and still less rule society in general, this fact means that actually Europe is suffering from the greatest crisis that can afflict peoples, nations, and civilization."[13] The best-selling book attracted a wide audience and became a classic in conservative thought, even though Ortega y Gasset considered himself a modern-day European liberal.

In the 1930s, conservatism was not a rigorous political philosophy (those associated with it were too disparate ideologically) but a frame of mind opposed to two *isms:* socialism and internationalism. According to right-wing critics, Franklin D. Roosevelt personified both these ideological conceits, which were based on the illusion of a false equality—economic equality among people and international equality among nations. Both meant the ultimate subversion of the rule of law, civil liberties, property rights, and national sovereignty. Critics of Roosevelt argued that the New Deal already had taken the first steps toward socialism and the subordination of constitutional principles to executive powers.

With the outbreak of war in Europe in September 1939, Roosevelt's critics on the Right demanded American neutrality and nonintervention. For most anti-interventionists, the Soviet Union posed a greater threat to world order than did Germany. The journalist Freda Utley, a former Communist, maintained in 1940 that "the Russian brand of National

Socialism is even more oppressive and far more destructive of life and material prosperity." Although Senator Robert A. Taft (R-Ohio) and Representative Karl Mundt (R-South Dakota), moderate anti-interventionist members of Congress, favored limited aid to the Soviet Union following Germany's surprise attack on its former ally in June 1941, most noninterventionists opposed any aid to the Soviets. Charles Lindbergh, a leading opponent of American involvement in the war, declared: "I would a hundred times rather see my country ally herself with England, or even with Germany with all her faults, than the cruelty, the godlessness, and the barbarism that exists in the Soviet Union."[14] Indeed, the central theme uniting noninterventionists was that American entry into the war on behalf of England could only lead to Soviet expansion into Western Europe. The defeat of Germany would mean the creation of a vacuum in Europe, which the Soviet Union would rush to fill. In *Confessions of an Individualist* (1940), the journalist William Henry Chamberlin articulated this fear when he predicted that it would take three years to crush Germany, during which millions of people would be killed or wounded and many of the grand cities of Europe destroyed— and in the end the Red Army would seize all of Poland and much of the Balkans. Britain and France would then be confronted with a hostile landmass stretching from the Rhine to the Pacific.[15]

This threat of a Communist Soviet Union's dominating the European continent struck fear in the hearts of Roosevelt's opponents. When America entered the war following the Japanese attack on Pearl Harbor, many conservatives on the Right were suspicious that Roosevelt either engineered Japan's action through his foreign policy or knew of plans of the attack, but did not inform commanding naval officers in Hawaii to prepare for the air raid. Revisionist accounts of the American entry into the war continued to circulate in some circles in the postwar Right, but they did not find wide favor in the atmosphere of the Cold War.

The New Deal established a powerful administrative state that embodied a programmatic liberalism through the creation of the Social Security system and regulatory agencies with expansive supervisory powers. Roosevelt declared that the American tradition of individual self-reliance should be replaced by a new understanding of government as a resource that protected individuals from the uncertainties of the marketplace. American citizens, he said, were entitled to economic security. They had an inalienable right to useful and remunerative employment, adequate medical care, a home, a good education, and protection from economic fears of old age, accident, and unemployment. Roosevelt and the New Deal sought to fulfill this new role for government by translating the older tradition of natural rights into government benefits.[16]

Right-wing opponents of the New Deal were overwhelmed by what they saw as the New Deal revolution, but they offered no programmatic alternative to modern liberalism. Babbitt, Nock, Cram, and the Southern Agrarians were reactionaries, eloquent in their criticisms of democratic culture, pristine in their condescension toward the masses, and confirmed in their elitism. They offered little alternative to the industrialism or mass democracy that they so vehemently derided. They held little faith in the future, the dynamic quality of capitalism, or the character of the American people. At heart, they remained pessimists. The success of New Deal liberalism in the 1930s deepened this sense of defeatism and confirmed their expectation that the advance of the collectivist state was inevitable. By the war's end, New Deal liberalism stood indomitable, a Gulliver untied, able to ignore its Lilliputian critics.

The Intellectual Renaissance of the Postwar Right

Even as the New Deal political order stood triumphant, a diverse group of intellectuals was mixing a heady brew of anticollectivist thought. Although they shared opposition to modern-day liberalism and a fear of centralized government, whether it be in the form of Communism or fascism, these thinkers were contentious about what conservatism meant. Ferocious debates broke out concerning the nature of liberty, individual rights and responsibility, the place of religion in the conservative order, and the extent to which the Right should accommodate itself to the Cold War military-industrial complex. Fundamental philosophical differences separated these intellectuals, and the Cold War intensified debates over an array of questions: How much should the Right compromise its principles in support of the Cold War? Did opposition to Soviet Communism mean that the United States had the right to intervene militarily and politically in the affairs of another country? Should government restrict the civil liberties of Communists in the United States? These debates were largely philosophical in nature and, until the 1960s, usually did not involve specific legislation. They gave vibrancy to the Right and appealed to a young generation of students and activists no longer satisfied with the Freudianism or French existentialism fashionable among intellectuals of the day.

For many of these young students, their first introduction to conservative thought came from two figures who loomed large in the postwar Right: the economist Friedrich Hayek and the novelist Ayn Rand, both European émigrés. Hayek, an Austrian-born economist, gained worldwide fame for his book *The Road to Serfdom,* which appeared in 1944 while he was a professor at the London School of Economics.[17] First published in England by Routledge, *The Road to Serfdom* became a best seller. Believing that England was poised to nationalize its industries, Hayek intended the book to reach a large audience of educated men and women who would be warned about the dangers that centralized planning posed to liberty. The point of the book was that private ownership in a society was essential to freedom and democracy. Socialism, in any guise, would lead to a totalitarian state, even if it was brought about by democratic means. He believed that free-market capitalism was essential to the maintenance of democracy. In a socialist economy, he warned, the individual would become little more than the means for realizing the schemes of a planner. He argued that socialism was inimical to liberty because it devalued individual rights, personal freedom, and economic choice.[18]

Hayek believed that individualism lay at the core of Western civilization, as demonstrated in the Hebrew conception that all men and women were equal in the eyes of God, the Christian conception of Christ's love for all, and the Roman belief in equality before the law.[19] In his view, the government could play an essential role in maximizing individual liberty. Thus the belief that government should not interfere in society or set rules and regulations was misguided. Still, he maintained, a liberty-maximizing society should make "the best possible use of the forces of competition as a means of coordinating human efforts . . . It is based on the conviction that where effective competition can be created, it is the better way of guiding individual efforts than any other." In making this argument, Hayek disclaimed any role as defender of the status quo. The fundamental principle of a society that preserves liberty should be to make the best "use . . . possible of the spontaneous forces of society" and resort "as little as possible to coercion." This principle was capable of infinite variation, and Hayek stressed "the difference between deliberately creating a system within which competition will work as beneficially as possible and passively accepting institutions as they are."[20]

Within weeks of publication, Routledge had to print more copies of *The Road to Serfdom* to meet popular demand. When Hayek failed to find a commercial press in America to publish the book, he turned to the University of Chicago Press, whose edition appeared six months after the British edition. The book received wide attention in the American press. A lead review in the *New York Times Book Review* by the conservative economic journalist Henry Hazlitt compared the book to John Stuart Mill's essay "On Liberty." Hazlitt observed that it was a "strange stroke of irony that the great British liberal tradition, the tradition of Locke and Milton, and Adam Smith and Hume . . . should find in England its ablest contemporary defender—not in a native Englishman but in an Austrian exile."[21] After Hazlitt's review, sales of the book took off. Further notice came when a *Reader's Digest* version of the book appeared in 1945. When the Book-of-the-Month Club picked it up, sales skyrocketed to more than 600,000 nationwide. The National Association of Manufacturers began recommending the book to businessmen throughout the country.

In 1948, Hayek accepted a faculty position at the University of Chicago in the Committee for Social Thought program. The position was sponsored by the William Volker Fund, created by William Volker, a Kansas City, Missouri, window shades manufacturer who had become a critic of the New Deal. Under the direction of Volker's nephew Harold Luhnow, the Volker Fund had begun in 1944 to promote free-market economics. The fund had supported an earlier proposal of Hayek's while he was still at the London School of Economics. With support from the Volker Fund and a group of Swiss businessmen, thirty-nine economists from the United States and Europe met in Mont Pèlerin, Switzerland, in March 1947 to discuss a long-term intellectual project to prevent Western democracies from entering a "new kind of serfdom" through socialism. Hayek wrote to the invited participants that "if we can regain that belief in the power of ideas which was the mark of liberalism at its best, the battle is not lost."[22]

The meeting ran for ten days in April, and participants included a distinguished group of economists and philosophers, among them Henry Simons of the University of Chicago, Ludwig von Mises, Hayek's former colleague in Austria who had immigrated to the United States in 1945, and the philosopher Karl Popper. Four of the economists attending the meeting would later receive Nobel Prizes in economics, including Hayek, Milton Friedman, George Stigler, and Maurice Allais. Participants drafted a "Statement of Aims" which declared that "the central values of civilization are in danger. Over large stretches of the earth's surface the essential conditions of human dignity and freedom have already disappeared. Even that most precious possession of Western Man, freedom of thought and expression, is threatened by the spread of creeds which, claiming the privilege of tolerance when in the position of a minority, seek only to establish a position of power in which they can suppress and obliterate all views but their own."[23] The Mont Pèlerin Society began to meet annually and served as a network for conservative and libertarian economists. As Milton Friedman later observed, "The importance of that meeting was that it showed us that we were not alone."[24]

Arriving at the University of Chicago in 1949, Hayek found many familiar faces in the coterie of free-market economists who had colonized the university in the 1930s. A number of them had helped to organize and attend the Mont Pèlerin Society, including Henry Simon, Aaron Director, and the young Milton Friedman, who a decade later would publish his influential book *Capitalism and Freedom* (1962).[25] Director, who landed a job at the University of Chicago Law School in 1946, introduced free-market economic analysis to legal studies. Director had been a socialist, but as a graduate student at Chicago he had changed his views under the influence of his mentor, Jacob Viner. Director turned to free-market economic analysis with missionary zeal. In 1958, he and his colleague Herbert Simon founded the *Journal of Law and Economics,* a publication that changed the course of conservative legal thinking in the United States. Shortly after the establishment of the journal, Director brought Ronald Coase, an English economist and future Nobel laureate, to the university to help him coedit the journal.[26] Through their editorship, Director and Coase offered a direct challenge to Keynesian macroeconomics by introducing microeconomic analysis to legal studies. By the 1960s, many law schools had adopted their views, establishing Law and Economics Centers sponsored by the Olin Foundation. Director and Coase influenced a new generation of legal scholars including the jurists Robert H. Bork and Richard A. Posner.

By the time Hayek left the University of Chicago in 1961 to resume teaching in Europe, *The Road to Serfdom* had become a classic in the canon of conservative thought. Still, Hayek did not receive universal acceptance on the Right. Criticism came sometimes from unexpected quarters. Ayn Rand, a best-selling author and leading figure on the Right, considered Hayek "dangerous," because he had declared that government had the right and even the responsibility to regulate private industry. Rand also rejected Hayek's concept of "maximizing" liberty. For Rand, liberty either existed or it did not; private enterprise was either unfettered or it was not. While government had the responsibility to safeguard the rule of law and protect the nation from outside threats, she believed that the state by its very nature was an intrusion on the individual's liberty.

Rand's own philosophy, which she labeled "Objectivism," had been shaped by her experience growing up in Bolshevik Russia, which she fled in 1926 at the age of twenty-one to come to the United States. A woman of immense creative drive, she moved to Hollywood, California, where she began writing screenplays and short stories while working for RKO Studios.[27] In 1936 she published her first novel, *We the Living,* set in Russia just after the Communist revolution. More personal than her later novels, *We the Living* focused on three idealistic young people caught in the middle of a totalitarian system. Rand's anti-Communist message was carried into her next novel, *Anthem,* which was published in England after she was unable to find a publisher in the United States. Her break came with the appearance of *The Fountainhead* in 1943. Although the manuscript had been rejected by a dozen publishers, *The Fountainhead* became a best seller. It told the heroic story of a young architect, Howard Roark, who triumphs over the "herd mentality" that afflicts big business and politics. In 1949, a movie based on the novel was released starring Gary Cooper and Patricia Neal; it brought Rand's message to millions. In 1957, she published her last novel, *Atlas Shrugged.*

While popular, these novels were didactic platforms for Rand's passionate defense of individualism against the collectivist mentality. Radically uncompromising in her paean to the individual ego, Rand rejected the altruistic ethos of the welfare state and regulated capitalism. Her power as a literary writer and essayist in portraying heroes, who with mythic fortitude stood against the rapacious state and the demands of an egalitarian society for conformity, found a receptive audience, including Alan Greenspan, then a young economist and later chairman of the Federal Reserve, who joined her inner circle for a while. In all probability, only a few of her most devoted acolytes understood her criticisms of Hayek, but her views indicated inherent ideological tensions over doctrine within the postwar Right.

Hayek's rejection of tradition and custom as the basis of liberty proved to be a contentious issue in the intellectual Right. Two of the most eloquent defenders of the Western tradition were colleagues of Hayek's at the University of Chicago, Richard Weaver in literature and Leo Strauss in political science. Both men were severe critics of modernity and sought a return to the knowledge of the ancient philosophers. Weaver articulated his criticism of modernity in *Ideas Have Consequences* (1948). He concluded that the decay of Western civilization lay in a metaphysical error that occurred during the Middle Ages, that is, the rejection of philosophical realism and universal truths for nominalism, a doctrine which held that "truth" exists only in words and has no corresponding reality.

Leo Strauss, a German émigré who fled Nazi Germany in 1932, espoused a return to the study of classical political thought, which in his view offered the knowledge necessary to combat the consequences of an intellectual crisis in modern society. Strauss argued that the ills of modernity were evident in the philosophy of Niccolò Machiavelli, who upheld political power as superior to philosophical knowledge.[28] Strauss saw the roots of totalitarianism in modern philosophy, with its dismissal of imperfect human nature, its faith in modern physical science as an instrumental means to perfection, and its presumption that all thought derives from changing historical circumstances. He maintained that classical philosophers, especially Aristotle, understood that the creation of a perfect regime is impossible, but that through contemplation knowledge could be derived that produced standards to judge and improve actual regimes. Through his lectures, seminars, and writings, Strauss provided a sharp critique of historical relativism and "value-free" social science. Although he promoted no original philosophy of his own nor a specific ideology, his thought provided a common intellectual framework for many conservatives.[29]

Other conservative thinkers defended the Western tradition as a basis for liberty, while disclaiming modern philosophy. The German émigré and philosopher Eric Voegelin at Louisiana State University offered a substantive philosophical critique of modernity in *The New Science of*

Politics (1952), part of his expansive *Order and History* series. He found the error of modernity in the doctrine of Gnosticism, a belief that rejected the transcendent order for the creation of a paradise on earth and was found in fascism and Communism. He also argued that liberal democracy had a pronounced tendency to replace transcendent faith with a type of secular faith.

In 1953 Russell Kirk, a young instructor in the history of civilization at Michigan State University, published *The Conservative Mind*. Kirk had taken a leave from Michigan State to complete his doctorate at St. Andrews University in Scotland. While in Scotland, Kirk wrote his doctoral dissertation, "The Conservatives' Rout." Acquired by Henry Regnery, a small conservative publishing house in Chicago, the dissertation renamed *The Conservative Mind* gained immediate national acclaim.[30] In the book, Kirk defined a conservative as a person who is convinced that "civilized society requires orders and classes, believes that man has an evil nature and therefore must control his will and appetite," and accepts that "tradition provides a check on man's anarchic impulse, and maintains a belief in a divine intent that rules society as well as conscience."[31] Before the publication of the book, members of the American Right had rejected the label conservative because they saw themselves as vigorous defenders of the nineteenth-century liberal tradition of individual rights, property rights, and distrust of centralized government. Franklin D. Roosevelt and the New Deal had usurped this liberal tradition and redefined it to mean the regulation of capitalism by centralized government, state welfare, and social equality.

The Conservative Mind offered a sweeping account of the conservative tradition, which Kirk found rooted in the "moral imagination" of Edmund Burke and his defense of tradition, order, and "permanent things." He believed that conservatives had been routed by "a world that damns tradition, exalts equality, and welcomes changes" and a "world smudged by industrialism; standardized by the masses, consolidated by government." He refused to condense the conservative tradition into "a few pretentious phrases," but outlined the canons of conservatism as a belief in a transcendent order, affection for "the proliferating variety and mystery of human existence," a conviction that civilized society requires orders and classes, a faith that "man's anarchic impulse" needs to be checked, and "recognition that change may not be salutary reform."[32]

The Conservative Mind was beautifully written and intellectually quirky in its inclusion of conservatives. Kirk revealed a fondness for the pastoral life and radical Jeffersonian agrarianism. He dismissed Alexander Hamilton as "a straggler behind his age, rather than a prophet of a new day." Kirk saw in Hamilton a man who believed in "planned productivity" and a follower of seventeenth-century views that government should "encourage and enrich particular classes and occupations."[33] Kirk found the conservative tradition in early nineteenth-century southerners like John Randolph of Virginia and John C. Calhoun of South Carolina, who defended states' rights and slavery. He praised romantic novelists such as Walter Scott and lauded Nathaniel Hawthorne for his understanding of the imperfections of men and women. He devoted a chapter to the New Humanists of the 1920s, Irving Babbitt and Paul Elmer More, and the twentieth-century philosopher George Santayana. In the final section of his book he explored the poet as conservative, concluding that "if men of affairs can rise to the summons of poets, the norms of culture and politics may endure despite the follies of time. The individual is foolish; but the species is wise."[34]

For those on the Right who considered themselves individualists—the followers of Hayek and Rand—Kirk's derision of the individual revealed an unfathomable political and philosophical ignorance. Nonetheless, Kirk's definition of conservatism as resting on custom and tradition found widespread acceptance in American intellectual and public life. An editorial in the *Wall Street Journal* in 1955 opined that "conservatism is not a policy; nor is it a program . . . It is hardly more than an instinctive belief that today's society is built on several thousand years of tradition and that in those years men have found things they should fasten to."[35]

The Conservative Mind laid down a gauntlet to right-wing intellectuals, who upheld the liberal tradition of the philosophy of John Locke, James Madison, John Stuart Mill, and neoclassical economics. These people did not define themselves as conservatives who wanted to preserve the status quo; they dismissed Edmund Burke as anachronistic and not central to the shaping of the American republican tradition of small government, property rights, and individual liberty. They believed that Kirk had invented a conservative tradition that revolved around obscure figures who were little read, and sometimes not even known previously by intellectuals on the Right. Contrary to Kirk, they held that custom and tradition should not be preserved for its own sake, but should be derived from the philosophy of John Locke as expressed by James Madison in the Federalist papers. By rooting conservatism in a Burkean defense of longstanding custom and tradition, Kirk revealed ideological and political tensions in the postwar intellectual Right.

These tensions were apparent in a fierce debate that emerged in the 1950s between what became known as libertarians (represented by Hayek, Rand, and others) and traditionalists such as Russell Kirk. Libertarians declared themselves to be classical liberals upholding the Lockean tradition of property rights and contractual government. Traditionalists stressed the importance of long-standing custom, the rule of law, social order, and hierarchy as guiding principles of good government. Exchanges between the two groups took place in small right-wing magazines and remained largely confined to the intellectual Right. There were few such publications in the immediate aftermath of the Second World War; H. L. Mencken's *American Mercury* with its dwindling readership went through a series of editors and owners before it drifted off in the 1950s to the conspiratorial and extreme anti-Semitic Right.[36] In 1946, *Plain Talk* was founded to promote anti-Communism under the editorship of the journalist Isaac Don Levine, who attracted a distinguished group of writers, including Eugene Lyons, Suzanne La Follette, and the black anti-Communist journalist George S. Schuyler. It failed to gain a large readership and folded in 1950. Shortly before *Plain Talk* closed, Levine joined with newspaper columnists John Chamberlan and Henry Hazlitt to start *The Freeman* (taking the name from Nock's old magazine).[37] *The Freeman* set out to revive John Stuart Mill's concept of liberalism. In 1954, Frank Chodorov, a sixty-eight-year-old writer known for his uncompromising libertarian, antistatist politics, became its new editor.

Before coming to *The Freeman*, Chodorov had edited *analysis,* a monthly magazine that lasted only two years from its inception in 1951. Although its readership never reached beyond 4,000 subscribers, the magazine's uncompromising stance against big government and collectivism, and its adamant distinction between the state and society, gave it a nearly mythic presence for a later generation of conservatives. Chodorov's equally important contribution to the American Right before coming to *The Freeman* was the establishment of the Intercollegiate Society of Individualists (ISI) in 1953.[38] William F. Buckley, Jr., recently graduated from Yale University, served as its first president. The ISI later changed its name to the Intercollegiate Studies Institute and continued to expand its presence on college campuses. But despite the unrelenting libertarianism that Chodorov brought to *The Freeman,* he was unable to revive the magazine's circulation from its high point in 1952, when circulation reached 22,000 subscribers, and in 1955 the magazine was taken over by the Foundation for Economic Education, a libertarian organization founded in 1946 to promote free-market economics. Shortly before the change in ownership, Chodorov joined the board of the newly established *National Review,* a biweekly magazine that made the monthly *Freeman* superfluous.

National Review was the brainchild of William F. Buckley, Jr. He envisioned the magazine as a source of conservative news analysis for the educated public. He wanted it to present different perspectives on the Right, unlike the only other mass-circulation conservative newspaper, the hard-edged *Human Events,* whose target audience was largely the anti-Communist grassroots.[39] Buckley had earlier gained national attention for his book *God and Man at Yale* (1951), a scathing attack on the faculty of his alma mater for having betrayed the university's original Christian mission through their espousal of antireligious, anticapitalist, and collectivist messages. Born to a wealthy Roman Catholic family in Connecticut, Buckley drew upon his family wealth and other private donors to fund his new publication. He gathered an impressive editorial board including James Burnham, former Communists Frank Meyer and Whittaker Chambers, Russell Kirk, novelist John Dos Passos, Buckley's brother-in-law L. Brent Bozell, Yale University political scientist Willmoore Kendall, and Frank Chodorov.[40] This group was joined by a former New York corporate attorney, William A. Rusher, who became publisher of the magazine.[41] With Rusher's managerial hand and Buckley's intellectual inspiration, the magazine reached a circulation of 30,000 by 1960 and would continue to grow.[42]

National Review was hard-core anti-Communist and anti–New Deal, and it supported American Cold War interventionist foreign policy. In this regard, the magazine made a clear break with the prewar isolationist Right. Nonetheless, Buckley wanted the magazine to serve as an umbrella for both traditionalist and libertarian perspectives, a desire reflected in the makeup of the magazine's editorial board and staff: Frank Chodorov was a libertarian, Russell Kirk a traditionalist; James

Burnham was a committed Republican and a pragmatist in his approach to politics, while William Rusher, who had worked in the New York state Republican party, was less sanguine about the possibilities of transforming the GOP into a conservative party. Frank Meyer, who served as the book review editor and a regular columnist for the magazine, called for the fusion of the libertarian and traditionalist perspectives within a broad conservative movement that would uphold the principles of minimal government and the worth of the individual while recognizing the moral order and the authority of God and truth.[43]

In seeking a conservative movement that embraced libertarianism and traditionalism, Meyer leaned toward libertarianism and the high regard it placed on individualism. Ideological fissures within the Right were not so easily pasted over in Meyer's call for unity. Indeed, even before he joined *National Review,* Meyer had crossed swords with Kirk in a 1955 *Freeman* article in which he criticized the author of *The Conservative Mind* for lacking "clear and distinct" principles. Meyer took issue with Kirk's denunciations of individualism and his faith that institutions, longstanding and prudently established, should be preserved. Meyer accused Kirk of failing to provide an analytical framework for judging which institutions or traditions should be maintained. Meyer quipped that it was no wonder that liberals had greeted Kirk's "new conservatism" so enthusiastically.[44]

Kirk replied a year later in *National Review* in an attack on John Stuart Mill's *Essay on Liberty,* published nearly a century before in 1859. Kirk argued that Mill had reduced liberty to a "few simple formulas to be applied universally and inflexibly," while "in truth the great mysterious incorporation of the human race is infinitely subtle and complex, not governed by neat abstractions." Kirk saw in Mill's concept of liberty the plight of the modern age. Mill and his school, Kirk wrote, assumed that "every man is the best judge of his own actions and welfare, competent to choose for himself what he will read or hear, to be restrained only by his own enlightened self-interest" from "indulging depraved tastes or entertaining fallacious notions." But, Kirk argued, "the mind has its own slums; and the society which does not object to these slums is liable to find itself overwhelmed." He warned that the masses, if left unguided, would turn to cultural and political evil.[45]

At issue in Kirk's essay was whether government had an obligation to regulate morality through the censorship of pornography. Did government have the right to deprive Communists of their civil liberties, or should such subversive doctrines be left to the free market of ideas for final determination? The essay was ostensibly about Mill's concept of liberty, but Meyer understood correctly that it was an explicit attack on him and the principles of libertarianism. His reply came two months later in the March issue of *National Review*. In an essay titled "In Defense of John Stuart Mill," Meyer wrote that he was prepared to defend a position more absolute than Mill's.[46] He declared that only "the individual person, whose fate it is to choose, can be free, for freedom is no more nor less than the possibility—and responsibility—to choose." The virtue of social and political institutions, Meyer wrote, can be judged "by the degree to which they expand or contract the area of freedom." He charged Kirk with advocating "the claims of power over spirit, blind force over right reason, matter over man." He maintained that the use of force—censorship or depriving individuals of freedom—is wrong, "not because it is inexpedient but because it is an outrage upon the freedom of man, and, in that, upon the nature of man." He concluded that conservatism could remain consistent only if it remained libertarian.

The Kirk-Meyer debate was left unresolved, but the question of government regulation of public morality would continue to divide the American Right into the twenty-first century. It would be at the heart of such controversies as abortion, prayer in schools, the Pledge of Allegiance, same-sex marriage, and wiretapping of terrorists. Kirk spoke for government's obligation to protect public morality through censorship, and for its right to restrict civil liberties of subversives, in this case Communists, he believed posed a threat to democratic society. Meyer expressed a faith in individual choice and the marketplace of ideas as fundamental to a free society. As a fervent anti-Communist, he defended, though with some qualification, Senator Joseph McCarthy's campaign to root out alleged Communist infiltration in government. As a libertarian, however, he opposed censorship of pornography and government regulation of personal morality.[47]

The Kirk-Meyer debate posed a fundamental dilemma for conservatives in the postwar period: They agreed that the charge of government was to uphold and protect the natural rights of its citizens, but the responsibility of government to maintain a well-ordered society was problematic. A free and civil society could be preserved when its citizens remained virtuous. Kirk believed that government had an obligation to enforce and regulate morality within a democratic polity; Meyer held that such enforcement belied a collectivist mentality. Only the individual, he said, could make such choices.

Conservatives, including Kirk and Meyer, agreed that the major responsibilities of government should be to uphold the rule of law and that government was responsible for protecting the nation from foreign enemies. In light of the threat posed by the Soviet Union at the outset of the Cold War, the editors at *National Review* supported an internationalist foreign policy and a well-armed United States willing to use military force, including nuclear weapons, if necessary. Support of the Cold War was unanimous within *National Review*. This position was agreed to overwhelmingly within the American Right throughout the Cold War period, even though it entailed the expansion of the military-industrial complex, huge expenditures for defense, and military intervention abroad.

A distinct minority within the Right, mostly libertarians, warned of the implications these policies held for longstanding right-wing principles of small government, fiscal responsibility, and opposition to foreign entanglements. Criticism of *National Review*'s hard-line Cold War foreign-policy position was found throughout the libertarian Right in the 1950s and grew more strident during the Vietnam War in the 1960s. Doctrinaire libertarians such as the economic historian Murray Rothbard were vociferous in their accusations that William F. Buckley and his fellow "new" conservatives had betrayed the Right in their support of the Cold War. Rothbard was not alone in his position, though it was shared by only a small circle of libertarians. In 1961 Ronald Hamowy, a former student of Hayek's at the University of Chicago, publicly attacked Buckley in the pages of the *New Individualist Review,* a short-lived quarterly journal published by the University of Chicago chapter of the Intercollegiate Society of Individualists from 1961 to 1968.

In his essay, "*National Review*: Criticism," Hamowy accused Buckley of leading "true believers in freedom and individual liberty down a disastrous path." Whereas the Right had once wanted "America to exert its moral effect upon the world by being a beacon-light of freedom," Buckley and other conservatives wanted to "turn America into an armed camp to crush Communism where ever it appears." The position of Buckley and the new conservatives, Hamowy declared, could be summed up as favoring a "belligerent foreign policy likely to result in war," while supporting a "suppression of civil liberties at home." Hamowy saw in *National Review* a tendency toward the conviction that "the community was superior to the individual."[48]

Buckley's rejoinder, which appeared in the same issue, was ironic and pointed. He observed that "national security is a proper concern for the libertarian because without it he stands to lose—in this case—all his freedom." He urged Hamowy and other libertarians to "face reality": Freedom existed in the United States because "we have a formidable military machine which keeps the Soviet Union from doing to us what it did to the Hungarians." He sardonically concluded that there is room in any society for "those whose only concern is for tablet-keeping," but they should realize that it was because of "the conservatives' disposition to sacrifice in order to withstand the enemy" that tablet-keepers like the libertarians were "able to enjoy their monasticism, and pursue their busy little seminars on whether or not to demunicipalize the garbage collectors."[49]

Buckley's position showed the dilemma faced by Cold War conservatives. Although they proclaimed small government as an essential tenet of their faith, their support of the Cold War necessitated the further expansion of government through a massive military buildup. As conservatives weighed the threat posed by what they saw as an expansionist Soviet Union set on world conquest and the defeat of the United States, they concluded that the struggle against Communism required ideological and political compromise of their principles. They continued to inveigh against New Deal collectivism, the welfare state, and government regulation of business, but as the Cold War deepened, the leviathan state continued its advancement in the United States. In their support of the Cold War, the American Right became consumed with the struggle against Communism. At the same time, conservatives used the issue of Communism as a means to attack liberalism politically. The threat of Communism became a way to mobilize voters and lay the foundations for an insurgency against the New Deal political order.

Spies at Home

Anti-Communist activists at the grassroots level supplied the first wave of troops that assaulted the liberal edifice, which had seemed so impregnable in the aftermath of the Great Depression and the Second World

War. These troops drew much of their political inspiration from a small group of conservatives in Congress and a coterie of journalists writing in anti-Roosevelt newspapers. These grassroots anti-Communists turned to conservative newspapers such as the *Chicago Tribune* and the *Washington Times-Herald.* In the *Chicago Tribune,* published by Colonel Robert McCormick until his death in 1955, conservatives read original reporting on national politics by Willard Edwards and Walter Trohan, and editorials by George Morgenstern on foreign affairs which were uniformly anti–New Deal, anti-Soviet, and anti-Communist. In addition, anti-Communist activists drew inspiration from a number of congressional leaders, including Robert Taft (R-Ohio), Kenneth Wherry (R-Nebraska), Styles Bridges (R-New Hampshire), William Jenner (R-Indiana), and William Knowland (R-California). These leaders called for outlawing the Communist party, instituting loyalty oaths, banning Communists from employment in the federal government, and restricting foreign travel. By the 1940s, these conservative Republicans had accepted key components of the welfare state, particularly Social Security, but they opposed further expansion of the New Deal, including national health insurance, full-employment work programs, and deficit spending. They had little, if anything, to say about civil rights for blacks, though as northerners they were opposed to de jure racial segregation in the South and said as much in their political campaigns.[50]

After a four-year struggle to defeat totalitarian Nazi Germany, Americans reacted with profound fear to the Soviet Union's expansion into Eastern and Central Europe. When the Soviet Union exploded an atomic bomb in 1949, American anxiety about the Soviet threat abroad and Communist subversion at home intensified. The American Right seized upon these issues to attack the Truman administration for its unwillingness to admit the extent of Soviet infiltration in the United States. The anti-Communist mindset cannot be grasped without understanding the shock waves that followed the news of Communist spy rings deep inside the American government.[51]

The first spy case broke in the summer of 1945, when six people, including the Asian expert John Stewart Service, were arrested for giving classified government documents to the left-leaning journal *Amerasia,* edited by Philip Jaffe, a friend of the Communist party chieftain Earl Browder. *Amerasia* was founded and funded in 1936 by two patrons of the Communist party, Frederick Vanderbilt Field and Philip Jaffe. The case against Service would be dropped for tainted evidence collected in illegal Federal Bureau of Investigation (FBI) and Office of Strategic Services (OSS) searches. Later evidence from FBI files reveals that Lauchlin Currie, an aide to Franklin D. Roosevelt, arranged to have Democratic party insider Thomas Corcoran intervene with top Justice Department officials, including Attorney General Tom Clark, to prevent Service from being indicted on the grounds that the evidence against him was circumstantial.[52] Plea bargains were reached with two of the others involved in the case, while charges were dropped entirely against the rest.

Further evidence of Communist infiltration of the federal government came directly from American and Canadian government interviews with Elizabeth Bentley, an American courier for a Soviet spy network; Igor Gouzenko, an intelligence officer working in the Soviet Embassy in Canada; and Whittaker Chambers.[53] Following the death of her lover, the Soviet spy Jacob Golos, Bentley broke with the party and confessed to the FBI in 1945. She provided names and details of two spy rings operating in Washington, D.C.—one headed by the Treasury Department employee Nathan Gregory Silvermaster, who counted among his agents Assistant Secretary of the Treasury Harry Dexter White and White House aide Lauchlin Currie. The other ring, headed by the Marxist economist Victor Perlo, included his fellow economist Harry Magdoff, Senate aide Charles Kramer, and OSS agent Donald Wheeler.[54]

Liberals claimed that Bentley's accusations were exaggerations on her part, but information given by Igor Gouzenko, a Soviet defector, was not so easily set aside. Documents taken by Gouzenko provided incontrovertible evidence that the Soviets had been operating a spy ring in Canada. His information led to the arrest of eight Canadians, including Fred Rose, a Communist member of parliament; Sam Carr, organizing secretary of the Canadian Communist party; and Dr. Allan Nunn May, a nuclear scientist.[55]

Gouzenko's information also pointed Canadian intelligence officers to the British nuclear scientist Klaus Fuchs as a Soviet agent. When arrested, Fuchs confessed to having provided the Soviet Union with extensive information on his work at Los Alamos in building the atomic bomb. Fuchs's arrest led to others, including that of his contact Harry Gold, who then implicated David Greenglass, an American soldier working at Los Alamos. Greenglass's trail led to Julius Rosenberg, who, along with his wife, Ethel, was arrested in 1950 and charged with providing the Soviet Union with vital information that led to its early development of the atomic bomb. Conducted during the heat of the Korean War, the Rosenberg trial drew international attention. Although Ethel Rosenberg's participation in the ring was not as extensive as her husband's, they were both convicted as spies and executed in 1953.[56]

Under pressure from Republicans, Truman sought to cover his right flank by signing an executive order establishing a government loyalty program that provided for investigation of every federal employee and the dismissal of any employee on "reasonable grounds to suspect disloyalty." This program led to the dismissal of 378 individuals within a short time. Truman's response, however, did not quiet Republicans, who continued to press the Communist issue. In 1948, the House Committee on Un-American Activities (HUAC) called Elizabeth Bentley and former Communist Whittaker Chambers to testify. Bentley repeated information she had previously given to the FBI about the operation of the Nathan Gregory Silvermaster and Victor Perlo spy rings. Again, she named Harry Dexter White as having passed on information to Silvermaster. Bentley's charge was especially serious given White's close association with Treasury Secretary Henry Morgenthau, Jr. In 1946, Truman had promoted White to executive director of the newly created International Monetary Fund (IMF), even though Truman had received an FBI report describing White as "a valuable adjunct to an underground Soviet espionage organization operating in Washington D.C." When White retired from this post for health reasons in 1947, Truman wrote him a letter praising his service. Following Bentley's testimony, White appeared before the committee and denied Bentley's charges. After his appearance, he returned to his home in New Hampshire, where he suffered a fatal heart attack on August 16, 1948. For many years afterward, White's defenders hailed him as a martyr to the Red Scare. Recent evidence confirms that he was a Soviet agent.[57]

HUAC created even more of a sensation when it called the former Communist and *Time* magazine editor Whittaker Chambers in 1948 primarily to corroborate Bentley's story. Chambers testified that he had been assigned to assist Communists working in federal agencies in Washington, D.C. He named as Communists many of the same people Bentley had mentioned, but one name stood out—Alger Hiss, who had accompanied President Franklin D. Roosevelt to the Yalta Conference with Josef Stalin and Winston Churchill in 1945 and then headed the

American delegation to the founding conference of the United Nations in San Francisco. Soon after, Hiss left the State Department to become director of the prestigious Carnegie Endowment for International Peace.

Called before the HUAC, Hiss categorically denied Chambers's charges. Tall, slim, polished, and charming, Hiss presented a different image from the rumpled, balding, overweight Chambers. He won over most of the committee members; following his testimony, John Rankin, a leading Democrat from Mississippi who had prevented liberals from disbanding the committee at the close of World War II, rushed to shake Hiss's hand. Newspapers praised Hiss and denounced HUAC and Chambers. In the middle of a presidential campaign in 1948, Truman called HUAC a "red herring" meant to keep from the public what he called the "do-nothing" record of the Republican-controlled Congress.[58]

Even after Chambers revealed secret government documents, the so-called pumpkin papers given to him by Hiss, Harry Dexter White, and other Soviet agents working in the federal government, he failed to convince large numbers of liberal-minded people that Hiss had been a Soviet agent.[59] The Hiss case was potentially damaging to the Democrats, but grassroots conservative anti-Communists found it unforgivable that Truman continued to dismiss the case as "mere politics." Truman's refusal to fire his secretary of state, Dean Acheson, after he defended Hiss only confirmed for conservatives that Truman was willing to gamble with the nation's security in order to protect the Democratic party. These fears intensified with the fall of China to the Communists in 1949.

Following the arrest of Klaus Fuchs in early 1950, the Republican National Committee issued a "Statement of Republican Principles" charging that Communists and fellow travelers had been employed to "a dangerous degree" in important government positions.[60] Republicans openly accused the Truman administration of allowing Communists to continue in government. The Republican senator from Wisconsin, Joseph R. McCarthy, gained national attention in February 1950, when in a Lincoln Day speech before a Republican women's club in Wheeling, West Virginia, he declared that Communists were employed in the State Department.[61] McCarthy's influence and popularity with the American public grew rapidly after the Korean War broke out in June 1950 and the United States intervened on behalf of South Korea to stop an invasion from the North.[62]

McCarthy provided a national voice for anti-Communism until he was censured by the U.S. Senate in a vote of sixty-five to twenty-two in December 1954.[63] The censure came after televised hearings in which McCarthy made unsubstantiated claims about Communist infiltration into the U.S Army. Yet even after he was condemned in a Senate resolution in December 1954 for not cooperating with the Senate Subcommittee on Rules and Regulations, McCarthy remained popular among a sizeable segment of the population. A Gallup poll taken immediately after the hearings showed that McCarthy was viewed favorably by 34 percent of the American people and unfavorably by 45 percent, while 21 percent declared that they did not have an opinion one way or the other.[64] Among liberals, McCarthy came to represent an irresponsible form of demagoguery that threatened individual civil rights.

McCarthy became a national symbol of anti-Communism in the 1950s and helped to fuel an active popular culture of anti-Communism in America.[65] Anti-Communist themes were found in movies, television programs, pulp books, and even comic books. The movie *The Iron Curtain* (1948) concerned Igor Gouzenko's defection to Canada, while *I Was a Communist for the FBI* (1951) told the story of Matt Cvetic, as first revealed in the *Saturday Evening Post*. That same year, 1951, moviegoers might have seen *Walk East on Beacon* or, the following year, *My Son John* (1952), a melodrama about a family ripped apart when it is revealed that their son is a Communist. From 1953 to 1956, Americans could watch *I Led Three Lives*, a syndicated television series based on Herbert Philbrick's best-selling book about his infiltration into the Communist party in the Boston area. The largest conveyor of the anti-Communist message was the popular magazine *Reader's Digest*, edited by the fervent anti-Communist Eugene Lyons. As the most widely read magazine in America, found in many private homes as well as in waiting rooms across the country, *Reader's Digest* inundated Americans with anti-Communist messages through a variety of human-interest stories and political articles.

On the Sabbath, Jews and Christians continued to hear anti-Communist messages from their religious leaders. Anti-Communism found in synagogues and churches imparted an odd ecumenical spirit to the movement. For example, in 1948, New York Rabbi Benjamin Schultz started the American Jewish League against Communism, which drew a national audience of Catholic, Protestant, and Jewish clergy. Past prejudices and theological differences among Protestant, Catholic, and Jew were downplayed in the face of a common enemy, presaging the religious cooperation that would appear two decades later in what became known as the Religious Right. Such ecumenicalism sought to counter the virulent anti-Semitism expressed by such religious bigots as Gerald L. K. Smith, who had run for president in 1948 on the Christian Nationalist party ticket.

Most leading anti-Communist leaders espoused racial and religious tolerance as a way to unify sentiment against a common enemy. They understood that their opponents could use expressions of religious or racial prejudice to portray anti-Communists as bigots, and they warned against introducing these prejudices into the movement. Fred Schwarz, a Jew who had converted to evangelical Christianity, was especially sensitive on this point, as was Robert Welch, the founder of the John Birch Society (JBS). Although anti-Semitic and segregationist sentiment had always been present on the Right, especially before World War II, most conservative leaders now pointed out that Communists routinely played on racial and social divisions in American society. Robert Welch, in his three-day seminar on Communism, devoted an entire lecture to an explanation of how "three-quarters" of racial and religious division in the world was stirred by "the Reds."[66]

A more graphic warning of Communist diversionary tactics came in the form of a forty-two-page comic book titled "Is This Tomorrow? America under Communism," published by the Catechetical Education Guild Society in 1947. In this futuristic tale about a Communist seizure of power in the United States, an early frame shows a heavy-mustached Communist leader telling his followers, "We have done an exceptional job of making different classes and religions hate one another." The next frame shows a Communist whispering to a dull-looking worker at a union meeting, "And the first thing you know, they'll have us working with a Jew and Nobody's gonna make me."[67]

Some Do Call It Conspiracy

This popular anti-Communist culture spawned grassroots activities across America. Anti-Communist fervor manifested itself in patriotic rallies, parades, petitions and letter-writing campaigns to government officials, controversies with school boards over textbooks and curriculum, and study groups. In small towns and urban centers across the nation, average Americans became involved in anti-Communist activities. They were driven by a conviction that a Communist conspiracy did exist. In their eyes, Communist activities in the United States were planned by the Kremlin and controlled by agents operating under secret orders with the purpose of subverting American democracy. If this was not conspiracy—a secret cabal to commit an illegal or evil act—then what was? In this crusade, average citizens were called upon to learn about the nature of the Communist threat and then become involved in community activities to strengthen American democracy. Self-education about Communism was touted in pamphlets, brochures, and newsletters as the first step in the confrontation with the worldwide Communist conspiracy. One anti-Communist tract declared, "The remedies we suggest are undramatic . . . First, study Communism." Another brochure urged readers to study Communism because "only an expert can tell who is a Communist." However, the belief in an imminent Communist threat led some activists to hurl charges of Communism against liberal opponents, which provoked a backlash and limited their impact.

In the 1950s, grassroots anti-Communism was not a national movement. Rather, it consisted of many small organizations that operated separately from one another. A few national organizations, such as Fred Schwarz's Christian Anti-Communism Crusade and Billy Hargis's Christian Crusade, gave the appearance of a well-organized movement, but both organizations operated through local, nonaffiliated sponsors. While Hargis's organization took in huge amounts of money through the sales of its publications, Hargis did not form local chapters. Schwarz's national organization consisted of his wife and one assistant.[68]

Born in Texarkana, Texas, in 1925, Hargis became an ordained minister at the age of nineteen in the Disciples of Christ Church, after dropping out of Ozark Bible College in Bentonville, Arkansas. He was a pastor at several churches in Oklahoma and Missouri before becoming a radio preacher in the early 1950s. He gained international attention when he traveled to West Germany to release thousands of balloons bearing Biblical passages with the hope of reaching the people of Eastern Europe. As his popularity grew, however, his extreme and often unsubstantiated charges of Communist infiltration into government, labor, entertainment, and philanthropic foundations led the Disciples of Christ to remove him as an accredited minister in 1957. Nevertheless, his Christian Crusade against Communism continued to grow as he crisscrossed the country to deliver his message. The Christian Crusade became a multimillion-dollar enterprise, publishing pamphlets, books, and a monthly newsletter. At the height of Hargis's popularity in the 1960s, his daily and weekly programs were broadcast on 500 radio and 250 television stations, mostly in the South. In 1966, he established the David Livingston Missionary Foundation, which operated medical clinics and orphanages in Asia and Africa.

The revenues generated by the Crusade and its overt political stance led the Internal Revenuc Service to withdraw Hargis's tax-exempt status in 1964. A court ruling in 1969 under the fairness doctrine forced stations carrying his controversial programs to air rebuttals from his opponents. As a consequence, many stations dropped the programs. A huge scandal struck in 1974, when Hargis was charged with having sexual relations with students of both sexes. Although he continued to deny these accusations, his reputation was severely tarnished.[69]

While Hargis was building his empire, George S. Benson, a man of definite right-wing views, transformed Harding College, a small school in Searcy, Arkansas, into a major center of anti-Communist propaganda.[70] Affiliated with Church of Christ, Harding College provided local anti-Communists with literature, films, study programs, books, and speakers. Born in 1898, Benson was raised in a hard-working but poor family in the Indian Territory of eastern Oklahoma. He had worked his way through grade school and high school before completing his college education at Oklahoma A & M. Shortly before graduation he joined the newly established Harding College as an administrator. In 1925, he and his wife undertook missionary work in China, where they spent the next nine years building orphanages and schools.

Benson returned to the United States in 1936 to assume the presidency of Harding College, which was then on the verge of bankruptcy. Benson bcgan an extensive fundraising campaign among local and state businessmen, promoting the importance of free enterprise and Christian education. At the same time, he expanded the college's agricultural and business enterprises, so that by 1948 the college owned 1,500 acres of farmland. The college also operated a concrete-block plant, an industrial laundry, and a dry-cleaning plant. It had a dairy and a farm that produced strawberries, grapes, and bushels of potatoes and sweet potatoes. In 1946, the college purchased a Memphis radio station, WHBQ, that later became a television station. Benson initiated a speaker's series that brought to campus leading corporate and industrial executives, including Sterling Morton, head of the Chamber of Commerce, James L. Kraft, president of Kraft Cheese Company, Lewis Brown, president of Johns-Manville Corporation, and many others. These executives became major contributors to Harding College. At the same time, Benson became a popular speaker on the lecture circuit, appearing before civic and business groups on the need for economy in government.

After the Second World War, Benson invested Harding with a new mission—to educate Americans on the dangers of Communism. He joined with the Advertising Council to organize an anti-Communist seminar program for chief executives in business and industry. The program sought to provide senior executives with the tools to educate their own employees about the benefits of free enterprise and the dangers of Communism. Benson invited leading anti-Communists to address these seminars, including Minnesota congressman Walter H. Judd; former U.S. commander in China during the Second World War General Albert C. Wedemeyer; the president of Metro-Goldwyn-Mayer Louis B. Mayer; syndicated radio host Clarence Manion; director of the Foundation for Economic Education Leonard Read; the president of Eastern Airlines Eddie Rickenbacker; and *Christian Economics* editor Dr. Howard Kershner.

The program was expanded to alert regular Americans to the dangers of Communism, primarily through films and filmstrips. During the Second World War, Harding College had produced a series of cartoons promoting free enterprise. By 1964, the college had produced more than fifty films on free-enterprise economics and anti-Communism that became a staple of grassroots anti-Communist activism. The films were shown by churches, schools, anti-Communist organizations, women's clubs, movie houses, and television stations. In 1964 Harding produced *Communism on the Map,* which was narrated by the well-known anti-Communist speaker Herbert Philbrick. Equally popular, although more tempered in its argument, was *The Truth about Communism,* narrated by Ronald Reagan. Through these programs and films, Harding College became a kind of mecca for anti-Communist activists.

In the 1950s other anti-Communist lecturers also rose to prominence. One of the most popular of these was Dr. Fred Schwarz, an Australian who gave up his medical career to bring a Christian anti-Communist message to the world. While practicing medicine and psychiatry in Sydney, Schwarz began to preach at local churches about the threat that Communism posed to Western Civilization. In his lectures, he portrayed

Communists as insidious foes who operated directly under orders from Moscow and skillfully employed words such as "peace" and "justice" to cloak a well-designed plan for world conquest.

Dr. T. T. Shields of Toronto and the American fundamentalist Carl McIntire met Schwarz on a tour of Australia. Impressed with his medical background, they invited Schwarz to the United States for a two-month lecture tour. Once in America, Schwarz joined the fundamentalist minister Dr. William Pietsch in founding the Christian Anti-Communism Crusade in 1953. Three years later Schwarz moved to California, where he set up a national program of anti-Communism seminars lasting three to five days. Schwarz gave the majority of lectures, but his programs also included speakers on specialized topics such as Soviet foreign policy, the nature of the Communist party in the United States, court decisions pertaining to Communism, and ways in which average citizens could become involved in the epic battle against Communism in their communities, schools, labor unions, and workplaces. Schwarz emphasized education and cautioned those attending his seminars that indiscriminate denunciations of Communists would play into the hands of their opponents. Warning about anti-Semitism and racism within segments of the grassroots anti-Communist movement, Schwarz rejected talk of a Jewish-Communist conspiracy. One of his favorite speakers was George Schuyler, a popular black anti-Communist author and lecturer. At its height in 1961 the Christian Anti-Communism Crusade reported a gross income of $1.2 million.[71]

Schwarz's group was only one of several organizations that provided educational materials to anti-Communists working in their local communities. Many of these organizations were family-run and few could support a full-time paid staff. Such groups included Kent and Phoebe Courtney's Conservative Society of America; Edgar Bundy's Illinois-based Church League of America; the Circuit Riders headed by Myers G. Lowman; and LifeLine Foundation sponsored by H. L. Hunt in Texas. In St. Louis, Fred and Phyllis Schlafly and Fred's sister Eleanor formed the Cardinal Mindszenty Foundation, named for an imprisoned Hungarian priest, to educate American Catholics about the persecution of priests and Christians in Communist countries. Its activities involved tens of thousands of people, but it remained an essentially family-run operation. Although all these groups produced anti-Communist literature, the combined circulation of their publications did not reach more than 100,000 subscribers.

Only a few lecturers were able to sustain full-time careers as speakers at patriotic rallies, seminars, and local civic clubs. The former FBI agent and author of *I Led Three Lives* Herbert Philbrick was unrivaled in his popularity. He had a set fee of $750 per speech and had to turn down two out of every three requests in the 1950s.[72] Other stars on the speaking circuit included W. Cleon Skousen, a former FBI agent and Brigham Young University faculty member who became chief of police in Salt Lake City from 1956 to 1960. In 1958, he published *The Naked Communist,* which portrayed Communists as brutal thugs. It became a best seller in anti-Communist circles and was reprinted many times. Philbrick and Skousen were frequently joined on the podium by the self-acclaimed brainwashing expert Edward Hunter, who had worked as a foreign correspondent for the *Chicago Tribune* in the 1930s.

These anti-Communist speakers were not of one mind on many issues. For example, not all of them believed Major George Racey Jordan's story that while in the Army Air Corps during the Second World War he had discovered a conspiracy that appeared to have been organized by Harry Hopkins to ship enriched uranium and cobalt to the Soviet Union.[73] Tensions were especially pronounced between Fred Schwarz and Robert Welch. Schwarz felt that Welch did a great disservice to the anti-Communist movement with his exaggerated claims of Communist infiltration into the federal government. When word got back to Welch that Schwarz had derided him, Welch blasted Schwarz in a heated letter. Schwarz replied that he thought highly of many members of the John Birch Society, adding that he might have misspoken when he had "sometimes unwisely used the word 'fascist' in describing the monolithic central organization of the John Birch Society." He added, "You and I stand together in an awareness of the vastness and the imminence of the Communist danger" facing America today.[74] Despite the strong convictions of such leaders, fervid anti-Communists remained a relatively small minority in Dwight D. Eisenhower's America. Though most Americans opposed Communism, they were moderate in their political views.

The Struggle to Remake the Republican Party

Conservatives despised the collectivism of the New Deal liberal order, but their immediate goal was to transform the Republican party into a voice of conservatism. A few right-wingers held that such a change was impossible, but most northern conservatives maintained that the battle against modern liberalism must begin with the Republican party. (In the South, most conservatives remained in the Democratic party. They were primarily identified with support for "states' rights," or the power of the state over federal authority, which was perceived by most northerners as a euphemism for continuing racial segregation.) With few exceptions, conservatives in the North were Republicans. Party loyalty was often as important as ideology.

For the GOP Right, the major enemy within the party was found in the eastern wing, which tended toward liberalism on economic and welfare issues and internationalism on foreign affairs. The strength of the GOP Right could be found in the Midwest and the western segments of the party, which opposed foreign aid and the United Nations, as well as the welfare state and government intervention in the economy. The right wing of the party tended to look to Senator Robert Taft (R-Ohio), the son of the former president, as the man they would most like to put in the White House. These conservatives were proud of the accomplishments of the Republican-controlled 80th Congress elected in 1946. Led by conservatives such as Taft, Senator Kenneth Wherry of Nebraska, Senator Styles Bridges of New Hampshire, and Speaker Joseph Martin of Massachusetts, Republicans had pushed through tax cuts, a balanced budget, a two-term limit for presidents, and reform of the National Labor Relations Board through the Taft-Hartley Act, all measures dear to their hearts. The 80th Congress showed conservative party activists what the GOP could accomplish if it were untethered from the eastern wing of the party, dominated by bankers and financiers and public-opinion makers from the liberal establishment. It was this wing that alienated conservatives when it rejected Taft and nominated Thomas Dewey as the party's presidential candidate in 1948.

Dewey's nomination to head the GOP ticket in 1948 had not come easily. He won only on the third ballot against Taft, after Harold Stassen, Earl Warren, and Arthur Vandenberg threw their support behind Dewey. More important, Taft had failed to win the support of several key conservative leaders in Congress, including Representative Charles Halleck of Indiana, Representative Joseph Martin of Massachusetts, and Representative James Kem of Missouri. Taft was bitter about losing the nomination, but as a good party man he rallied to Dewey's candidacy. Right-wingers pressed Dewey to pursue the issue of Communist infiltration into government, which had broken open with Whittaker Chambers's and Elizabeth Bentley's recent testimony before Congress.[75] Instead, Dewey and his running mate, Earl Warren, the Republican governor of California, played it safe. In doing so, they allowed Truman to go on the offensive. He accused the Republicans of being a party of big business, interested only in "the welfare of the better classes." Truman warned that if the "Republican reactionaries" got control of government, this might be the "end of our democratic institutions of free labor and free enterprise."[76] Dewey refused to respond to these attacks, for he was confident that based on the polls he would win the election hands-down. With his deep baritone voice, Dewey called for national unity, bipartisanship, and more efficient government. He tried to stand above the fray, believing that he would win decisively.

The decisive victory was Truman's. He won 303 electoral votes, 37 more than needed to win the presidency, and the Democrats regained control of the House. Taft supporters quickly drew the conclusion that 1952 would be the year for their candidate. The Eastern Establishment had been given three campaigns to win the White House and had failed each time. As one Republican in Houston wrote, "The Republicans lost in 1940, 1944, 1948—three times—with candidates other than Senator Taft. Yet they have the unmitigated gall to spread the sing-song statement: Taft cannot win."[77]

Many Republicans believed that 1952 would be Taft's year, and that he deserved the Republican nomination after supporting Dewey. As a result, they brought to the 1952 convention high hopes that Taft and the right-leaning conservative agenda would prevail. Taft, however, faced a major challenge from the war hero General Dwight D. Eisenhower, the commander of the Allied forces in Europe during the Second World War. When Eisenhower won on the first ballot, Taft's loss at the 1952 convention took on mythic proportions for many on the Right who believed that the nomination had been stolen, once again, by the eastern wing of the party.

Many conservatives suspected even before Eisenhower entered the White House that he was not a man of the Right. Once in office, Eisenhower revealed himself to be a moderate who accepted much of the New Deal, tempered by a fiscal conservatism that prevented the administration from supporting further expansion of the welfare state. As Eisenhower's second term drew to a close, conservatives became more pointed in their criticism of the administration. Eisenhower had not turned back the New Deal welfare state; in fact, the Social Security program had grown, farmers continued to receive agricultural subsidies, and the federal government had expanded public housing and other social-welfare programs. In foreign policy, the Eisenhower administration had voluntarily banned atmospheric nuclear testing and supported expanded trade and cultural exchanges with the Soviet Union. Conservatives saw in Eisenhower's invitation to the Soviet leader Nikita Khrushchev to visit the United States in 1959 further signs of the administration's acceptance of peaceful coexistence with the Soviet Union. For the American Right, peace with the USSR was impossible because the Communists could not be trusted to keep treaties or relinquish their designs for world conquest.

The Right remained only a dissident voice within the GOP and not a coherent faction. Indeed, many right-wingers were unconvinced that the GOP could be made into a party of conservatism. As one conservative observed, "It seems to me that the leftwing element in both political parties, including various socialists, liberals, and New Dealers and Fair Dealers of every stripe, are making steady gains . . . The country is sliding slowly into International Socialism."[78] The GOP stood as a party of moderation, but by 1960 there was a sense among the American public that change was needed to address the problems of poverty in the inner city and rural areas, to end segregation in the South, and to make some accommodation with the Soviet Union. Conservatism had found a voice in a small group of intellectuals, but its influence was limited intellectually and politically. A strident anti-Communism had gained popular acceptance among grassroots activists, but its fervor was never shared by the majority of Americans. Conservatism had advanced in the immediate aftermath of the Second World War, but as the 1950s drew to a close, the future of the American Right within the Republican party and the larger political order was by no means certain.

2

Triumph and Travail in 1964

In 1964, the conservative faction within the Republican party flexed its muscles and placed one of its own, Barry Goldwater, U.S. senator from Arizona, at the head of the GOP presidential ticket. Goldwater's nomination marked a major triumph for the GOP Right, and euphoria swept through conservative ranks. The liberal eastern wing of the party—the so-called Rockefeller wing—had been defeated by a popular insurgence in the ranks of the GOP. Conservatives were convinced that millions of potential voters were "out there" waiting for an opportunity to vote for a conservative. The days of Tweedledum and Tweedledee were over.

The letdown was severe. Incumbent president Lyndon Baines Johnson easily thumped Goldwater in the general election. Goldwater lost by more than sixteen million votes and carried only six states, his home state of Arizona and five Deep South states. Moderates and liberals in the Republican party, angered by their defeat at the GOP National Convention in 1964, joined in an attack on Goldwater as representing "a whole crazy-quilt collection of absurd and dangerous positions."[1] Following the election, a shell-shocked Republican party swung toward the center, purging Goldwaterites from high party positions. GOP conservatives were once again placed on the defensive.

Most political observers saw Johnson's triumph as a clear repudiation of conservatism. Johnson had run as a liberal and a successor to Kennedy's New Frontier. He proclaimed that his own legislative agenda, the Great Society, was the fulfillment of the Kennedy promise. Johnson launched the Great Society with much fanfare. The welfare state was expanded to include health insurance for the elderly and the poor through Medicare and Medicaid. He promised to end poverty in his lifetime through new community-action programs, training and employment programs, and new education programs that extended from preschool through graduate school. In 1964, civil rights legislation had been enacted to protect citizens from discrimination on the basis of race, ethnicity, gender, age, or religion. The following year another civil rights act was passed to protect the voting rights of African Americans. There seemed to be no end to Johnson's energy or his vision.

The election of 1964 marked an apogee for liberals. By 1966, the Johnson administration was in deep trouble. Racial riots and growing opposition to a war in Southeast Asia brought a backlash from the general public on both the left and the right. In these circumstances, conservatives knew liberalism was weak, but they were unsure how to capitalize on the situation. They did not, as in 1964, have a clear candidate to rally around. Some saw Ronald Reagan, the new governor of California, as a rising star in the conservative heavens, while others believed that Nixon had the best chance of winning the nomination and defeating the Democrats. Goldwater supporters had not forgotten that in 1964 Nixon had campaigned for their candidate, while Rockefeller and other moderate and liberal Republicans had sat out the campaign. The future course was by no means clear. Moreover, Goldwater's support for states' rights and freedom of association and his opposition to federally enforced integration of public accommodations placed conservatives on the defensive. Conservatives had won a major victory in nominating Goldwater in 1964, but the question remained whether this was an aberration or the start of a sustained movement.

The 1960 Election

To understand fully the dilemma faced by the GOP Right as the 1964 election approached, we need only recall the debacle of the 1960 GOP Convention. In 1960, conservatives made a vain attempt to take over the GOP, only to discover that Richard Nixon, who had won the nomination, was more concerned with placating the Rockefeller wing of the party than with extending power to the Right.

Throughout the 1950s, the GOP Right had become increasingly dissatisfied with the Eisenhower administration. Though conservatives appreciated Eisenhower's fiscal discipline in balancing the federal budget, they disapproved of his foreign policy. In 1956, they were troubled by the administration's weak reaction to the Soviet invasion of Hungary to suppress a popular uprising against the Russian-backed regime. More troubling, however, was Eisenhower's voluntary ban on atmospheric testing of nuclear weapons, his support for trade with Eastern-bloc countries, and his call for nuclear arms control negotiations with the Soviet Union.

Conservatives tempered their criticism of Eisenhower out of party loyalty. Nonetheless, undercurrents of complaint could be heard in conservative circles. Five years into Eisenhower's presidency, the conservative Edgar C. Bundy, president of the Abraham Lincoln National Republican Club, confided that he believed "the so-called Republican leadership is giving the country a bigger New Deal program and people cannot recognize it because it is being dished out under the guise of Republicanism!" By the end of the Eisenhower administration, the anti-Communist author and lecturer Herbert Philbrick had reached an even more pessimistic conclusion, telling friends that "we lost all during the Eisenhower administration." He added that at the end of eight years of Republican rule in Washington, "we lost still further ground while the communists gained."[2]

For many on the Right, the problems with the GOP were deeper than Eisenhower's failure to roll back New Deal programs at home and Communism abroad. Conservatives held that when it came to policy, there was little difference between the Republicans and the Democrats. William A. Rusher, publisher of the *National Review*, declared that "both major parties, as presently constituted are simply highly efficient vote-gathering machines," while the rightwing journalist Tom Anderson, whose column "Straight Talk" appeared in 375 newspapers, labeled the Democrats and the Republicans "Socialist Party A and Socialist Party B."[3] Conservatives felt forsaken by their party leader and the party itself.

The conservative faction within the Republican party wanted a genuine conservative to head the GOP ticket in 1960. For many this meant nominating Barry Goldwater because of his espousal of individualism, anticollectivism, and personal liberty. He favored right-to-work laws and an aggressive American foreign policy that cut off foreign aid to socialist countries, ended trade with the Eastern bloc and the Soviet Union, and sought to roll back Soviet Communism. He called for nuclear superiority, a first-strike nuclear strategy, and opposition to arms control treaties with the Soviet Union. The Soviet regime, he argued, could not be trusted to uphold treaties.

Not all conservatives were for Goldwater, however. Many believed that Vice President Richard Nixon had the nomination sewn up, and they did not want to engage in useless infighting.[4] This is not to say that those conservatives who favored Nixon for the nomination were enthusiastic about him. In fact, neither the liberal Republicans nor the hardliners on the Right were enthralled by the prospect of a Nixon candidacy in 1960. Nixon's dubious role in winning the California delegation for Eisenhower in 1952 was not easily forgotten by the Right. Many conservatives were convinced that Nixon had arranged a secret deal at the 1952 GOP convention with California Governor Earl Warren to throw his state's delegates to Eisenhower at the last moment, thereby winning the nomination for Eisenhower over his rival, Senator Robert Taft. In exchange for this favor, Eisenhower appointed Warren as chief justice to the U.S. Supreme Court. Conservatives distrusted the Warren Court, especially because it overturned a set of state and federal sedition and anti-Communist laws.

However mixed their feelings about Nixon, the Republican Right despised the alternative, Nelson Rockefeller, who typified in their eyes all the faults of the eastern, internationalist-minded establishment. The tough choice was between Nixon and Rockefeller, and for conservatives this meant no choice at all. They turned to Barry Goldwater as their candidate in 1960, but they faced a major problem. Goldwater had made it clear that he would not accommodate any movement to draft him. He had endorsed Nixon for the 1960 nomination and he was not about to break his pledge.

Such sentiment might have convinced most people that a campaign to draft Goldwater in 1960 was quixotic. Clarence Manion was not one of those people, however. He devised an audacious plan to draft Goldwater, even if the candidate made it clear that he wanted no part of such a movement. Manion, the former dean of the University of Notre Dame Law School, hoped to rally conservatives behind a Goldwater nomination, with the expectation that when the nomination fell through, it would lead to the formation of a new, conservative third party. Manion believed that Goldwater could be enlisted to head the new third party's ticket, joined by an unnamed southern Democrat. Only Manion's prestige and conservatives' discontent with the Eisenhower administration and distrust of Nixon prevented this plan from being dismissed as a cockamamie scheme with no chance of succeeding.

Manion's prominence reflected the rising status of Roman Catholics in the conservative movement. Born into a working-class family in Henderson, Kentucky, the precocious Manion attended St. Mary's, a local Catholic college, and then Catholic University in Washington, D.C., where he received an M.A. in Philosophy. After receiving his law degree, he took a position teaching history and government at the University of Notre Dame in Indiana. In 1941 he became dean of the law school. Manion had been active in Indiana Democratic party politics in the 1920s and 1930s, making a run for Congress in 1932 and an unsuccessful bid for the party nomination for the U.S. Senate in 1934.

Manion's politics were largely anticorporate in sentiment and Roman Catholic in orientation. In early 1929, before the great stock market crash, he formed what he described as "a group of militant old-fashioned individualists" to publish a monthly magazine, *The Independent Citizen*. The purpose of the magazine was to protect "the little fellow in business and politics." The group sought to counter the "trend toward consolidation and centralization in business as in government." In his efforts to recruit well-known authors for his magazine, Manion told the former progressive reformer Gifford Pinchot that there could be "little or no personal or civic self-government as long" as business and government remained centralized. The stock market crash in October of that year dashed the hopes for the monthly, but the nature of this publication was suggested by the articles Manion had commissioned before his plans fell through. Prospective authors included Columbia University President Nicholas Murray Butler on the importance of "individualistic education"; Missouri Senator James Reed on Prohibition as a manifestation of "parasitical" big government; and a piece on how "the chain store carries a threat to local community life."[5]

Manion's philippics against "big government" continued into the 1930s. In his civics textbook prepared for Catholic junior high schools, *Lessons in Liberty: A Study of American Government,* he attacked the ideology of "the pagan all-powerful state," which rejected the belief that government needed to be founded on "self-evident principles of God."

He warned that fascism and communism were the inevitable results of a denial that "God is the masthead of every properly constituted political system." He drew from Catholic social teachings the need for workers to receive a "living wage," but this was not a call for socialism or big government; rather, it was an affirmation that society, including "big business," needed to follow Christian principles.

Manion's populist distrust of "big business," "big government," and socialism led him to oppose Franklin Roosevelt's interventionist foreign policy. Manion believed that Roosevelt's pro-British policies served the financial interests of WASPs who dominated both the Democratic and the Republican parties. He believed that war meant the erosion of democracy at home and the militarization of American society. War benefited big business and promoted centralized government. Like other noninterventionists, he feared that the Soviet Union would dominate postwar Europe. In 1939, he left the Democratic party and became a registered Republican. In 1941, Manion accepted an invitation from Sears, Roebuck Chairman Robert E. Wood to join the America First Committee and its campaign to oppose participation in another European war and to "extend democracy at home."

Following World War II, he carried on his battle against centralized government and Communism with a message that included a strong anti–big business undertone. Manion's opposition to the Second World War and his passionate anti-Communism after the war led the new president of the University of Notre Dame, Reverend Theodore Hesburgh, to remove Manion as dean of the law school on the grounds that he wanted to improve the quality of the school. (He was replaced by a well-known Ohio lawyer, Joseph O'Meara, whose lack of academic credentials was compensated for by his work for the Democratic party and the American Civil Liberties Union.) Manion then turned to full-time writing and lecturing.[6] His bestselling book *The Key to Peace* (1950) gained him a national following which he used to launch a fifteen-minute nationally syndicated radio program in 1952.

By 1959, Manion had become one of the most visible and respected figures on the Right. Thus when he began organizing a Goldwater for President committee, he was joined by a number of prominent conservatives, a kind of Who's Who of the American Right.[7] He persuaded the committee to go along with a two-stage plan. Stage one was to publish a campaign book by Barry Goldwater outlining his conservative philosophy. This was to be followed by stage two, a grassroots campaign organized around the projected popularity of the book. The only hitch in this two-skip waltz was Goldwater's outright refusal to join the dance. Manion did convince Goldwater to have a book produced under his name, ghost-written by William F. Buckley's brother-in-law, Brent Bozell.[8]

Privately, Manion felt that even if Goldwater was persuaded to run, the Eastern Establishment would prevent him from securing the nomination, at which point all "Hell will pop." Throughout 1959, Manion believed that the GOP nomination would likely go to Nelson Rockefeller. He was convinced that if Rockefeller won the nomination, conservatives within the GOP would break to form a new party.[9] Although some people around Manion spoke of running Orval Faubus of Arkansas (best known for his opposition to school integration in his state), Manion doubted the viability of a Faubus candidacy.[10] For a while Manion hoped that South Carolina Governor Ernest Hollings might lead a southern revolt in the Democratic party, but in the end Hollings refused to go along with the scheme.[11] Although Manion did not support forced racial segregation in the South, either in public or in his private correspondence, he saw civil rights as an Achilles' heel of the Democratic party in the South. Anti-Communism and anti–big government drove Manion's politics, but he was willing to seize upon dissension within the Democratic party, apparent in the formation of the States' Rights party in 1948 headed by South Carolina Governor Strom Thurmond. Manion's opportunism prevented him from grappling with a policy alternative to federal enforcement of court-mandated integration of public places. Given the demands by blacks to end segregation, any argument that rested its claim on the need to protect the federal balance between central government and state governments gave the appearance of supporting segregation, even if this was not the intent of the argument. As a result, the states' rights argument carried heavy political baggage.

States' rights became an even more important issue for Manion in 1960, when states'-rightists Kent Courtney of Louisiana and right-wing radio commentator Dan Smoot of Texas called for a national convention in Chicago to form a new, third party, the States' Rights party. Although leading conservatives such as William F. Buckley, Jr., John Birch Society founder Robert Welch, and the former governor of Utah J. Bracken Lee spoke at the convention, the party never gained traction. In 1960 independent electors appeared on the ballot in New Jersey and Louisiana, but the States' Right party effort in 1960 was a failure.[12]

Manion sighed in relief at the failure of the Courtney-Smoot third-party effort, only to discover that he had dissension in his own ranks over Robert Welch's attempt to use the Draft Goldwater Committee to proselytize on his behalf his personal brand of anti-Communism and to recruit members for JBS. Welch, a long-time anti-Communist activist and Massachusetts candy manufacturer, founded the John Birch Society in 1958, about the same time that Manion organized his Goldwater campaign. Welch established the JBS as an educational organization with the clear purpose of thwarting internal Communist subversion in the United States. He had written a privately circulated manuscript "The Politician" that suggested President Eisenhower was either an incredibly slow-witted dupe of the Communists or their conscious agent. Many found Welch's allegations shocking and irresponsible, especially when it appeared that Welch was using Manion's organization to promote his peculiar form of anti-Communism. Stuart Thompson, a well-known conservative in Seattle and one of the early enlistees in Manion's Draft Goldwater movement, resigned in outrage after he received two letters and a loose-leaf book from "Robert Welch of Belmont, California [sic]." Welch's material offended Thompson, who wrote to Manion, "Frankly, the [Welch] book frightened me, and not for the reason it was intended. It seemed to me that, by innocently expressing my respect for Goldwater, I had allied myself with a campaign of vilification, in which camp I do not want a part." Others on the committee wrote to Manion denouncing the book.[13] Those who complained about what they saw as Welch's dual loyalties did not realize that Manion was sympathetic to the JBS and would later accept an invitation to join the society's council.

Meanwhile, a highly reluctant Goldwater gave the go-ahead for a book to be written in his name outlining the conservative philosophy, although he made it clear in a private meeting with Manion in early November 1959 that he had no wish to run for president. In fact, Goldwater continued to publicly promote Richard Nixon for the 1960 nomination.[14] Nonetheless, Manion proceeded with the arrangement for Brent Bozell, Jr., to ghost-write under Goldwater's name. Unable to receive an advance contract for an unfinished manuscript, Manion decided to publish and distribute the book through his newly formed nonprofit company, Victor Publishing.[15] Batches of the manuscript were sent to

Manion and Goldwater's political operative Stephen Shadegg in Arizona for review as soon as pages rolled off Bozell's typewriter. As astounding as this sounds, it remains unclear whether Goldwater read any of the manuscript, but when the book appeared in March 1960 it became an instant best seller.

In what was many Americans' first introduction to the topic, *The Conscience of a Conservative* defined conservatism as a philosophy that upheld "the dignity of the individual human being" and was "at odds with dictators who rule by terror, and equally those gentler collectivists who ask our permission to play God with the human race." The book gave much attention to the necessity of winning the Cold War against the Soviet Union. It warned, contrary to the liberal perspective, that winning the Cold War was not simply a matter of domestic reform at home and foreign aid abroad. It called for an aggressive foreign policy that began with American military superiority. *The Conscience of a Conservative* declared that "the Communists' aim is to conquer the world," even though few in the West seemed willing to believe this "central political fact of our time."[16]

This was an indirect criticism of the Eisenhower administration's foreign policy, especially its support of a ban on nuclear testing, cultural exchanges and foreign trade, and summit meetings with Soviet Premier Nikita Khrushchev. The book also implicitly criticized Eisenhower's domestic program, including the expansion of Social Security during his administration. Goldwater (Bozell) defended states' rights against "modern Republicans" such as Arthur Larson, a liberal Republican who had maintained in his book *A Republican Looks at His Party* (1956) that when states failed to fulfill the needs of the people, the federal government must step in. He pointed to the erosion of state power by the federal government in education, slum clearance and urban renewal, and enforcement of health and safety standards related to the atomic energy program. Goldwater maintained that the federal government was not sovereign—only the people in the states were—and that the federal government's failure to recognize that line has been "a crushing blow to the principle of limited government."[17]

This defense of states' rights was remarkable given recent events in the struggle for civil rights in America. The Supreme Court decision in *Brown v. Board of Education* (1954) had intensified the struggle over racial integration in the South. Pro-segregationist organizations such as the

Citizens' Council and the Ku Klux Klan encouraged opposition to deseg-
regation that expressed itself in violence against black and white civil
rights activists. Moderates in the South were left isolated and politically ineffective, thereby increasing demands for federal intervention.
The conflict came to a head when the public schools in Little Rock,
Arkansas, attempted to integrate Central High. In response, Governor
Orval Faubus encouraged some white parents to resist. When a white
mob attacked a young black girl outside the school, President Eisenhower called out the 101st Airborne under General Edwin Walker to
forcibly open the high school to black students.

Goldwater supported racial integration in principle. As a young city
councilman in his home city of Phoenix, Arizona, he had led the struggle
to end segregation in the city's public schools. When he went to the U.S.
Senate, his first staff assistant was a black woman. He was a member
of the National Association for the Advancement of Colored People
(NAACP). He had voted for the Civil Rights Act of 1957, declaring that
voting rights for African Americans needed legal protection that could
be provided by the establishment of a Civil Rights Commission and a
Civil Rights Division in the Department of Justice to provide relief in
civil rights cases. Speaking in favor of the act, Goldwater declared, "I do
not think any man, after having listened to the debate, can say that the
right to vote has not been abused—nay, even denied—in certain sections
of our country. I do not condone this. It is reprehensible."[18]

Richard Nixon, an exceptional politician whatever his personal flaws,
understood that the GOP must appear to take a strong stand for civil
rights. As vice president, he pressed the Eisenhower administration to
promote the Civil Rights Bill of 1957, the first major piece of civil rights
legislation since Reconstruction. In one interview Nixon declared, "I
think it proper to emphasize that both of our political parties, Republican and Democratic, have a record in the field of civil rights that leaves
much to be desired." As the 1960 Republican National Convention approached, Nixon sought to unify party factions and avoid, at whatever
cost, a fight over a civil rights plank in the party platform.[19] Civil rights
was the kind of issue that Nelson Rockefeller could seize upon to rally
moderates and liberals within the Republican party to his banner. At
one point, Rockefeller had apparently bowed out of the presidential
race, but on the eve of the convention, in May 1960, he suddenly reentered, seizing on the failure of an Eisenhower-Khrushchev summit and

the shooting down of a U.S. spy plane piloted by Francis Gary Powers, who was captured by the Soviets. Rockefeller had avoided running in the primaries but was prepared to fight Nixon at the convention. When Rockefeller issued a press release calling the GOP Platform weak on civil rights and defense, he laid down a glove, challenging Nixon to a contest for the nomination.[20] Rockefeller let Nixon know that liberal Republicans wanted a place at the table.

Nixon panicked and arranged to meet with Rockefeller, who set a high price for agreeing to speak with him. Rockefeller demanded that the meeting be held at his Park Avenue apartment in New York City, and that negotiations take place through a conference telephone call with the president of the electronics manufacturer Bell and Howell, Charles Percy, and Rockefeller's associate Emmett Hughes. Rockefeller required that the press release after the conference state that Nixon had insisted on the conference in the first place. The meeting was held on July 22, 1960, and what emerged became known as the "Compact of Fifth Avenue." This fourteen-point agreement included seven points on foreign policy and seven points on civil rights.

The announcement of the deal came just as the Republican party was convening in Chicago, and news of it shook the delegates. Conservatives were outraged by Nixon's capitulation to the eastern wing of the party. Rumors circulated that Goldwater was so outraged that he was prepared to throw his hat into the presidential ring. This rumor was fed by Goldwater's denunciation of the compact as an unnecessary concession to the liberals. He called Nixon's compromise self-defeating "immoral politics," nothing less than the "Munich of the Republican Party."

The confrontation between liberal and conservative Republicans surfaced in the platform committee over the civil rights plank. Rockefeller had demanded more "aggressive action to remove the remaining vestiges of segregation or discrimination in all areas of national life." The Rockefeller plank called for businesses to begin serving blacks at lunch counters. Conservatives counterpoised a plank drafted by John Tower of Texas that called for orderly progress toward full rights for black Americans, even while expressing opposition to a permanent Federal Employment Practices Commission. The difference between the Rockefeller plank and the Tower plank was fairly negligible in the larger scheme of things; the difference was symbolic. Both sides called for the end of segregation and for racial integration of public places. The real fight was over Rockefeller's influence within the Republican party. Conservatives, angered by the Fifth Avenue Compact, wanted to reject Rockefeller's plank.

With war about to break out within the Republican party, Nixon stepped in to persuade the conservatives to accept Rockefeller's civil rights position.[21] Hopes remained among the faithful that Goldwater still might come forward to challenge Nixon. Goldwater had allowed his name to be placed in nomination, and when he stepped to the podium for his acceptance speech, a spontaneous demonstration broke out among the delegates. Further demonstrations erupted when he announced he was withdrawing his name. Goldwater admonished the delegates: "We had our chance . . . Let's grow up, conservatives. If we want to take this party back—and I think we can someday—let's get to work."[22] And go to work he did. During the campaign, Goldwater gave 126 speeches for the Nixon-Lodge ticket. When John F. Kennedy edged out Nixon for the White House, Goldwater became the front-runner for the 1964 Republican nomination.

For Manion, 1960 was his moment in the sun. His nationally syndicated radio program remained an outlet for voices on the Right, but his association with the John Birch Society estranged him from mainstream Republican conservatives. Still, Manion's radio program gave vent to Kennedy's right-wing critics—a message that reached tens of thousands of Americans and helped build opposition to the liberal regime.

Kennedy and His Critics

While journalists proclaimed the Kennedy White House a modern-day Camelot—King Arthur's court of mythic times—conservatives grew to despise Kennedy and both his domestic and foreign policy. They saw his domestic agenda and its high costs, especially his proposals for federal funding of public education, national health insurance for the elderly, and new civil rights legislation, as evidence of America's continuing march toward centralized government. When civil rights disturbances broke out, Kennedy blamed economic inequality and racial discrimination. To remedy this situation, he proposed an ambitious liberal domestic program called the New Frontier, which aimed to spur education, job training, and employment opportunities through an array of federally supported programs.[23] Conservatives saw in Kennedy's proposals a further expansion of the welfare and regulatory state, including the socialization of medicine and the centralization of government. Anti–income tax crusader Tom Anderson, popular in right-wing circles for his wit, captured conservatives' view of Kennedy when he told an audience in Jackson, Mississippi, "Our menace is not the Big Red Army from without, but the Big Pink Enemy within. Our menace is the KKK—Kennedy, Kennedy, and Kennedy."

Kennedy's domestic agenda met with resistance in Congress from the southern wing of his party, as well as from his Republican opponents. The Right was equally unsparing of his foreign policy. They especially despised Kennedy's espousal of what would become an article of liberal faith in the 1960s: the belief that international Communism was caused by poverty in developing nations. Kennedy called for a strong American defense policy, but he maintained that the best means of combating international Communism in the end was to eliminate the social causes that allowed Communists to plant their seeds of destruction. Moreover, Kennedy eased American anxieties over an inadvertent nuclear exchange with the Soviet Union by calling for arms control with the USSR. Kennedy's critics on the Right—and there were many, including Senators Barry Goldwater and Strom Thurmond, Generals Bernard A. Schriever and Albert Wedemeyer, defense experts Stefan Possony and Edward Teller, popular writers Phyllis Schlafly and Admiral Chester Ward U.S.N. (ret.)—were not reassured by Kennedy's message. They described his foreign policy as misguided and accused the president of posturing on national defense.

Astounded and annoyed by Kennedy's charisma and his apparent popular appeal, conservatives accused the administration of manipulating a sympathetic news media. For the activist Tom Anderson and other conservatives, presidential character was the issue: "I'm for Jack Kennedy showing less profile and more courage . . . and the other super-rich-by-inheritance, built-in-guilt-complex do-gooders should share their own wealth and not mine."[24] Nonetheless, conservatives also sensed a change in public opinion toward the Soviet Union and the arms race. The American public had grown wary of the arms race. By the late 1950s, many Americans—although not the majority, if polls are to be believed—found the attitude "better dead than Red" disconcerting and even dangerous.

A series of books and movies had captured popular fears of nuclear holocaust should the Cold War turn hot. Most right-wingers argued that these books and movies contributed to a growing campaign to disarm America. A few even suggested that this campaign was part of a Soviet plan to weaken the United States. Nevil Shute's novel *On the Beach* (1957), about the last days of society following an atomic war, became an instant best seller. *Two Hours to Doom* (1958) by the British novelist and nuclear disarmament activist Peter Bryant painted a frightening portrait of impending nuclear doom caused by a renegade general. Later, the film director Stanley Kubrick translated the book into the dark comedy *Dr. Strangelove; Or How I Learned to Stop Worrying and Love the Bomb*. Fletcher Knebel's *Seven Days in May* (1962) kept readers spellbound with a plot centered around an attempted military coup led by the chairman of the Joint Chiefs of Staff. Also in 1962, *Fail-Safe* introduced readers to an even more frightening scenario in which the president of the United States is forced to order a nuclear bomb to be dropped on New York after a computer error led to the bombing of Moscow. These anti-nuclear books and movies suggested that the world would be a safer place if the United States and the Soviet Union improved their relations.[25]

Conservatives did not accept these doomsday scenarios. They remained convinced that nuclear war could be prevented through a strong American defense policy, which would deter the Soviet Union from launching a first-strike nuclear attack for fear of massive retaliation. Conservatives rejected the concept of peaceful coexistence or arms control with the Soviet Union. They viewed Nikita Khrushchev, the premier of the Soviet Union, as a devious Communist ideologue bent on destroying the capitalist West. Khrushchev might have denounced his predecessor, Josef Stalin, in his secret speech to the party congress in early 1956, but he had not repudiated Lenin's missionary zeal to bury the West; nor had Khrushchev confessed to the treacherous role he had played as Stalin's personal emissary in Ukraine and Byelorussia from 1939 to 1941, when more than a million people, nearly 10 percent of the total population in these nations, were deported, and fifty thousand people executed or tortured.[26] Khrushchev's talk of "peaceful coexistence" was taken by conservatives as a typical Communist ploy to get an enemy's guard down before striking a deadly blow.

The theme repeated over and over in conservative literature was that the Soviets could not be trusted to uphold treaties. Titles of right-wing publications captured this sentiment: Fred Schwarz, *You Can Trust the*

Communists (to Be Communists) (1962); Robert Morris, *Disarmament: Weapon of Conquest* (1963); and Admiral C. Turner Joy, *How Communists Negotiate* (1955). These publications projected a view of the Soviet Union as incapable of substantive change. Conservatives saw Communism as a monolithic movement without nationalist divisions. With news of a Sino-Soviet split, many on the Right expressed skepticism or dismissed tensions within the Communist bloc as implausible. The John Birch Society took a radical position when it alleged that the split was really a Communist ploy to beguile the West into lowering its guard. Even the more temperate *National Review* declared as late as 1965 that "Moscow and Peking (everyone tells us) are at each other's throats, pursuing diametrically opposed international policies ('peaceful coexistence' vs. 'revolutionary struggle'). Can you prove it, we ask?"[27]

For conservatives, proof of the Soviets' intention to conquer the world could be found in Fidel Castro's takeover of Cuba in 1959. Castro was a revolutionary who never hid his intense hatred for American imperialism. Conservatives were convinced that Communism had advanced another step in its quest for encirclement of the United States. Conservatives had warned even before Kennedy came into office that the Soviet Union would try to place missiles in Cuba and that Castro would target Panama in order to seize control of the canal.[28] If conservatives had known that Castro's first offer of foreign aid went to a Chilean senator, Salvador Allende Gossens, a Marxist physician, and that Castro had lent $5 million to Cheddi Jagan's leftist government in British Guyana, they would have been even more fearful.[29]

Conservatives drummed a steady warning that Castro intended to spread revolution throughout Latin America. They pointed to Castro's nationalization of Cuba's sugar industry and two American-held utility companies. In August 1960 Castro announced a "new stage" of revolution to be led by "new Communists." Intelligence sources would later reveal that Castro had developed a secret "parallel" Marxist government alongside his official government. In developing this parallel government, Castro had worked with his brother Raul Castro and the Cuban Communist party intellectual Carlos Rafael Rodríguez to train a disciplined Marxist cadre to take over the administrative reins of the new state. Conservatives did not believe that Kennedy was directly supporting Castro, but they maintained that liberals, acting in the press and in the government, supported Castro over the former dictator Fulgencio

Batista, even though they knew Castro was anti-American and perhaps even a Communist. William F. Buckley, Jr., labeled the *New York Times* coverage of Castro before he came to power as "stubborn propaganda."[30] The failure of the CIA-sponsored invasion of Cuba in April 1961 confirmed the American Right's worst fears about the Kennedy administration: liberals in the State Department sabotaged the invasion in its planning stages, and Kennedy's refusal to provide air support during the landing doomed the invasion from the start.[31]

Shocked by the establishment of a Communist dictatorship in Cuba, conservatives responded by organizing grassroots groups such as the Committee to Defend Cuba and the Committee for the Monroe Doctrine.[32] Clarence Manion declared on his syndicated radio program that "the Communists in Cuba mean business . . . Either the government of the United States acts now to dissolve the menace of Communism in Cuba, or we—the people of the United States—must prepare ourselves for the same kind of conquest of Communism that overtook Czechoslovakia and Eastern Europe."[33] This was radical talk, indicating the urgency that the Cuban situation imparted to conservatives. In the face of the Soviets' unrelenting march forward, right-wingers perceived the Kennedy administration as incapable of taking the initiative to stop the Communists. It seemed capable only of responding to situations created by the Soviet Union in Laos, Berlin, and Vietnam. The American Right was convinced that the Soviets had placed the United States on the defensive and were, at this rate, bound to win the fight. Fred Schwarz predicted that by 1973 the Soviet Union would dominate the world, while the United States would become a third-rate power.[34]

The John Birch Society Forms and Young Conservatives Awaken

The John Birch Society manifested this sense of fatalism and the proclivity to see conspiracy in government.[35] Whatever sense of pessimism the Right felt in the late 1950s and early 1960s, the John Birch Society embodied a militant anti-Communist fervor. Members pledged that the battle against Communism would continue until the last American patriot had died with a sword in hand. Named after an American soldier who had been killed by Chinese Communists during the Second World War— "the first death of the Cold War"—the JBS brought to the anti-Communist movement an intensity not seen since the first days of the Cold War.

For members of the John Birch Society, known as Birchers, this was a life-and-death ideological battle against an insidious, well-organized Communist conspiracy that threatened every value they held dear—faith, family, and nation. The John Birch Society resonated with many grassroots conservatives and emerged as the first truly viable anti-Communist organization with a national membership and chapters throughout the country. Although membership never reached the 100,000 alleged by its critics, the JBS exerted a powerful early influence on grassroots conservatism by promoting a hyper anti-Communism that tended to lump European democratic socialism with Communism and to view every aspect of American foreign policy through the lens of anti-Communism. As the conservative Clare Boothe Luce told Buckley, "Birchers refuse to believe that sheer stupidity and ignorance of history have an enormous amount to do with our foreign policy, and that the increasing secularization of a pluralistic society naturally favors the Left."[36]

The John Birch Society grew rapidly and found particular strength in California and the Sun Belt states, though its financial statement to the attorney general of Massachusetts reported only 24,000 members nationwide. Birchers, who were mostly middle class and white, were organized into chapters that met weekly. Residents of areas without local chapters were made members-at-large. Although the Birch Society defined itself as an educational rather than an activist organization, it became involved in petition drives to impeach Supreme Court Justice Earl Warren for the Court's decisions to overturn state and federal antisubversion legislation. It also joined campaigns calling for U.S. withdrawal from the United Nations and encouraging people to "Support Your Local Police." Birch Society members did not participate in partisan campaigns in an organized way, though Birch members were omnipresent in many local and state political campaigns.

Chapter meetings were organized around anti-Communist films, lectures, and discussions of the weekly bulletin issued by the national office, located in Belmont, Massachusetts. The organization was highly centralized with Welch in complete control of publications, the national staff, and regional and state coordinators. Welch brought to his members a message that Soviet Communism was winning the Cold War through influence and infiltration at home and Soviet imperialism abroad. In his privately circulated manuscript *The Politician,* Welch intimated that Dwight D. Eisenhower was a Communist agent, an accusation Welch himself later publicly retracted.[37] Welch also claimed that the Soviet Union was too economically backward to pose a military threat to the United States. Indeed, some Birch members argued that the artificial satellite Sputnik launched by the Soviets in October 1957 was a hoax perpetrated by the Soviet Union to deceive the West. The real Soviet threat, Welch argued, was through infiltration, takeover, and puppet regimes.

In his two-day seminar conducted for high-level potential recruits—later reprinted as *The John Birch Society Blue Book*—Welch maintained that Communism had spread through subversion in Eastern Europe and China. The Communist takeover of China, he argued, was possible only because Communists in the State Department and the Treasury Department had prevented the Nationalist government in China from crushing the Communists. When the Communists broke the truce, those same forces in the United States government prevented aid from reaching the mainland. Once China fell, as Welch told the story, Tibet, North Vietnam, and North Korea came under Communist control. He warned that the Communists controlled, or were rapidly acquiring control of, Syria, Lebanon, Egypt, Libya, Tunisia, Algeria, and Morocco. In addition, "for all practical purposes" Finland, Iceland, and Norway were under Communist dominion, and the Communists were in "complete control in British Guyana, Bolivia, and Venezuela."[38]

These excessive claims, coupled with the secrecy of the JBS, made the society a target for liberals eager to paint the entire Right as extremist. This was more than smart politics: the Left actually believed that the John Birch Society was a threat to democracy owing to its centralized nature and what liberals considered Welch's demagoguery.[39] As a result, liberals exaggerated the size of Birch membership and its influence on the Right. Nonetheless, as the attacks on the JBS intensified, establishment conservatives sought to distance themselves from the Birch Society in the belief that it was hurting the conservative cause and would damage the nomination of a conservative in 1964. William F. Buckley, Jr., editor of *National Review*, openly denounced Robert Welch and the John Birch Society in the early 1960s. Buckley described Welch as a "likeable, honest, courageous, energetic man" who nevertheless, "by silliness and injustice of utterance," had become "the kiss of death" for any conservative organization and threatened to divert "militant conservative action to irrelevance and ineffectuality." Other conservatives joined with Buckley in trying to distance themselves from Welch, including the former Minnesota congressman Walter Judd, radio commentator Fulton Lewis, Jr., anti-Communist crusader Fred Schwarz, and the former American Bar Association president Frank E. Holman.[40]

Still, even after Buckley's "excommunication" of Welch, the John Birch Society remained a strong presence in the conservative movement. In a confidential memorandum to *National Review* publisher William Rusher, one Republican strategist observed that "fortunately or unfortunately, the Birchers are contributing a substantial portion of our workers and some of our leaders in many important areas and can be expected to be increasingly in evidence as the campaign progresses." The strategist recommended that Goldwater not be mouse-trapped into denouncing the John Birch Society lest he alienate many of his campaign workers.[41]

The relationship of the John Birch Society to the Republican party presented the larger problem that GOP leaders faced with their activist constituents on the Right. Party leaders recognized that grassroots activism was necessary to win elections. Conservative leaders, eager to transform the GOP into a voice of conservatism, also understood that right-wing activists could play an important role within local and state party organizations. Thus both party leaders and conservatives maintained an uneasy relationship with right-wing activists found in groups such as the John Birch Society. This led them to denounce Welch as a fanatic while proclaiming the good intentions of his followers.

At the same time, Buckley and other establishment conservatives sought to extend the activist base by forming a new organization, Young Americans for Freedom (YAF). Buckley and William Rusher believed they could win over a generation of college students to the conservative cause. First organized in 1960, YAF brought a youthful presence to the conservative movement, while providing a pool of talent for the next two decades. Young Americans for Freedom took shape when Buckley invited ninety young conservatives, mostly from the East, for a weekend at his estate in Sharon, Connecticut. The meeting culminated in the Sharon Statement, the founding document of YAF, which declared, "In this time of moral and political crisis, it is the responsibility of the youth of America to affirm certain eternal truths." Foremost among these transcendental values, the statement declared, is "the individual's use of his God-given free will, whence derives his right to be free from the restrictions of arbitrary force."[42] Some followers of Ayn Rand attending the meeting objected to the use of "God" in the statement. They adhered to the philosophy of objectivism, which upheld "rational egoism" as their moral philosophy and rejected the belief in a Supreme Being. Later, sharp factionalism would erupt as libertarian chapters challenged the traditionalist conservative leadership of YAF, but in the fall of 1960, ideological differences were downplayed in the excitement of forming this new vanguard organization.

Over the next decade, YAF organized hundreds of chapters across the country. By 1963, YAF had grown large enough to host its first national convention in Florida, which drew 450 delegates from across the country. When the convention hotel refused a room to Jay Parker, a black national board member, YAF delegates threatened to leave the hotel unless the management changed its segregationist policy. The hotel capitulated. The politics of protest came easily to YAF in these years. Its "Stop Red Trade" campaign targeted major American corporations for trading with the Soviet enemy. Among the corporations that drew YAF's fire were IBM, Mack Trucks, and Firestone Tire and Rubber. When YAF threatened to distribute a half-million pamphlets at the Indianapolis 500 Race denouncing Firestone for proposing to build a synthetic rubber plant in Romania, the corporation withdrew its plans. YAF members also organized boycotts of retail stores that sold Communist-produced goods, including clothing, foodstuffs, and wine. As the election of 1964 approached, YAF chapters became spearheads in the Draft Goldwater campaign. The group's 1963 rally for Goldwater at Madison Square Garden drew more than eighteen thousand people and attracted national attention. YAF's activity on college campuses led the national media to speak of new radicals on campus (this was before the left-wing organization Students for a Democratic Society made its presence felt). *Life* magazine published a feature story on the new college rebels, while M. Stanton Evans, a young editor at the *Indianapolis News*, authored *Revolt on the Campus* in 1961.[43]

Kennedy Attacks Right-Wing Extremism

The growth of the Right through groups like the John Birch Society and Young Americans for Freedom alarmed high officials in the Kennedy administration. In particular, Arthur Schlesinger, Jr., presidential aide Myer Feldman, and Attorney General Robert Kennedy expressed concern about burgeoning growth of political activism on the Right. They understood the political benefits of linking the new activism to the Republican party, especially Barry Goldwater, but they also believed that the Right's influence on public opinion could hinder efforts to establish better relations with the Soviet Union. In addition, the administration worried that the U.S. military was being politicized by right-wing anti-Communist propaganda through Defense Department Directive 5122, issued under the Eisenhower administration to educate troops about Communism and American values. Under this directive, some commanding base officers invited civilian speakers to give lectures to their troops or conduct classes on anti-Communism. Liberals viewed these addresses as nothing more than right-wing propaganda. As a consequence, the Kennedy administration decided to launch an attack on the extreme Right in America. In doing so, the president and his supporters set the stage for the 1964 election.

The campaign against the Right began in March 1961, when Deputy Secretary of Defense Roswell L. Gilpatric issued a memorandum announcing that the Defense Department had established a new office for "evaluating materials designed for indoctrination of personnel." Gilpatric ordered that popular anti-Communist films such as *Operation Abolition* were not to be used for training. This memorandum was followed shortly afterward by another order banning the purchase of the anti-Communist filmstrip *Communism on the Map*.[44]

The *New York Times* picked up the story on June 18, 1961, with the front-page headline "Right-Wing Officers Worrying Pentagon."[45] The article described dozens of militant educational programs on military bases being conducted by "extremist" civilians. Even more shocking, the article revealed that the commander of the Twenty-fourth Infantry Division in Germany, Major General Edwin A. Walker, had been officially admonished by Pentagon officials for conducting a troop indoctrination program that extolled the John Birch Society and denounced Harry S Truman, Eleanor Roosevelt, and Dean Acheson as "definitely pink." In a subsequent Kennedy-ordered investigation, Walker was exonerated from the charge of distributing John Birch Society materials, but he was found to be "injudicious" in his statements about prominent Americans. Angered by the investigation, Walker resigned his commission. His resignation set off a storm of protest in right-wing circles, which charged the Kennedy administration with "muzzling the military." Conservative newspapers and pamphlets spilled forth denunciations of Defense Secretary Robert McNamara for suppressing anti-Communist educational programs on military bases. Reports were circulated that anti-Communist educational officers were being relieved of their duties or threatened with dishonorable discharges if they continued using "extremist" anti-Communist propaganda materials.

Suspicions that the Kennedy administration was purging the Right from the military were confirmed when Senator Strom Thurmond (D-South Carolina) learned that Senator William Fulbright (D-Arkansas) had sent a secret memorandum to President Kennedy condemning "radical extremism" in the military. Fulbright urged Kennedy to instruct the Department of Defense to take swift action to correct this problem before it became an obstacle to Kennedy's foreign policy goals. In a congressional investigation of the matter, Senator Thurmond forced a reluctant Fulbright to reveal the full contents of the memorandum.[46] Fuel was added to the fire when General Arthur Trudeau and Admiral Arleigh Burke charged that their speeches had been censored by Pentagon officials. Strom Thurmond stoked these flames by telling his constituents that his congressional investigation had revealed a "disturbing and potentially disastrous conspiracy" to "discredit and discourage our military leaders" in the worldwide struggle against Communism.[47]

Under attack, the Kennedy administration tried to back away from the issue and let Fulbright handle it himself. McNamara told Kennedy that "Senator Fulbright has gotten himself into a somewhat untenable position with this matter and has given his political opponents quite an opening." At the same time, the Right tried to exploit the issue to embarrass the administration and to flay the liberal Fulbright.[48] Some conservatives began to see Walker as a viable presidential candidate for the GOP. The Right seemed to have found a new hero.[49]

The only problem with the Walker crusade was Walker himself. With great expectation, conservatives waited for him to appear before Strom Thurmond's congressional hearing on "muzzling the military." The older generation of conservatives remembered MacArthur's eloquence when he had appeared before Congress after being fired as supreme commander of the U.N. forces by President Truman in 1951. Conservatives believed that Truman had "muzzled" General MacArthur after he had called for an American military attack on mainland China if the Chinese did not lay down their arms. Conservatives wanted to see in Walker another MacArthur. When Walker appeared before Congress in April

1951, it became apparent that he was not, in fact, another MacArthur. His testimony was disorganized and at times incomprehensible. Any lingering hopes that he might emulate MacArthur were dashed when he spoke a few weeks later to an overflow audience in Chicago. Even the title of the speech, advertised widely to the press, had a comical ring to it: "The American Eagle Is Not a Dead Duck." The talk, which ran nine single-spaced pages, was full of inflated language and lacked substance.[50] The speech was intended to launch Walker's political career as a candidate for governor of Texas and then perhaps for president. When he came in fifth in the Texas gubernatorial primary, his political career was over.[51]

Two months later, when Barry Goldwater learned that Walker was to appear with him at a YAF rally at Madison Square Garden on March 7, 1961, Goldwater withdrew his name. Robert Welch reported that at least one-third of JBS members wanted to disassociate themselves from Walker.[52] Although conservatives rallied to Walker's defense when he was arrested in 1962 for his alleged involvement in a riot at the University of Mississippi over the admission of the African-American civil rights activist James Meredith, which he categorically denied, Walker remained unwelcome in most conservative circles.[53]

The Right presented Kennedy with both a political problem for reelection and a potential obstacle to his foreign policy goal of better relations with the Soviet Union. In late 1961, Kennedy responded by ordering a White House aide to prepare monthly reports on the Right, and he directed the Internal Revenue Service to begin gathering data on conservative organizations holding tax-exempt status.[54] He also made a calculated decision to attack publicly the extreme Right. In a speech at the Hollywood Palladium in southern California, he openly parodied the Right's view of Yalta and the "loss" of China: "It was not the presence of Soviet troops in Eastern Europe that drove it to Communism, it was the sellout at Yalta. It was not a civil war that removed China from the free world; it was treason in high places." Kennedy told his audience that those who uttered such historical nonsense offered only the "counsels of fear and suspicion." The Right played into Kennedy's hands—at least in the eyes of the mainstream press—by picketing the president as he spoke. Protesters carried signs reading "Clean Up the State Department," "Disarmament Is Suicide," and "CommUNism Is Our Enemy."[55] When Kennedy spoke at a Democratic party fundraiser later that evening, he was even more explicit to the party faithful when he told them that the rightist groups were a direct threat to the nation's liberty.

Shortly after Kennedy returned to Washington, D.C., the administration stepped up the campaign against the Right by releasing sections of a lengthy report produced by the labor leaders Victor and Walter Reuther and the founder of the liberal group Americans for Democratic Action, Joseph L. Rauh. The report, known as the Reuther Memorandum, warned of the growth of the extreme Right in America. Conservatives viewed the report as biased and hysterical. For them, asking the Reuther brothers and Rauh to investigate the right wing in America was like asking Chicken Little to report on whether the sky was falling.

Much of this attack on the Right reflected genuine concern about the growth of grassroots conservatism in America, but it also revealed Kennedy's strategy for the upcoming presidential election. Kennedy wanted to cast the Republican party as dominated by extremists, in sharp contrast to the centrist Democratic party under his leadership. Shortly before Kennedy's assassination, in November 1963, presidential aide Myer Feldman told the president that "the radical right-wing constitutes a formidable force in American life today." He urged a federal investigation into the Birchers and other extremist groups.[56] Enclosed in Feldman's memorandum was a longer memorandum drafted by the liberal senator from Wyoming Gale McGee (D-Wyoming) in which he warned that a "wide open investigation in the Congress of right wing groups now might have the effect of killing them dead before next fall [the presidential election]. I am personally convinced that the issue is such a good one that we need to keep the villain alive and kicking for a year from now."[57]

The White House was not alone in worrying about the growth of the Right. The mainstream press spoke of the "rampant right" and the "rampageous right" invading the GOP and multiplying spore-like across the country. Writing in the *New York Times Magazine,* the liberal academic Alan Barth noted that "one of the common denominators characterizing the Right-Wing groups is a deep distrust of democratic institutions and of the democratic process—a distrust, in short, of the people." He described conservatives as being "in a rage to destroy," not conserve. He also predicted that Barry Goldwater, "the darling" of the Right, would be "obliged" to "choose between the support of the Right and the support of real Republicans who will not care to forsake the traditions of their party for a forlorn kind of fascism." Two years later, in 1963,

Look magazine spoke of "a fierce new breed of political activists" who called themselves conservatives in public but in private "put on another label: Right Wing."[58]

Members of the Left charged that their opponents on the Right were racially prejudiced, xenophobic, and easily manipulated by dema-gogues—all the qualities that made for fascism.[59] In 1963, Daniel Bell joined other social scientists to examine the emergent Right in American politics. In a book of essays titled *The Radical Right,* Bell and his col-leagues maintained that the American Right was not ideological. What really bothered these ultra-rightists, they claimed, was not the Commu-nist threat per se but a changing modern world that left no place for them.[60] With the authoritative voice of the postwar social scientist, Bell wrote that "what the right wing is fighting, in the shadow of Commu-nism, is essentially 'modernity.'" Among those who were "dispossessed" (to use Bell's term) were the older generation of Americans from small towns and rural areas, the managerial executive class, and members of the military establishment.[61] The concept of status anxiety that was prev-alent throughout the essays came under attack by other social scientists in the 1970s.

Popularizers of this social science analysis of the Right showed less cir-cumspection. Arnold Forster and Benjamin R. Epstein, in their widely read book *Danger on the Right* (1964), described the Right as a witch's brew whose very vapors threatened democracy.[62] Writing in *The Nation,* the well-known leftist Fred J. Cook warned in a thirty-page jeremiad "The Ultras" that the "portrait of the Radical Right" was not the "face of fascism as we have known it in Europe. But unmistakably it is a face bearing the marks of a sickness that could develop into fascism."[63] La-bels such as the "Far Right," "the Extremist Right," and the "Radical Right" entered the political vocabulary.

For the American liberal, the Far Right was equated with racism as African Americans struggled for voting rights and racial integration. In 1962, the *Saturday Evening Post* ran a photo of the John Birch Soci-ety founder Robert Welch next to that of the neo-Nazi George Lincoln Rockwell. Welch was outraged by this association because he had con-sistently warned his followers about the dangers that racism and anti-Semitism posed to the political success of the JBS.[64] He devoted an entire half-day of his two-day seminar to explaining how "three-quarters of ra-cial and religious prejudice is agitated by Reds." He warned that the primary goal of the Communists was to create dissension in the United States, especially racial and ethnic tension. "The Communists," he declared, "use race hatred to stir up trouble among good Americans. These people are not Jews but Communist troublemakers."[65]

Welch's disapproval of racial and religious prejudice, however, failed to screen segregationists from entering the John Birch Society in the South, especially as the civil rights movement began to gain momentum. Welch did try his best to disassociate himself and his organization from racial and religious bigotry. In doing so, he expelled the University of Illinois classics professor Revilo Oliver for anti-Semitic remarks. Welch also expelled Robert DePugh for organizing the paramilitary group the Minutemen, whose members believed that armed resistance was the only alternative to a Communist takeover of the United States.[66] Nonetheless, as a substantial body of racist literature began to appear in the late 1950s and early 1960s in response to racial integration in the South, the Right became associated with the racist label. This occurred even though the Republican party remained weak in the South and northern conservatives ignored the civil rights question by continuing to see Soviet Communism as the most critical issue facing America.[67]

The Election That Failed: 1964

The attacks on the Right set the tone for the presidential campaign of 1964. The possibility that a conservative might capture the White House alarmed liberals. The Right was firmly convinced that if a conservative could win the Republican nomination, the GOP had a good chance of winning the White House. Thus the key to the success of the party lay in securing the nomination of Barry Goldwater in 1964. This meant blocking Nelson Rockefeller within the party. Rockefeller at first tried to court the right wing of the party, only to turn on conservatives with the ferocity of a jilted lover. He initiated the courtship by attacking Kennedy's proposal for a new federal department of urban affairs, then denouncing the nuclear test ban treaty. This position won a few conservatives to his cause, including some key leaders in the newly formed Young Americans for Freedom.[68]

Rockefeller's bid to become the next Republican nominee ground to a halt on May 4, 1963, when the liberal governor announced that he had married Margaretta (Happy) Murphy, a recent divorcee who had left her husband and four children to marry Rockefeller. Before the marriage a Gallup poll found him leading Goldwater 43 to 26 percent; after the marriage the poll reported Goldwater ahead by about the same margin. Goldwater had become the man to beat, as other liberal-to-moderate candidates stepped forward to try to stop the conservative juggernaut.[69]

As Goldwater gained momentum, Nelson Rockefeller decided to reenter the race in order, he said, to save the Republican party from the threat of an extreme right-wing takeover. The political operative Graham T. Molitor was hired to develop a strategy based on portraying Goldwater as an extremist backed by even more extremist elements within the Republican party. In a confidential memorandum, Molitor told Rockefeller that Goldwater should be hammered on his failure to recognize that the Soviet Union was evolving—a failure that placed the entire world in peril.[70] In midsummer, Rockefeller intensified his campaign against extremists within the GOP. He told audiences that the party was on the verge of falling to "subversion by a radical, well-financed, and highly disciplined minority." He warned that the Right had its eye on the Young Republicans (YR) as part of a plan by a "lunatic fringe" to "subvert the Republican party itself."[71] At the YR convention in San Francisco, Goldwater supporter Donald E. Lukens won the presidency in a close second ballot, defeating the Rockefeller candidate. The editors of *National Review* rejoiced.[72] The battle between Rockefeller and Goldwater for control of the party was fierce, but the entire race changed when John F. Kennedy was assassinated in Dallas, Texas, in November 1963. Any opportunity for the Republicans to regain the White House in 1964 collapsed with Kennedy's death.

Kennedy's successor, Lyndon Baines Johnson, drew upon the tragedy to push an aggressive liberal agenda through Congress. Whereas Kennedy's death inspired liberals to fulfill the Kennedy dream, his death deflated Goldwater.[73] Following Kennedy's assassination, Goldwater's eagerness for a presidential race vanished. He had looked forward to a race against Kennedy, whom he had known in the Senate and personally liked. Recalling his mood in 1963, he later recorded in his private diary that Kennedy and he had talked about running an "old-fashioned" cross-country debate on the issues of the day "without Madison Avenue, without any makeup or phoniness, just the two of us traveling around on the same airplane, but when he was assassinated that ended that dream." In the end, he decided that he was obligated to enter the race after his supporters had worked so hard for his nomination.[74] In early January 1964 Goldwater wired his supporters across the country to inform them that he was officially seeking the nomination of his party.

In the beginning, the fight for political control of the GOP was a battle of words. Goldwater's *Conscience of a Conservative* (1960) inspired the first salvo of conservative books promoting his candidacy. In 1964, grassroots conservatives published three books that reached millions of Americans. All three were self-published. J. Evetts Haley's book *A Texan Looks at Lyndon: A Study of Illegitimate Power* (1964) was a vociferously partisan attack on Johnson by a conservative activist in the GOP. Its heated language appealed to conservatives already opposed to Johnson. John Stormer published *None Dare Call It Treason* under his own imprint, the Liberty Bell Press, with a P.O. box address in Florissant, Missouri. Within a month of its publication in February 1964, Stormer's paperback had sold 100,000 copies. By August 1964, the book was in its thirteenth printing, having sold 2.2 million copies.[75]

Stormer's book encouraged another conservative activist and president of the Illinois Federation of Republican Women, Phyllis Schlafly, to pursue the same path to publish and market *A Choice Not an Echo*. Of these books, Schlafly's was the most influential because it presented a conservative brief to Republican delegates to mobilize on behalf of Goldwater to prevent a Rockefeller nomination. It convinced many Republicans to support Goldwater, especially in the decisive California primary in June 1964.

A Choice Not an Echo appeared in April 1964. This short, 128-page book presented a common view in the GOP Right that in every election since 1936 a small group of eastern Republican liberals, whom Schlafly labeled "kingmakers," had selected the party's presidential nominee.[76] The villains in her book were "me-too" Republicans who accepted the liberal Democratic program, especially its internationalist foreign policy. What the party needed to win elections—and to put the nation on the right path—was a genuine conservative, a man like Barry Goldwater. By November 1964 the book had sold 3.5 million copies.[77]

When Goldwater entered the race, Republicans were a minority at every level.[78] In 1960, there were only fifteen Republican governors. In 1961, John Tower of Texas had won a seat in the Senate, but his victory was due in large part to deep divisions within the Democratic party in the state. Republican strength had eroded in most states. In order to win the nomination, Goldwater counted on winning western and southern delegates at the Republican National Convention. His campaign got off to a rocky start when he lost the New Hampshire primary to former GOP vice presidential nominee Henry Cabot Lodge, who surprised both the Goldwater and the Rockefeller campaigns by winning the primary with 35.2 percent of the vote, while Goldwater and Rockefeller each garnered less than 25 percent.[79]

With the two leading candidates, Goldwater and Rockefeller, in trouble, the door opened for others to enter the race, including Pennsylvania governor William W. Scranton and Michigan governor George Romney. After much flurry and press activity the race came down to what people expected—a contest between Goldwater and Rockefeller. Although Lodge won write-in victories in Nebraska, New Jersey, and Massachusetts, he was always somewhat of a dilettante when it came to campaigning, and he fell out of contention when he refused to leave his post as U.S. ambassador to South Vietnam. The Romney campaign was revealed to be mostly hot air generated by the press. Goldwater and Rockefeller had reached a draw by the time of the California primary. Whoever won the state was assured the nomination.

Political observers at the time saw the California primary as a toss-up. The northern part of the state, with its moderate-to-liberal Republican vote, favored Rockefeller. Rockefeller also gained the support of former governor Goodwin Knight, Senator Thomas Kuchel, and San Francisco mayor George Christopher. Southern California leaned toward Goldwater, but more important, conservatives had captured control of important statewide party organizations, including the California Young Republicans and the California Federation of Republican Women. In addition, they had established their own Republican organization, the United Republicans of California (UROC), which carried clout in conservative circles, even though, or perhaps because of, considerable JBS influence.[80]

The influence of the Birch Society in California placed Goldwater in a delicate position. Nixon's denunciation of the JBS had damaged his gubernatorial race in 1962, so Goldwater understood the costs of alienating Birchers. On the other hand, too close an association with what was publicly perceived as an extremist organization might alienate many Republican primary voters.[81] Therefore, Goldwater's campaign made a decision to use activists who might be members of the John Birch Society—as long as they did not reveal themselves to be members. Goldwater pursued a don't ask, don't tell policy.

Rockefeller knew that the way to defeat Goldwater was to portray him as an extremist who was out of touch with the common voter and posed a danger to the GOP, if nominated, and to the nation, if elected. Rockefeller campaign literature asked if voters really wanted Goldwater near an H-Bomb. The Goldwater campaign responded to these attacks by rallying the conservative grassroots in the state. Tens of thousands of copies of Schlafly's *Choice Not an Echo* were distributed door to door. Rockefeller might have won the state, but in the final days of the campaign things turned sour when what should have been a felicitous event in his life inflicted severe political damage: The announcement that his wife, Happy, had given birth to a child reminded everyone that he had broken up two homes to satisfy his desires. That the divorce cost Rockefeller a state well known for its high divorce rate was ironic, but Goldwater swept southern California by such a large margin that his losses in the North were negated.

Although Rockefeller failed to win the California primary, his campaign strategy against Goldwater provided a model for Goldwater's opponents within the party and in the general election. Set on denying Goldwater the nomination, the moderate-liberal wing of the GOP intensified its attack on Goldwater as an extremist. In a nationally televised address on June 28, William Scranton declared that "an hour of crisis" had arrived for the GOP and the nation. He depicted Goldwater's vote against the Civil Rights Act of 1964 as a vote in favor of segregation.[82] Such attacks carried into the convention in San Francisco, where Goldwater was denounced as a warmonger, racial bigot, and potential Führer.

Goldwater delegates were greeted in San Francisco by a march of 40,000 civil rights demonstrators who took over City Hall Plaza and denounced Goldwater as the next Adolf Hitler.[83] This association with Nazism was reinforced the next day, when the CBS reporter in Germany, Daniel Schorr, broke a story that Goldwater was planning to travel to Bavaria, a former stronghold of the Nazi party, to meet with Germany's right wing and to visit Berchtesgaden, "once Hitler's stomping ground, but now an American recreational center." Schorr told Germany's leading newspaper, *Der Spiegel,* that this pilgrimage was Goldwater's way of appealing to right-wing elements in the United States and abroad.[84] Schorr's report was distributed freely to convention delegates by

Scranton and Rockefeller aides to counterattack the conservative dominance in the Republican party. In fact, Goldwater had planned a trip to Germany after the convention, but he had no plans to meet with right-wing leaders. Goldwater was of Jewish ancestry and hated Nazism.

Prestigious magazines like *Life* and *The Reporter* spoke of a "tide of zealotry" and the "conquest" of the GOP by fanatics. The nationally syndicated columnist Drew Pearson told readers that the "smell of fascism has been in the air at this convention."[85] Such sentiments continued to find expression following the convention. The civil rights leader Reverend Martin Luther King, Jr., declared, "We see dangerous signs of Hitlerism in the Goldwater campaign." Postmaster General John Gronouski said that Goldwater's extremism was reminiscent of Joe McCarthy, while *New York Times* publisher Arthur Ochs Sulzberger said that after the GOP convention a "powerful detergent" was going to be needed to clean out the stench.[86]

Goldwater delegates, at times, played into their opponents hands by making rambunctious remarks to reporters. For many this was their first convention, and they shared a fevered enthusiasm. The battle over the GOP platform reflected the moralistic fervor of the Goldwater conservatives: It called for victory over Communism; denounced Johnson for not being tough enough in South Vietnam; criticized the administration for reducing America's nuclear strength; and called for the full implementation of the Civil Rights Act while opposing federal "reverse discrimination" through what later would be called affirmative action. The platform also warned of a decline in public morality and promised to restore the moral fiber of the nation through laws curbing pornography and a constitutional amendment restoring prayer in schools.[87] Accurately seeing the 1964 platform as an attempt to repudiate earlier GOP platforms, Rockefeller, Scranton, and Romney supporters joined forces to attempt to inflict more political damage on the Goldwater faction. The Rockefeller planks were intended to deepen the rift over "extremism" in the party, but Goldwater delegates beat back every plank in committee votes.

A defeated Rockefeller brought the issue of the platform to the convention floor. He held little hope that delegates would overturn the committee-recommended platform, but he wanted to publicly damage the Goldwater wing of the party. In his speech, he deliberately taunted the delegates by speaking of "goon squads and Nazi methods." He was quickly drowned out by shouts of "We Want Barry." In response, Rockefeller looked directly at the television camera and declared, "This is still a free country, ladies and gentlemen."[88] The image of rampant extremism was planted in the minds of the average American.

There was little that Goldwater could do to erase this image without appearing defensive, so in his acceptance speech he tried to impart a new meaning to extremism: It was all right if it was in defense of freedom. He declared, "Extremism in the defense of liberty is no vice. Moderation in the pursuit of justice is no virtue." The quotation allegedly came from the ancient Roman orator Cicero, but to many Americans it suggested a defense of extremism, a threat of using nuclear weapons, and inaction on civil rights.

Goldwater tried to backtrack by pursuing a moderate campaign strategy. Under the direction of American Enterprise Institute president William Baroody, his campaign now aimed at winning the center by staying away from issues such as the privatization of Social Security, the war in Vietnam, and civil rights, even when racial riots broke out in the summer of 1964 in Harlem, Brooklyn, and Rochester, New York; Jersey City, Paterson, and Elizabeth, New Jersey; Toledo, Ohio; Kansas City and St. Louis, Missouri; and Philadelphia. President Johnson believed he was vulnerable on the issue of race riots and his inability to maintain law and order. When he met with Goldwater in late July, however, his opponent told him that he would not bring up the issue of racial rights or Vietnam. This was the cost of moderation.

Nonetheless, Goldwater's vote against the Civil Rights Act of 1964 haunted him throughout the campaign. Speaking on the Senate floor on June 18, Goldwater explained why he was opposed to the act. He based his opposition on constitutional grounds, declaring that while the federal government had a responsibility to protect civil rights, he did not support titles II and VII of the bill, which allowed federal regulation of public accommodations and employment. He maintained that these parts of the bill represented an undue and unconstitutional interference in private enterprise. Arguing that he would support the legislation if these two sections were deleted, he warned that enactment of the bill would require "the creation of a federal police force of mammoth proportions." He concluded, "If my vote is misconstrued, let it be, and let me suffer its consequences."[89] His vote would tar both him and the Republican party for years afterward.

Goldwater represented a minority voice among Republican senators. Major opposition to the passage of Kennedy's bill came from southern Democrats, who threatened a filibuster. Senate Minority Leader Everett Dirksen (R-Illinois) had taken a forceful stance in favor of civil rights legislation throughout the Kennedy administration, and he would prove critical in mustering the Republican votes necessary to force an end to the debate. Six Republicans opposed cloture, and 67 votes were needed to invoke it. This meant that Dirksen needed to win about four-fifths of the Republicans in the Senate, who would join with their Democratic colleagues to support the bill. Dirksen played a key role in broadening the legislation in order to win over moderate Republicans for the bill.[90] When the civil rights bill reached the Senate floor, southern Democrats launched a filibuster against it. After 67 days, the Senate voted 71 to 29 to end debate. Dirksen delivered 27 of the 33 votes on his side of the aisle.

In the Senate, northern Republicans voted overwhelmingly for the bill, 27 to 5 (84 percent to 16 percent). The South had only one Republican, John Tower of Texas, and he voted against it. All in all, 6 Republicans voted against the Civil Rights Act of 1964 and 27 voted for the measure. Twenty-one Democrats, nearly half of the Democratic caucus, voted against the act. Of these 21 Democrats, 20 came from the South. As a result, southern Democrats voted nearly unanimously against the Civil Rights Act of 1964, 1 to 20 (5 percent to 95 percent). When the act came before the House, northern Republicans voted in favor 138 to 34 (85 percent to 15 percent), although all 10 southern Republican House members voted against the bill. Southern Democrats in the House also voted against the bill, 7 to 87 (7 percent to 93 percent). In short, major opposition to the act came from southern Democrats, not Republicans.[91]

It is less clear where the majority of rank-and-file conservatives stood on the 1964 Civil Rights Act. Goldwater's views were echoed by the editors of *National Review*, who from the inception of the magazine in 1955 opposed federal involvement in enforcing equal access to public accommodations and protecting black voting rights in the South. They based their opposition on constitutional grounds and conservative resistance to radical social change. However principled their justifications, their rhetoric overstepped the bounds of civility and was racially offensive. In a March 1960 unsigned editorial, *National Review* declared, "We offer the following on the crisis in the Senate and the South: In the

Deep South the Negroes are, by comparison with Whites, retarded ('unadvanced' the National Association for the Advancement of Colored People might put it) . . . Leadership in the South, then, quite properly, rests in White hands. Upon the White population this fact imposes moral obligations of paternalism, patience, protection, devotion, and sacrifice." The editorial added that "the attempt to hand over to the Negro the raw political power with which to alter it is hardly a solution. It is a call to upheaval, which ensues when reality and unbridled abstractions meet head-on."[92]

As the civil rights struggle heated up in the summer of 1963, the editors of *National Review* expressed alarm. William F. Buckley, Jr., described Governor George Wallace's refusal to integrate the University of Alabama as tragic, "tragedy here defined as an irresistible force moving on a collision course toward an immovable body." Still, Buckley warned that trying to change people's opinions about race through legislation was as futile as trying to change human nature. What was needed, he said, was "to stimulate man's capacity for love, and his toleration, understanding and respect for other, different people."[93] On a theoretical level, Buckley might have been correct, but in the heat of 1963, calling for love seemed naïve and obfuscating.

The *National Review* columnist Frank Meyer was more direct. He warned that a revolutionary situation was being created by black leaders who called for riot and violence unless their demands were met. Meyer declared that laws "enforcing segregation have always been a monstrosity," but those wrongs should not be "righted by destroying the foundations of a free constitutional society." He concluded by warning that "under the pressure of rioting mobs, intemperate demagogues and rampant ideology, we are in [danger] of depriving private citizens of their protection of their property; of enjoining, under threat of federal armed power, the police power from preserving order in our communities; of disrupting and catastrophically lowering the standard of an already enfeebled education system; of destroying the constitutional separation of powers."[94] Anxious about what they perceived as a fundamental issue of preserving the balance of power between centralized government and state governments, the editors of *National Review* opposed the civil rights demands of African Americans and supported southern white opponents of integration.

Grassroots conservatives gave higher priority to the battle against Soviet communism than to the civil rights issue, which they tended to downplay. Nonetheless, Goldwater's vote against the Civil Rights Act of 1964 was applauded by conservatives as principled politics, but its effect was rocking-chair politics: For all its motion, it created a sitting target for opponents, did not advance the conservative cause one iota, and perhaps even moved it back. Some conservative Republican politicians, sensing that Goldwater's position was a loser, attempted to mitigate its impact. In the GOP Convention, Senator Dirksen, a Goldwater supporter, worked successfully with Representative Melvin Laird of Wisconsin, chairman of the Platform Committee, to include a plank in the Republican National Platform calling for the "full implementation and faithful execution of the Civil Rights Act of 1964."[95]

Goldwater's staff realized from early polls that the campaign was over even before it had begun.[96] The polls proved accurate. In November, voters gave Johnson 43 million votes to Goldwater's 27 million, a difference of 16 million votes. This translated into 486 to 52 Electoral College votes.[97] The Goldwater debacle was costly to the Republican party and would continue to haunt it for the next decade and a half. In the Senate, George Murphy won in California and Roman Hruska in Nebraska. Liberal Republicans did somewhat better. John Lindsay won a New York seat in the House. George Romney won reelection as governor in Michigan.

In subsequent campaigns, Democrats continued to exploit the extremism issue. Typical in this respect was the scurrilous campaign waged against the incumbent New York congressman Steven Derounian (R) in 1964. His Democratic opponent, Les L. Wolff, a peppery public relations man, described Derounian as being "tied up" with the Birchers. The allegation stemmed from an incident that occurred in 1961, when Derounian joined Robert Michel (R-Illinois), Peter Frelinghuysen (R-New Jersey), and Melvin Laird (R-Wisconsin) on a Republican Congressional Committee tour of the far West. At a meeting on October 5, 1961, in Los Angeles, the congressional delegation was asked whether it supported the reelection of Rep. John Rousselot (R-California), whose Birch membership had become a matter of public knowledge. Derounian, speaking for the delegation, declared, "We're here to sell Republicanism and there's room in our party for all shades of opinion." Three years later, when Derounian ran for reelection to a seventh term, Wolff accused him of having traveled to California to support Rousselot.

Derounian responded later in the campaign by publishing ads in district newspapers declaring himself a conservative, not an extremist. Placed on the defensive in the last days of the campaign, he lost by 2,600 votes out of more than 190,000 cast.

The 1964 election left the GOP sharply divided. Following the debacle of 1964, moderates within the party sought to regain control and move it toward the political center. This meant purging Goldwater supporters from high-level positions within the party hierarchy. While right-wingers proclaimed that 27 million people had voted for a conservative Republican presidential candidate despite an unprecedented media smear, the election returned the GOP Right to the fringes of the party.

3

Trust and Betrayal in
the Nixon Years

Lyndon Johnson's victory in 1964 carried the seeds of destruction of the New Deal political coalition. Johnson viewed his landslide as both a mandate to expand liberal social and civil rights programs and a political cushion to increase America's involvement in Vietnam without leaving him vulnerable to attack from the Right. The New Deal coalition did not collapse on its own accord—conservatives mobilized to defeat it—but liberals were not helped by Johnson's inflated rhetoric. Johnson raised expectations enormously with promises to end poverty within his lifetime, to create true racial equality, and to defeat Communism in Vietnam. Most attracted to these promises of a better life were African Americans, who voted overwhelmingly for Johnson in 1964, as well as many moderate and liberal whites. When Johnson's Great Society failed to meet their expectations, angry emotions erupted in race riots in America's inner cities.

At the same time, the escalation of the war and the body count in Vietnam led to campus protests and mass demonstrations, sometimes resulting in violent confrontations with the police. The rise of a "hippy" counterculture that fostered drug use and easy sex heightened middle-class anxieties about a breakdown in American society. Urban riots caused further erosion of the Democratic party among southern voters. These voters did not stream directly into the Republican party, however. Indeed, in the South, where the backlash was greatest, the Democratic party still held sway. As a consequence, the liberal administrative state under Johnson had expanded and become further entrenched, seemingly impenetrable to conservative attack.

In this volatile political environment, the GOP Right was unable to take full advantage of the waning fortunes of liberalism; conservatives were too embattled in the Republican party in the immediate aftermath of the Goldwater debacle, and they lacked a declared presidential candidate of their own to rally around. One possible conservative candidate, the newly elected governor of California, Ronald Reagan, refused to declare himself in the race. Amid the uncertainty, many conservatives turned to Richard Nixon, who promised to pursue a strong defense policy and to quell violent protest on college campuses and riots in the inner cities. Once he entered the White House, Nixon proved not to be a conservative at all.

By 1968, after nearly a decade of social experimentation by a liberal Democratic administration, the liberal agenda was losing its appeal. The time seemed ripe for conservatives to step forward and establish a new political order, but this was not to be. The history of the conservative movement was not a Whiggish advancement toward predestined victory but a story of defeat after defeat.[1] The years 1965 to 1976 were not good for liberals or conservatives. American politics had become polarized, but neither end of the political spectrum seemed to benefit from the electorate's disillusionment.

Purge within the GOP

Following the 1964 election, Republicans were eager to move the party to the political center and reestablish it as a party of moderation. GOP moderates moved to replace Goldwaterites in the chairmanship and staff of the Republican National Committee (RNC). Conservatives saw where things were headed and pushed back. Ronald Reagan, who had been co-chairman of California Citizens for Goldwater, declared, "We don't intend to turn the Republican party over to the traitors in the battle that just ended." South Carolina's Senator Strom Thurmond, who had bolted to the Republican party in 1964, predicted that the GOP would become a conservative party "in spite of Rockefeller and his ilk." Moderates and liberals in the party were equally direct. Senator Hugh

Scott of Pennsylvania, who just barely survived reelection, told the press that "the present party leadership must be replaced—all of it."[2]

The fight centered on replacing Goldwater's appointee to the chairmanship of the RNC, Dean Burch, an attorney from Tucson. Conservatives saw control of the RNC as the key to dominating the Republican party for years to come. As the Goldwater staff member Karl Hess later observed, conservatives believed that if Goldwater could win the nomination, "he would also win control of the Republican National Committee, and for this, the future of the party."[3] This agenda had become evident once Burch stepped into the chairmanship following his selection by Goldwater at the 1964 convention. Working with his executive director, John Grenier, Burch began replacing moderate and liberal members of the RNC executive committee with conservatives. He also fired or demoted RNC staff members who were not ideological conservatives. One of the disgruntled staff members circulated a bumper sticker that read, "Better LBJ than John Grenier."

As soon as the November presidential election was over, moderates counterattacked. The Michigan national committeeman John Martin called for Burch's removal, a sentiment echoed by the former RNC chairman Thruston Morton, a senator from Kentucky, who said, "We have got to change the national committee and we have got to change the party's image, by broadening the base of the party's appeal." Burch, however, refused to resign, reigniting the battle between conservatives and moderate-liberals within the party. Rockefeller lieutenant George Hinman was instrumental in organizing the anti-Goldwater forces to oust Burch. Through his efforts, they selected Ray Bliss, the chairman of the Ohio Republican party. Bliss was seen as "non-ideological" and a superb "nut and bolts" manager. At the same time, the moderate-dominated Republican Governors Association joined the call for Burch's removal at their December 5 meeting in Denver by calling for "inclusion" not "exclusion." It did not take a close reading of the statement to see that the governors meant that Burch and his conservative gang were exclusionists. Goldwater responded by declaring that any removal of Dean Burch would be "a repudiation of a great segment of our party, and a repudiation of me."[4]

The campaign against Burch gained further momentum when midwestern Republicans swung to Bliss in large numbers. The 1964 election took a heavy toll on Republicans in the nation's midsection, who lost nineteen of the total thirty-eight states that went to the Democrats in 1964. In Iowa alone, Republicans lost five of the six House seats they had controlled in the state. These losses led Senate Minority Leader Everitt Dirksen of Illinois to work actively to replace Burch with Bliss. Dirksen joined House Minority Leader Jerry Ford to denounce the John Birch Society in a press conference, maintaining that the JBS's position on the United Nations, civil rights, and meeting the threat of Communism was "irreconcilable with the stand taken by the Republican party and there is no room in the Republican party for the John Birch Society."[5] With the GOP about to rupture, Goldwater finally agreed to ask Burch to resign and have Bliss take over the RNC. The announcement came on January 12, 1965. Many conservatives on the RNC were outraged by what they saw as a liberal coup. As one national committeewoman observed, "For thirty years it's been conservatives who had to make concessions. If the others [Burch opponents] feel sincerely about unity, why don't they make concessions once in a while?"[6]

Bliss was not an ideologue but a party pragmatist who developed a national reputation for building the GOP in Ohio. Once in the chairmanship, he openly attacked "extremists" in the party.[7] His major accomplishment, however, was reinvigorating party organization at the national, state, and local levels. Under his leadership, the Republican National Finance Committee increased its income from $4.2 million in 1965 to $29.6 million in 1968. Bliss also restored party discipline, which limited the Right's ability to seize control of the GOP.

At the same time, party moderates moved to prevent further gains by the Goldwater faction within other party organizations. In particular, they were concerned that Phyllis Schlafly might win the presidency of the National Federation of Republican Women (NFRW), the largest female GOP group in the nation. The organization's election was approaching in 1966, and the image of Schlafly, well known for her denunciation of eastern Republicans, whom she labeled "the Kingmakers," gave the GOP regulars cause for unrest. The defeat of Goldwater in 1964 had thrown the presidential nomination in 1968 wide open, reviving from the ashes the political careers of Richard Nixon and Nelson Rockefeller. In Michigan, George Romney's landslide reelection as governor placed him on the national stage as a GOP presidential contender.

Regardless of who won the 1968 GOP presidential nomination, the

Republican establishment did not want the author of *A Choice Not an Echo* serving as president of the NFRW in an election year. From the outset, the battle for the NFRW presidency was seen as a struggle for control over the Republican party. *National Review* publisher William Rusher warned that the liberal eastern wing of the party had targeted the NFRW and the Young Republicans as the battle lines for control of the party.[8] To prevent Schlafly from winning election to the 400,000-member body, moderates led by Elly Peterson, a Romney operative in Michigan, engineered the nomination of Gladys O'Donnell, a Californian Republican who had warned earlier of "extremism" within the National Federation. In the bitterly fought campaign, O'Donnell defeated Schlafly by only 516 votes out of 3,404 cast. Schlafly charged that the voting had been rigged and that Ray Bliss and the RNC had worked behind the scenes to defeat her.[9] The NFRW election reinforced the view among conservatives that Republican insiders had undertaken a campaign to purge the party of conservatives.[10]

Meanwhile, Republican party organizations at the state level began to clear out extremist elements from their ranks. Typical of these purges was the state of Washington under the newly elected Republican Dan Evans, a liberal who had served two terms in the House before winning in the highly Democratic state. Working through Charles "Gummie" Johnson, whom Evans had appointed as the first full-time chairman of the Washington State Republican Central Committee, Evans initiated a systematic purge of Birchers within the state GOP. Johnson defended the expulsion of Birchers from the GOP in the press. "We had to make the term 'conservative' respectable again," he contended. "The only way to do it was to get the far-right off the backs of conservatives. The Republican Party is not far-right."[11] Neither Evans nor Montgomery were conservative, but such rhetoric was meant to appeal to conservatives within the GOP who were also wary of Bircher influence.

Liberalism in Crisis

While Republicans sought to return their party to the center, President Lyndon Baines Johnson launched the Great Society, a program that called for the expansion of the welfare state. Johnson promised that through the Great Society initiative, poverty would be eliminated in ten years. Moreover, American cities would be rebuilt, highways beautified, meaningful jobs provided to everyone who desired work, and race relations improved. A war in Southeast Asia hobbled the Great Society politically and financially, and racial riots following the 1964 election forced Johnson to retreat from his domestic program. Republicans in the House attacked Community Action Program (CAP) workers for participating in these social disturbances. In response, Johnson ordered the CAP funds cut.

Race riots did irreparable damage to Johnson's domestic program. Surveys showed consistently improving attitudes by whites toward blacks in both the North and the South, including a growing acceptance of school integration. Racial riots did not derail improving racial attitudes, but they raised apprehension among whites about social order and lessened support for Johnson's Great Society programs.[12] A Gallup poll taken in 1967 revealed that 45 percent of whites (10 percent of blacks) blamed racial riots on outside agitators, while 16 percent of whites (36 percent of blacks) believed that "prejudice, promises not kept, and bad treatment" were behind the riots. Only 14 percent of whites (28 percent of blacks) believed that poverty, slums, and ghetto conditions caused the riots. Attitudes toward law and order at the time were revealed in a Harris poll that asked respondents whether "people who throw fire bombs in riots should be shot." Sixty-eight percent of whites said "yes" and 22 percent replied "no." Blacks, meanwhile, were nearly evenly divided on the issue, with 47 percent answering "yes," and 42 responding "no."

A racial riot in the Watts section of Los Angeles just five days after Johnson signed the Voting Rights Act of 1965 shocked the nation. There was no link between the legislation and the Watts riot, but the disturbance suggested that progress on civil rights was not necessarily a remedy for social problems in northern inner cities. The Watts riot lasted a full week and left 34 people dead, 1,110 injured, and an estimated $40 million in property damage. The following year, there were 38 riots that resulted in 7 deaths and 500 injuries. In the first nine months of 1967, there were 164 riots. Public disturbances in Newark and Detroit lasted for a week each and left a total of 64 people dead. In Detroit, federal troops were called out to suppress the rioting, just the third time in American history that they had been sent in to quell a local insurrection.[13] These riots undermined white blue-collar and middle-class support for the Great Society. A Harris poll in August 1967 revealed that twice as many whites as blacks believed that the riots had been organized by outside agitators. As a leading historian of law and order in this period concludes, "In the eyes of critics on the left and the right, the riots had discredited the entire liberal enterprise."[14]

Support for the liberalism of the Great Society fell further with Johnson's expansion of the war in Vietnam following the 1964 election. In general, conservatives supported the war, but not unanimously. Although division within conservative ranks was not as deep as it was among liberals, the war in Vietnam placed the Right in a difficult position. For twenty years conservatives had called for a tougher stand against Communist expansion, and during the 1964 campaign Goldwater had called for a military escalation of the war in Vietnam. But confronted with increased U.S. involvement in the war under Johnson in 1965, right-wingers found themselves in an awkward position, ideologically and politically.

Conservatives backed a war against Communist aggression, but they also saw Vietnam as "Johnson's war." Though they supported the troops fighting in the jungles of Southeast Asia, they accused the administration of refusing to unleash the full power of the American military to win the war.[15] Right-wingers called for the administration to bomb Hanoi and mine its harbor; expand the war into the North; and use the threat of nuclear weapons to bring the Communists to the negotiating table. Conservatives also criticized Johnson for pursuing détente with the Soviet Union. *National Review* described his foreign policy as "Hard-Soft Schizophrenia."[16]

By 1968, polls showed that the majority of Americans did not favor escalation of the war in Vietnam. American support for the war had already been waning when, in the spring of 1968, the Communists launched the so-called Tet offensive, which only accelerated the decline of public support for the conflict. Later, conservatives would argue that the Tet offensive was a major military defeat for the North Vietnamese, but in the spring of 1968 American confidence in the war effort had collapsed.[17] For months the administration had been telling the American people that the war was being won. Now, after thirty-four months of active military involvement, America seemed no closer to winning the war than when it had begun. The Tet offensive in 1968 proved to be a military defeat for the Communists, but Americans had enough of a war that seemed to be an endless quagmire.

This reaction set the stage for Senator Eugene McCarthy (D-Minnesota), a little-known liberal from the Midwest, to enter the Democratic primary in New Hampshire as a viable antiwar candidate. When the underfunded McCarthy campaign, which relied heavily on youth volunteers, received a surprising 42 percent of the primary vote, Robert Kennedy, the younger brother of the late president, threw his hat into the ring. Faced with a Kennedy challenge, Johnson made the stunning announcement in a televised address on Sunday, March 31, that he would not seek or accept the nomination of his party for another term as president. The Democratic nomination became a free-for-all as McCarthy, Kennedy, and Johnson's heir apparent, Vice President Hubert Humphrey, battled it out for the presidential nomination. Joining the fray was George Wallace, who as the governor of Alabama had opposed a federal court order to integrate the University of Alabama.

On April 4, two days after Eugene McCarthy won the Wisconsin primary, the civil rights leader Martin Luther King, Jr., was gunned down by a lone assassin in Memphis. Rioting broke out in dozens of American cities, including the nation's capital, where the night skies were lit by fires across the city. Most politicians, as well as established black leaders, denounced the rioting as an insult to Martin Luther King, Jr.'s message of nonviolence, but by 1968 some black radicals had rejected King's leadership. Black nationalists like Stokely Carmichael called for "black power" to counter white power, while H. Rap Brown cried, "Burn, baby, burn!" In April and May, students at Columbia University went on strike. They occupied the president's office and demanded that the university stop its threatened expansion into surrounding urban areas.

The reaction in the United States was predictable: Republican politicians began calling for "law and order."[18] The law-and-order issue captured and reinforced the public's anxieties about rising street crime, campus disturbances, urban riots, and civil rights protests. The Johnson administration responded with legislation to alleviate economic and social conditions, which they believed caused crime. At the same time, Johnson also enacted a major piece of crime-control legislation, the Safe Streets Act of 1968. He declared the act his greatest achievement to control crime, but liberals appeared hesitant to tackle the issue of street crime. Indeed, many liberals were reluctant to support the Safe Streets Act because of its wiretapping provisions. If this position made them appear "soft" on street crime, they often seemed even worse on urban riots. Following racial rioting in the summer of 1968, Hubert Humphrey told the press that if he had been born in a ghetto he might have staged a pretty good riot himself, to which his Democratic challenger, George Wallace, answered that he had grown up in a house without running water but had never started a riot.

The more politically astute Robert Kennedy began emphasizing that as attorney general of the United States, he had prosecuted the corrupt Teamster leader Jimmy Hoffa and put him in jail. Kennedy might have presented a different image for liberals on the crime issue, but his assassination following his victory in the California primary ended this possibility. With Kennedy's death, McCarthy seem to lose heart in the campaign, and Hubert Humphrey won the Democratic party nomination in Chicago. But bloody riots between radical antiwar protesters and the Chicago police outside the convention all aggravated discord within the severely divided Democratic party. Newspapers across the country blamed the rioting on an unrestrained Chicago police force that had been unleashed by Chicago mayor Richard Daley, a Humphrey supporter.

Sensing the first signs of cracks in the liberal regime, George Wallace left the Democratic party to exploit working-class white resentment toward African Americans, rising crime rates, growing welfare rolls, inner-city riots, and the war dragging on in Southeast Asia. Running on the American Independent ticket, he appealed to less-educated white voters, who shouted with rollicking enthusiasm at his attacks on pointy-headed intellectuals, government bureaucrats, black militants, hippies, welfare mothers, and "bearded anarchists." Despite Wallace's popularity among poor and lower–middle class whites in the North and the South, few right-wing leaders rallied to his campaign, with the exception of John Schmitz, a southern California community college instructor and John Birch Society member.[19] Most Republican conservatives refused to support Wallace even though he called for law and order and expressed open disdain for welfare and opposed court-ordered busing. For all of his conservative rhetoric, the GOP Right did not see Wallace as a conservative at all. Rather, right-wingers viewed him as a typical New Deal southerner who welcomed federal monies for public works and welfare in his state, while demanding that the federal government recuse itself from enforcing civil rights laws concerning voting rights and integration of public places.

Wallace's overt appeal to supporters of racial segregation held little attraction for most conservatives in the Republican party. The civil rights movement in the South and racial riots in the North had sharpened segregationist opinion, but the white supremacist movement stood largely outside the mainstream political arena. Although Wallace drew a few GOP Right leaders into his party, and the press at the time tried to associate his campaign with the conservative movement, sharp differences in class and political outlook separated the two movements.[20] Wallace's third-party try and the surprising support it drew revealed the volatility of the political climate at the time.

There were indications that Republicans could win the South from the Democrats. In 1952, Eisenhower secured some southern states including Florida, Texas, North Carolina, Virginia, and Tennessee. In 1956, he won these states plus Louisiana. In the Goldwater campaign of 1964, Republicans penetrated the Deep South for the first time since Reconstruction by winning Louisiana, Mississippi, Alabama, Georgia, and South Carolina. Responding to the potential Republican threat, many local Democratic leaders in the South became more conservative, and some even vociferous in their pro-segregationist stands, but they still remained within the party. The Voting Rights Act of 1965 and the Supreme Court's one-man-one-vote decision, which had been top priorities on the liberal agenda, succeeded in loosening the Democrats' hold on the South. In response, by the late 1960s some Democrats sought to accommodate the changing South by building biracial coalitions to hold off a rising Republican party.[21]

Nixon and the 1968 Election

Divisions within the Democratic party encouraged Republicans to believe that they could win the White House. Only four years earlier, the party had suffered its worst defeat since the election of 1932. In the midterm elections of 1966, Republican hopes for a comeback brightened when the GOP gained four seats in the Senate and 47 seats in the House. By 1968, Richard Nixon had emerged as the odds-on favorite to win the Republican nomination. After losing the California gubernatorial race in 1962, he had returned to center stage in American presidential politics, a comeback comparable only to that of James K. Polk, who had lost his bid for election as Tennessee's governor in 1841 and 1843 before winning the Democratic presidential nomination in 1844.

On the sidelines stood George Romney, a former automobile executive who had breathed new life into American Motors and then used this success to win election as governor in Michigan. Romney's candidacy showed that divisions within the GOP were far from healed. In 1964 he had staked his claim as a moderate by refusing to support Goldwater in the general election. This act had won him the support of liberal Republicans such as Senator Jacob Javits (New York) and Senator Hugh Scott (Pennsylvania), but it had also caused the Right to distrust him nearly as much as they disdained Rockefeller.[22] Romney's bid for the nomination came to an abrupt end when he lost the New Hampshire primary after declaring that he had earlier been "brainwashed" by the State Department into supporting the war in Southeast Asia, which he now opposed. Romney's withdrawal from the race created an opportunity for Nelson Rockefeller to pick up the liberal banner. When Nixon soundly defeated Rockefeller in the Oregon primary in late April, Nixon's nomination appeared sewn up. Sitting in the background, however, was Ronald Reagan, the recently elected governor of California. Acting on the advice of his campaign manager, Clifton White, Reagan did not declare his candidacy, but instead hoped for a deadlocked convention that would turn to him as the compromise candidate.

Such a strategy was clearly antiquated, given that delegate counts had become so precise as to eliminate dark-horse insurgent campaigns. Still, many on the GOP Right distrusted Richard Nixon because of his support for liberal-backed Eisenhower over conservative Taft in 1952, his internationalist foreign policy outlook, and his denunciation of the John Birch Society in 1962. To reassure his right-wing base, Nixon carefully cultivated Senator Strom Thurmond and the grassroots activist Phyllis Schlafly by pledging a strong stance on national defense, including a restoration of America's nuclear superiority. He also promised Strom Thurmond that his first two nominations for the Supreme Court would be from the South. Thurmond wanted a Supreme Court to thwart forced busing in the South. His support for Nixon proved critical in keeping the southern and conservative delegates in Nixon's column.

The sixty-five-year-old Thurmond represented the emergent Republican party in the South. In his early political career as a judge and governor of South Carolina, Thurmond had distinguished himself by his relatively moderate views on race (compared with the virulent racism of other state judges). He opened his courtroom to black lawyers and called for dramatically increased funding for black schools in his state. In 1948, however, he broke with the national Democratic party over integration by federal law and declared himself a States' Rights party presidential candidate. Elected to the U.S. Senate in 1954 as a Democrat, he switched parties in 1964 to support Goldwater. Thurmond was one of the most admired Republican politicians in the South, and his endorsement helped win Nixon the nomination at a time when some conservatives were looking to Ronald Reagan.

To shore up his support on the Right, Nixon picked Maryland governor Spiro Agnew as his running mate. Only nine years earlier Agnew's highest political ambition had been a seat on the Loch Raven Community Council. Agnew started his career as a Rockefeller Republican, and because of his support (albeit lukewarm) for open housing in Maryland, he was characterized in the 1966 gubernatorial election as a liberal. He defeated a Democrat who had narrowly won his party's nomination running as an opponent of integration. Once in the governor's mansion, Agnew took a strong stand for law and order when a riot broke out in Baltimore following the assassination of Martin Luther King, Jr. Agnew told black leaders, "I call on you to publicly repudiate all black racists. This, so far, you have been unwilling to do." His rhetoric and law and order stance garnered him national attention and sufficed to win him support among conservatives at the Miami Republican National Convention who were eager to prevent Nixon from placing a liberal Republican on the ticket. Nixon saw Agnew as a counter to the Wallace threat.

Nixon courted southern whites, working-class ethnics, and the suburban middle class. This strategy entailed support for law and order, reform of the welfare state, and the promise of a secret plan to end the war in Vietnam. His opponent Hubert Humphrey faltered in the early stages of the campaign, but as the prospect of Nixon's winning the White House grew, Democrats disgruntled about the war in Vietnam and the assassination of Robert Kennedy rallied to the Democratic nominee's campaign. This surge came too late, though it made for a tight election. More detrimental to the Humphrey campaign was the Wallace campaign, which drew white southerners, ethnic Catholics, and union members from the Democratic party to the American Independent party. On Election Day, Nixon barely won, receiving 43.5 percent of the vote to Humphrey's 42.7 percent and Wallace's 13.5 percent.

Even though Nixon made heavy inroads into the white ethnic vote in the Northeast and Midwest, he failed to achieve a major breakthrough in the South. In large part this was due to George Wallace's appeal in the Deep South. Nixon won only North Carolina, South Carolina, Tennessee, Florida, Virginia, and Kentucky. Nixon cut into the northeastern and midwestern blue-collar, white ethnic vote, but Republicans still needed to break through in the South.[23] Still, many voters once aligned with the Democratic party increasingly began to see the party and its liberal agenda as hostile to their interests. Their allegiance to the Democratic party had been substantially shaken.

The course of history might have been different had the Democrats won. Liberals might have kept the White House if Humphrey had won in 1968. Bobby Kennedy might have been an even stronger candidate if he had lived. The burning question remains, if Bobby Kennedy had not been assassinated in Los Angeles, would he have won the Democratic nomination? After his victory in the California primary, he was headed into his home state of New York, where he was certain to win. He would have gained momentum going into the Democratic Convention, but he probably did not have enough delegate votes to win the nomination. President Johnson had kept tight control of the delegates who remained committed to his candidate, Vice President Humphrey. Johnson despised Bobby Kennedy and would never have accepted his nomination to head the Democratic ticket in 1968. Nonetheless, Johnson might have been forced to accept a Humphrey-Kennedy ticket, and with this the Democrats would in all likelihood have kept the White House in 1968.

If this had happened, Nixon's political career would have been over. Nelson Rockefeller would have had a strong claim to the 1972 nomination, especially in light of the fact that another conservative-backed Republican in 1968 had given the party a back-to-back loss. Instead, Nixon won in 1968. Many conservatives believed that Nixon owed the election to them and were confident that he was one of their own. Not all conservatives felt this way, however. Watching Nixon during the campaign and his first days in office, William Rusher confided to a friend that he doubted whether conservatives had made a "wise" choice in supporting Nixon.[24] Brent Bozell, writing in the ultra-Catholic magazine *Triumph,* intoned that by supporting Nixon the conservative movement had "ceased to be an important political force in America."[25]

If some conservatives were ambivalent about Nixon, liberals were certain that he was an anti-Communist reactionary at heart, too devious to put his authentic beliefs on display. Liberals despised Nixon for what they considered his questionable methods of defeating the liberal Jerry Voorhis for Congress in 1946 and the liberal Helen Douglas for Senate in 1950, as well as his involvement in the Hiss case.[26] The Hiss case in particular convinced many conservatives and most liberals that Nixon was a man of the Right. In reality, however, Nixon was above all an opportunist. He was an anti-Communist and a cold warrior, but his outlook proved to be remarkably flexible. As an avid reader of English history, Nixon saw himself as a Disraeli, the nineteenth-century conservative prime minister who had undertaken liberal reforms as necessary steps for the survival of the Tory party. Nixon had entered the Republican party as a "Modern Republican," eager to disassociate the party from the isolationism of Robert Taft. He wanted to transform the GOP into the party of internationalism. Nixon's views on domestic policy were determined by what he thought could garner political strength. As vice president under Eisenhower, he had played a pivotal role in pushing through the Civil Rights Act of 1957, the most important such legislation enacted since Reconstruction. Nixon believed that the GOP could regain the African-American vote that had been lost to Franklin Roosevelt in the 1930s. But following the 1960 election, when blacks overwhelmingly voted for Nixon's rival, John F. Kennedy, Nixon retreated from a strong civil rights stance, and during the 1968 election he criticized forced busing to integrate schools.

While Nixon appointed some conservatives to his administration, from the outset he saw the key to his reelection as beating liberal Democrats at their own game by usurping their program.[27] There had been early indications of Nixon's distrust of the Right within his party. In October 1965, for example, *National Review* reported that Nixon had told a group of reporters that when it came to the GOP's rebuilding efforts, "the Buckleyites" were "a threat to the Republican party even more menacing than the Birchers." The editors of *National Review* demanded an explanation through Pat Buchanan, a St. Louis columnist known for his contacts with the Right who had been hired as Nixon's full-time speechwriter. A coherent explanation of this comment never came because Nixon would not be distracted from his major goal of creating a majority party, however opportunistic the means. Indeed, at one point he suggested that this new political alignment might include black militants who rejected welfarism for a program of self-help. [28]

Nixon was the first president since Zachary Taylor to have come into office with both houses of Congress controlled by the opposing party. Under Nixon, the Democratic-controlled Congress became increasingly liberal. Conservative Republicans who played a critical role in nominating and electing Nixon were not sympathetic to his political dilemma. The Senate had fifty-seven Democrats and forty-three Republicans. Republicans had not held so many seats since the Eisenhower years, but liberals were becoming a dominant force in the Senate, as older southern conservatives dwindled and northeastern liberals rose in seniority. In the House, conservatives dominated key military and foreign policy committees, but liberals were on the rise there, too. In special elections held in 1969, conservatives took some joy in the victories of Barry Goldwater, Jr. (the presidential candidate's son) in California and Philip Crane in Illinois. Crane won the North Shore Chicago suburban district that had opened when Donald Rumsfeld left to join the Nixon administration. Philip Crane's campaign as a free-market conservative attracted national attention and offered a glimmer of hope to the conservative movement, but Democrats remained in control of Congress throughout Nixon's presidency.[29]

Even if Nixon had wanted to move in a conservative direction—which he did not—Democratic control of Congress would have blocked such a strategy. Under pressure from a liberal Congress, Nixon pursued a serpentine course that mostly veered toward the left on both domestic issues and foreign policy, with the important exception of the war in Vietnam. In Vietnam, he intensified bombing, while his national security adviser and later secretary of state, Henry Kissinger, began secret negotiations with the North Vietnamese. Nixon kept congressional Democrats off balance, but the general perception remained, reinforced by the news media, that Nixon was a conservative. Even after he opened relations with mainland China, entered into an unprecedented arms-control agreement with the Soviet Union, and expanded the welfare and regulatory state, liberals believed that Nixon, albeit a clever politician, was an ideological conservative.

Nixon brought his own fears about liberals into the White House. Ultimately, his deep-seated paranoia proved to be his undoing. As the presidential speechwriter Patrick Buchanan, a dedicated, loyal, and honest Nixonite, admitted, Nixon could be exceptionally vindictive. Presidential aide John Ehrlichman was more blunt in his assessment when he observed that there was a side to Nixon that was "like the flat, dark side of the moon."[30] The president's pathological concern with the opposition led to a flagrant misuse of power by his subordinates. During the presidential campaign of 1972, several of his supporters attempted to burglarize the offices of the Democratic National Committee at the Watergate building complex in Washington, D.C. This abuse of power galvanized Nixon's opponents, who believed that the president was directly involved in ordering the break-in. In the highly charged climate of the early 1970s, however, many conservatives rallied behind Nixon as a victim of the Left, while liberals viewed his machinations and policy twists and turns as dangerous manifestations of the Republican Right in power.

Nixon's politics were designed to keep his opponents off guard, while ensuring his place in history. He derided the "welfare mess" and then proposed a guaranteed national income for the poor; when this failed to muster support, he pushed through a supplemental-income program for the poor and a food stamp program.[31] He curried favor with Catholics by proclaiming the importance of parochial schools, but he also pushed through the Family Planning Services Act, which expanded the government's role in family planning services. He attacked forced busing to end segregation, while at the same time encouraging the Equal Employment Opportunity Commission to begin instituting affirmative-action programs for African Americans on federal projects. He pressured corporations to contribute to his reelection campaign, while pushing through Congress a series of environmental regulatory laws that often interfered with their profit-making. His support for the Equal Rights Amendment (ERA) passed in 1972 by Congress was lukewarm after its passage, but he publicly endorsed the legal affirmation of women's equality. He declared himself a believer in free-market capitalism yet instituted wage and price controls as the election approached. And, for all his talk about cutting the budget, by 1975 social services financed by the federal government had grown greatly under his administration, especially for the middle class.[32] Nixon expanded universal coverage of social benefits through programs such as Medicare and Social Security, which benefited primarily the middle class, while cutting funding for many programs aimed at the poor. In his administration, social expenditures totaled approximately $338.7 billion. Speaking from the conservative perspective, the recently elected U.S. senator from North Carolina, Jesse Helms, observed, "It pains me to say this, but the current administration [Nixon's] cannot escape a large measure of blame for the current easy acceptance of Leviathan-like government expansion. This expansion has, if anything, become even faster under the current administration."[33]

Moral Decline and the 1970 Election

As the 1970 midterm elections approached, Republicans hoped to reverse the liberal gains in Congress that had occurred in the 1960s. Polls revealed a growing antiwar sentiment among the American public, which led some segments of the Democratic party to move to the left. Democrats sensed that Nixon was in political trouble and might be defeated for reelection. They looked to Senator Edward Kennedy of Massachusetts to run against Nixon, but catastrophe struck in 1969, when Senator Kennedy's car went off a bridge on Chappaquiddick Island, killing his staff worker Mary Jo Kopechne. The senator's failure to call the police immediately and his changing stories destroyed his presidential chances.[34] The American Right saw Chappaquiddick as a symbol of Kennedy family decadence, set within a declining moral climate in which the elite eschewed traditional values and personal responsibility in favor of self-indulgence.

Chappaquiddick occurred within a growing counterculture of youth which rejected materialistic values and sought an intensity of experience through drugs, mysticism, and sexuality. Representing this counterculture were the hippies, young people who sought an alternative lifestyle by rejecting political involvement, taking drugs, wearing their hair long, and living communally. The drug culture was closely associated with a sexual revolution which had been gathering speed since World War II. This revolution had been made possible by the development of artificial contraception—the pill—as well as by changing cultural mores. Sexual relations outside of wedlock became more common, and young couples increasingly chose to live together outside of marriage. Homosexuality, which had been hidden in "the closet," became more visible and tolerated. In 1969, states began to allow unilateral divorce without allegation of fault, in acknowledgment of a divorce rate that had jumped precipitously from around 10 percent of marriages in 1960 to more than 30 percent in 1970.

Conservatives lashed out at these cultural changes. Suzanne Labin's book *Hippies, Drugs, and Promiscuity* (1972) summarized the right-wing jeremiad against the breakdown of morality in America. This fear of cultural erosion was widespread and sometimes reached bizarre manifestations, as seen in David A. Noebel's pamphlet "Communism, Hypnotism, and the Beatles," published by the Christian Crusade in 1965. In the pamphlet, which reached a printing of 35,000 copies, Noebel cajoled parents, "Let's make sure four mop-headed anti-Christ beatniks don't destroy our children's emotional and mental stability and ultimately destroy our nation as Plato warned in his Republic." He maintained that the Beatles were part of a Communist "music master plan" aimed at "rendering a generation of American youth useless through nerve-jamming, mental deterioration and retardation."[35]

Such sentiment reflected the far fringes of the Right in America and was not taken seriously by most conservatives, though moderates and right-wingers did agree that the counterculture was indicative of a general disorder in American society.[36] Such views contrasted sharply with visions found on the cultural left in 1970. In his best-selling book *The Greening of America,* published in 1970, Yale University law professor Charles Reich foresaw a coming revolution that "promises a higher reason, a more human community, and a new and liberated individual. Its ultimate creation will be a new and enduring wholeness and beauty—a renewed relationship of man to himself, to other men, to society, to nature, and to the land."[37]

Contrary to Reich's prediction of a new utopia of harmonious life, America in 1970 appeared polarized politically and culturally—a phenomenon that would characterize national life through the end of the century. Republicans, certain that the majority of Americans were silently angered by what they perceived as undisciplined student protesters, sexually free hippies living off the fat of the land, demanding blacks, and urban crime, sought to mobilize this polarization through a "law and order" theme in the congressional elections of 1970. Statistics showed that violent crimes like random murder, mugging, armed robbery, and rape were on the rise, and Republicans sought to capitalize on Americans' anxieties by linking crime rates to the rise of the counterculture.[38] This strategy meant downplaying economic problems as the country experienced recession.

The 1970 midterm election could have been worse for Republicans, but as it was they lost two seats in the Senate and twelve in the House. These losses revealed fissures within the GOP as some conservatives began to openly criticize the administration's domestic and foreign policy. There was a growing belief among conservatives that Nixon had betrayed the GOP Right—whom he had promised to restore American nuclear supremacy—by pursuing arms control negotiations with the Soviet Union.[39] The GOP Right continued to believe that the Soviet Union was a serious military threat and that it was intent on achieving first-strike nuclear superiority either to intimidate the United States or to launch a surprise attack against it. Conservatives rejected the belief that the Russians had given up on their goal of world domination.

The Right was already uneasy with the administration's foreign policy when Nixon revealed in the spring of 1971 that his administration had opened relations with mainland China. Upon hearing the news, the Right exploded. After decades of calling for the defense of Taiwan and keeping China out of the United Nations, not to mention warning about the threat that Communist China posed to the free world, conservatives were left stunned by Nixon's pursuit of relations. The conservative radio commentator Clarence Manion told Eugene Lyons, a longtime foe of Communism, "This is madness, of course, but it reveals that Nixon is a politician first, statesman second, and anti-communist 'also ran.'"[40] William F. Buckley, Jr., asked in the August 1971 issue of *National Review* how long Nixon could postpone the widening gulf between conservatives and his administration "before the American right comes to the conclusion that he is not one of us."[41] Representative John Ashbrook echoed this sentiment in early 1972 in a speech to the House titled "How the U.S. Lost Military Superiority," in which he warned Nixon to "repudiate" his defense strategy.[42] The administration's answer came in the summer of 1972, when Nixon and Soviet premier Leonid Brezhnev signed the Strategic Arms Limitation Treaty (SALT) and a separate Anti-Ballistic Missile (ABM) Treaty. Conservatives concluded that Nixon had betrayed them.

The Failed Coup of 1972

By 1972, many conservatives were openly talking about challenging Nixon for reelection. Conservatives were not willing to support George Wallace in 1972, but the Right agreed that Nixon must go.[43] Some conservatives believed, incorrectly, as it turned out, that Nixon could be defeated in the GOP primaries; if he was not, then more than likely a liberal would win the White House and carry on where Nixon had left off. (Nixon, too, thought he might be vulnerable and initiated a chain of events to do anything and everything to ensure his reelection, a decision that ultimately led to his downfall.)

When Rep. John Ashbrook (R-Ohio) announced that he was a candidate for president, some conservatives believed that he could knock Nixon off the ticket. Ashbrook argued that Nixon had pushed liberal policies even though liberalism was being discredited with the electorate.[44] By attacking Nixon as a liberal acting in the guise of a conservative, Ashbrook hoped to do what few had accomplished: defeat an incumbent president seeking his party's nomination for a second term. Only five sitting presidents had lost their bid for nomination: John Tyler (1841–1845), Millard Fillmore (1850–1853), Franklin Pierce (1853–1857), James Buchanan (1857–1861), and Chester Arthur (1881–1885). Still, the attempt to remove Nixon from the Republican ticket in 1972 was downright quixotic given Nixon's actual support within the party.

Ashbrook drew support from the nation's leading conservative organization, the American Conservative Union (ACU), which he had helped organize in December 1965. The ACU had been formed as a vehicle to carry on the conservative cause following the devastating Goldwater defeat. Ashbrook had joined Frank S. Meyer, William F. Buckley, Jr., Brent Bozell, William Rusher, and former YAF president Robert E. Bauman in this effort. It was not surprising that the ACU should back Ashbrook's challenge. Indeed, the organization's hostility toward the president was probably behind Ashbrook's decision to run in the first place.

The ACU's strained relations with the administration typified the sense of betrayal that many conservatives felt toward Nixon. By 1968, after years of struggle, the ACU under Ashbrook's leadership had become a force on the Right. It was financially solvent, and through its political action committee, headed by William Rusher, the ACU had mobilized at the grassroots level. During the election of 1968, the ACU exerted its influence by urging conservatives to support the Nixon-Agnew ticket. ACU leaders felt that Nixon owed the organization and conservatives for his closely won election. Relations between the two quickly soured, however. Difficulties first arose when the ACU refused to support the administration's Family Assistance Plan, basically a guaranteed annual income program. Conservatives also opposed Nixon's revenue-sharing plan, fearing that it meant higher government spending, even though liberals correctly warned that it would mean cuts in social programs for the poor. By 1970, relations with the Nixon administration had grown so poor that the ACU felt compelled to publicly attack the administration in its report "The Nixon Administration: The Conservative Judgment," prepared by Henry Hazlitt and M. Stanton Evans. In July 1971, the ACU, now under the leadership of Ashbrook's replacement, M. Stanton Evans, announced that it was suspending its support for the Nixon administration. Shortly afterward, the ACU declared its support for Ashbrook's challenge to Nixon's reelection. The political operative Richard Viguerie, who had emerged as a major fundraiser in conservative circles through his direct-mail business, promised to raise funds for the challenge to a sitting president.

In the end, Ashbrook's support in the Republican party proved paper-thin. In fact, Nixon's most serious challenge came not from the Right but from the Left, when Representative Paul McCloskey (R-California), running as an antiwar Republican, entered the GOP primaries. McCloskey was a single-issue candidate, but he showed the continued, albeit declining, strength of the liberal wing of the Republican party. In the New Hampshire primary, McCloskey received close to 20 percent of the vote, while Ashbrook received less than half that amount, even though he had been endorsed by William Loeb's *Manchester Union Leader*. After New Hampshire, Ashbrook's campaign completely fizzled so that by the time of the Republican National Convention, Ashbrook refused to have his name placed in nomination. At the convention, conservatives defeated resolutions that would have allowed for proportional representation for women and minority delegates—measures that had been instituted in 1968 by the Democrats—but there was no stopping the Nixon juggernaut. In September 1972 the ACU, facing the perennial problem of a minority faction confronting political disregard, reluctantly endorsed the Nixon-Agnew ticket.

At the time, Ashbrook's challenge was seen as courageous by his supporters; however, it was politically naïve to think that Nixon could be replaced by a challenger within his own party. The GOP Right overestimated its own support within the party and misread the success of Wallace's 1968 campaign as indicative of deep discontent within the electorate. Events proved that the Wallace vote never translated into votes for a Republican conservative. Although there were signs of erosion within the Democratic party in the South, as well as fraying along the edges in some northern industrial states, the time was not yet right for a conservative Republican candidate. It would take another twelve years, a failed Carter presidency, and a Reagan candidacy before these voters could be won decisively to the Republican banner.

Within the Democratic party, South Dakota's liberal senator George McGovern capitalized on the prevailing antiwar sentiment among Democrats to win the nomination. McGovern's nomination reflected the Democratic party's drift to the left since 1968.[45] At the Democratic Convention, new party rules required every state delegation to include a proportionate number of minorities, women, and young people, which startled television audiences accustomed to seeing conventions dominated by older, affluent, white males. These new delegates stood well to the left of the general American electorate, and their nominee reflected this leftist outlook. McGovern called for defense cuts, the immediate withdrawal of U.S. troops from Vietnam, amnesty for draft evaders who had fled to Canada, and income redistribution through new inheritance taxes and corporate taxes. McGovern's campaign faced immediate disaster when it was revealed that his running mate, Senator Thomas Eagleton (D-Missouri), had undergone electric shock therapy for depression. After some vacillation, McGovern decided to replace Eagleton with Sargent Shriver, John F. Kennedy's brother-in-law. The McGovern campaign never recovered.

McGovern proved a pushover for a well-organized and effective Nixon campaign. As the McGovern campaign stumbled, few recalled that in the spring of 1972 the polls had shown that McGovern might be able to defeat Nixon in a general election. Aware of these poll numbers, Nixon left little to chance. His Committee to Reelect the President (CREEP), operating independently of the Republican party, raised millions of dollars by targeting corporations and executives with close ties to government, while at the same time launching a dirty-tricks campaign. One of those dirty tricks involved the break-in of the Democratic National Committee headquarters at the Watergate complex. When the burglars were caught in the act, the Nixon White House denied all links with what it described as a "bizarre incident," but it secretly provided $400,000 to buy the silence of those arrested. The administration, acting under orders from Nixon, surreptitiously pressured the FBI to halt its investigation of the Watergate break-in, using national security as a pretext to block the probe. McGovern tried to link the break-in with Nixon's alleged favoritism toward big business, but the Watergate break-in had less to do with big business than with sheer abuse of presidential power and privilege. Throughout the campaign, McGovern was kept on the defensive answering Republican charges that he supported abortion-on-demand, amnesty for draft-evaders, and legalized drugs.

Nixon gained an advantage from the absence of Governor George Wallace following an assassination attempt during the Democratic primaries, which had left Wallace paralyzed. Behind the scenes Nixon had pressured Wallace to enter the Democratic party primaries in 1972 instead of running as a third-party candidate. After barely winning the 1968 election, Nixon feared that a third-party challenge from Wallace might cost him reelection. Initially, Nixon undertook a direct assault on Wallace by funneling money to Wallace's challenger in the 1970 Alabama gubernatorial race, but when this strategy failed, he pressed the Internal Revenue Service to investigate Wallace and several of his aides, including Wallace's brother Gerald. The IRS investigation snarled Wallace's closest aide, Seymore Trammell, who was subsequently sent to prison for four years for IRS violations. Shortly after Attorney General John Mitchell announced in January 1972 that the government would not pursue its prosecution of Gerald Wallace, George Wallace announced that he would run as a Democrat and not as a third-party candidate.[46]

Without Wallace in the general election, Nixon carried every one of the thirteen states of the formerly solid Democratic South by a sizeable margin. (In 1968, Wallace had carried five southern states, while winning 13.5 percent of the popular vote and forty-six electoral votes.) On election day, Nixon swamped McGovern, winning 60 percent of the popular vote and the Electoral College with 520 votes to 17. McGovern won only Massachusetts and the District of Columbia.

It would be easy to conjecture that voters were taken with Nixon's Machiavellian twists and turns, but there is no empirical evidence that this was the case. Polls showed that voters liked him better than McGovern, but their affection for Nixon was shallow. This fact was further evident in Nixon's short coattails in the election. For the first time in a national election, a party that won 60 percent or more of the presidential vote failed to add seats in Congress. Instead, Democrats widened their control of the Senate to 57–43 (a gain of two seats). The Democrats controlled the House 243–192. At the same time, Democrats added another statehouse to their rolls, for a total of 31 to the Republicans' 19. Senator Robert Dole (R-Kansas) accurately described Nixon's reelection as "a personal triumph for Mr. Nixon but not a party triumph."[47]

While the party might not have triumphed, conservatives took major solace in the election of the conservative radio and television commentator Jesse Helms to the U.S. Senate from North Carolina. Helms was greatly influenced by his father, a Piedmont village police and fire chief who had gained the respect of his small community for his fairness and integrity, even though he had only a fourth-grade education. As a radio-television commentator for WRAL television in Raleigh, Jesse Helms established a statewide reputation for fiery, ultraconservative editorials. Helms, who had only recently changed his party registration, entered the Senate race at the urging of his friends, who saw an opportunity for the Republicans to make a historic gain by electing North Carolina's first Republican senator. The incumbent senator, B. Everett Jordan, was ill with cancer, and in the May Democratic primary he was upset by Nick Galifianakis. In the general election, Helms coasted to an easy victory, winning 54 percent of the vote. When Republicans also took the governorship, Democratic hegemony in the state was shattered.[48] Republicans smashed the Democratic grip that had lasted since Reconstruction by capturing antiliberal sentiment in the state.

Nixon did not have much time to celebrate his historic victory. The Watergate cover-up was exposed by *The Washington Post,* which kept the scandal in the spotlight. In January 1973, seven men, including White House political operatives Jeb Magruder, G. Gordon Liddy, and E. Howard Hunt, were convicted for their role in the break-in. In March 1973, U.S. District Court Judge John Sirica received a letter from the convicted Watergate felon James McCord implicating White House Counsel John Dean and Magruder in a cover-up. Under questioning, both Dean and Magruder broke, testifying that former Attorney General John Mitchell had approved the break-in with the knowledge of White House domestic adviser John Ehrlichman and Chief of Staff H. R. Haldeman. In late April, Nixon forced the resignation of Haldeman and Ehrlichman, who would ultimately go to prison for their involvement in the affair.

In May 1973 the U.S. Senate opened a special investigation chaired by Senator Sam Ervin (D-North Carolina). Attorney General Elliot Richardson appointed Archibald Cox as a special prosecutor to investigate the entire affair. In July 1973 it was revealed that the administration had secretly recorded conversations in the White House since 1971. When Cox sued to obtain the tapes, Nixon ordered him fired, leading to the resignation of Attorney General Richardson and his assistant William Ruckelshaus. Finally, Solicitor General Robert Bork fired Cox in what became known as the "Saturday Night Massacre." At this point the House of Representatives began an impeachment investigation.

The Watergate scandal, as it became known, consumed the American public in the summer and fall of 1973. Congress appeared headed toward impeachment when in October 1973, in a separate investigation, Vice President Spiro Agnew was forced to resign his office in a plea bargain after being charged with accepting bribes as governor of Maryland. Nixon disliked Agnew and had considered dropping him from the 1972 ticket. As the Watergate investigation intensified, Nixon saw Agnew as his insurance policy against impeachment. Nixon understood that though congressional Democrats despised him, they feared Agnew because he was mean-spirited, played political hard ball, and was corrupt.[49] Agnew's resignation doomed any chance that Nixon might avoid impeachment, because it removed the specter of Agnew succeeding him as president. Republican Representative John Rhodes (R-Arizona) later recalled that when he heard of Agnew's resignation, he could almost hear the sighs of relief from his Democratic colleagues on the House floor.[50] With Agnew gone, members of Congress from both political parties persuaded President Nixon to select Representative Gerald R. Ford (R-Michigan) to assume the office of vice president. Nixon selected Ford as a "safe" candidate because he was considered unlikely to seek the presidency in 1976 and therefore did not pose a political threat to the administration. Nixon had considered Nelson Rockefeller and Ronald Reagan as Agnew's replacement, but concluded that both were too risky and would fail to secure Senate confirmation.[51]

The Watergate investigations revealed that Nixon had betrayed the public trust and had ordered a cover-up of the investigation, but the threat of Agnew in the White House was a terrifying prospect. As Rhodes later conjectured, Agnew was politically tough and personally disliked Nixon, so he would not have pardoned him. If Agnew had become president (presuming he had been cleared of criminal charges), he would have sought the party's nomination in 1976. His rival for the conservative vote would have been Ronald Reagan. Republican leadership would probably have prevented Agnew's nomination, but the primary campaign would have split the party. If Reagan had won the GOP nomination—not an unlikely scenario given his popularity—he would surely have lost the general election in the Watergate backlash. This would have been an irreversible loss for conservatives and would have undermined the argument—heard after the Ford defeat in 1976—that a conservative could have won the general election.

Whatever might have been, Agnew was forced to resign. Eight months later, Nixon resigned when the Supreme Court ruled unanimously that the White House must turn over all tape recordings of conversations relevant to Watergate. The tapes revealed a conversation between President Nixon and his chief of staff, H. R. Haldeman, in which the president ordered the Central Intelligence Agency to stop the Federal Bureau of Investigation probe into the Watergate burglary on the basis of "national security." This was the "smoking gun" that Nixon's opponents had been looking for. When Senator Barry Goldwater told Nixon that the administration did not have the votes in Congress to prevent impeachment, Nixon resigned from office on August 9, 1974. As the valiantly smiling but humiliated Nixon boarded the helicopter that took him away from the White House, Gerald Ford assumed the presidency.[52]

The Watergate crisis accelerated changes that were already occurring on the political landscape. Watergate allowed the Democratic party to unite, while causing the Republican party to fall apart. More important, Watergate encouraged the Democratic party's march to the left. This was especially apparent in the emergence of an insurgent left-wing Democratic leadership in Congress. The takeover of the Democratic leadership began in 1972, when Whip Hale Boggs (D-Louisiana), a foreign policy hawk and a traditional political operator, was killed in a plane crash while campaigning in Alaska. His death allowed Tip O'Neill (D-Massachusetts) to become House Democratic whip and two years later House speaker. O'Neill joined forces with the liberal wing of his party, led by Philip Burton (D-California), a self-righteous defender of the downtrodden. Under O'Neill and Burton, the House Democrats shifted to the left at a time when the Republican minority stood in disgrace. In the 1974 midterm elections, Democrats extended their control of the House by picking up forty-nine seats. In the Senate, Democrats picked up four additional seats, even winning the once hardcore GOP state of Vermont, which had never in its history elected a Democrat. The seventy-four new Democratic representatives elected in 1974 entered Congress eager to reassert power over the executive branch.[53]

Nixon left a shattered Republican party. Its liberal wing was in paralysis and conservatives were generally demoralized.[54] Shortly before Nixon's resignation, the conservative activist Howard Phillips summed up the feelings of the Right when he told the press, "Under Richard Nixon, our ideological opportunity has been squandered, our loyalties have been unreciprocated, and our party's reputation for integrity has been virtually destroyed."[55] Many Republican insiders spoke of the party as going the way of the Whigs. In reality, however, the old Whig party may have enjoyed more political support in the electorate before its demise than the Republican party did in 1974: polls revealed in 1974 that only 18 percent of voters identified themselves as Republican. In this environment, the GOP Right had become a minority within a minority party.

4

The Power of Ideas and Institutions

The Bolshevik leader Leon Trotsky observed that the first stage of revolution begins with the disaffection of intellectuals and their construction of duplicate institutions, counterparts to established organs of power.[1] This process, Trotsky notes in his *History of the Russian Revolution*, is accompanied by the revolutionary vanguard's mobilization of the masses, who will ultimately provide the fatal force to overthrow the ruling elite. Trotsky was obviously a man of the radical Left, but he understood how established regimes can be weakened and removed from power.

The disaffection of some intellectuals from the American liberal regime became evident when a small group of university professors and public intellectuals, who later became known as neoconservatives, began criticizing President Johnson's Great Society for its domestic policy failures. Neoconservatives were not of one mind about politics or political ideology; many refused to accept the conservative label, and many remained Democrats. Nonetheless, they exerted a subtle intellectual influence on American conservatism. Leo Strauss, a political science professor at the University of Chicago, served as an intellectual godfather to the new dissenters. Strauss was a scholar *par excellence,* far removed from contemporary partisan politics. He was interested in the knowledge that could be derived from the study of classical philosophy and Judeo-Christian tradition. Though he was a critic of modern liberalism, it is impossible to derive any specific conservative ideology from his writings. Yet his influence on two generations of neoconservatives, including Irving Kristol and his son William Kristol, was immense.

Just as neoconservatives were voicing their disaffection, conservative think tanks emerged to provide technical expertise to the GOP. The Goldwater campaign and the Nixon regime taught conservatives that they needed specific policy proposals to combat the hegemony of liberalism in the policy arena and to present a case to voters (and Republican party leaders) that there were real alternatives to the status quo. Policy entrepreneurs such as William Baroody, Edwin Feulner, and Paul Weyrich began to institutionalize conservatism through research institutes, fellowship and student-training programs, and new publications. They brought to these endeavors a single goal: to erect countervailing sources of power to undermine the liberal establishment. The Left had the prestigious Brookings Institution and the liberal academy to influence policy makers and public opinion, and conservatives wanted to create their own sources for what Washington insiders called "policy innovation." To this end, they expanded established moderate-conservative research institutes such as the American Enterprise Institute and launched the Heritage Foundation. Drawing support from philanthropies such as the Scaife Fund, the John M. Olin Foundation, and the Bradley Foundation, as well as from wealthy conservative benefactors such as Joseph Coors, these research institutes emerged as vital centers for conservative policy innovation.[2]

The development of think tanks marked an important shift in the history of conservatism and would have important implications for the shaping of the GOP Right in subsequent years. A kind of "managerial conservatism" arose that reoriented conservative thinking on actual governance toward a more ready acceptance of the exertion of federal government power acting within the broad principles of conservatism. Neoconservatism was not welcomed in some right-wing circles, but it imparted energy and expertise to the conservative movement in the 1980s.

Breaking Ranks

Any understanding of neoconservatism must begin with the leftward shift of the Democratic party that began when George McGovern won the party's nomination in 1972. In order to win the nomination against an old guard of traditional New Deal Democrats represented by Hubert Humphrey (D-Minnesota), Edmund Muskie (D-Maine), and "Scoop" Henry Jackson (D-Washington), who were anti-Communist defense hawks, McGovern strategically reached out to new voters, mostly young cultural leftists who were antiwar activists, feminists, and New Left sympathizers. To challenge the Democratic establishment built on the urban, blue-collar, labor-union wing of the party, McGovern mobilized voters outside the traditional base of the party. In doing so, he introduced new constituencies into the Democratic party and moved it to the left. This transformation was made possible by the changes enacted at the 1968 Democratic Convention and implemented four years later in 1972. The rule changes, proposed by a commission headed by McGovern, aimed to democratize the party by ensuring a wider representation of ethnic minorities, women, and homosexuals among convention delegates.[3] Many of the delegates selected under these new rules were activists. They came to the 1972 convention with a politics that was anti-imperialist, anti-racist, pro-feminist, pro-abortion, and pro-homosexual rights.

The veteran political reporter Theodore White, who covered the convention, wrote that a parade of women crossed the podium insisting that "they be allowed to control the fruit of their bodies." They were followed, he observed, by homosexuals demanding that "the coupling of males be accepted not furtively, but as a natural and legal right."[4] White found all this a bit strange; at the time, such views seemed out of touch with the general American electorate. Nonetheless, these issues reflected a growing liberalization of values that would eventually cause fission within American politics and lead to what became known as the culture wars of the 1980s.[5]

The McGovern turn to the left indicated a shift in American culture in the late 1960s and early 1970s. While the majority of the population remained religious—roughly 20 percent of Americans were Roman Catholic and 50 percent were Protestant—their practices had become more diverse. Mainstream Protestant denominations began to decline in membership, while evangelical churches attracted more members with their focus on individual religious salvation and traditional morality. These evangelical Protestants perceived themselves in opposition to secular American culture. They were joined in this opposition by traditional Roman Catholics and Mormons. The result was a cultural divide. Although not all traditionally minded religious people became Republicans, many evangelical Protestants, traditional Catholics, and Mormons shifted their allegiance to the GOP as the Democratic party moved to the left. Politics was becoming increasingly polarized.

For religious traditionalists who became Republicans, religion informed, and even motivated, their politics. This world view contrasted with the secular values of the new activists mobilized by McGovern. Surveys revealed that Democratic party activists shared a secular outlook.[6] They supported a sharp separation between church and state. Their political views were shaped by secular values such as equality, recognition of ethnic and sexual diversity, and a belief that men and women could shape their own destinies.[7] Translated into actual political policy, this meant support of affirmative action for minorities and women; reproductive rights for women; gay rights; and support for the banning of religious symbols in public places. At the same time, the Democratic party under McGovern swung to the left in foreign policy by supporting the downsizing of the military, arms control negotiations with the Soviet Union, and a greater reliance on international organizations to further peace in the world.

Changes in American culture and within the Democratic party prompted two leading public intellectuals, Irving Kristol and Norman Podhoretz, to desert liberalism. Their turn to the right resulted from a disillusionment with the McGovern Democratic party and its support for the expanded welfare state, affirmative action, anti–Vietnam War sentiment, and strategic disarmament. Both Kristol and Podhoretz expressed hostility to New Left student protests, the sexual revolution, radical feminism, and gay liberation. Both were defense hawks who supported the Vietnam War. Their desertion of the Left drew fire from their former allies, but because they disassociated themselves from Goldwater Republicanism and grassroots conservatism, they were not ostracized as had been an earlier generation of intellectuals who abandoned the Left: Whittaker Chambers, John Dos Passos, James Burnham, and many others. Kristol and Podhoretz brought respectability to conservatism in the liberal-dominated worlds of publishing and universities, even though both men were hesitant at first to call themselves conservatives.

Kristol, who was ten years older than Podhoretz, first broke ranks when he founded the magazine *The Public Interest* in 1965. Kristol started *The Public Interest* as a scholarly antidote to what he considered the increasing utopianism of leftist intellectuals. As an editor at Basic Books in 1965, he had reached the conclusion that a new breed of intellectuals had emerged on the scene who disregarded empirical studies for self-righteous ideological proclamations against American racism, capitalism, and imperialism. Kristol had begun his life in politics as a Trotskyite in the 1940s, but by the 1950s he had come to reject Communist ideology. Throughout the 1950s and 1960s, he remained critical of liberal group-think, especially its inability to see that Soviet Communism posed a serious danger to the United States.

Kristol's experience within the Communist movement, which began when he was a student at City College of New York in the 1930s, had an important influence on his intellectual development, as well as on his personal life. While attending a Trotskyite meeting in Brooklyn, he met his future wife, Gertrude Himmelfarb, who was just beginning her career as a historian. Trotskyism in the United States combined a hyper-intellectual faith in the cause of the world socialist revolution and a highly insular world of sectarian radical politics. Trotskyites were deeply anti-Stalinist and focused on the deformities of the Soviet system under Stalin, the betrayal of world revolution, and the political assassination of their own (including Trotsky himself in 1940). For Trotskyites such as Kristol, it was a small step from Trotskyism to anti-Communism.

The nature of the Soviet Union under Stalin haunted the American Trotskyite movement from the beginning, and debates over the Soviet Union caused continuous ruptures within the leading Trotskyite party, the Socialist Workers party (SWP), founded in 1937. Trotsky described the Soviet Union under Stalin as a degenerate workers' state that nonetheless must be defended by all revolutionaries. This view was challenged by James Burnham, a member of the SWP and a professor of literature at New York University who had only recently converted to Trotskyism. In a direct challenge to Trotsky, who was living in exile in Mexico, Burnham maintained that the Soviet Union should not be defended by revolutionaries. During this intense sectarian squabble (which Trotsky loyalists magnified into epic battles), Burnham developed a theory that a new political order, which he labeled "bureaucratic managerialism," was emerging in all advanced industrial societies, whether they claimed to be fascist, communist, or democratic capitalist. He maintained that an inexorable drive toward managerial hierarchy and centralization existed in all such societies. His views were articulated in *The Managerial Revolution* (1940), which became a best seller.

This debate between Burnham and Trotsky had all the hairsplitting abstraction of medieval scholasticism, but the signing of the Stalin-Hitler Pact in August 1939 gave the issue particular importance for the Left in America. At stake was whether the Soviet Union was a progressive state in any regard, and whether it should be defended in case of attack by the Western powers. In 1939, Trotsky, for all his animosity toward Stalin and his caustic denunciations of the Soviet leader as having betrayed the international socialist revolution, concluded that the Soviet Union still must be defended in the event of an attack. Trotsky, with his augural understanding of dialectics, haruspicated that the Nazi-Soviet Pact, and the Soviet invasion of Poland, and Finland a month later, was an advance for world socialism. Many American Trotskyites were disgusted by Trotsky's line of defense, among them Burnham and SWP leader Max Shachtman, who led a faction out of the party to form the Workers party, a "Third Camp" of world revolutionaries standing between Western capitalism and Soviet Communism. Burnham left this group within a year as he began a march to the right that would eventually take him to the editorial board of Buckley's *National Review.*

In 1942, this revolutionary faction within the Socialist party, led by Philip Selznik, later a distinguished sociologist at the University of California-Berkeley, launched a new magazine called *Enquiry.* The editor of this party magazine was young Irving Kristol, who wrote under the name of William Ferry. Kristol's infatuation with the revolutionary socialist party did not last long. By the time he entered the army in 1944 his disaffection with the radical Left had become evident. The army cemented his conclusions that revolutionary socialism was not only impossible but wrong-headed. In the army, he developed a distrust of the masses and their potential for revolution.[8] Though he abandoned his Marxist politics, he did remain a man of the Left, but a decidedly independent-minded one.

While in England after the war, Kristol began writing for a liberal anti-Communist magazine, *The New Leader,* and the newly founded magazine *Commentary,* sponsored by the American Jewish Committee. He joined the *Commentary* staff as an editor when he returned to the States the next year, entering into the world of the New York literati. Kristol soon showed, however, that he was not a camp-follower of the intellectual fashion-setters of postwar America.

In 1952, he took his fellow liberals to task for their adamant defense of Communists who refused to testify before congressional hearings on the grounds that they might incriminate themselves. When the essay "Civil Liberties 1952—A Study in Confusion" appeared in the March issue of *Commentary,* a firestorm of controversy exploded in New York literary circles. Kristol was typically eloquent and provocative. He wrote, "There is one thing that the American people know about Senator McCarthy. He, like them, is unequivocally anti-Communist. About the spokesmen for American liberalism, they feel they know no such thing."[9] The essay was aimed at liberals like the historian Henry Steele Commager, the journalist Alan Barth, and Supreme Court Justice William O. Douglas, who had defended this use of the Fifth Amendment by suspected Communists. Kristol argued that Communists were manipulating civil liberties, even though they abhorred these rights as bourgeois falsities. Communists, he maintained, were not dissenters protesting a specific policy or issue but revolutionaries who insidiously operated under the command of a foreign power that conspired to overthrow the system.[10]

Shortly after the publication of his *Commentary* article, Kristol resigned to take a job at the Committee for Cultural Freedom. This job had been arranged for him by the philosopher Sidney Hook, who had helped found the organization as a liberal social democratic voice against Soviet totalitarianism. Unfortunately for Kristol, who was given the job of executive director, the committee was in the middle of a crisis over Senator Joseph McCarthy. On one side stood the historian Arthur Schlesinger, Jr., and the journalist Richard Rovere, who believed that the committee should be anti-McCarthy; on the other side was James Burnham, who represented a small group that was less hostile to McCarthy. Kristol, caught in the middle trying to keep tempers in check, accepted an offer to become coeditor with the poet Stephen Spender of a new liberal anti-Communist magazine, *Encounter,* in London. Neither Kristol nor Spender realized at the time that the magazine was being funded by the U.S. Central Intelligence Agency.

Kristol's intellectual formation took shape during these years. He became fiercely anti-Communist under the influence of Sidney Hook and the literary critic Lionel Trilling. He was introduced to Leo Strauss, a

German émigré from Nazi Germany who moved to the University of Chicago in 1949. At Chicago, Strauss introduced several generations of students to a philosophical perspective that divided the intellectual world between the ancients and the moderns. Strauss was on the side of the ancients and thus was exceptionally critical of modern Enlightenment thought.[11] More important, through Strauss, Kristol began to understand the Aristotelian art of the politically possible and the prudent, in contrast to the unattainable and the utopian. He had taken the first steps toward conservatism. While in England he and his wife were becoming gradually more discontented with social democracy and liberalism, owing, among other things, to "the Left's predisposition to see Communists as, in some sense, a wayward extremity of the Left, ultimately redeemable by therapeutic strategies."[12]

Kristol returned to the United States in 1958 to take a position as editor for *The Reporter;* shortly afterward, he became an editor at Basic Books, then a small publishing company specializing in psychoanalytical books. Kristol expanded the press's list of authors to include a number of the most prominent social scientists of the day, many of whom shared Kristol's growing disillusionment with Lyndon Johnson's Great Society. Kristol began to write op-ed pieces for *The New Leader* in which he expressed his skepticism, but he felt there was a need for another magazine. He believed that the conservative *National Review* was "insufficiently analytical and too stridently hostile to the course of American politics since 1932."[13] At a dinner party hosted by Sidney Hook, he met Warren and Anita Marshel, who agreed to provide $10,000 to launch a new magazine edited by Kristol and Daniel Bell. Working out of his Basic Books office, Kristol began *The Public Interest,* which provided an outlet for Daniel Moynihan, Nathan Glazer, James Q. Wilson, Edward C. Banfield, Aaron Wildavsky, and other social scientists critical of liberal social and economic programs devised by the "new class" of university intellectuals and government bureaucrats. Those contributing to the magazine had similar criticisms of the Great Society and the fashionable Left, but they refused to accept the label conservative, which at that point was associated with Barry Goldwater. For the most part, those writing in *The Public Interest* still considered themselves liberals and voted Democratic. Still, the establishment of *The Public Interest* revealed the first cracks in the liberal orthodoxy and the rightward turn of these public intellectuals.

Meanwhile, the fissure within the liberal ranks widened with a decided shift to the right in *Commentary* under its editor Norman Podhoretz.[14] Like Kristol, Podhoretz came from Brooklyn. He was born in 1930, the son of a milkman. He attended Columbia University, where he quickly earned a reputation among his teachers and classmates as brilliant and conspicuously ambitious. With the support of Lionel Trilling, Podhoretz won a scholarship to Cambridge University, where he spent two years earning another B.A. While in Cambridge, Podhoretz began writing book reviews for *Commentary,* eager, as he put it, "to see my name in print, to be praised, and above all attract attention."[15] He went out of his way to be a contrarian, purposely deflating egos in order to inflate his own reputation for cleverness. He created a stir when he criticized Saul Bellow's critically acclaimed novel *The Adventures of Augie March* (1953) as solipsistic and marred by one-dimensional characters, including its eponymous Jewish hero. In another review, he pontificated that the southern novelist William Faulkner had been "bamboozled by irrelevant religiosity."[16] After a stint in the U.S. Army, where he ran a compulsory lecture program titled "Democracy versus Communism," Podhoretz returned to New York and *Commentary.*

In 1960, the thirty-year-old Podhoretz became editor of *Commentary,* moving it temporarily to the cultural left in the next few years. Many of the essays published in *Commentary* in the 1960s do not read well forty years later, but at the time Podhoretz placed the magazine on the avantgarde left, the so-called New Left. Paul Goodman published chapters from what became *Growing Up Absurd,* a Rousseauian attack on institutional public education and contemporary democratic society. Published in three installments, the essay caused a sensation and reversed the magazine's financial fortunes. Circulation rose from 20,000 to 60,000. Other voices from the Left followed, including socialist Michael Harrington, historians Staughton Lynd and H. Stuart Hughes, and James Baldwin, author of *The Fire Next Time.* These authors became required reading for the new generation of Kennedy liberals. These were the voices of anger that emerged in the 1960s as civil rights and antiwar protests swept across the nation. Podhoretz began calling himself a radical, accusing friends such as Lionel Trilling of being hypocrites and cowards. Yet for all his posturing (and sincerity), Podhoretz's radicalism was tempered by his own life experiences.

This fact was evident in his 1963 essay "My Negro Problem—And

Ours," a pointed analysis, drawn from his own childhood experiences, of why whites feared and admired blacks, and why white liberals, expressing feelings of guilt, romanticized and pandered to blacks, allowing them, in his opinion, a moral license to be deceitful and exploitive. Podhoretz claimed that the essay was a critique of "liberal ideas and pieties," but it caused an explosion in left circles, where he was charged with racism.[17] There were other signs that Podhoretz was not one of the radical faithful. He was troubled by Harvard University professor H. Stuart Hughes's call for unilateral disarmament, and he refused to publish the Port Huron Statement by the Students for a Democratic Society because he thought it was a mishmash of derivative themes, "stripped of all complexity, qualification, and nuance."[18]

By the late 1960s, Podhoretz showed signs of breaking with the Left. He found its social and cultural styles repugnant. He condemned what he considered the disingenuous ideology of the New Left, espoused by privileged white students who called for an authentic democratic society in the United States while supporting repressive Communist governments in Cuba, North Vietnam, and China. He questioned the new cultural liberation in which proponents of radical change—blacks, Hispanics, Asians, feminists, and homosexuals—proclaimed themselves the authentic voices within their own minority cultures. As a Jew who had broken into the world of literary and academic respectability, Podhoretz was sensitive to the persecution of minorities, but he felt that this new generation was inauthentic. He concluded that the black radicals, feminists, and others of the New Left were not true visionaries who commanded respect and authority but phonies who hid behind a rhetoric of intimidation, violence, and intellectual nihilism.[19]

His alienation from the New Left, as well as differences with Johnson's Great Society, drove Podhoretz and others to break ranks with liberals in the late 1960s and early 1970s, although the break was not complete or irrevocable. Many neoconservatives remained in the Democratic party, even though they supported Richard Nixon in 1972. Podhoretz joined Democrats like Senator Henry Jackson, Hubert Humphrey, journalists Max Kampelman, Ben Wattenberg, international relations professor Jeane Kirkpatrick and her husband, Evron Kirkpatrick, and Daniel Moynihan to form the Coalition for a Democratic Majority with the intention of taking back the Democratic party from the McGovernite wing. This group was openly critical of the "New Class" of radicals who held antibourgeois values and had captured the Democratic party in 1972. Jeane Kirkpatrick spoke for the coalition when she declared in *Commentary* in February 1973 that "an embattled revolutionary elite united under the banner of George McGovern" had transformed liberalism into an "ideology of the privileged." She maintained that McGovernites were upper-middle–class feminists, high-income homosexuals, and college-educated whites who despised blue-collar ethnic workers, white southerners, and traditional American values. As a consequence, she observed, conservatism had become the "position of the less privileged."[20] Conservatives, she suggested, upheld traditional values of hard work, family, and patriotism. From this perspective it was a short step to Republicanism.

Within the Democratic party, neoconservative critics remained isolated. McGovern liberals had their own perspective of the world. For them, fervent anti-Communism had led the United States into a tragic war in Vietnam that had cost tens of thousands of American lives and untold numbers of Vietnamese lives. Claims of the virtues of the white ethnic blue-collar workers were negated by their exclusion of other ethnic groups, particularly African Americans. Blue-collar values often meant sexism, intolerance toward gays, and a nationalism that tended toward xenophobia. Capitalism had given wealth to a few but had led to great disparities in income and wealth. Social justice in a democracy called for redistribution of wealth, protection of the environment from greedy corporations, and policies such as preferential employment to rectify past discrimination against blacks and women in the workplace.

The issue that caused the greatest divide between McGovern liberals and neoconservatives was foreign policy and how to deal with Communist nations. Anti-Communism united Podhoretz and Kristol intellectually. Both men believed that many on the McGovern left misunderstood the imperial nature of Communism and overestimated the good intentions of Soviet leadership. Both agreed on the need to fight for democracy in the world, and it was this belief that became a defining characteristic of what became known as "neoconservatism." Neoconservatism also rejected the counterculture of the 1960s as self-indulgent, thoughtless, and immoral. While Podhoretz initially embraced, and even furthered, this counterculture in the early 1960s, his reaction against it went deeper and was more vociferous than Kristol's. Podhoretz and his wife, Midge Decter, moved much further to the right on cultural and social issues when they accused youth culture of the 1960s of promoting hedonistic and relativistic values which threatened democratic society.[21]

Neoconservatism was a label placed on Kristol and Podhoretz by their enemies.[22] Yet, as Kristol observed, neoconservatism was not an organized movement but a "current of thought" represented by a few dozen people who were disenchanted with the prevailing liberal-left orthodoxy at a time when "liberalism itself was crumbling before the resurgent left."[23] Many individuals within this "current of thought" were not genuine conservatives.[24] Neoconservatives still favored the welfare state and regulated capitalism. In 1968, Kristol still spoke in favor of a "modified form of capitalism"—hardly the enthusiastic and unqualified cheers he would give to free-market economics ten years later.[25]

For many old-time conservatives who had fought in the anti-Communist trenches in the 1950s and struggled through the Goldwater campaign in 1964, the neocons were Johnny-come-latelies who were not serious conservatives. Traditional conservatives held that society rested on transcendent values derived from a Supreme Being who imparted order and cohesion to the universe and its laws prior to human history. They upheld the sacred, nonrational, and non-utilitarian aspects of social existence found in evangelical Protestant, traditionalist Roman Catholic, and Mormon teachings. Traditionalists believed in the fundamental importance of maintaining social order based on a constellation of historically given beliefs, customs, norms, and institutions derived from the experience of a free people.[26] Such assumptions often appeared contrary to the views of neoconservative writers who intimated that religious belief was a utilitarian instrument to provide social order and, as such, was not central to their movement.

Some neoconservatives were devout and practicing Christians and Jews, but religious belief was not at the core of their thinking. Neoconservatism was an evolving political perspective that moved gradually to the Republican party and the political Right. In the process, neoconservatives came to express greater, and at times hyperbolic, appreciation of free-market economics, property rights, and the rule of law. Yet in certain respects, many of their assumptions about politics, governance, and policy remained liberal. Although neoconservatives did not speak with one voice, and clear individual exceptions were evident, most people in the movement tended to distrust what became known as the Religious Right. Moreover, the heavy influence of classical thought found in their

Straussian training imbued them with a faith in elite leadership. While they denounced the "New Class," liberal government bureaucrats and academic intellectuals, the neoconservative complaint was not so much against elitism as against liberal elitism and Great Society policies. They sought to displace liberal expertise, which they described as ideologically based, with their own, empirically based expertise.

The neoconservative current was rife with personal ambition and intellectual arrogance. While projecting themselves as a new force in the political debate, neoconservatives were elitists who upheld the seemingly oxymoronic theory of democratic rule by elites.[27] In effect, they offered managerial conservatism at a time when bureaucratic liberalism was under attack.

The World of Think Tanks

Kristol's and Podhoretz's criticism of the Great Society drew the attention of the small but rapidly expanding world of conservative research institutes operating in Washington, D.C. Here were liberals, many from places considered alien to conservative thought—the Ivy League and New York's Jewish intelligentsia—providing devastating critiques of Johnson's War on Poverty, affirmative action, and American foreign policy. The breaking of ranks within the liberal intelligentsia attracted the attention of conservative philanthropic organizations, especially the John M. Olin and Bradley foundations, which provided sizeable grants to support Kristol's journal. In the process of establishing relations with these foundations, these ex-liberal intellectuals discovered the expanding world of conservative groups eager to enlist what they considered the best and the brightest. For all their complaints about liberal academia, conservative foundation officers, many from the Ivy League themselves, were impressed with people credentialed by Harvard, Yale, Columbia, and Princeton.

Conservatives since the New Deal had been concerned with public policy, but quite often their involvement in policy discussions was reactive and abstract. The world of the think tank, by contrast, was empirical and intended for immediate policy consumption. The result was the emergence of a form of managerial conservatism that would challenge the bureaucratic liberalism that had reigned since the turn of the twentieth century.

Think tanks, a peculiarly American phenomenon, had been closely associated with the emergence of the modern liberal state in the early twentieth century. The complexity of a modern industrial system had required an enormous range of specialized knowledge and administrative expertise. Centralized government bureaucracies in Western Europe and Japan provided expertise to public officials. The United States had limited reliance on centralized bureaucracy because of its federal system of government, sectional politics, and long-standing distrust of centralized government. The emergence of industrialism in the late nineteenth century encouraged progressive reformers to call for greater state and federal government involvement in regulating business, ensuring public health, and providing pensions to veterans, widows with children, and others. These demands paved the way for a new bureaucratic liberalism, grounded in social empiricism, the social sciences, and expertise. As they enlarged the role of the state, progressive reformers were limited by tradition and politics from enlarging government bureaucracies to fully satisfy the requirements of the new liberal regime they envisioned.[28] To meet the needs of the new administrative state, reformers established nonpartisan research institutes (think tanks) on the local, state, and national levels.

The establishment of the nation's first think tank, the Brookings Institution (1916), reflected the aspirations of progressive social science reformers who were critical in shaping the ideology of the new administrative state. The founders of the Brookings Institution held a deep conviction that the polity had been corrupted by partisan interests, especially in those urban political machines that operated in flagrant disregard for any notion of public morality or the public interest in government. The measures proposed by reformers at the institution included the elimination of party labels in municipal elections, the shortening of the ballot, the weakening of the legislative branch of government, the enacting of an executive budget system, and the shifting of decision-making as far as possible from elected bodies. These reforms were intended to depoliticize the political process. Underlying these proposals were strong antimajoritarian values fused with antiparty perspectives.

These university-trained and highly specialized social scientists used scientific methodology to mask their preoccupation with political matters in the terminology of scholarly objectivity and empirical research. The new professional social scientists were not disingenuous in their concerns with social issues. They saw the proposed administrative solutions to social problems as an avenue to address larger questions such as industrial relations, distribution of wealth, and stability in the political order. They were concerned about political corruption found in party machines controlled by thuggish bosses. They sought to better the lives of the urban poor, factory workers, and women and children. For them this meant placing the "best men" into government through the creation of a new bureaucratic state. With typical academic modesty, they saw themselves as fulfilling the requirements of "the best" because they brought into government nonpartisan expertise, social science knowledge, and understanding of the new administrative state from their studies in Germany or under German-trained social scientists at American universities.

As the administrative state emerged in the early twentieth century, large numbers of experts entered government. While professing the ideology of social science objectivity and nonpartisanship, these experts assumed the expansion of government as a natural development necessitated by industrial capitalism. The new administrative state failed to bring nonpartisan government to Washington, D.C., however. In the 1930s, administrative expertise became an extension of Roosevelt's New Deal agenda. Experts came to represent partisanship, special interest groups, and, of course, their particular agencies within the government itself.

As partisanship became evident in the community of specialists, a group of American businessmen established a new think tank, the American Enterprise Institute (AEI), initially named the American Enterprise Association, in 1943. Led by Lewis Brown, the chairman of the Johns-Manville Corporation, the AEI reflected corporate business's general accommodation with the New Deal in some areas, notably Social Security, but expressed opposition to any further extension of federal power through the enactment of compulsory national health insurance or a full-employment work program. Brown was not a reactionary; he did oppose what he perceived as an antibusiness attitude of the New Deal and its pitting of the wealthy against the poor. Instead, he called for industrial cooperation as a way "to break down class consciousness and the battle spirit." At the same time, he warned that it was impossible to reconcile "the principles of democracy" with "the principle of government omniscience." To continue to follow the path of New Deal bureaucratic government, he maintained, would mean "the loss of freedom and dictatorship." He established the AEI to provide Congress and the public with objective summaries and analyses of current legislation and legislative proposals.[29]

The conservative AEI declared in one of its early publications that the sole standard for judging the public interest should be whether it strengthened or weakened the individual enterprise system. In its early years, the AEI remained primarily reactive. It did not propose or write new legislation, but instead examined current public policy or laws within a context of free-market ideology. The AEI's National Economic Problems series generated hundreds of pamphlets published by conservative scholars critical of farm price supports, social welfare, Social Security, full-employment legislation, and antitrust regulation. The death of Lewis Brown in 1951 left the AEI without major financial support, so that by 1954 the institute was nearing collapse. The AEI was saved when A. D. Marshall, the head of General Electric, assumed the presidency. Marshall hired William Baroody, Sr., and W. Glenn Campbell, both staff economists at the U.S. Chamber of Commerce, to head an invigorated research program at the AEI.[30] Baroody, son of a Lebanese immigrant and an economist with academic training, brought to the AEI an intellectual vibrancy and a conviction that conservative ideas and traditional values would prevail in the marketplace of ideas. He was a Lebanese Catholic who emphasized economic enterprise, property rights, and the centrality of religious values in maintaining social and political order in America. Baroody slowly attracted a small coterie of conservative scholars to the AEI. Still, even by 1960, the AEI employed only twelve full-time people and had an annual budget of $230,000.[31] In 1961, Baroody persuaded the board of trustees to change the name to the American Enterprise Institute, although they rejected his proposal to drop "Enterprise" altogether because he felt the word too value laden.

In 1964, Baroody took a leave of absence to participate in Barry Goldwater's campaign for the presidency. Among many conservatives, Baroody was seen as a moderate who tempered Goldwater's ideological conservatism during the general election campaign. Baroody alienated many within the campaign by his behind-the-scenes power plays and his unwillingness to work as a team member. Baroody was aggressive, egotistical, and ambitious, qualities that were seen in his leadership at the AEI. AEI's reputation for scholarly objectivity still had not been established as the decade of the 1960s drew to a close. A multiyear grant from the Ford Foundation to study business and economics in 1972, however, marked a major turning point for the AEI. The Ford Foundation grant, totaling $300,000, validated Baroody's claim that the AEI was providing high-quality policy research. Major financial support for the AEI ensued from conservative organizations such as the Lilly Endowment and the Scaife, Earhart, and Kresge foundations; and from corporate donors including General Motors, U.S. Steel, Republic Steel, Mobil, and Standard Oil. The institute's reputation was further enhanced when the Nixon administration drew on a number of AEI associates to staff government positions, including Paul McCracken to head the Council of Economic Advisors, Murray Weidenbaum at the Treasury, Robert Bork at the Justice Department, and Robert Pranger at the Defense Department.

By 1977, the AEI was spending $1.6 million on its public outreach program, which included 118 publications that were received by 400 universities. Its public affairs programs were being sent to more than 700 televisions stations across the nation. The AEI, under Baroody, became a command center for a movement to deregulate the economy. In 1975, the AEI had published Murray Weidenbaum's important economic study *Government-Mandated Price Increases: A Neglected Aspect of Inflation.* This study tied the problem of inflation to government-regulated industries by showing that federal regulation favored large established corporations that were protected from price competition from smaller companies, who were then forced out of the market by federally approved prices. Further scholarly criticism of the regulated economy came from two other AEI economists, Marvin H. Kosters and John C. Miller. Through such studies, the AEI placed itself on the cutting edge of policy research by looking at economic efficiency on a microeconomic level, thereby examining questions of equality within a larger context that weighted economic costs against economic rewards. This methodology, located squarely in the mainstream of quantitative economic analysis, was a far cry from the work of earlier conservative economic tracts by such authors as the journalist Henry Hazlitt or Leonard E. Read at the Foundation for Economic Education. AEI research introduced into the policy arena specialists who articulated free-market perspectives and proposed conservative policy recommendations.

Shortly before his retirement in 1977, William Baroody invited Irving Kristol to become an associate fellow at the institute. Other neoconservative appointments to the AEI followed, including political scientist Jeane Kirkpatrick, former Catholic seminarian Michael Novak, and political commentator Ben Wattenberg. Thus emerged a new type within the conservative movement—the policy expert. These new conservative policy experts came on board at a time when the AEI was undergoing a tremendous expansion. The AEI was tempered in its conservatism and eager to prove that it was a respectable research institution.

In 1977, William Baroody turned over the presidency of the AEI to his son, William Baroody, Jr., an aide to Melvin Laird while he was in Congress and later secretary of defense in the Ford administration. Baroody, Jr., set out to expand the corporate donor base from 200 companies in 1977, which contributed 25 percent of the institution's revenue, to more than 500 corporations that would provide 57 percent of its revenue by 1982. By this time the AEI's annual budget was close to $11 million, supporting a staff of 140. Under Baroody, Jr., the research program was expanded to include seminars on health, taxation, legal affairs, the environment, foreign policy, and defense. In addition, four new periodicals were initiated that targeted the scholarly and policy communities: *AEI Economist, AEI Defense Review, Regulation,* and *Public Opinion.* The staff of the AEI was one of the most prestigious in Washington and included former cabinet members Melvin Laird and William Simon, economist Herbert Stein, legal scholar Robert Bork, and political scientists Norman Ornstein and William Fellner. In the 1980s, gifts from a rejuvenated Bradley Foundation and the John M. Olin Foundation allowed further expansion of the AEI.

The AEI was a formidable conservative intellectual presence in the nation's capital. In the 1970s, it provided expertise to the Nixon and Ford administrations. This marked a coming-of-age for conservatives in the policy arena and in government, but for some conservatives, the AEI was too much like the Brookings Institution in its lengthy analysis and hesitancy to challenge the liberal establishment. The AEI was at the forefront of calling for deregulation of the economy, but within the conservative movement there were demands for cutting the size of government, abolishing entire government agencies, slashing the budget, and redirecting American foreign policy to confront Soviet expansion.

Two former congressional aides, Edwin Feulner and Paul Weyrich, represented this more assertive conservatism when they established the Heritage Foundation in 1973. In starting the foundation, Feulner and

Weyrich sought to consciously influence Republican legislators. The Heritage Foundation received major funding from the beer magnate Joseph Coors and the Mellon heir Richard Scaife. Both donors sought to stem the tide against what they considered antibusiness sentiment in the country. Coors provided an initial donation of $250,000, while Scaife gave an estimated $3.8 million over the next eight years. The Heritage Foundation was to be an "activist version of the Brookings Institution" able to turn out policy papers with an explicit conservative point of view. These brief policy papers were short, two- or three-page reports that could be read quickly by congressional staffers. The Heritage Foundation's ability to articulate conservative values in economic, defense, and social policy quickly placed Heritage at the forefront of conservative policy thought in the 1970s.[32]

While the AEI and the Heritage Foundation were establishing a presence in the policy arena, other organizations were striving to institutionalize conservatism and libertarianism. In 1977, Edward H. Crane, the former national chairman of the Libertarian party, joined with libertarian Murray Rothbard to establish the Cato Institute. Major funding for the institute came from Charles G. Koch, a wealthy Kansas businessman and dedicated libertarian. The Cato Institute was established for the purpose of pushing a libertarian perspective of limited government, individual liberty, and free-market economics into the policy arena. The institute considered itself "classical liberal" and not conservative. As libertarians, its founders believed that the only role of government should be to provide for the protection of property rights, individual liberty, and national security. The Cato Institute opposed the "military-industrial complex" and American involvement abroad. It believed that the free market could provide solutions to social problems, and it opposed government regulation of social behavior, including homosexuality and abortion.[33]

The emergence of neoconservative policy experts and the institutionalization of conservatism through think tanks brought a direct challenge to the liberal regime. Conservatives believed that to achieve power the Republican party needed to be revived ideologically and electorally. Without political power in Congress or the White House, conservatives would have only the voice of dissent to offer, important in some intellectual and policy circles, but still just one voice among many. Liberalism remained the dominant voice in American politics, though few realized that the United States stood at the cusp of ideological change.

5

The Accident of History

In 1976, Ronald Reagan came within an inch of defeating incumbent President Gerald Ford for the Republican nomination for president. Reagan's challenge split the Republican party and helped cost Ford the general election, which he lost to Democrat Jimmy Carter.

The Watergate spill-out had left the GOP Right demoralized and isolated within the Republican party. In general, the Ford White House continued to marginalize conservatives, dismissing their threat to Ford's nomination in 1976. A few lone voices in the Ford administration, most notably Chief of Staff Richard Cheney, suggested reaching out to Reagan to head off a 1976 challenge, but Ford remained contemptuous of the sixty-five-year-old former governor of California, who had been out of office for two years. As a result, Ford seemed impervious to the political sea-change that was occurring in American politics.

Democrats appeared equally complacent about the shifting tides of American politics. The Democratic party aggressively supported legalized abortion, feminism, gay rights, and affirmative action. These issues had awakened a sleeping giant—evangelical Christians, traditional Roman Catholics, and Mormons—constituencies that strategists of the Republican Right would eventually mobilize to revive the GOP. Arguably these constituencies could have been co-opted into the GOP in 1976 if the Ford administration had backed away from its support of the Equal Rights Amendment and showed stronger opposition to legalized abortion. Instead, Ford lost this bloc, which went largely to his rival, Jimmy Carter.

Would Reagan have done better than Ford in 1976 if he had won the Republican nomination? Conservatives believed so, but the answer is probably not. Although the electorate had become increasingly conservative in outlook, the American public was not yet ready to elect a conservative. Had he been defeated in 1976, Reagan would have found it difficult, if not impossible, to win the Republican nomination four years later. Losing the 1976 nomination saved his political career and, with it, the GOP Right.

Gerald Ford and the Dilemma of Moderation

In the mid-1970s, the world of the liberals was one of confidence. Richard Nixon had been disgraced and forced out of office, and the Democratic party had strengthened its power in Congress. Paying the price for Watergate and two years of economic decline, the Republicans suffered in the 1974 midterm elections. Democrats gained forty-three seats in the House and three in the Senate.[1] Moreover, this new class of congressional Democrats in the House was more ideologically liberal than its own party leadership. Moderate and liberal Republicans meanwhile strengthened their position in Congress relative to their conservative Republican counterparts. Moderate-liberal Republicans posted gains in the House with victories by Paul N. McCloskey, Jr. (California), Gilbert Gude (Maryland), and Ronald A. Sarasin (Connecticut). In the South, Republicans lost ten House seats, while also faring badly in the Midwest, a Republican stronghold. In the Senate, the only conservative Republican who was elected easily was Barry Goldwater, while Peter H. Dominick of Colorado and Marlow W. Cook of Kentucky lost. Senator Bob Dole barely won reelection in Kansas. His seat was saved at the last stage of the campaign when he attacked his opponent, Representative William R. Roy, for supporting abortion. Dole won with only 50.8 percent of the popular vote.

In their victory, the new Democrats who entered Congress displayed antagonism and arrogance toward the Republican minority. Nearly a quarter of House Democrats were freshmen; half of them had been elected in 1970 or after. Through this critical mass, House rules were changed to end the power of southern Democrats in controlling committee chairmanships. By assuming committee chairs, liberal Democrats—"Watergate Babies"—seized control of the Democratic party in Congress and pursued their agenda with little input from their GOP colleagues. Bipartisanship remained in the Republican vocabulary of necessity, but it became, for the most part, a forgotten word in the lexicon of post-Watergate Democrats. Democrats restricted debate; changed House rules for their own benefit; and exacted penance from the Republicans for the sins of Watergate and political defeat. These actions allowed liberals to exercise control over executive branch agencies and departments, ensuring the continuation of the liberal regime.[2]

As a consequence, though Ford pursued a moderate course, he found his presidency thwarted in both houses of Congress, as well as within the federal bureaucracy. Ford was a moderate Republican who believed, in principle, in balanced budgets and free enterprise, but he was a moderate to the core. He was consistent in this regard. He was first elected to Congress in 1948 by challenging an incumbent Republican, Bartel Jonkman, who had been a prewar noninterventionist. Ford was a Republican internationalist who supported Eisenhower's Europe First policy. As House minority leader, he had opposed much of Lyndon Johnson's Great Society program, but he was no Goldwater conservative. As the old southern Democratic–Republican coalition in the House began to break down in the 1970s, Ford prepared to retire from politics. He changed his mind only when Nixon selected him to replace the disgraced vice president, Spiro Agnew.[3]

From the moment Ford came into the presidency he pursued his natural inclination to chart a centrist course. This tendency was reflected in his cabinet, White House staff, and policies. He came to rely on the moderate-liberal wing of his party represented by Nelson Rockefeller, Senator Charles Percy (Illinois), and Senator Jacob K. Javits (New York). Ford appeared oblivious to the rumbles coming from the right wing of the party. Instead, he seemed to go out of his way to alienate conservatives through his appointments, his equivocation on abortion, his support of the Equal Rights Amendment, and his endorsement of SALT II negotiations with the Soviet Union. At the same time, he estranged much of the general electorate with his pardon of his predecessor, Richard Nixon. The pardon convinced many that Nixon had struck a secret deal with Ford before turning over the vice presidency to him.

The problems Ford faced as he stepped into the White House seemed insurmountable. Confronted with an economy shredded by runaway inflation and a severe recession that followed a steep rise in interest rates initiated by the Federal Reserve, Ford considered himself a steady helmsman. He believed he could heal the nation's wounds from Watergate and Vietnam and steer an even course on domestic and foreign policy issues. He sought to provide continuity in American foreign policy by keeping Henry Kissinger as his secretary of state. Although admired by some conservatives, Kissinger was for most right-wingers the man who had opened relations with China, reversed a long-held pro-Taiwan policy, abandoned South Vietnam to the Communists (Saigon fell in the spring of 1975), and pursued an appeasement policy toward the Soviet Union through nuclear arms treaties.

The Republican Right's opposition to what it considered the Kissinger-Rockefeller continuum in Ford's foreign policy was intense. Here, too, Ford was limited by a Democratic Congress eager to restrict presidential powers in the conduct of foreign policy. In June 1973, Senators Frank Church (D-Idaho) and Clifford Case (R-New Jersey) wrote into the 1974 fiscal budget an amendment forbidding the use of any American forces in Indochina, thus eliminating the possibility of U.S. support for South Vietnam if it were attacked again. This amendment was followed by legislation introduced by Senators Adlai Stevenson III (D-Illinois) and Charles Mathias (R-Maryland) terminating aid to South Vietnam. Two months before this legislation was to take effect, the North Vietnamese captured Saigon, renaming it Ho Chi Minh City.

Meanwhile, Ford tenaciously sought an arms control agreement with the Soviet Union. In late 1974 he met with Soviet Premier Leonid Brezhnev in Vladivostok to work out the details of a treaty. To ensure that relations between the United States and the Soviet Union remained on the right course, Ford refused to meet with the dissident Russian author Aleksandr Solzhenitsyn in the White House, much to the dismay of the Republican Right, which interpreted this move as another sign of appeasement toward the Soviet Union. In the summer of 1975, Ford signed the Helsinki Accords, in which the Soviet Union pledged to protect civil liberties in the Soviet bloc. The accords, as critics were quick to observe, did not include measures to enforce this pledge.

Ford aroused fierce opposition from his party's right wing when he nominated Rockefeller to become his vice president. In making this nomination, Ford sought to gain favor with eastern Republicans, whose financial support would be crucial to a reelection campaign in 1976.[4] The Republican Right immediately organized a campaign to defeat the nomination.[5] When charges were leveled that Rockefeller had bribed the head of the New York Republican party, Congress forced an angry Rockefeller to reveal his financial records. Although he easily won confirmation, the process had humiliated Rockefeller and stunned the Ford administration, which had been caught off-guard by the backlash.

Facing a huge Democratic majority in Congress, Ford had little room for political maneuvering and little incentive to appease the right wing of his party. To counter the liberal Democrats in the House, he relied on Republican moderates and liberals in the House, including Paul McCloskey, Jr., of California, Gilbert Gude of Maryland, and Ronald A. Sarasin of Connecticut. In the Senate, Ford found support in Robert W. Packwood of Oregon, Richard S. Schweiker of Pennsylvania, Jacob K. Javits of New York, and Charles Mathias of Maryland. By aligning himself with the liberal wing of the party, he sought to tack a centrist course, restraining a spendthrift Congress on budgetary matters. Ford vetoed more bills than any president since Harry Truman, but he received little credit from conservatives. While taking a strong position on fiscal issues, he sought to sidestep social issues, though that became increasingly difficult after the Supreme Court's decision in *Roe v. Wade* (1973) legalizing abortion.

While Ford appeared reluctant to take a strong stand on abortion, he came out strongly in favor of the ERA, which would write equality for women into the constitution. From Ford's perspective, support for the ERA looked safe. The amendment passed Congress in 1972 with overwhelming support and was quickly ratified by a large number of states. The amendment read, "Equality of rights under the law shall not be denied or abridged by the United States or by any state on account of sex." The ERA looked to be on its way to easy passage, and early polls indicated that most women supported ratification. Ford's wife, Betty, was a vociferous supporter of the amendment. In short, Ford had every reason to back the amendment when he came into office. But once again he miscalculated. A small group of women activists on the Right believed that the polls were wrong and that support for the amendment was weak among mainstream women. These activists thought the amendment was unnecessary and so broad that it presented potentially dangerous implications. They wanted to fight ratification and found their leader in Phyllis Schlafly, a right-wing activist from Alton, Illinois.

Ford's centrist policies created a political vacuum on the Right that was quickly filled by a groundswell of grassroots activism. From this activism emerged the New Right—a term coined by the longtime activist Paul Weyrich. The media identified the leaders of the New Right as Richard Viguerie, Howard Phillips, Paul Weyrich, and Terry Dolan, but these people were certainly not new conservatives. Phyllis Schlafly's involvement in conservative Republican politics and anti-Communism went back to the 1950s, before other leaders of the New Right had become politically active. Viguerie, Phillips, and Weyrich were children of the 1960s who became involved in right-wing politics through Young Americans for Freedom. By 1978 the National Conservative Political Action Committee (NCPAC), founded by three young conservatives— Charlie Black, Roger Stone, and Terry Dolan (the chairman)—became the largest conservative political action committee in the country, distributing more than $1.2 million in cash and in-kind contributions to political campaigns in its first five years.[6]

The New Right's ability to tap into grassroots discontent over social and moral issues such as abortion, prayer in school, and the ERA caught both liberals and the Republican establishment off-guard. These New Right activists challenged the status quo and the power structure in both parties.[7] They saw themselves as radicals who wanted to overthrow entrenched elites and professional experts. Paul Weyrich later declared, "We are radicals who want to change the existing power structure. We are not conservatives in the sense that conservative means accepting the status quo." They believed that liberalism was a dying force in American politics and that the political future belonged to conservatism. "The liberals have not only lost confidence in themselves but in their ideas," Viguerie declared. "We're convinced we have the ability to govern and will govern in the not-too-distant future."[8]

New Right leaders recognized that much of their ideology was not new. Viguerie admitted that "in many ways, there's not a great deal 'new' about the New Right. Our views, our philosophy, our beliefs are not that different, if at all, from the Old Right. It is our emphasis that is different." The emphasis was on social issues and a populist impulse to challenge the GOP establishment by organizing the grassroots. To accomplish this goal, the New Right developed new political organizations funded largely through direct-mail campaigns focused on controversial issues that had immediate emotional appeal.

The New Right targeted average Americans, many of whom felt that their culture was under attack by the Left, with its demands for liberation from traditional moral constraints. In this campaign, conservative activists stepped in where the Republican establishment dared not tread. Paul Weyrich liked to tell the story of how he had worked for the Republican party in Wisconsin in 1962 when the Supreme Court ruled in the Madalyn Murray O'Hair case that prayer in public schools was unconstitutional. Upon hearing of the decision, he had excitedly phoned the state party chairman, a "relatively conservative fellow," to tell him, "Here is an issue which a lot of people are concerned about, and I think it would be good for you to make a statement on it." The chairman railed that he would not be "caught dead making a statement on prayer in schools, nobody could care less, and why on earth should anyone want to get involved in an issue like that?" It was just such seemingly personal issues that the New Right would use for political mobilization.

These activists brought to the political arena the organizing skills necessary to build coalitions. Weyrich proved critical in this insurgency. A former aide to Senator Gordon Allott (R-Colorado), Weyrich gained the financial backing of the beer magnate Joseph Coors in founding the Committee for the Survival of a Free Congress (CSFC) in 1974. The purpose of this organization was to support the election of conservatives to Congress. By 1978, CSFC had spent $400,000 helping to elect thirty-one conservative candidates, including Senators Orrin Hatch (R-Utah) and Malcolm Wallop (R-Wyoming), as well as many in the House. Weyrich's principal talent was teaching conservatives how to form and make use of coalitions involving antitax groups, antiabortion groups, veterans' organizations, small business associations, and conservative pro-family advocates.

In his work, Weyrich was joined by Howard Phillips, the founder of the Conservative Caucus, in late 1974. The mission of the caucus was to recruit conservative leaders, organize the grassroots, and help set the conservative agenda. Phillips developed his political skills as a Harvard University undergraduate and as one of the founders of the Young Americans for Freedom in 1960. In 1964, he became Republican party chairman in Boston and then managed Richard Schweiker's successful race in

Pennsylvania for the U.S. Senate in 1968. In 1970, he lost his own race for Congress in Massachusetts and accepted an appointment by Richard Nixon as head of the Office of Economic Opportunity (OEO). Nixon had talked about shutting down OEO, but a Democratic-controlled Congress prevented Phillips from doing so. By 1979 the Conservative Caucus had a base of 300,000 contributors. It also launched the Religious Roundtable, which reached out to evangelical Protestant leaders and brought them together for briefings on public policy issues.

Richard Viguerie brought new technical skills to the Right through his use of sophisticated computer technology to raise money and garner support among the grassroots. Viguerie had gained valuable experience in mass fundraising by working in the 1950s for Marvin Liebman, whose Committee of One Million had pioneered the use of fundraising on the Right through mass mailing.[9] Viguerie took direct mailing to new levels of effectiveness through the use of the computer. In doing so, he advanced the conservative cause well beyond the technological capabilities of the Left.

Born in 1933 in a small town outside Houston, Viguerie grew up in a devout Roman Catholic family. His father began as a construction worker for Shell Oil Company and eventually worked his way up to top management. While in college in Texas, Viguerie became involved in Young Republican politics. In 1960, he worked for John Tower's unsuccessful race for the U.S. Senate seat held by Lyndon Johnson, who won reelection before resigning to become vice president under John F. Kennedy.

In 1961 Viguerie went to work as the account executive for Young Americans for Freedom, where he quickly developed his fundraising abilities. In 1964, he withdrew his life savings of $4,000 to start his own direct-mail company in Washington, D.C. Using the public files on record with the clerk of the House of Representatives, he compiled a list of 12,500 donors who had given $50 or more to the Goldwater campaign. With the help of Edward N. Mayer, Jr., he became a direct-mail expert. His only client was Young Americans for Freedom, but in 1966 he showed the power of direct mail when he helped Senator Robert Griffin (R-Michigan) win election to a full term in the U.S. Senate. The following year he worked on Max Rafferty's primary campaign to unseat Republican senator Thomas Kuchel in California. During the primary race, Viguerie's firm mailed more than five million letters. Although Rafferty lost the general election, Viguerie showed he was a skilled political operator.

Other clients followed, including Phil Crane, who won the Republican primary in an upset against thirteen other candidates in a 1969 special election for Congress. In 1972 he went to work for George Wallace to help retire his presidential campaign debt. By 1976, he had raised about $7 million for Wallace. By the late 1970s, Viguerie's company had 250 employees, a multimillion dollar computer, and a subsidiary that published the *Conservative Digest,* a monthly founded in 1975 and edited by another former member of YAF, John Lofton. Viguerie started the *Conservative Digest* in part as an outlet to overcome what he considered the liberal bias of the media. His major enemies were liberalism and moderate Republicanism. To overthrow the GOP establishment, Viguerie rallied the grassroots sentiment to vote for conservative Republican candidates. He sought a revolution from below.

Because members of the New Right were a minority within a minority party, they were able to press with impunity an agenda that interjected new issues and policies into the political arena. They seized upon moral and national defense issues, which genuinely reflected their views of the world, as a means of exerting their influence within the party and turning the GOP into a voice of conservatism. They realized instinctively that their success rested on tapping into additional constituencies that would broaden the appeal of the entire Republican party. They brought to their politics traditional issues combined with the new techniques of political persuasion to mobilize new voting blocs. They projected a vision of America as a place where people upheld traditional values, mothers placed primary value on their homes and their children, and parents protected their children from social evils that came from a secular culture in disarray. They envisioned a nation with a strong social fabric; a culture that looked to past tradition as necessary to the preservation of its future; and a country protected by a powerful military willing to exert its strength when necessary.

Arise Ye Christians of Salvation!

New Right leadership proved critical in transforming the Republican party into a voice of conservatism. The Republican Right was ideologically prepared to press those issues that the GOP establishment was eager to avoid, namely, the cultural issues. They were prepared to wage ideological battle with the GOP and their opponents on the Left: the feminists who demanded the ratification of the Equal Rights Amendment; the radical civil libertarians who worked to drive the expression of Christian belief from the public square; and homosexuals who sought not only to decriminalize sodomy but also to gain legal recognition as a minority group. By mobilizing the grassroots, these activist leaders sought to transform the GOP into a voice of strict conservatism and to end the dominance of the Democratic party and liberalism in American political life.

Postwar conservatives had long lamented the decline of traditional values and Christian morality in America, but what gave these moral issues poignancy was the Supreme Court's ban on school prayer, its decision to legalize abortion, and the rise of the feminist movement.[10] While controversies over abortion and the ERA in the 1970s were later viewed as sparks that ignited Christian evangelical involvement in politics, the issue of school prayer had been smoldering since the Supreme Court banned prayer in public schools in the early 1960s.

Traditionally, the First Amendment had been interpreted narrowly as providing for the free exercise of religion and a prohibition against the federal government's favoring one Christian domination over another.[11] Before the 1960s, the Court had confined itself to protecting the rights of religious minorities. In 1961, however, the Court took the first steps in providing equal standing to non-Christian religions and to nonbelief. Led by Chief Justice Earl Warren, Justice Hugo Black, and Justice William O. Douglas—all members of a local Washington, D.C., Unitarian Church—the Court began to erect an impermeable barrier between church and state. In 1961, the Court ruled that a Maryland law requiring an employee to declare his belief in God was unconstitutional. The following year the Court ruled in *Engel v. Vitale* (1962) that state and local governments were prohibited from requiring children to pray in school. This decision was followed in 1963 by two cases, *Abington School District v. Schempp* and *Murray v. Curlett,* in which the Court banned Bible reading and the recitation of the Lord's Prayer in schools as unconstitutional.

These rulings shocked and angered many American Christians. Senator Strom Thurmond (D-South Carolina) declared in his November 1963 newsletter that at the bottom of "this drive to root God out of our national life is the realization that America cannot be effectively social-ized until it is secularized."[12] Thurman Sensing, vice president of the Southern States Industrial Council, declared in 1964, "It was a tragic day in the life of our Nation when atheists were allowed to veto recognition of Almighty God in our public schools. Isn't it strange that it took the Supreme Court of the United States 186 years to find prayer and Bible reading in our public schools unconstitutional?"[13] Adolph Bedsole, a Baptist minister in Florida, circulated *The Supreme Court Decision on Bible Reading and Prayer: America's Black Letter Day* (1966) to evangelical Christians.[14]

Some Christian literature perceived the decision as a sign that the world was in its last agonies before coming to an end, as foretold in the Book of Revelation. Congress was flooded by demands for a constitutional amendment to reverse these Court rulings. By 1964, 117 representatives had introduced 154 resolutions proposing 35 different constitutional amendments.[15] These amendments faced immediate opposition from Representative Emanuel Celler (D-New York), chairman of the House Judiciary Committee. Celler was joined by other liberals such as Representative B. F. Sisk (D-California), who accused right-wing Christians like Carl McIntyre of heading a crusade to limit American freedom of religion. School prayer amendments remained bottled up in the Judiciary Committee.

Following the 1964 election, Senator Everett Dirksen (R-Illinois) introduced an amendment resolution allowing school administrators to permit voluntary prayer but explicitly prohibiting them from prescribing the content or form of the prayer. The amendment received the endorsement of the American Legion as well as nearly two thousand other organizations. The Senate Judiciary Subcommittee under liberal senator Birch Bayh (D-Indiana) opposed the amendment. Bayh invited the Jesuit Robert Drinan, dean of the Boston College Law School, to testify against the bill. Fr. Drinan denounced the Dirksen amendment as a "truly pathetic desire of Congressmen to be identified in the popular mind" as wanting "more godliness in our schools and more fervor in our public piety."[16] In September 1966 Dirksen's amendment appeared all but dead. In 1971 the prayer amendment was resuscitated when Representative Chalmers Wylie (R-Ohio) persuaded the House to discharge it from committee. Nonetheless, in a 240 to 162 majority vote in favor, the bill fell 28 votes short of the two-thirds required for passage.

Openly disobeying the Court's ban on prayer in schools, many schools in the South and East continued to conduct Bible readings and prayers. Resentment toward the Court's ruling remained widespread among Christian evangelicals. Groups such as the National Committee to Restore Prayer in Schools, chaired by Judge Robert Morris, continued to keep the issue alive in evangelical circles.[17] Joining the effort were groups such as Americans for God, Campus Crusade for Christ, Catholic War Veterans, Concerned Citizens for God and Country, Connecticut Back to God Movement, Florida Back to God Movement, Fort Wayne Prayer Group, Iowans for Moral Education, Lions Club, Ohio Citizens for Parental Rights, Oklahoma Back to God Movement, and Young Americans for Freedom.

While the constitutional ban on prayer in schools stirred the passions of evangelical Protestants, the movement to legalize abortion laws in the states, culminating in the *Roe v. Wade* decision (1973), ignited a grassroots fire that spread across local Catholic communities. For Roman Catholics the abortion issue went to the core of their religious beliefs. They saw life as a gift from God and conception as a link among living persons. To end life through abortion, traditional Roman Catholic theologians argued, was to attack fundamental human good, to intrude on God's domain. As a divine gift, life in its temporal phase reflected God's promise for eternal life.[18]

For feminists who came of age in the 1960s, such views on abortion seemed scholastic and male-centered, and they indicated an attempt to impose personal religious beliefs on an entire citizenry. In the feminist view, the option to terminate a pregnancy should be considered a woman's right. Although in the late 1960s feminists disagreed about exact restrictions on abortion, there was general agreement that it should be allowed in cases of rape, incest, or mental incompetence, or when the woman's life was endangered, or if there was a good chance that the fetus would be born severely deformed or mentally retarded. Feminists saw reproductive choice as a fundamental right within a democracy.

By 1967 states began to liberalize abortion laws. Their efforts coincided with the emergence of a feminist movement. Under the slogan "My Body Belongs to Me," feminists began staging "speak-outs," street theater and other demonstrations in support of abortion rights, adding to the groundswell for the repeal of laws criminalizing abortion.[19] Hawaii became the first state to repeal its law, followed by New York, which enacted legislation, signed into law by Governor Nelson Rockefeller, that removed all restrictions on abortions performed in the first twenty-four weeks of pregnancy.[20] Fifteen other states enacted liberalized abortion laws, while in twenty-nine states abortion remained unlawful except to save the life of the mother.[21] In many states bills to liberalize abortion laws were defeated. In New York, the state legislature repealed its abortion-on-demand law, but the repeal was vetoed by Governor Nelson Rockefeller. In November 1972, pro-abortion referendums were overwhelmingly defeated in North Dakota by 78 percent and in Michigan by 61 percent.

Opposition to abortion reform from religious groups began on the state level through grassroots activism. During the fight over legalized abortion in California in 1967, when Ronald Reagan was governor, activists organized the Right to Life League and Mothers Outraged at the Murder of Innocents (MOMI) to lobby against the bill. Although under heavy pressure from these local activists, as well as from Roman Catholic James Francis Cardinal McIntyre of Los Angeles, Governor Ronald Reagan signed the act into law in 1967.[22] The hierarchy of the Catholic Church supported the antiabortion movement as it grew in the late 1960s, but the impetus for the movement came from local activists who often organized without official Church support.[23]

Women played critical roles in these organizations, both as leaders and as foot soldiers. In terms of demographics, they mirrored their counterparts in the pro-abortion movement. Both the National Right to Life Committee (NRLC) and the National Association for the Repeal of Abortion Laws (NARAL), the leading pro-abortion organization, drew largely from white, suburban, middle-aged, college-educated women.[24] The one critical difference between the pro- and antiabortion activists was religious faith. Many of these early antiabortion activists were Roman Catholics, though a significant number of the most prominent female leaders were Protestants. Approximately 70 percent of the NRLC's members were Roman Catholic—two and one-half times the proportion in the general population—compared with only 4 percent of NARAL's members. NARAL's membership was 17 percent Jewish, eight times the general population, while NRLC had few Jewish members. Each organization attracted some African Americans, but not in significant numbers.[25]

As the election of 1972 approached, Nixon sought to direct this growing antiabortion movement to the Republican party.[26] George Wallace's dramatic showing as a third-party candidate convinced Nixon that the northern ethnic Catholic vote—the backbone of the Democratic party in urban areas—could be won to the GOP column.[27] Further evidence of this possibility was revealed when James Buckley, the brother of William F. Buckley, Jr., won a U.S. Senate seat in New York running on a third-party ticket, the Conservative party, against two liberals. Nixon felt that the key to winning the Catholic vote lay in his support of parochial schools and his opposition to abortion.

As the abortion issue emerged in the late 1960s and early 1970s, the GOP began to shift its position. Before the early 1970s, Republicans had promoted global and national population control through family planning, including contraception, sterilization, and abortion. With the mobilization of antiabortion groups, family planning became politicized and support for abortion divided along partisan lines. Members of the New Right—many of whom were Roman Catholic themselves—saw the abortion issue as a wedge to lure traditional Roman Catholic and evangelical Protestants away from their Democratic loyalties.

In May 1972, Nixon shifted his views on abortion when he issued a public statement condemning "unrestricted abortion policies." He declared, "I consider abortion an unacceptable form of population control. In my judgment, unrestrictive abortion policies would demean human life." Shortly afterward, Nixon released a letter that he had sent to Terence Cardinal Cooke of New York supporting his campaign to repeal the recently passed New York abortion law.[28] The *Roe v. Wade* Supreme Court decision the following year changed all this, but in the meantime, Nixon's "Catholic strategy" paid off. That November, Nixon captured 60 percent of the Catholic vote, 59 percent of the working-class vote, and 57 percent of the union vote.

The Supreme Court's decision in *Roe v. Wade* on January 22, 1973, transformed American politics by polarizing the electorate and the two major political parties. At the federal level, opponents of abortion in Congress sought to repudiate *Roe* by amending the constitution and preventing federal funding of abortion. At the state level, antiabortion groups undertook efforts to limit legalized abortion through restrictive regulations. By early 1976 more than fifty different constitutional amendments to ban or limit abortions had been introduced in Congress.[29] Led by Representative Henry J. Hyde (R-Illinois), a rider was attached to an appropriations bill banning federal funding for abortions for any reason. The measure became law, albeit it with less restrictive language, in 1976.[30] Pro-abortion activists immediately challenged the Hyde amendment in court, but the Supreme Court upheld the decision in *Harris v. McRae* (1980).[31]

Abortion divided the Republican party. The GOP Right feared that Ford was not strongly opposed to abortion. Their fears were heightened when the First Lady, Betty, declared in her first public interview that she supported legalized abortion—as well as the legalization of marijuana and the ratification of the Equal Rights Amendment. Even after Ford instructed his solicitor general, Robert H. Bork, to file an *amicus curiae* brief with the Supreme Court in support of the Hyde amendment, conservatives remained convinced that Ford was soft on the issue and that they still needed to battle their own party.[32]

The Right Attacks Ford

In addition to the abortion debate, Ford encountered a grassroots revolt over the issue of the Equal Rights Amendment.[33] Support for the ERA came from both Republicans and Democrats. Indeed, both parties had endorsed the amendment in its various forms in their party platforms dating back to the 1940s. Following Republican policy, President Dwight Eisenhower had endorsed the passage of the ERA in his message to Congress in 1957, though opponents pointed out that the ERA then included the Hayden provision, which protected rights previously conferred on women by law.

The emergence of the women's movement in the late 1960s revived the drive for an ERA. In October 1967, the newly formed National Organization for Women (NOW) voted to endorse the amendment. In Congress, the head of the House Judiciary Committee, Emanuel Celler (D-New York), a pro-labor Democrat, refused to vote the ERA out of committee because he believed that such an amendment would undermine labor legislation designed to protect women. Finally, in the summer of 1970, Representative Martha Griffiths (D Michigan) cajoled her House colleagues into discharging the ERA from Celler's committee. On August 10, 1970, after only one hour of debate, the House approved the amendment in a vote of 352 to 15. Differences with the Senate held up the bill, but the House again passed the ERA on October 12, 1971, after rejecting the Wiggins amendment, which would have exempted women from compulsory military service and preserved established laws protecting the health and safety of women. The ERA passed the Senate with surprisingly little controversy. Attempts by Senator Sam Ervin (D-North Carolina) to modify the amendment to exclude issues of the military draft and combat, marital and family support, privacy protections and exemptions, and homosexuality failed to attract support from his fellow senators. As a result, the Senate passed the amendment by 84 to 8 in the spring of 1972, granting seven years for the amendment to be ratified by three-fourths of the states. Nixon expressed a phlegmatic attitude toward the amendment, but after he won reelection he allowed White House staffer Anne Armstrong to lobby state legislators to support the ERA.[34]

Whereas Nixon had been indifferent to the Equal Rights Amendment, Ford threw himself and the White House fully into the fight for the ERA. Although ratification of the amendment had slowed by 1974, Ford believed that it could not be stopped. He was not willing to waste political ammunition on what appeared to be a foregone conclusion. Moreover, he had voted for the amendment when he was House minority leader in 1970, so it would have looked like political opportunism if he reversed course. The following year, after his House office was overwhelmed with negative mail, he abstained from voting on the ERA. First Lady Betty Ford, however, vocally supported the amendment.[35]

A former New York model, Betty Ford saw herself as a feminist setting an example for the women of the country. She began appearing at pro-ERA rallies, speaking at fundraisers, and writing and telephoning state legislators when ERA ratification came up in their states. This activism did not ingratiate her to state legislators, who resented her intrusion into state issues; nor did it win her favor from the public. Indeed, mail sent to the White House ran three to one against her. This negative reaction did not give Betty Ford pause. She told the press that she expected this kind of reaction and was not bothered by it one bit. She was following her own conscience and was not about to conform her actions to the political goals of her husband. "Besides," she noted, "he's a male chauvinist." There appeared to be no end to Betty Ford's activities on behalf of the ERA. At one point she sent out a memo to the entire White House staff requiring their attendance at a White House briefing on the ERA held by the paid consultant John D. Deardourff.[36]

Betty Ford's efforts did not help her husband politically, nor did they win her support among feminists. The ERA issue was as much about partisan politics as it was about feminist ideology. Most pro-ERA Democratic women were not going to support Republicans whatever their stance on the ERA, and radical feminists would not find in Betty Ford, with her sprayed bouffant hairdo, a model for feminism. Most important, the First Lady's efforts failed to win over average American housewives. She told a reporter from *Good Housekeeping* that she recognized "the low status of the homemaker in today's society and would like to find ways to raise it."[37] Betty Ford did not seem to realize that most American "homemakers" did not consider themselves "low status" and did not like being told they were by the president's wife.

When first passed by Congress and sent to the states for ratification, however, the ERA had looked like a sure thing. The very day that the Senate passed the ERA, Hawaii became the first state to ratify it, followed in the next few days by Delaware, Nebraska, New Hampshire, Idaho, and Iowa. Within a year of its passage by Congress, twenty-four states had ratified the ERA. At this point, the amendment ran into trouble at the grassroots level, when Phyllis Schlafly started a movement called STOP ERA. She warned that ratification of the ERA would result in women being drafted into the military, abortion on demand, same-sex marriage, and loss of legal protections for wives, mothers, and female workers.[38]

Schlafly opened her attack in the February 1972 issue of her newsletter with a trenchant polemic, "What's Wrong with 'Equal Rights' for Women?" She began her assessment of the ERA by arguing that the traditional family was "the basic unit of society," ingrained in "the laws and customs of our Judeo-Christian civilization." The family, she maintained, assures a woman the "most precious and important right of all—the right to keep her own baby and to be supported and protected in the enjoyment of watching her baby grow and develop."[39] She claimed that the amendment was unnecessary because Congress had enacted the Equal Pay Act (1963); Title VII of the Civil Rights Act (1964); equal opportunity through the Equal Employment Opportunity Act (1972); education opportunity through Title IX of the Education Amendments (1972); and credit protection through the Depository Institution Amendments of 1974. Other inequalities in the law, she maintained, could be handled through further incremental legislation.

Such arguments inevitably angered proponents of the ERA, who contended that without a constitutional amendment, the legislation that had been enacted through their efforts in recent years could be repealed. ERA advocates could not understand opposition to the amendment, especially when it came from women. As a result, Indeed, they were caught off guard by the anti-ERA movement, which spread like wildfire among traditional women who were offended by what they called the "women's libbers." The anti-ERA campaign tapped into a growing resentment among traditional religious women that their values were being threatened.[40]

By 1973, STOP ERA organizations existed in twenty-six states, with the most active chapters in states critical to ERA ratification, including Arizona, Florida, Illinois, Louisiana, Missouri, Ohio, Oklahoma, Utah, Nevada, North and South Carolina, and Virginia.[41] Schlafly appointed the state directors, but individual states pursued their own tactics and undertook their own fundraising. This organizational structure was different from that of the major pro-ERA organizations, NOW and ERAmerica. NOW had taken a leading role in the fight for ratification of the ERA, but as Schlafly gained momentum, pro-ERA groups decided that a more concerted effort needed to be waged on behalf of the amendment.

ERAmerica was formed in 1976 as an umbrella organization representing 120 groups, including labor unions, the American Civil Liberties Union, and professional, religious, and political groups. NOW, however, refused to join ERAmerica, and as a consequence the two groups often found themselves at loggerheads over strategy and tactics. ERAmerica wanted to emphasize lobbying state legislators, while NOW's approach called for demonstrations and, later, political boycotts of states that refused to ratify the amendment. Moreover, ERAmerica believed that it was a fundamental mistake on NOW's part to link ratification of ERA to demands for legalized abortion and gay rights. *Roe v. Wade* (1973), which legalized abortion, had followed shortly after the ERA passed Congress and set the context for much of the debate over the amendment.

This radicalism dismayed ERAmerica leaders, who wanted to focus on lobbying efforts rather than street demonstrations. As younger leaders such as the radical feminist Gloria Steinem replaced an older generation of feminists such as Betty Friedan, NOW became more obstreperous in its rhetoric.[42] In 1975, NOW elected as its president Karen DeCrow, who had run on the slogan "Out of the Mainstream: Into the Revolution." DeCrow insisted that NOW's goals should include preferential hiring of women and homosexual rights, in contrast to the older strategy of "equal opportunity for women."

The call for lesbian rights and abortion on demand was especially powerful in mobilizing opposition among Christian women. As state campaigns got under way, anti-ERA leaders at the state level began to tap into other religious constituencies—evangelical Christians and Mormons. The influence of these groups in STOP ERA organizations varied from state to state. In Oklahoma, STOP ERA drew heavily from the Church of Christ, while Mormons provided key activists in Utah, Nevada, and Arizona. Evangelical Christians were especially important in North Carolina, Georgia, and other southern states, as anti-ERA activists fanned out to rally traditional women to become involved in the movement. Evangelical churches were obvious places to organize women concerned about what they considered an assault on their family values. Remarkably, surveys showed that 98 percent of anti-ERA activists claimed church membership, in sharp contrast to 31–48 percent of pro-ERA activists.[43] For these fundamentalist and evangelical Christian women who opposed the ERA, the place of wives and mothers in the family and in society came from biblical injunctions to uphold the authority of husbands and fathers; manmade legislation like the ERA threatened the essence of what they believed as God-fearing, Christian women.

When the anti-ERA campaign began, few if any political pundits believed that ERA ratification could be stopped. The leadership of NOW and ERAmerica were confident that Schlafly—in their opinion, just a small-town housewife—could not do much damage to their cause. Overconfident, they did not take the campaign as seriously as they should have in 1973. Three more states ratified in 1974, one in 1975, and another in 1977, bringing the total to thirty-five states of the necessary thirty-eight. By this point, however, the ERA had ground to a halt. In this same period, 1973–1976, five states rescinded their previous ratification of the amendment. By 1976, ERA proponents were admitting that they had failed to win over the average homemaker.[44]

By 1976 momentum for ERA ratification had been halted. In 1974, ERA proponents won in Maine, Ohio, and Montana, but they lost in seventeen other states. With a total of thirty-three states having ratified the amendment, only five more were needed for final ratification. At the same time, Nebraska had rescinded its ratification in March 1973, and Tennessee did the same in April 1974. In the course of the ERA fight another three states would also rescind their ratifications.[45] The battle had succeeded in making feminism a suspect term for mainstream America. Feminists believed that their struggle had forced the expansion of economic and social opportunities for women. For this reason, the defeat of the ERA was especially painful for them.

In supporting the ERA, Ford underestimated the growing strength of the Right within his own party. He found equally vociferous opposition from conservatives in what they considered his unrestrained pursuit of détente with the Soviet Union. Promising that "America can regain its pride," Ford anxiously pursued better relations with the Soviet Union, even while the Democratic-controlled Congress systematically enacted measures to limit presidential powers in foreign policy and to cut defense expenditures. Ford kept Henry Kissinger as his secretary of state at Nixon's urging, thereby ensuring a continuation of accommodation with the Soviet Union through trade and arms control treaties.

During this time, the North Vietnamese began their military descent on South Vietnam, in clear violation of the Paris Peace Accords of 1972.[46] Supported by significant Soviet military aid, North Vietnam prepared to conquer the rest of South Vietnam. In November 1973, Congress passed the War Powers Act restricting presidential war-making powers, and three months earlier, in August, Congress had voted to prohibit further U.S. military activity in Indochina. In subsequent years, Congress cut military aid to South Vietnam from $2.2 billion to a little more than $700 million for 1975. In April 1975, the North Vietnamese captured Saigon and renamed it after the Communist leader Ho Chi Minh. In 1975, Cambodia also fell to the Communists, the Khmer Rouge under Pol Pot. Once in control, the Communist regimes in Vietnam and Cambodia—though soon at war with each other—massacred hundreds of thousands of opponents. In Cambodia, an estimated two million people died under the abominations of the Pol Pot regime.[47]

In the mid-1970s, the Soviet Union pursued an adventuristic foreign policy in Africa and Latin America. In civil war–racked Angola, it began sending advisors and heavy arms shipments to the Marxist group Popular Movement for the Liberation of Angola (MPLA). When Ford asked for funds to aid the anti-Communist faction, Congress rejected the request. In Nicaragua, the Soviets provided training and advice to the revolutionary Sandinistas seeking to overthrow the corrupt dictatorship of Anastasio Somoza Debayle.

Conservatives feared that America was losing power to the Soviet Union in Asia, Africa, and Central America. Estimates from military experts indicated that the Soviet Union was quickly surpassing—some said it had already surpassed—the United States in conventional and nuclear weapons. By 1974 the Soviet Union had 500 more Intercontinental Ballistic Missiles (ICBMs) than the United States; an equal number of submarine-launched missiles; five times as many tanks; and an army twice the size.[48] While administration officials assured the American public that the United States military and nuclear weapons were adequate and more efficient than the Soviet Union's, conservative Republicans—and an increasing number of Democratic hawks—believed that America was headed toward disaster. Most experts agreed that the Soviet Union had continued a massive nuclear arms buildup following the signing of the Strategic Arms Limitation Treaty (SALT I) in 1972. In fact, as the historian Steven Hayward observes, SALT I did not prevent "a single offensive weapons system from being developed or deployed."[49]

Criticism of SALT I remained unabated when President Ford and Soviet leader Leonid Brezhnev met in Vladivostok in November 1974. From this meeting, the Vladivostok agreement emerged, setting the framework for SALT II. At Vladivostok, Ford and Brezhnev agreed to limit nuclear delivery vehicles to 2,400 for both sides. In addition, the agreement set a limit of 1,320 Multiple Independently Targeted Reentry Vehicles (MIRVs), a ban on construction of new land-based ICBM launchers, and limits on deployment of new types of strategic offensive weapons. The Vladivostok Interim SALT II allowed the Soviets to keep their heavy missiles, while deferring for further negotiation the American cruise missile and the Soviet Backfire bomber.[50]

The GOP Right blasted the interim SALT II agreement as soon as it was announced. Criticism of détente policy heightened when Ford and Kissinger met with Soviet leader Leonid Brezhnev in Helsinki, Finland, in 1975. The Helsinki Accords were signed with much fanfare—and an explosion of conservative criticism at home in the United States. The accords recognized the "inviolability of frontiers," in effect providing *de facto* recognition of Soviet control of Eastern Europe. The phrase "inviolability of frontiers" was inserted at the insistence of the Soviet negotiators, who had agreed in principle to language suggesting the eventual reunification of Germany. For critics of the language, this was an unconscionable reversal of thirty years of American foreign policy.

This issue alone would have been enough to draw criticism from the Right, but other aspects of the Helsinki Accords proved equally provocative. Conservatives were aghast at the trade concessions offered to the Soviet Union, including favorable credit terms to purchase American goods. The Ford administration replied that trade between nations encouraged peace and that the Soviet Union had agreed to respect human rights within its borders. This did little to placate the Republican Right, which viewed the Soviet Union as inherently repressive and run by apparatchik thugs. As a consequence, the Helsinki Accords were greeted with disdain by conservatives. Ronald Reagan declared, "I am against it [Helsinki Accords], and I think all Americans should be against it."[51]

The Shot Heard around the GOP

When conservatives began to coalesce around a Ronald Reagan challenge to the GOP nomination, the Ford presidential campaign dismissed the threat. Having once urged Ford to reach out to Reagan, White House Chief of Staff Dick Cheney now assured Ford that he had an "enthusiastic following among grassroots conservatives," so he did not need to worry about the nomination.[52] This sentiment was reinforced by others in the Ford campaign. The president was told that the voters considered Reagan "too slick" and "too much a politician."[53] Ford decided to tack to the center, giving little heed to the winds blowing from his right. As part of this strategy, he forced the resignation of Secretary of Defense James Schlesinger in November 1975; at the same time, Kissinger encouraged the resignation of Daniel Moynihan as U.S. ambassador to the United Nations. Moynihan had delighted conservatives with his acerbic confrontation of Third World ambassadors to the United Nations.[54]

Reagan's staff began to think about a presidential race as early as 1974.[55] Mike Deaver and Peter Hanaford, former aides, had established a public relations firm with Reagan as their major client. They estimated that through his writings and speeches Reagan earned approximately $400,000 a year, of which half could support a small staff preparing the ground for a presidential challenge. Although members of his staff, especially Lyn Nofziger and Michael Deaver, encouraged Reagan to run for the presidency, Reagan held back on making a full commitment to the race. Early polls in 1974 and 1975 showed him trailing badly in a head-to-head race with Ford. Even many conservatives felt that Reagan could not win the nomination. William Rusher, publisher of the *National Review,* wanted Reagan to lead a new third party that would bring Goldwater Republicans and southern Democrats into the same party. This was an old dream of the American Right, but Rusher brought a keen intelligence to the proposal, so he was not to be cavalierly dismissed.

In early 1975 Rusher wrote to William Loeb, the strident conservative publisher of the *Manchester Union Leader* who believed that neither Wallace nor Reagan could win the nominations of their respective parties, "I concur in your feeling that Wallace is probably not going to be able to carry off the Democratic nomination, and that he will thereupon go the third-party route. I also appreciate your concerns about Reagan. But if (as I expect) Ford and Goldwater slowly paint him into a corner, I do not rule out the real possibility that he too may decide to teach them a lesson by taking our advice and stepping outside the GOP altogether." He added that in such a case, high-level diplomacy would be needed to bring Wallace and Goldwater forces together. Therefore, he concluded, "it is important for us 'radicals' in such a context to put forward as reassuring a foot as possible."[56] In the end, Reagan decided not to go the third-party route. He feared that American voters might not accept a candidate who had broken with the Democratic party, only to desert the Republican party twelve years later. He remained cautious, however, about declaring his candidacy for the presidency.

As months passed and Reagan failed to declare his intentions, conservatives became increasingly impatient with him. They asked, was Reagan serious or not? Typical was a letter from Mickey Edwards, a national board member of the American Conservative Union and an Oklahoma Republican who had failed twice in his bid for elected office. He wrote to Reagan in the spring of 1975, "The Republican Party is in serious danger of extinction because it has ceased to represent anything more than a broad based pragmatism . . . If Gerald Ford becomes the Republican nominee, I see a disastrous defeat that will end the Republican Party. Because the Republican Party is, at its roots, a party of conservative principle, I believe that would be tragic." With your nomination, he declared, will come "a resurgence of conservative philosophy of government. I urge you to run for President."[57] Reagan received hundreds of similar letters urging him to challenge Ford for the GOP nomination. Finally, on November 19, 1975, Reagan declared that he was seeking the GOP presidential nomination. His announcement was greeted with enthusiasm by conservatives and with derision by the liberal media. James Reston of the *New York Times* mockingly described Reagan's challenge as a "frivolous fantasy," while John Osborne in *The New Republic* described Reagan as an "essentially mindless and totally unconvincing candy man," whose declaration should not be taken seriously.[58]

Reagan's entrance into the primary divided Republicans. Although the division was primarily ideological, some conservatives remained with Ford. Harry Dent, a well-known southern Republican, joined the Ford campaign and worked assiduously to win the South for Ford. Barry Goldwater, once the hero of the Right, remained a faithful Ford supporter and simply could not understand why conservatives were not backing Ford. Moreover, it made no sense to him that he himself was, in his opinion, being driven out of the conservative movement for his support of the president. "I can appreciate," he wrote to the actor Efrem Zimbalist, Jr., "the fact that there are strong feelings within the party, and though I have been the target of the more emotional assaults, I can understand it. What is getting tougher to understand by the minute, however, is how we can finally come so close to achieving what we set out to achieve three elections ago and risk it all now over a hair-splitting debate within the party about which of two genuine and bona fide conservatives is more conservative."[59]

Zimbalist, a Goldwater delegate in 1964, replied that he was disappointed in Goldwater's inability to discern "any difference between the two candidates in question, in degree of quality, idealism or intention; who can with equanimity accept, on the one hand, a Kissinger foreign policy and, on the other, the largest federal budget in our nation's history." In a sharp note, he concluded, "I am, to be blunt, astounded that, as a Republican, you can see no difference, either with respect to philosophy or the ability to implement it, between the two years of this appointed administration and the eight years of the Reagan mandate in California."[60]

Reagan launched his campaign by proposing a plan to streamline government by transferring programs to the states. He promised that his plan would save the American taxpayers more than $90 billion. What he did not explain in the plan was how the states were going to pay for these programs—other than by raising state and local taxes. The Ford campaign immediately seized upon this deficiency and turned it against Reagan in New Hampshire, where the first Republican primary was fought. Reagan entered New Hampshire as a favorite to win the election, but he was soon defending himself against Ford's allegations that the Reagan plan meant raising taxes in the state. Reagan's set campaign speech soon became a $90 billion albatross hanging around his neck.

Under heavy attack from Ford, Reagan stuck to his guns in defending his proposal to devolve federal power to the states. By January, a month before the primary, Reagan had taken a twelve-point lead, but it soon dissipated under heavy campaigning by Ford in the state. Reagan's general campaign manager, John Sears, knew the race would come down to the wire, but he allowed Reagan to leave the state on the last day to campaign in Illinois. When the vote came in the next day, Ford won New Hampshire by a mere 1,300 votes out of more than 108,000 cast. It was a bad start for the challenger.

As his campaign failed to gain traction with the voters, Reagan turned to attacking Ford, specifically on détente policy and the administration's alleged acquiescence in the face of the diplomatic and military decline of the United States. Reagan found crowds cheering when he attacked the proposed turnover of the Panama Canal to the left-wing Panamanian regime headed by General Omar Torrijos, who had come to power in 1968. Reagan maintained that the turnover of the canal, which the Ford administration was proposing, threatened national security because it deprived the United States of easy access between the Pacific and Atlantic oceans. Reagan appealed to American nationalism. The recent fall of Saigon had heightened Americans' anxiety about the power of the United States in the world. He drew cheers from the crowd with the line, "We built it, we paid for it, and it's ours, and we should tell Torrijos and company we are going to keep it." Still, Ford won Illinois, Massachusetts, Vermont, and, more important, Florida.

Ford was confident that the nomination was his, and so he spent only two days campaigning in North Carolina. Concerned that he might lose the conservative women's vote because of his pro-ERA stance, he devoted his speech to the State Annual Convention of Future Homemakers of America in Charlotte on March 20 to a defense of the American housewife. White House staff member David Gergen had been brought in to help write the speech. Ford emphatically declared, "I regret that some people in this country have disparaged and demeaned the role of the homemaker. I say—and say it with emphasis and conviction—that homemaking is good for America."[61] Reagan, for his part, downplayed any hopes of winning North Carolina. He knew that the state was critical to any chance of reversing what had been a disappointing campaign premised on early victories. Reagan willingly turned the North Carolina campaign over to Senator Jesse Helms's well-oiled political machine. In his speeches, Reagan began attacking "Dr. Kissinger and Mr. Ford."

Reagan won the North Carolina primary 52 percent to 46 percent. The loss of North Carolina was a serious blow to Ford. The race became wide open. Instead of being able to turn to the Democrats he would face in the general election, Ford was forced to spend resources and attention fending off Reagan. For the next two months, Ford and Reagan traded blows, as the campaign shifted to the West. Reagan beat Ford easily in Texas, winning every congressional district to take all ninety-six delegates. Then he won the next three primaries, Indiana, Alabama, and Georgia. He won Nebraska. Ford bounced back in his home state of Michigan. And so it went, back and forth. As the battle became more heated, Ford swung between a strategy of denouncing Reagan as an extremist and moving toward the right himself. As the primaries came to a close, it appeared to be a dead heat, with Reagan winning in California, while Ford won Ohio and New Jersey.

The delegate count was too close to call, as both candidates scurried to pick up uncommitted delegates. Both sides admitted that they did not have the 1,130 votes needed to secure the nomination. Ford was about 100 votes short, while Reagan was estimated to be 200 votes short. At this point John Sears, who early in the campaign, when Reagan had lost five straight primaries, had opened secret negotiations with the Ford camp for Reagan to withdraw from the race, proposed that Reagan announce his selection of U.S. Senator Richard Schweiker (R-Pennsylvania) as his running mate. Schweiker, the reasoning went, was from the key state of Pennsylvania, which had a large number of uncommitted delegates. Furthermore, Schweiker was a well-established liberal in the GOP, a fact that might reassure the moderate-liberal wing of the party. His voting rating from the Americans for Democratic Action was 89 percent, the same as George McGovern's.[62]

When the Schweiker choice was announced by the Reagan camp, conservatives reacted with outrage. Congressman Henry Hyde (R-Illinois) likened Reagan's selection to "a farmer selling his last cow to buy a milking machine."[63] Only conservatives' deep loyalty to Reagan kept the GOP Right from deserting the campaign. But the Ford staff was not to be outdone. Ford brought in a wily Texas lawyer, James A. Baker 3rd, to round up delegates. He was joined by the southern political operative Harry Dent. Working behind the scenes, Baker and Dent convinced Clarke Reed, head of the Mississippi delegation, to declare for Ford. Congressman Trent Lott had already declared for Reagan after the Schweiker announcement, and others followed. The hope that northeastern delegates would swing to Reagan failed to materialize. Reagan then tried to split the Ford delegates by inserting conservative planks into the GOP platform. Led by Senator Jesse Helms, Reagan forces proposed a strong, anti-détente foreign policy plank called "Morality in Foreign Policy." The plank took clear aim at the Kissinger-Ford foreign policy by praising the Russian dissident Solzhenitsyn and criticizing the Helsinki Accords. Ford, anxious to avoid a floor fight, accepted the plank.

At the same time, conservatives decided not to press an anti-ERA resolution. The anti-ERA plank won endorsement in a platform subcommittee, only to be overturned in an exceedingly close vote in the full platform committee.[64] (This was the last GOP convention platform that contained a pro-ERA plank.) Still, conservatives won other victories in the platform that testified to their increased strength. Planks were approved calling for constitutional amendments restoring prayer in school and prohibiting racial busing, and the abolition of the Department of Education was supported.

More important, the convention platform pledged to seek the enactment of a constitutional amendment to restore the protection of the right to life for unborn children. This was a victory for conservatives, though the plank was somewhat equivocal: "There are those in our party who favor complete support for the Supreme Court decision which permits abortion on demand. There are those who share sincere convictions that the Supreme Court's decision be changed by a constitutional amendment prohibiting all abortions." The platform added that the Republican party supported "a continuance of the public dialogue on abortion and . . . the efforts of those who seek enactment of a constitutional amendment to restore protection of the right to life for unborn children."[65]

Reagan's maneuvering on the platform was not enough to swing a sufficient number of delegates to win the nomination. By the time of the convention, it was clear that Ford was the winner. This was confirmed when a jubilant Ford won the nomination by a narrow margin. At this point the president was so eager to unite the party that on the final evening of the convention he invited Reagan to join him on the stage. A reluctant Reagan left his box and worked his way to the stage amid cheers from his supporters. Once on the stage, Reagan gave one of the greatest speeches of his life. His natural eloquence left many Republicans wondering if they had nominated the wrong man. After warning of the dangers of nuclear war and reaffirming his own commitment to preserve liberty in a dangerous world, he concluded, "We must go forth from here, united, determined that what a great general said a few years ago is true, 'There's no substitute for victory,' Mr. President." It was a masterly speech.

The Democrats turned to an outsider after winnowing the field of candidates. Jimmy Carter, a one-term governor of Georgia and a wealthy peanut farmer, entered the Democratic primaries as the southern Democrat who could best stop George Wallace from winning the nomination. In a hotly contested Democratic race, Carter decided to concentrate on winning the Iowa caucuses, an unprecedented strategy at the time. He presented himself as a Washington outsider who promised to break with "politics as usual" by restoring virtue and trust to government. While campaigning in the Iowa primary he emphasized his roots as a "bornagain" Christian, a Baptist who found personal salvation in Christ. He said that religious values were essential to the nation and that he opposed abortion. After he won Iowa, he clarified his antiabortion stance, declaring that he was against abortion on demand but opposed to a constitutional amendment overturning *Roe*. Nonetheless, at the Democratic Convention he alienated many feminists within the party by declaring categorically that "abortion is wrong." During the campaign against Ford, Carter downplayed social issues and emphasized economic issues and the loss of confidence in government. Carter's avoidance of the social issues was made easier by Ford, who likewise did not want to talk about abortion during the campaign.

Neither the Ford nor the Carter campaign was inspiring. Carter's equivocation on many issues left voters confused as to where he stood on domestic and foreign policy. On the campaign trail, Carter described himself as a benevolent conservative who would downsize government through reorganization and impose fiscal responsibility by cutting operation costs. Ford, for his part, defended his record and emphasized, rightfully, that he had provided the nation with responsible leadership in the aftermath of Watergate.

Most conservatives, however, refused to rally to Ford and his "unity" message. Doubts about Ford and his naïve views about Communism and the Soviet Union were confirmed when, during the presidential debate, he declared, "There is not Soviet domination of Eastern Europe." He maintained further that Yugoslavians, Romanians, and Poles did not consider themselves dominated by the Soviet Union: "Each of those countries is independent, autonomous." He added, "And the United States does not concede that those countries are under the domination of the Soviet Union."[66] His statement confirmed conservatives' worst suspicions of Ford as an obstinate fool.

When the final votes were tallied, Carter narrowly won the election with 50.8 percent of the popular vote to Ford's 48.02. Carter swept the South, while winning evangelical Christians to the Democratic party. This was the first time many evangelical Christians had voted in a presidential election. Carter believed he had won the election because he called for a new politics different from the extremes of both parties. He felt that the abortion issue had been critical to his victory, and he was convinced that Betty Ford's strong pro-abortion views and Gerald Ford's ambivalence on the abortion issue had alienated religious voters. These views soon put Carter at odds with the Left of his party, while his pro-ERA stance and foreign policy based on détente fueled the growing conservative movement.

Arguably, if Ford had done more to placate the Right by winning Reagan to his side, he might have unified the party going into the 1976 presidential election, and a united Republican party probably would have defeated Jimmy Carter. After all, Carter won the popular vote by only 2 percentage points. Ford's centrist policies, while upsetting the small but vocal Right in his party, appeared to be good politics at the time. Ford was driven, however, by concerns larger than politics. Having assumed the office of president, he wanted to become a statesman, a leader for the entire nation. He sincerely believed that Americans needed time to heal from the wounds inflicted by the Vietnam War and the loss of confidence brought about by Watergate. Ford wanted to stabilize the nation and renew people's faith in the democratic system. This was his primary motivation in granting clemency to Richard Nixon in order to avoid a long trial, and for granting amnesty to draft evaders who had fled to Canada during the war. This is also why he supported the Equal Rights Amendment.

The GOP Right had failed to win the Republican nomination, though Ford's defeat in the general election revived their hopes of taking control of the Republican party. Ronald Reagan appeared to hold the future of the GOP Right in his hands, but he was old and considered too right-wing by many to win the presidency. With control of Congress and the White House, however, Democrats had been given yet another opportunity to keep the GOP Right from the reaches of power. In the end, the Carter presidency proved to be a disaster for the Democratic party and a godsend for the Republicans.

6

Forward to the Promised Land

As it turned out, Carter's election to the presidency in 1976 marked a high point for Democrats in the sixteen years that followed. The 1976 election had been a squeaker, with no decision until the early morning hours. But Carter won. A change of a little more than 23,000 votes in Ohio and Wisconsin would have given the election to Ford. As it was, Carter received only 1.6 million more votes than Ford out of nearly 80 million cast. He won the bare majority of the popular vote, 50 percent to 48 percent. The 1976 election gave Democrats control of the White House as well as both houses of Congress.

The election left the GOP a divided party. Ford's loss was critical in sustaining Ronald Reagan's political career. With Ford's defeat, the conservative wing of the party believed that Reagan would win the 1980 nomination. He had revived the fortunes of the GOP Right. The realists among the conservatives understood that a Reagan candidacy had its problems, however. Reagan would be sixty-nine years old in 1980. Conservatives admired him for his outspoken conservatism, but conservatism was not necessarily a political advantage. Although the electorate had shifted to the right since 1964, and the number of self-identified liberals had declined as a percentage of the overall electorate, most voters considered themselves moderates. Reagan needed to win this bloc in order to win the presidency. Conservative strategists also knew that the 1980 election stood four years away, and four years in American politics was an eternity. A lot could happen in the meantime.

Carter, too, realized that the key to his 1976 election lay in the moderate vote, which counted for about half the electorate. He won roughly 51 percent of the moderate vote, leaving Ford the other 48 percent. He also took nearly a third of the conservative vote, while Ford took nearly 70 percent of it. At the same time, Carter won only 47 percent of the white vote, compared with Ford's 52 percent. If Carter was to keep the White House, he needed to maintain his support among moderates and conservatives, while perhaps extending his support among white voters.[1]

Carter had run in 1976 as an outsider and a centrist. By announcing that he was a born-again Christian who accepted Jesus Christ as his personal savior, he had won the evangelical Protestant vote in the general election. Once in office, however, Carter appeared to distance himself from these voters and actually seemed to go out of his way to incense them. Evangelical Christian leaders were particularly upset in 1978, when the Internal Revenue Service threatened to deprive all private schools established after 1953 of their tax-exempt status if they were found guilty of discriminatory practices against blacks. Tim LaHaye, an evangelical minister who had helped found the Moral Majority with Jerry Falwell, met with Carter to resolve the IRS threat, and left the meeting vowing to defeat Carter for reelection. He prayed, "God, we have got to get this man out of the White House and get someone in here who will be aggressive about bringing back traditional moral values."[2] The rumor in Washington, D.C., was that Jerry Falwell and the Moral Majority had initially offered their support to the Democratic party. Whether this was true or not, Carter's policies and his inability to distance himself from left-wing activists played into the hands of Republican operatives eager to capture this vote.

In losing the evangelical bloc, Carter provided additional proof of his political ineptitude. Some of his incompetence must be attributed to his lack of experience. Before coming to the White House he had served as a state representative then a one-term governor in his home state of Georgia. When he was governor, his major opposition had come from the Right, and he had little experience dealing with the Democratic Left. In pushing through what would be his major legislative achievement, the reorganization of state government, he faced opposition from his lieutenant governor, Lester Maddox, a segregationist who had served as governor from 1967 to 1971. When Carter ran as Maddox's successor to the governorship, he aligned himself with Maddox, who was then seeking election as lieutenant governor. Once in office, Carter and Maddox fell out. Observers at the time said the clash was as much over egos as it was political principles, but whatever the case, Carter successfully pushed through his legislative program over Maddox's opposition.[3]

Carter showed that he could handle the segregationist Right in his party in Georgia politics; he revealed less adeptness at dealing with the Democratic Left on a national level. As a result, Carter's political experience was with opponents to the right of him. In the White House, he confronted the left wing of his party. He alienated the Left because of his equivocation on abortion, his acrimonious relations with feminists, his budget cutting, and his unwillingness to move forward on national health insurance. Lacking political skills that might have come with a more experienced politician or a less moralistic man, Carter failed to head off a revolt in his own party when U.S. Senator Ted Kennedy challenged him for the Democratic nomination. Carter won his party's nomination, but he entered the general election campaign with a divided party, an economy experiencing double-digit inflation, and a foreign policy crisis precipitated by the seizure of the American Embassy in Tehran, Iran, by militant Islamic students and the resulting hostage crisis. His crushing defeat on Election Day was predictable in hindsight, but the election was not lost until the final weeks of the campaign.

Jimmy Carter's Moralism

Carter projected in his presidency a moralism reminiscent of Woodrow Wilson, also a southerner and devout Christian. Much like Wilson, Carter tended to filter the world in moral terms, usually placing himself on the side of light and his enemies on the side of darkness. His critics accused him of being self-serving in his moral outlook. He showed flexibility during the 1978 Camp David negotiations, which brought peace to Israel and Egypt, but at the same time, critics pointed out that Carter had too easily accommodated anti–U.S. revolutions in Nicaragua under the Sandinistas and the early stages of the Iranian revolution led by militant Muslims.[4]

Carter viewed himself as an idealist. Whereas other politicians and heads of government might pride themselves on their pragmatism, their ability to wheel-and-deal, their legislative or political skills, Carter prided himself on his morality. He was a born-again Christian who came to

Christ following his defeat for the Georgia governorship in 1966. During the primary campaign, a race riot broke out in Atlanta that suddenly gave momentum to segregationist candidate Lester Maddox, an Atlanta restaurant owner who had closed his establishment rather than serve blacks. On Election Day, Carter finished third behind Maddox and the former liberal governor Ellis Arnall. Maddox went on to win the election after a deadlock that threw it to the state legislature. The Democratic-controlled legislature elected Maddox.

Carter was devastated by the loss. In his entire career he had experienced success, as an outstanding high school student in his small town of Plains, as a graduate of Annapolis Naval Academy, as a naval officer on a nuclear submarine, and as a peanut farmer. Although the events leading up to his becoming a reborn Christian remain unclear, sometime following the 1966 defeat he turned to Jesus Christ as his personal savior. As a born-again Christian, Carter was not hesitant to reveal his religious faith. It was on display when he won the governor's race four years later, in 1970. When his four-year term was over in 1974, he decided to run for president of the United States.

Carter spent the next two years campaigning, offering himself as a southerner who could stop Wallace from winning the Democratic nomination, an outsider to Washington politics, and a man who could return integrity to government. After winning his party's nomination, he carried this theme of idealism into the general campaign. He told audiences that he wanted an American government "as idealistic, as decent, as competent, as compassionate, as good as its people."[5] He was critical of Washington insiders, as evidenced in a typical refrain in his campaign speeches: "I'm not a lawyer, I'm not a member of Congress, and I've never served in Washington."[6] He promised to transform Nixon's imperial presidency into a people's presidency. When he won the election, he brought to the nation's capital a down-home presidential style. He staffed the White House with advisers from Georgia who took great pride in their lack of experience in Washington, D.C.

Hamilton Jordan, White House chief of staff, was typical of these brash young men who surrounded Carter. Jordan openly disdained the power establishment in the nation's capital and seemed to go out of his way to offend Washington insiders. When Speaker of the House Thomas "Tip" O'Neill complained about being given a poor seat at Carter's inaugural dinner, Jordan offered to give him back his money. Such antics alienated the Democratic-controlled Congress to such a degree that Carter found his major opposition coming from those within his own party rather than from the small Republican minority that was struggling to survive. Unable to exert leadership over Democrats in Congress, or to distance himself from them, Carter squandered his political capital over the next four years.

The Carter presidency was a missed opportunity for the man and his party at a time when Republicans appeared to have become a permanent minority in Congress. In 1976, Republicans lost only 1 House seat, but they had lost 43 seats in 1974. They were a pitiable 292–142 minority. The Senate remained 62–38 Democratic. At the state level, matters were not any better for Republicans. Democrats controlled state legislatures by a two-to-one margin. With only 24 percent of the electorate registering as Republicans, the GOP seemed to be facing extinction. Other losses extended beyond numbers, though. One of the great conservative disappointments of the election was the defeat of incumbent U.S. senator James L. Buckley in New York by Daniel Moynihan. Buckley had been elected U.S. senator from New York in 1970 as a member of the Conservative party. He won that three-way race with a plurality of 38 percent, defeating Republican incumbent Charles Goodell and Democrat Richard Ottinger. In the Senate, James Buckley emerged as one of the leading voices against abortion. Although Moynihan ran as a Catholic and appeared conservative on many issues, once elected he moved to the left.[7]

Carter's legislative initiatives met all too frequently with opposition from a Democratic-controlled Congress. Carter found that congressional Democrats combined a strong sense of ideological conviction with a powerful instinct for good-old-boy pork barrel politics. He noted later in his memoirs: "I learned the hard way that there was no party loyalty or discipline when a complicated or controversial issue was at stake—none . . . It was every member for himself, and the devil take the hindmost!"[8] For his part, Carter appeared to bring to the legislative arena high moral principles without any sense of politics. Carter's moralism was evident in his foreign policy: Though he appointed the hardliner Zbigniew Brzezinski to be his national security adviser, he made Cyrus Vance, an anti–Vietnam War liberal, his secretary of state. To emphasize the importance of human rights in his foreign policy, he made Patricia Derian, a former Mississippi civil rights activist, his assistant secretary of state with the charge of inserting human rights into every aspect of foreign policy. The civil rights activist Andrew Young was appointed United States ambassador to the United Nations, where he often sided with the Third World bloc against Western nations and Israel. When Carter nominated Paul Warnke to be director of the Arms Control and Disarmament Agency and chief negotiator of SALT II, Democratic party hawks led by Senator Henry Jackson and Paul Nitze organized to prevent the nomination. Concerned that the United States had fallen behind the Soviet Union in nuclear forces, and fearful that SALT II, based on the Vladivostok Accords, allowed the Soviet Union to increase its advantage over the United States, Paul Nitze joined Eugene Rostow and David Packard in organizing the Committee on the Present Danger, only seven days after Carter won the White House.

Nitze and others feared that by nominating Warnke, a well-known dove, Carter was conveying to the Soviets that his administration was desperate for an arms control treaty at any price. As a consequence, Warnke's confirmation hearings became a forum to debate SALT II and American nuclear policy.[9] Nitze wanted to organize congressional opposition to SALT II out of concern that the treaty would freeze the Soviets' nuclear advantage for the next ten years. He was convinced that the Soviets saw "their relative military position improving as they deployed their new family of weapons, especially a new series of ICBMs and a new missile, the SS-20, all of which they had been developing and testing over recent years." It was against this background that Nitze assessed the Vladivostok Accords in November 1974, when President Ford met with General Secretary Brezhnev. Nitze was convinced that Brezhnev, who had headed the Soviet missile program for many years before replacing Khrushchev as chief of the Soviet Union, had out-negotiated Ford and Kissinger. As Nitze recalled, "It was difficult to see how the accord reduced, in any meaningful way, the U.S. strategic defense problem posed by the new panoply of Soviet missiles and bombers which were completing development and whose large-scale deployment was then beginning."[10]

Nitze's break with the Carter administration was followed by that of other defense hawks who had thrown their support to Carter after Senator Henry Jackson's campaign faltered in 1976. Jackson, the senator from Washington, had run as a hardliner on American foreign relations and a liberal on domestic policy, but his message did not have wide appeal among rank-and-file Democrats in the post-Vietnam era. Those supporting Carter included the neoconservatives Norman Podhoretz, Irving Kristol, and Georgetown University professor Jeane Kirkpatrick. Their support of Carter had come with a good deal of reservation and uncertainty. Following the election, when only a few hawks were invited to join the administration and Carter nominated Warnke, these reservations toward Carter hardened into opposition.

In testimony before the Senate, Nitze portrayed Warnke as a McGovernite dove and noted that Warnke had opposed almost every effort to modernize or improve U.S. strategic systems, including building the B-1 bomber, the Trident submarine and the Trident II missile, the submarine-launched cruise missile, the mobile ICBM, MIRV deployment, and on and on. If Warnke's advice on defense policy was followed, Nitze warned, the United States would find itself in "such clear inferiority we would be in serious trouble."[11] Nevertheless, in a vote of seventy to twenty-nine, the Democratic-controlled Senate confirmed Warnke as director of the Arms Control and Disarmament Agency.

While facing opposition from the right wing of his party on his foreign policy, Carter faced criticism from the left wing on social issues. Feminists within the Democratic party were ambivalent about Carter from the beginning of his administration owing to his equivocation on abortion. At the same time, Carter was eager to bring women into high-level and cabinet positions, and he promised to use the power of the presidency to ratify the Equal Rights Amendment, which had come to a grinding halt under a conservative counteroffensive. The feminist movement had experienced its own divisions over whether to focus on legal issues, such as the Equal Rights Amendment and defending *Roe v. Wade,* or to emphasize cultural issues such as gay and lesbian rights. There were divisions among black and white women, professional and working-class women, heterosexual and lesbian women, and other interest groups and ideological positions. By 1977, when Carter entered office, the women's movement was so factionalized that his support of a single issue such as the ERA would not have been enough to earn him full support of the movement—or what had in effect become many movements.[12]

For all his good intentions, Carter failed to win the full support of the feminists, even though he went all out for the ERA and appointed feminists like Midge Costanza to important government positions. As one of Carter's chief policy advisers, Costanza pledged to support gay rights, abortion, and the decriminalization of marijuana use. One of her first acts as domestic policy advisor was to invite fourteen gay rights advocates to the White House, including Jean O'Leary, co-executive director of the National Gay Task Force, the predecessor of the National Gay and Lesbian Task Force. During the Democratic party Convention, Costanza worked with O'Leary in a failed attempt to insert an even stronger gay rights plank into the 1976 party platform. Within the context of singer Anita Bryant's antihomosexual campaign, "Save Our Children," this highly visible meeting with gay and lesbian delegates drew immediate media attention and criticism from the Right.

Costanza's declining position in the White House accelerated when she took issue with Carter's show of support for the Supreme Court decisions of June 20, 1977, that upheld local and state restrictions on abortion (Maher v. Roe, Beal v. Doe, and Poelker v. Doe). Carter's relations with women activists within his administration did not improve when he signed legislation banning federal funds for abortions except to protect the life of the mother or in cases of rape or incest. Costanza left the administration in August 1978 to become executive director of the actress Shirley MacLaine's High Self Seminars.[13]

Nonetheless, Carter remained eager to establish positive relations with feminists. This desire was apparent when, against the advice of White House aides, he appointed Bella Abzug and Carmen Delgado Votaw as co-chairs of the President's Advisory Committee for Women on June 22, 1978. Abzug, a former congresswoman from New York, represented the left wing of the Democratic party. Relations between the Carter White House and Abzug were never good, but they ruptured completely when she released a ten-page memorandum, "The First Eighteen Months: A Status Report of the Carter Administration Action on International Women's Year Resolutions," that was openly critical of the administration. At a well-publicized meeting in mid-January 1978, Carter confronted Abzug, who heatedly defended herself. Following the meeting, Jordan called Abzug into his office to ask for her resignation.

Abzug's firing drew the wrath of the feminist movement and revealed the kinds of problems that Carter faced with the left wing of his party. Abzug took to the lecture circuit, telling audiences that "it was as though every woman in this country was fired." She warned that in Carter's America, "women have no power. We are on the fringes of democracy looking in."[14] In May 1978 Carter named Lynda Robb, the daughter of

Lyndon Baines Johnson, to chair a reconstituted President's Advisory Committee for Women. At the same time, he pushed for ratification of the Equal Rights Amendment to reinforce his support for women's rights. He appointed his daughter-in-law to head up a White House lobbying campaign to secure ratification of the ERA.[15] Carter's wife, Rosalynn, a strong and articulate woman, joined these efforts to lobby state legislators to vote for ratification. These actions backfired, as had Betty Ford's earlier, because local legislators resented what they saw as heavy-handed White House interference in state matters.[16]

By 1978, the movement for ratification had just about come to a dead stop, and pro-ERA activists became desperate to save the amendment from defeat. Celebrities including Hollywood actor Alan Alda, comic actresses Lily Tomlin and Carol Burnett, actress Candice Bergen, television producer Norman Lear, columnists Ann Landers and Erma Bombeck, and Christie Hefner, the daughter of *Playboy* publisher Hugh Hefner, joined in what had become a struggle to ratify the ERA. Publishers and editors of leading magazines joined in the crusade by printing pro-ERA stories. Feminist activists in the states organized rallies and marches to pressure state legislators to ratify the ERA.

Eager to win support for the amendment, the pro-ERA movement began linking abortion and homosexual rights to ratification of the ERA. This was especially apparent in resolutions passed at the International Women's Year (IWY) Conference in November 1977. The Carter White House had given full support to the conference, but it turned into a media disaster when Phyllis Schlafly organized a counter-conference that drew twenty thousand people to a "Pro-Family Rally" at the Astro Arena. ERA opponents seized on the homosexual rights issue and turned it to their advantage.

With the deadline set for March 22, 1979, it appeared in 1978 that the ERA had been defeated. Democrats began calling for an extension of the ERA deadline. Representative Elizabeth Holtzman (D-New York) introduced a resolution to extend the ratification period another seven years. The time-frame was pared down to a thirty-nine-month extension, to June 30, 1982. In the fall of 1978, Carter and Vice President Walter Mondale managed to get votes to pass the extension of the ERA deadline, and Rosalynn Carter held a White House briefing for key administrative officials on the importance of the extension.[17] At the signing of the congressional resolution extending the deadline, Carter told the press that though the resolution did not require a presidential signature, "I particularly wanted to add my signature to demonstrate as strongly as I can my full support for the Equal Rights Amendment."[18]

Bitter battles remained to be fought over ERA ratification in Illinois, Florida, and North Carolina, but not a single state ratified the amendment after the time extension. In fact, not a single state ratified the ERA after the feminist extravaganza for International Women's Year in Houston in November 1977. State legislators, after years of political pressure from both sides, wanted to get rid of the issue once and for all. The struggle had gone on too long, and now it was too late for proponents to mount an effective counterattack. Efforts at writing Equal Rights Amendments into state constitutions also faced hurdles. In November 1980, a referendum in Iowa for a state ERA was soundly defeated by a 55 percent majority of voters. By 1980, feminists had broken totally with Carter and refused to endorse him for a second term, blaming him for a defeat whose deeper roots they still had not grasped.[19] In 1982, *New York Times* correspondent John Leonard came closer to the truth when he concluded that "the backlash against feminism looks more like a tidal wave."[20]

Signs of an Awakening: The 1978 Election

The ERA battle taught conservatives three important lessons that changed the course of American politics from its leftward drift to the right: First, the STOP ERA organization and the antiabortion movement showed the importance of social issues in mobilizing unheard numbers of average Americans. Second, the anti-ERA campaign provided a casebook example of how evangelical Protestants, Roman Catholics, and Mormons could be united into a single cause. In particular, the antifeminist crusade revealed that there was a huge reservoir of potential voters in the evangelical Protestant revival of the 1970s that could be tapped by the Republican party. Finally, the defeat of the ERA taught conservatives that they could win when they mobilized around the right causes. Ever since Barry Goldwater's defeat in 1964, the conservative movement had lacked confidence that it could ever win nationally, but on the issue of the ERA it had triumphed.

In the midterm elections of 1978, conservative operatives put these lessons to the test. Abortion proved to be an especially good issue to separate liberal Democratic congressmen from their more traditionally minded constituents. The actual gains from this strategy were not large—three new Republicans were elected in the Senate and eleven in the House. As *Congressional Quarterly* noted, this was not "the stuff of which a renaissance is normally made," but given the losses in the previous two elections, it was an important beginning of a Republican revival.[21] These gains came in an election in which Republicans were especially vulnerable because they were defending 17 of the 38 seats held by Republicans in the 95th Congress. The Carter administration still had a good numerical lineup after the election, with Democrats controlling the Senate 59–41 and the House 276–157. Republicans made gains, and conservatives reemerged as a potent force in GOP politics. They were not yet dominant, but they were no longer a disregarded, isolated faction within the party, begging for a seat at the table.

Moderate and liberal Republicans lost in the Senate. Edward W. Brooke (Massachusetts) lost in the general election, Clifford Case (New Jersey) lost in the primary, and James B. Pearson (Kansas) retired, but they gained William S. Cohen (Maine), David Durenberger and Rudy Boschwitz (Minnesota), and Larry Pressler (South Dakota). Nevertheless, liberal Republicans were gradually being replaced by conservatives.

The ascendant Right was able to take advantage of the post-Watergate campaign-finance reform that allowed the formation of political action committees (PACs). The Committee for the Survival of a Free Congress and the National Conservative Political Action Committee proved especially important in exerting conservative influence in the 1978 election. In particular, these two organizations played a major role in the successful campaigns of Gordon Humphrey (R-New Hampshire) and Roger Jepsen (R-Iowa). Both victories were especially sweet for conservatives because they meant the ouster of the liberal Democrats Dick Clark of Iowa (seen by some as the successor to Hubert Humphrey's leadership) and Thomas J. McIntyre of New Hampshire. It was not just that they lost; it was how they lost. Jepsen, a former lieutenant governor, defeated Clark by hammering him for his refusal to support antiabortion measures or tuition tax credits for parochial schools. Jepsen painted Clark as the most liberal member of the United States Senate, and as a result, Jepsen's support in traditionally Democratic Catholic areas declined. In New Hampshire, Humphrey, a thirty-seven-year-old airline pilot, zeroed in on McIntyre's vote in favor of the Panama Canal treaties and his liberal stance on social issues. Such victories gave credence to Richard Viguerie's claim that social issues were the key to unlocking a conservative resurgence. Once attacked for their positions on the social issues, both Clark and McIntyre raised charges of McCarthyism, redbaiting, and right-wing extremism, but such tactics tended to backfire, further suggesting a shift to the right in the electorate.

Conservative Republicans were victorious in other states in 1978 as well. In Colorado, the conservative William L. Armstrong, a three-term U.S. representative who had supported Ford in 1976, won his race for the U.S. Senate against Floyd K. Haskell, a liberal. In Wyoming, Alan K. Simpson, a former state representative, assumed the seat once held by his father, when the conservative Republican Clifford Hansen retired. In Mississippi, the first Republican ever chosen by popular vote, Thad Cochran, was elected. In Texas, incumbent Republican senator John Tower was reelected in an especially bitter campaign. Jesse Helms won reelection to a second term as U.S. senator by a narrow victory of 95,000 votes out of 1.1 million cast. Helms spent more than $6 million to defeat his Democratic challenger, John Ingram, who spent under $500,000. Democrats concluded from this race that Helms was vulnerable, thus setting the stage for an expensive and nasty challenge in 1984. Conservatives also welcomed the reelection of Strom Thurmond in South Carolina and the election of John Warner, running as a conservative, in Virginia.

Although the South had not gone fully Republican, these victories presented unmistakable signs of Democratic erosion. This decline was most apparent in the House races in the South, where Republicans reignited a party that had been deadened by Watergate. One of the most significant victories came when the college history professor Newt Gingrich won election in his third try in Georgia. In Texas, Ron Paul, a Christian libertarian-conservative, won back a seat he had lost in 1976 to Democrat Bob Gammage.

Amid this battle for Congress, a seismic shift occurred in California. By a margin of almost two to one, voters ratified the Jarvis-Gann initiative—Proposition 13—cutting property taxes by more than $6 billion. Proposition 13 shifted the tax burden away from property owners by taxing all property at a flat 1 percent of its actual value. Under the measure new taxes could not be raised by state or local government except by a two-thirds majority vote. In addition, property assessments were rolled back to 1975–1976 levels, except for a 2 percent annual hike for inflation. New homes were assessed at current market values.

The measure had been promoted by Howard Jarvis, a sixty-two-year-old, long-time conservative activist. Jarvis had served on the national board of the Liberty Amendment Committee to promote the repeal of the federal income tax. In 1964, he organized "Businessmen for Gold-water." Jarvis captured the discontent of California taxpayers who had been pushed into higher income tax and property tax brackets during the inflationary decade of the 1970s. Whereas incomes in California rose more than 50 percent between 1973 and 1977, personal income taxes increased by 150 percent and sales taxes by 188 percent.[22] By 1978, California under Governor Jerry Brown was running a $4 billion surplus. The Jarvis-Gann initiative had a simple appeal, but it drew opposition from California's liberal elite, including the AFL-CIO, the League of Women Voters, Common Cause, and Bank of America, as well as from consumer activists, environmentalists, police associations, school teachers, feminists, and African Americans because of its benefit to property owners and the loss of revenue for public services and social welfare.[23]

Jarvis-type amendments translated differently in other states. Idaho and Michigan passed similar measures in 1978, and Hawaii and Texas passed initiatives limiting future growth of public spending to the growth of the state economy. Missouri passed a Jarvis-like amendment in 1980. Oregon rejected Jarvis limitations.[24] Nonetheless, the popularity of the measure in California revealed a growing discontent among voters about inflation. In 1979 Lewis Uhler, a former aide to John Rousselot, the first Bircher elected to the U.S. Congress, and the National Tax Limitation Committee revealed their plan for a national balanced-budget amendment that proposed to limit future federal outlays to an increase in gross national product, except during specific periods of high inflation.

Not all conservatives supported the balanced-budget amendment because they were concerned about tinkering with the Constitution. Opposition to the amendment revealed tensions evident between social conservatives and economic conservatives. Economic conservatives tended toward a pro-corporate outlook, while social conservatives did not necessarily consider big business their natural ally. Differences among conservatives were often ignored, however, in their opposition to Soviet Communism and in their mutual desire to put a conservative in the White House.

The Fear of Decline

In the 1970s, conservatives thought that the United States was on an irredeemable path of decline unless the situation was reversed immediately. Nixon's foreign policy had heightened fears among the Right that America had lost its way. Writing in the August 21, 1971, issue of *Human Events,* the conservative commentator John Chamberlain noted, "We are a nation in retreat . . . Because we have been soft in the head and weak in will, our retreat is in danger of becoming a rout." The SALT I arms control agreement under Nixon offered further proof of America's retreat in the face of a Soviet enemy that had continued to advance since World War II. Conservatives saw American foreign policy under Ford and Carter as a continuation of U.S. appeasement of the Soviet Union. This anxiety about America's decline fueled conservative opposition to reverting control of the Panama Canal zone to Panama.

Conservative opposition to turning over the Panama Canal was not new. Accusations that the Soviet Union had a secret plan to wrest control of the canal from the United States had circulated in rightist circles since the 1950s. Anti–U.S. riots in Panama in 1964 were seen as part of a Communist plot to drive the United States from the Canal Zone. Further trouble came when the Panamanian dictator Omar Torrijos denounced the canal treaty as "unacceptable." As evidence of Communist influence in Panama, conservatives pointed to Rep. Daniel Flood (D-Pennsylvania), who warned in 1971 that the Torrijos dictatorship was actively helping the Soviets gain control of the vital waterway.[25]

This background set the stage for a battle over ratification of two treaties signed in August 1977 that would transfer legal title of the American Canal Zone to Panama in 1999. In light of the Soviet Union's military buildup, the projected turnover of the Panama Canal raised strategic issues concerning America's ability to defend itself in a two-front war. At the same time, the canal issue was framed by the grassroots Right as a battle between Wall Street and the American people. Grassroots conservatives maintained that eastern banks initiated the turnover in order to protect loans they had extended to Panama's government. Conservatives claimed that the only way the government of Panama could repay the loans was through revenue gained from control of the canal. As a consequence, they contended, powerful eastern banks had engineered the canal turnover and were supporting the two treaties that needed ratification by the Senate. Not all conservatives opposed the return of the canal, however. William F. Buckley, Jr., came out in support of the turnover, much to the chagrin of many of his magazine staff as well as other grass-roots conservatives.

Carter drew on pro-business interests to gain support for the treaties, including the U.S. Chamber of Commerce, banks, shipping companies, and large multinational corporations with investments in Panama. The Torrijos government in Panama hired F. Clifton White, a Republican party strategist, and Lawrence F. O'Brien, a former Democratic party chairman, to lobby for the treaties. Conservatives countered with their own campaign to paint the Torrijos government as an ally of Castro's Communist government in Cuba. Conservatives also charged that Torrijos and Castro were involved in international drug-smuggling operations. They believed that American and European banking interests had lent the Torrijos government $135 million with the expectation that Panama would gain control of the canal. Books and articles spilled forth from the conservative press. In *Hands Off the Panama Canal* (1976), the anti-Communist journalist Isaac Don Levine warned of a Soviet takeover of the canal. The Arizona conservative Denison Kitchel echoed this warning in *The Truth about the Panama Canal* (1978), claiming that if the canal treaties went through, the Soviets would gain control of the canal through their surrogates, the Cubans. The American Conservative Union launched a series of massive mailing campaigns against the treaties, including one letter signed by Ronald Reagan that brought in more than $700,000 in contributions. Although polls showed that the majority of Americans opposed the turnover, the Senate ratified the Panama Neutrality treaty in March 1978 with a single vote to spare, and in April the Panama Canal Treaty was ratified. Carter rightly counted this as a major victory, but the close vote also revealed how vulnerable he was in the area of foreign policy. This vulnerability quickly became evident when SALT II was brought before Congress the following year.

By the time SALT II reached the Senate in 1979, the Carter presidency had been wounded by dissension within the Democratic party, the alienation of feminists, a stagnant economy experiencing runaway inflation, and a disgruntled public that had lost confidence in the president. Expert opinion in both Democratic and Republican circles warned that the Soviet Union was on the verge of overtaking the United States in the nuclear arms race. Many critics feared that Carter's injection of morality into American foreign and defense policy had displaced any realistic assessment of the Soviet Union.

The neoconservative Jeane Kirkpatrick was especially critical of Carter's moralism. Born in Oklahoma in 1926, she began her college education at Stephens College in Missouri before attending Barnard College in New York. In 1955, while studying at the Institut de Science Politique at the University of Paris, she met and married Evron Kirkpatrick. Although she postponed completion of her doctorate to raise a family, she remained active in scholarly circles. Her doctoral dissertation, published as *Leader and Vanguard in Mass Society: A Study of Peronist Argentina* (1971), was followed by *Political Women* (1974) and *The New Presidential Elite: Men and Women in National Politics* (1978). Kirkpatrick became a member of the anti-McGovern group the Committee for a Democratic Majority, which reluctantly supported Carter in 1976. Like others in the committee, she quickly became disillusioned with Carter because of his Cyrus Vance–Paul Warnke pursuit of arms control with the Soviet Union; his unwillingness to confront Soviet and Cuban imperialism in Africa; and his insistence that human rights should be the standard for judging foreign policy. From her position as a professor of political science at Georgetown University, she ridiculed the administration's foreign policy as "McGovernism without McGovern."[26]

Even more worrisome to Carter's critics were strong indications that the American intelligence community had been systematically underestimating Soviet strategic capabilities. This underestimation was due to faulty data as well as to a strong proclivity on the part of analysts to assume that the Soviets were pursuing détente.[27] Within this context, Paul Nitze, Eugene Rostow, and David Packard organized the Committee on the Present Danger to open a public debate on the proposed SALT II negotiations. The formation of this committee drew immediate attention from the press because these were the "wise men" of the American establishment; they were not ranting right-wingers warning of Soviet imperialism but defenders of previous arms control agreements dating back to the Eisenhower administration. Although they were not members of the right wing, their language employed hyperbole that matched any found on the Right: "Soviet expansionism threatens to destroy the world balance of forces on which the survival of freedom depends."[28]

On June 28, 1979, Carter met Soviet Secretary Brezhnev in Vienna to sign SALT II.[29] The treaty was in clear trouble when it reached the Senate in the summer of 1979. The Senate Foreign Relations Committee barely approved the treaty by a close vote of nine to six. For his part, Carter promised to increase defense spending and proposed placing intermediate-range missiles in Europe as a counter to the placement of Soviet SS-20 missiles in Eastern Europe. Even with these measures, the Senate Armed Services Committee voted down the treaty in December 1979. When the Soviet Union invaded Afghanistan two days later, Carter withdrew the treaty. He was shocked by the Soviet invasion. Soviet leaders, meanwhile, were surprised by Carter's angry response. From their perspective, Carter appeared to have given them *carte blanche* in Africa and Southeast Asia. He had opposed linking SALT II negotiations to Soviet-Cuban involvement in Africa, especially in the Ethiopian-Somali border dispute in support of Ethiopia's left-wing government.[30]

The World Turned Right: 1980

Given conservative anger toward the president, one of the great ironies of the 1980 election was that the left wing of the Democratic party, represented by Senator Edward Kennedy, antinuclear peace activists, feminists, and social liberals, contributed significantly to Carter's loss to Ronald Reagan, an avowed conservative. Carter expended campaign and political resources in fending off the Kennedy challenge, money and energy that could have been used later against Reagan. The Kennedy challenge left the Democrats divided and unenthusiastic about Carter. Given the political costs of the Democratic feud, it is surprising that Carter's crushing defeat stunned the Democratic Left. Carter himself was stunned because at the outset of the campaign he had been convinced that he would easily win reelection against the sixty-nine-year-old Republican. Like other opponents before him, Carter underestimated Ronald Reagan.[31]

Carter had much to feel confident about in August 1980 as the general election approached. The challenge to Carter from the Democratic Left had fizzled in a series of primaries that revealed the hollowness of the

Kennedy campaign. Before Kennedy declared he was running for president, polls suggested a neck-and-neck contest in a Carter-Kennedy race. Once Kennedy formally entered the race, however, these strong polling numbers began to dissipate. It quickly became evident that Kennedy did not have much to run on, other than the fact that he was a Kennedy and he was not Carter. Moreover, a takeover of the American Embassy in Iran by militant students on November 4, 1979, just three days after Kennedy declared he was running, initially boosted Carter's approval ratings as Americans rallied around the flag. These approval ratings did not last, but as the political analyst Michael Barone observed, the paradox of 1980 was that the Iranian hostage crisis saved Carter's nomination as the Democratic candidate but cost him the presidency in the general election.[32]

The seizure of the American Embassy in Iran was a serious violation of diplomatic immunity and international law. Carter might have used this flagrant breach of international law—an act of war even—to rally the American people to his side. Instead he and his advisers sought to mollify the student militants. Carter sent the former attorney general Ramsey Clark as an envoy—a clear sign that Carter was not going to take a tough stance. From the outset, the president decided against a military approach for fear of a military catastrophe and concern that he might alienate the Third World.[33] In the end, he got both—a military debacle and political alienation. In April 1980, Carter gave the go-ahead for a military rescue attempt that had to be aborted when the helicopters malfunctioned. The military had to launch an operation to rescue the helicopter crews. Meanwhile, the sixty-six Americans held hostage in the embassy remained in captivity throughout the rest of Carter's presidency.[34]

Nonetheless, Carter believed that he was in a strong political position for reelection. In the spring of 1980, he was able to fend off a challenge from Kennedy. Carter won in the Iowa caucuses by a two-to-one margin and then defeated Kennedy in his own backyard, New Hampshire, 47 to 37 percent. Kennedy won his own state of Massachusetts but then was trounced 65 to 30 percent in Illinois before Carter headed into the southern primaries, which, as expected, he won. As he considered possible Republican challengers, he believed that the field looked weak. Reagan stood out as the strongest candidate, having nearly upset Ford for the Republican nomination in 1976. From Carter's perspective the other Republican candidates did not seem any stronger. Former Secretary of the Treasury John Connally, a Texan, had only recently converted to the party. Representative John Anderson from Illinois was a well-known moderate whose call for hiking the gasoline tax to cut fuel consumption was audacious but hardly appealing to an electorate carrying the weight of a stagnant economy. Senate Minority Leader Howard Baker from Tennessee lacked support from the party's rank and file. His vote for the Panama Canal treaties hurt him. It turned out that Reagan's most formidable opponent was George H. W. Bush, the favored candidate of the Eastern Establishment. Although Bush had run unsuccessfully in Texas for Congress in 1964 as a Goldwater Republican, he opposed Reagan's call for tax cuts and had promoted population-control legislation while in Congress during the Nixon years. His connections to Yale, where he had graduated, and to the CIA raised immediate suspicions of his establishment ties among hard-core conservatives.

Bush surprised the Reagan campaign and political pundits when he won the Iowa precinct caucuses in late January 1980.[35] After Iowa, Reagan reevaluated his campaign strategy—and its strategist, John Sears. He turned to his good friend U.S. Senator Paul Laxalt (R-Nevada), who told him, "You were sitting on your ass in Iowa."[36] The Iowa defeat marked the end of Sears. After a victory in the New Hampshire primary, Reagan placed William Casey, a wealthy New York attorney, and long-time California supporter Edwin Meese in charge of the campaign. When campaign debts mounted, Reagan called in Stuart Spencer to head the campaign.

Reagan won New Hampshire and put Bush on a downward spiral that eventually cost him the nomination. Although his strong campaign organization and ample funds allowed him to win the Michigan and Pennsylvania primaries, Bush was forced to drop out in late May. New Hampshire also spelled the end for Howard Baker, who received 13 percent of the vote, followed by John Connally and Phil Crane, with 2 percent, and Robert Dole with 1 percent. In the end, Reagan won twenty-nine out of thirty-three primaries and 60 percent of the primary vote.

As the *New York Times* political analyst Jeff Greenfield observed, the key factor in the Republican primaries and the general election was not television images, soundbites, or quips that caught voters' fancy but Reagan's message. Reagan made plenty of gaffes during the primaries and the general election: he often got his facts wrong; at times he appeared insecure and indecisive at press conferences and on television talk shows. But what was crucial to the Reagan campaign was the message he brought to the voters and his obvious faith in it. The message was that of an ideological conservative: Big government weakens the will and the spirit of a free people, wreaks havoc on the free enterprise system, and replaces the power of families and local communities with distant bureaucrats. Reagan maintained that government activity should be scaled back; spending on social programs reduced; regulation of business eased; and defense spending increased to confront an aggressive Soviet Union. He brought a clear message into his campaign that the cultural revolution begun in the 1960s must be opposed through legislation of prayer in school, ratification of a human life amendment, and restoration of the place of the traditional family in American life.

Reagan's unapologetic message rejected the liberal turn in American culture and politics and called for a return to a simpler, more traditional way of life. It enabled Democrats (later called Reagan Democrats) and new voters to embrace the Republican cause. No other Republican candidate, including Representative John Anderson, who ran as a liberal Republican, presented an effective ideological alternative to Reagan's philosophy for the simple reason that the base of the Republican party had become more conservative.[37]

The power of Reagan's message went beyond conservative shibboleths. In the aftermath of the Vietnam War, and at a time when a second-rate power, Iran, held American citizens hostage, Reagan made it acceptable once again to express unambiguous patriotism. He reaffirmed a deep faith on the part of the American people that this nation was worth preserving and that the republican principles for which it stood were righteous. Reagan's affable personality, his ease on television, and his ability to communicate ideas appealed to average voters, but in the end it was his optimistic vision, based on a rock-hard faith in conservative principles, that enabled Reagan to win the GOP nomination and later the general election.

Reagan had a strong practical side as well. He was a politician who tempered ideology with a desire to achieve political and legislative success. Yet behind Reagan's realism lay a strong ideological foundation built on conservative principles. On core issues, Reagan remained inflexible to the point of being described as stubborn by those who knew him. He conveyed this sense of principle and commitment to voters, and this projection of firm belief compensated for his many gaffes, mistaken facts, and misremembered anecdotes.

In nominating Reagan, the Republican party continued its transformation into a party of conservatism. Not all Republicans had become conservative by 1980, and many in Congress could best be described as moderate in their views of the federal government, the welfare state, social programs, and relations with the Soviet Union. Moderate Republicanism remained a force in the GOP, but the liberal stars of the party who had garnered so much media attention in the 1960s and 1970s—Senators Jacob Javits (R-New York) and Charles Percy (R-Illinois)—were the dwindling remnants of a once-significant bloc in Congress. Nelson Rockefeller, the embodiment of liberal Republicanism, died in 1979 enjoying life as he always had. Liberal Republicanism was fading into history when John Anderson, an Illinois congressman, sought to pick up the fallen liberal banner within the party.[38] When he looked around, however, he found that the troops rallying to his cause were not Republicans but liberal Democrats—actor Paul Newman, authors Kurt Vonnegut and Gore Vidal, feminist Gloria Steinem, and cartoonist Garry Trudeau. Misreading their cries of support and the pre-election polls, Anderson decided to run as an independent, only to receive about 6 percent of the vote.

The conservatism of the GOP was apparent in the party platform adopted at the Republican Convention in Detroit. While the media was obsessed with the possibility of Ford being named as Reagan's running mate—newsman Walter Cronkite suggested a co-presidency in a convention interview with Ford (much to the anger of Reagan)—Republican delegates approved the most conservative platform in recent GOP history. The only area of controversy was over removing support of the Equal Rights Amendment from the platform. As the convention opened, 5,000 people, including Michigan Governor William Milliken and U.S. Senator Jacob Javits, marched on behalf of the ERA, but after the platform committee rejected the amendment, the pro-ERA forces did not have enough strength to bring the matter to the convention floor. In the end, the convention approved a platform without the ERA, but with an endorsement of a human life amendment and the promise to appoint federal judges who would "honor the sanctity of innocent unborn life."[39]

The GOP platform emphatically expressed the view that the less federal government the better. Opportunity instead of government entitlement emerged as the dominant theme.⁴⁰ The platform declared that contrary to the Democrats, who believed that it was the "duty of government" to solve every new problem, Republicans believed that government should "foster in our society a climate of maximum individual liberty and freedom of choice. Properly informed, our people as individuals or acting through instruments of popular consultation can make the right decisions affecting personal or general welfare, free of pervasive heavy-handed intrusion by the central government into the decision-making process." The platform denounced governmental regulation and called for the restoration of "the family, the neighborhood, the community, and the workplace as vital alternatives in our national life to ever-expanding federal power."

Feminists and abortion rights supporters quickly pointed to what appeared to be a contradiction between the Republicans' call for "individual choice" and smaller government and their antiabortion stance. They asked how Republicans could call for choice and personal freedom yet deny women what they considered the fundamental right to control their bodies through abortion. Conservative Republicans answered that the fetus had a fundamental right to life, but the seeming inconsistency in the Republican espousal of individual choice, as opposed to federal regulation and federal mandates, did not sit well with pro-choice activists.

On other issues, however, there was no ambiguity about where the Republicans stood in contrast to the Democratic party. The Democratic platform declared, "The Democratic party has long stood for an active, responsive, vigorous government . . . We must begin to think of federal expenditures as capital investments." In short, the Democratic party expressed faith in the federal government to protect its citizens from the vicissitudes of a free-market economy, unrestrained corporate exploitation, waning natural resources, technological dislocation, and the uncertainties of health and old age. This generous vision had been given greater meaning and eloquent articulation during the depression of the 1930s and the New Deal regime of Franklin D. Roosevelt. It was a vision that informed Lyndon Johnson's Great Society, which reached out to those in poverty and need. By 1980, however, this vision had lost its appeal for an electorate disgusted with runaway inflation, high unemployment, welfare abuse, and a weakened American image abroad.

The Reagan campaign realized that if Carter was successful in making the 1980 election into a replay of 1964, Republicans would lose. To prevent this outcome, Reagan needed to emphasize the poor economy while reassuring the public that he would not slash benefit programs indiscriminately. This was a tricky strategy because Reagan was on record as opposing many of the entitlement programs proposed to help workers hurt by economic dislocation. GOP strategists realized that the key to victory rested in winning traditional Democrats to their cause. As a result, when Senator Paul Laxalt nominated Reagan at the convention, he pointed to Reagan's record as governor of California in increasing aid to the truly needy, increasing funding to higher education, protecting the environment, and undertaking welfare reform.[41]

In his acceptance speech, Reagan also sought to reassure the political center, even while he conveyed a strong conservative message. He spoke in favor of restoring to the "federal government the capacity to do the people's work without dominating their lives," and he denounced the secular humanism that had led to the banning of prayer in schools, abortion rights, and family-planning clinics. He promised to build "a national consensus with all those across the land who share a community of values embodied in these words: family, work, neighborhood, peace, and freedom." At the same time, he declared himself in favor of the goals of equality, even while opposing the Equal Rights Amendment. He promised to encourage governors to "eliminate, wherever it exists, discrimination against women. I will monitor federal laws to insure their implementation and to add statutes, if they are needed." His rhetoric was one of compromise and moderation.[42]

At the same time, Reagan's campaign was determined to win the evangelical Christian vote that had gone to Carter in the previous presidential election. On August 21, 1980, Republican presidential nominee Ronald Reagan appeared before the Religious Roundtable to address a cheering throng that had gathered at the Reunion Arena in Dallas, Texas. Ed McAteer, the founder and chair of the Religious Roundtable, introduced Reagan to the fifteen thousand people who had gathered to hear such prominent speakers as the religious conservatives Jerry Falwell, Pat Robertson, James Kennedy, and James Robison.

These figures gave shape to what became known as the Christian Right. The rapid rise of the Christian Right in the late 1970s caught many political observers and journalists by surprise.[43] When the Christian Right appeared on the scene, much of the media tended to associate televangelists with Christian Right groups, often missing the grassroots nature of the evangelical movement and the sharp theological differences that divided organizations and their leaders. Estimates of Christian Right members varied from close to a half-million to three million. News reports did agree on the sharp rise of the Christian Right organizations that were formed in 1978 and 1979. Many of the leaders of these groups were Protestant fundamentalists, including Bob Billings of the National Christian Action Coalition, Ed McAteer of Religious Roundtable, Jerry Falwell of Moral Majority, Beverly LaHaye of Concerned Women for America, and Tim LeHaye of the American Coalition for Traditional Values. These organizations spoke of the need to restore "moral sanity" to American politics. They defined issues such as abortion and pornography as sins. Their tone and message were jarring to many in the mainstream press who were not used to hearing this kind of religious language used in politics.[44] Few doubted, though, that the Christian Right had emerged as an important force in American politics and that Ronald Reagan was eager to win the support of conservative Christians, beginning with an endorsement from McAteer's Religious Roundtable.

McAteer, a former district manager for a soap company who had gone to work for Viguerie, had formed the Roundtable to provide a nonsectarian forum for evangelical Christians concerned with the perceived liberal assault on traditional values and moral breakdown in America. These religious leaders were angry at what they saw as the promulgation of a disbelief in God, moral relativism, and antifamily values in public schools and the federal bureaucracy. Reagan understood the potential of capturing this audience and their emotion. He also knew that the crowd was eager to welcome him. Incumbent president Jimmy Carter had declined an invitation to address the Roundtable.

In a bid for the group's endorsement, Reagan spoke directly to their concerns: "I know you can't endorse me, but I want you to know that I endorse you and what you are doing." Then he got to the heart of the matter. "When I hear the First Amendment used as a reason to keep traditional moral values away from policy making, I am shocked . . . The First Amendment was written not to protect the people and their laws from religious values, but to protect those values from government tyranny."[45] As expected, Reagan won the group's enthusiasm. The evangelical vote proved important to Reagan's victory in the general election.

Polls following the convention showed Carter and Reagan running neck and neck, with neither candidate seemingly able to pull ahead. In the early stages of the general campaign, Reagan continued to make gaffes in his speeches and press comments, especially when he broke from his script. He called for establishing official relations with Taiwan, a statement implying that he wanted to reverse relations with China; he spoke of the Vietnam War as a "noble cause"; he suggested that creationism should be taught side-by-side with Darwinian evolutionary theory; and he told the press that the United States was in an economic depression.

These were minor mistakes compared with the controversy that followed a speech in Philadelphia, Mississippi, the place where three civil rights activists had been murdered in the summer of 1964. In his first speech following his nomination, Reagan declared, "I still believe the answer to any problem lies with the people. I believe in states' rights . . . I believe we have distorted the balance of our government today by giving powers that were never intended to be given in the Constitution to the federal establishment." Reagan's use of the words "states' rights" in a town known for the murder of civil rights workers gave immediate offense to black leaders. Following these remarks, Carter's secretary of health and human services warned that black voters "will see the specter of a white sheet" behind Reagan. Carter's former ambassador to the United Nations, Andrew Young, said that Reagan's remarks seemed like code-words implying "it's going to be all right to kill n——— when he's President." Coretta Scott King, the widow of Martin Luther King, Jr., told the press she was frightened that if Reagan won the election "we are going to see more of the Ku Klux Klan and a resurgence of the Nazi Party."[46]

In 1976, Carter had swept the South. Reagan's campaign strategists assumed that if Reagan could take the South, he would win the election. Mississippi was a good place to start because Carter had won the state by less than two percentage points of the popular vote. Also, the state had a young Republican rising star in Trent Lott, who had been elected to Congress in 1972. Reagan's comments on states' rights came in the context of calling for local communities to address their own problems rather than turning to the federal government, but Reagan did not attempt to mollify possible criticism by condemning, or even mentioning, the murder of the civil rights workers. What is not clear is whether such talk hurt him with voters; indeed, his pro-Taiwan policy, anti-Communism, and talk of a depression might have helped him with conservative-leaning voters. The vehemence with which his opponents and many in the media seized on his gaffes, however, left Reagan rattled in private. In September, Stuart Spencer began traveling with Reagan to help steady his nerves. The editors of *National Review* expressed the general sentiment among conservatives when it declared, "His [Reagan's] mind has an unfashionable and even home-made quality, he knows a lot more than people expect him to know, and he will win or lose as Ronald Reagan."[47]

Much more consequential to Reagan's bid for the presidency was his call for tax cuts. By May 1980 unemployment had reached 7.8 percent, inflation was running at nearly 18 percent, and the gross domestic product was falling precipitously. This was a clear indication that the classic Keynesian economic model, which postulated an inverse relationship between unemployment and inflation, no longer worked. Keynesianism had provided the foundation for economic policy for the liberal state since 1937, when Roosevelt failed to balance the budget. The question remained, What was to replace it? The University of Chicago economist Milton Friedman proposed monetarism, specifically, controlling the growth of the money supply in the economy. This was exactly the policy that was being implemented by Carter's chairman of the Federal Reserve Board, Paul Volcker, who had decided to raise interest rates. For Reagan, the problem was how to reconcile his proposal for a massive tax rate cut with the long-standing Republican position that deficits should be cut. Not everyone in the Reagan camp bought what became known as "supply-side" economics, the belief that tax rate cuts, by leading to economic growth, would increase government revenues, thereby reducing budgetary deficits. Among Reagan's economic advisers, however, there was agreement on the need to cut the income tax rate. In September, Reagan announced the details of his plan, which *Newsweek* dubbed "Reaganomics" (though the radio commentator Paul Harvey later claimed that he had coined the word).[48]

Reagan waited to spell out the details of his tax policy, but he never wavered during the campaign in his call for tax cuts. This was a matter of principle and an indication of his abiding faith that lower rates were good for business and good for the nation. He believed that high tax rates imposed economic burdens on taxpayers, stunted economic growth, and meant big government would grow bigger. Another article of faith was his belief in peace through military strength. He insisted that defense spending be increased and that America win the arms race against the Soviet Union. At the core of this policy rested a view held by conservatives since the early days of the Cold War: The Soviet economy stood on the verge of collapse; therefore the Soviets could not maintain a sustained arms race with the United States. Push the Soviets through an arms race and the USSR would tumble like a house of cards.

A poor economy, a failed attempt to rescue the American hostages in Iran, and Carter's own gaffes kept the race close. The electorate did not believe Carter's warning that a Reagan election would lead to ethnic, religious, and geographic division in American society, and probably nuclear war with the Soviet Union as well. Carter needed to restore the public's confidence in him, and this meant not projecting an appearance that he would say anything to get elected. This issue went beyond the matter of Carter's competence to whether voters fully trusted him. In 1976, he declared himself antiabortion to win Iowa, only to qualify his stance later; he declared himself a born-again Christian, only to give an interview in *Playboy* magazine; he spoke of his military experience, only to appear antidefense once he got into office; he presented himself as a traditional and devoted family man and then brought outspoken feminists into government. He pledged to bring smaller government to Washington, D.C., and then called for national health insurance and established a Department of Education. After four years, many Americans could not reconcile Carter's many contradictions in rhetoric and action. They suspected that he was not what he appeared to be.

When the two candidates met for their only debate, on October 18, polls showed they were dead even. Carter kept Reagan on the defensive for most of the debate with his firm grasp of issues and data, but his story about talking with his daughter, Amy, about nuclear war became national news the next day. It gave the impression to some voters that Carter was consulting with his daughter about nuclear strategy. Moreover, Reagan's ability to fend off Carter's attacks on him as an extremist with the response, "There you go again," made Reagan appear quick-witted and good natured, if not well informed on some specific issues. But the questions Reagan posed in his closing statement were critical— "Are you better off than you were four years ago? Is America as respected throughout the world as it was? Are we safer today than we were four years ago?"

On Election Day, Ronald Reagan won in one of the largest landslides in American political history. Virtually everyone had predicted a close outcome, but official returns gave Reagan a margin of 8.4 million votes (a 7 percent lead over Carter). He won 489 electoral votes to Carter's 49, taking 44 states. The third-party threat from Anderson garnered only 7 percent of the vote, and his run for the presidency quickly became only a footnote in history. Carter was the first Democratic incumbent president since 1888 to lose a bid for reelection, but more ominous for Democrats was a fact noted by the *Congressional Quarterly* in its post-election analysis: Since World War II, Democratic presidential candidates had won the majority of the popular vote only twice, in 1964 and 1976.[49]

Carter's defeat represented a severe loss for Democrats. His percentage of the vote from 1976 had dropped in every state, and in nearly half of the states it had fallen more than ten points. The vote had fallen in all regions and in all groups except among Hispanics and blacks. Carter won the Jewish vote and the labor union vote by less than 8 percent each. Reagan, by contrast, handily won the suburban vote, often exceeding Ford's vote in that area. In the South, white voters deserted Carter in droves. The results for Reagan were even better in other parts of the country. He won most of the southern states by five percentage points, and he took many midwestern states by more than ten points. For example, he won Ohio by more than 450,000 votes. Reagan cut heavily into the blue-collar ethnic vote in the industrial northern part of the state. He won the western region by nearly 20 points.

Reagan's victory in the South was especially important. The transformation of the South into a Republican stronghold had already begun on the presidential level, but more important was the shift on the district level that began in the 1960s. It is worth noting that from 1903 to 1960, there were no Republican senators from any of the eleven Old Confederate states. In 1961, John Tower won a special election in Texas as a Republican. More significant, a decisive class shift occurred in voting patterns among southern voters in the post-1960 period. Before 1960, the Democratic vote was drawn from the upper-income groups, while the few Republican votes came from lower-income groups. After 1960, upper-income groups switched to the Republican party. This shift coincided with demographic changes in the South, particularly the tremendous growth of suburbs outside of major southern cities and the large influx of northerners to the South. These suburban voters were concerned with issues such as low taxes, anti-unionism, and family values, and they moved into the Republican party. As the political scientists Byron Shafer and Richard Johnston demonstrate, economics, not race, won the South for the Republicans. The burgeoning suburban middle classes went Republican in 1980 and in the elections that followed because of promises of tax cuts and a smaller federal government.[50]

Especially interesting in this regard was the pattern of voting for Democratic presidential candidates George Wallace in 1968 and Jimmy Carter in 1976 and 1980. In 1976, when Carter first ran for president, he picked up majorities in 79 percent of the districts that had gone for Wallace, and 59 percent of the districts that had gone for Nixon in 1968. In 1980, in a Republican sweep of the South, the majority of districts that remained in Democratic hands were those that had gone for Wallace in 1968. This suggests that Wallace was not a bridge candidate for white voters in the South into the Republican party.

In a landslide election sixteen years after the Goldwater defeat and six years after the Watergate scandal, Reagan, an avowed conservative, stepped into the White House. At first stunned by the defeat, liberals responded that the vote was primarily anti-Carter rather than pro-Reagan. Polling data suggested, in fact, that voters cast their votes mainly as a rejection of Carter, specifically his economic record, rather than as a complete endorsement of Reagan. Pundits had a harder time explaining the inroads Republicans made in Congress, though these proved to be more transitory. For the first time in a quarter of a century, Republicans won the Senate, ending, as the *Congressional Quarterly* remarked, "the longest one-party dominance of the Senate in American history."[51]

Not only had the Republicans won a majority of Senate seats, but liberal Democrat after liberal Democrat fell as election returns came in: George McGovern in South Dakota, Warren G. Magnuson in Washington, John C. Culver in Iowa, Gaylord Nelson in Wisconsin, Birch Bayh in Indiana. Republican liberals joined the ranks of the fallen, having been beaten in GOP primaries by more conservative Republicans. Jacob K. Javits was defeated by Alfonse M. D'Amato, who won the endorsement of the Conservative party and the Right to Life party. Other conservative winners included Charles E. Grassley of Iowa, Steven Symms of Idaho, Don Nickles of Oklahoma, James Abdnor of South Dakota, Robert W. Kasten in Wisconsin, Paula Hawkins of Florida, and John P. East of North Carolina. Clearly, many Americans were rejecting the liberal vision of economic and social welfare.

Grassroots conservatives claimed credit for many of these defeats. The

National Conservative Political Action Committee had targeted six liberal Democrats, four of whom fell, including Birch Bayh of Indiana, Culver of Iowa, McGovern of South Dakota, and Frank Church of Idaho. Alan Cranston of California and Thomas Eagleton of Missouri were among those who were targeted but survived. Religious conservatives played an important role in the victories of Don Nickles in Oklahoma and Admiral Jeremiah Denton, a former prisoner of war in Vietnam , in Alabama.

The election results revealed further erosion of Democratic control of the South. From a Democratic perspective, the most disheartening aspects of the decline of the party were the cracks evident in the suburbs, the fastest-growing areas in a rapidly urbanizing (or suburbanizing) region. In Georgia, Republican Mack Mattingly defeated longtime Democratic senator Herman Talmadge by winning the suburban areas around Atlanta. Also disturbing from a Democratic point of view was the money that grassroots conservative organizations were able to pour into Republican campaigns. In North Carolina, Jesse Helms used his Congressional Club to mount a massive advertising and direct-mail campaign for John P. East, a deeply conservative university political scientist, to upset Robert Morgan.

Republicans also made gains in the House, though they remained twenty-six seats short of control. Democrats lost thirty-three seats as they came under a $9 million dollar media barrage launched by Republicans in the waning days of the campaign. The GOP targeted incumbents through the slogan, "Vote Republican for a Change." Those Democrats who fell included Majority Whip John Brademas (Indiana) and twelve-term Ways and Means Committee Chairman Al Ullman (Oregon). Other senior Democrats defeated included the chairman of the Public Works and Transportation Committee, the head of the Democratic Congressional Campaign Committee, the chair of the Banking Subcommittee on Housing and Community Development, the chair of the Commerce Communication Committee, and the chair of the Merchant Marine and Fisheries Committee. Democrats felt relieved that Majority Leader Jim Wright (D-Texas) and Interior Committee Chairman Morris K. Udall of Arizona survived the GOP hit list. Overall, conservative Republicans did quite well as incumbents and challengers. A major loss for conservatives occurred when Robert E. Bauman (R-Maryland), a former YAF leader, prominent American Conservative Union member, and pro-family conservative was defeated after being arrested for soliciting sex from a sixteen-year-old boy. Still, conservative Republicans fared well. Robert Dornan (R-California), Vin Weber (R-Minnesota), Steve Gunderson (R-Wisconsin), and Ron Paul (R-Texas) all won their elections.

Liberalism was not dead; nor was the Democratic party. Both would make a comeback in the next midterm elections. But liberalism had been battered severely by the 1980 election, and to many it appeared exhausted, intellectually and politically. The question Democratic strategists still ask is whether their fortunes could have been reversed. Could a politician more adept than Carter have saved the Democratic party in 1980? A debate raged among the Democrats as to whether the party needed to return to the center or move further to the left. While the Democrats debated, the GOP Right advanced. After wandering in the desert for nearly thirty-five years, conservatives had marched to the promised land and were prepared to enter the White House. The political war was not over—more battles were to be fought—but in 1980, conservatives rejoiced in splendid victory.

7

The Reagan Decade

In the early spring of 1985, a year after his landslide victory for reelection to the White House, President Ronald Reagan addressed his critics on the Right who complained that the Republican revolution had stalled. Reagan reassured them that the "tide of history is moving irresistibly in our direction" because liberalism had become "virtually bankrupt of ideas. It has nothing more to say, nothing to add to the debate. It has spent its intellectual capital, such as it was, and it has done its deeds." He concluded, "We in this room are not simply profiting from their bankruptcy; we are where we are because we're winning the contest of ideas. In fact, in the past decade, all of a sudden, quietly, mysteriously, the Republican party has become the party of ideas. All of a sudden, Republicans [are] not defenders of the status quo but creators of the future."[1]

Reagan's speech displayed his ability to inspire conservatives with a sense of historic destiny. He convinced them that they were the creators of change, the embodiment of the future, and the protectors of American liberty. Reagan was skilled at linking traditional Republican antistatist conservatism and patriotic nationalism with New Right positions on abortion, school prayer, and other social issues. In doing so, he maintained control of his conservative base, while broadening the appeal of the party to southern whites, the suburban middle class, and blue-collar ethnic groups. Since the 1930s the GOP in general had managed to maintain discipline within its activist ranks, but Reagan was particularly adept at keeping the lines of communication open to grassroots activists in the conservative movement. He relied on his popular national base to promote his agenda, often to the neglect of building a strong Republican party on the state and local levels.

Reagan accomplished much in his presidency. Although historians later would debate his specific contributions, during his administration the American economy boomed and the Cold War waned. Reagan did not pay close attention to many of the details of policy, but he brought into office a superb ability to communicate his ideas to the larger public and a realistic sense of what was possible. On some issues, such as tax reform and defense, he proved unbending, often to the dismay of his staff.

Reagan's administration was exceptionally well organized. Policy and legislative strategies were vetted at all levels of the bureaucracy, and an efficient White House staff organized presidential liaisons with Congress, state officeholders, public-interest groups, conservative groups, and ethnic leaders. Reagan was famous for conducting personal telephone conversations with critical members of the House and Senate, holding group meetings, and making public addresses. He actively joined in efforts to build the Republican party organization on the national level. In 1980, he posed with Republican congressional candidates on the steps of the Capitol, and as president he campaigned for Republican candidates. In 1983 and 1984 he made more than two dozen campaign and fundraising appearances for Republican candidates and the GOP at all levels.

Not all of Reagan's initiatives were successful, however. In 1986, in a bid to retain a Republican Senate, Reagan visited twenty-two key states and raised $33 million for the party and its candidates.[2] His efforts ultimately failed when Republicans lost the Senate. This defeat marked yet another setback in a second term marred by scandal. The Iran-Contra affair involving the sale of missiles to Iran to fund counter-revolutionaries in Central America, in particular, appeared to confirm critics' characterization of Reagan as a leader detached from the responsibilities of governance. Nonetheless, the Reagan presidency fulfilled much of its conservative legislative and policy agenda thanks to strong leadership and a White House organized to accomplish its goals.[3]

Whatever successes the Reagan presidency enjoyed, however, the liberal administrative state survived the Reagan "revolution" and blocked many of the president's initiatives. Reagan faced another obstacle in downsizing government—the American public. Although most Americans considered themselves conservative to moderate, they remained tenaciously committed to entitlements such as Social Security, Medicare, consumer protection, and health and safety measures.[4] Furthermore, as popular as Reagan was with voters, in 1980 he received only 2 percent more of the popular vote than Ford had in 1976. Public support for middle-class entitlement programs enabled Democrats in Congress to work with favored federal agencies to prevent government downsizing.

Reagan was genuine in his belief that the size and scope of the federal government should be reduced, but he also needed a strong federal government to defeat Communism. His strategy relied on a combination of executive action and mobilization of conservative groups outside of government. Reagan failed, however, to reshape government institutions that sheltered liberal programs. Moreover, he failed to impose a permanent conservative regime within the Republican party itself, a shortcoming that became evident in the policies of his successor, George H. W. Bush. Any celebration of the Reagan revolution, therefore, must be qualified by his successor's policies; and any assessment of the failure of liberalism must first consider whether the Democrats might have been successful had they not swung so far left.

Whatever qualifications are placed on the Reagan revolution, there is no denying that Reagan changed the political landscape of modern America. He tapped into a reservoir of anxiety felt by traditional Christians who feared that their values were under attack. By articulating these fears, Reagan brought religious voters into the Republican party; and in doing so, he reshaped the GOP by making the Religious Right a permanent feature of Republican politics. Republican strategists did not realize the full value of Christian voters and the important role of churches in mobilizing voter turnout until later, but in 1980, Reagan's election marked a historic step in fulfilling the conservative ascendancy.

Reagan's Vision and the Reality of Administration

Reagan brought to the White House a clear set of principles on core issues that shaped his administration for the next eight years.[5] He was an ideological conservative but showed a willingness to compromise in order to achieve legislative success. Writing to Clymer Wright, a Texas supporter, in the spring of 1982, Reagan observed, "Some in the media delight in trying to portray me as being manipulated and led around by the nose . . . Clymer, I'm in charge and my people are helping carry out the policies I set. Now we don't get everything we want and yes we have to compromise to get 75 or 80 percent of our program. We try to see that the 75 or 80 percent is more than worth the compromise we have to accept."[6]

This pragmatism was reflected in Reagan's choice of James Baker as his chief of staff instead of Edwin Meese, a staunch conservative loyalist who had been with Reagan since his first campaign for governor of California.[7] Drawing on the advice of many, including Richard Nixon, whose opinion he respected, Reagan appointed a politically diverse cabinet, indicating that he valued experience over ideology. His nominations also reveal a president confident in his ability to reconcile factional differences within the party.

At the center of Reagan's political ideology lay anti-Communism, drawn from his experience fighting Reds when he was president of the Screen Actors Guild in Hollywood in the late 1940s. Indeed, his work with the actors' union shaped his views not only of international Communism but of liberalism as well. Liberals, whom Reagan understood because he used to be one, appeared willing to accommodate themselves to Communists by including them in the "progressive" camp, while ignoring the ruthless, undemocratic, and repressive nature of the Communist party and the Soviet Union. Reagan's own transformation from liberal to conservative began with his unwillingness to accept this contradiction. His support of free-market ideology followed and was reinforced when he went on the lecture circuit for General Electric in the 1950s. During that time, he became an avid reader of *Human Events* and *National Review.* He also began reading conservative thinkers, and Hayek's *Road to Serfdom* exerted a major influence on his thinking.[8]

Reagan's core beliefs led him to the worldview that the best government is that which governs least so individual citizens can reach their full potential. Reagan believed that centralized government weakened a free people's self-reliance and capacity for self-government. In his inaugural address, he declared, "In this present crisis, government is not the solution to our problem, government is the problem. From time to time we've been tempted to believe that society has become too complex to be managed by self-rule, that government by an elite group is superior to government for, by, and of the people. Well, if no one among us is capable of governing himself, then who among us has the capacity to govern someone else?"[9]

Reagan was a pragmatist eager to achieve his policy goals. His insistence on legislative accomplishment led his chief of staff, James Baker, to cultivate a strong relationship with Senate Majority Leader Howard Baker (R-Tennessee). This relationship paid dividends in the early part of Reagan's administration. Despite being wounded in an assassination attempt in March 1981, Reagan carried through on many of his campaign promises. The Economic Recovery Tax Act (1981) cut federal income rates over a three-year period; nondefense spending was cut sizably; some welfare administration was shifted to the states; and many federal regulations were eliminated.

From the moment he entered office, Reagan placed highest priority on implementing tax and spending cuts.[10] He proposed $35 billion in domestic cuts and a multiyear program of nearly $750 billion in tax cuts. He joined these cuts with a 27 percent increase in defense spending over a three-year period. The revenue lost from the tax cuts greatly exceeded reductions in domestic spending and increases in defense spending. The administration argued that a large tax rate cut would stimulate economic growth, which in turn would lead to increased tax revenues. The theory that tax rate cuts would increase tax revenue was based on supply-side economic theory promulgated by Arthur Laffer, an economics professor, and Paul Craig Roberts, a former legislative aide to Representative Jack Kemp (R-New York). Few established economists accepted supply-side economics, but it provided a political rationale for tax cuts.

Most Washington insiders believed that Reagan's agenda had little chance of passing Congress. The new chairman of the Senate Budget Committee, Peter Domenici (R-New Mexico), doubted that the budget could be balanced while taxes were cut and defense expenditures increased. The Reagan administration lobbied hard for the president's plan, which was aided by sympathy and admiration after Reagan was shot in an assassination attempt. While recovering from surgery in the hospital, Reagan started calling members of Congress to ask them to support his program. When he returned to the White House on April 11, 1981, his lobbying efforts continued. He ultimately met with more than four hundred members of Congress.

Reagan had an advantage over his Democratic opposition owing to the near decimation of Democratic leadership brought about by the 1980 election. In the Senate, Minority Leader Robert Byrd (D-West Virginia) proved unable to provide the leadership the Democrats needed to counter a smooth-running White House machine. In the House, Speaker Tip O'Neill (D-Massachusetts) lacked a strategy to oppose the Reagan agenda effectively. Reagan, for his part, put together a coalition that supported his tax cuts. He convinced even Pete Domenici by appealing to party loyalty. The Economic Recovery Tax Act offered tax cuts, reduced capital gains taxes, and inflation-indexed tax rates. This was the largest tax cut in American history. Reagan also signed the Omnibus Budget Reconciliation Act, which cut spending for the next fiscal year.

Reagan made deregulation an integral part of his economic recovery program. He pursued regulatory relief mostly through administrative repeal and executive discretion rather than through legislation, with the important exception of the deregulation of the savings and loan industry.[11] Reagan's executive orders 12291 and 12498 mandated a review of proposed agency regulations by the Office of Management and Budget, an executive office. Reagan also appointed Vice President George H. W. Bush to chair a newly appointed task force on regulation. He then issued an executive order freezing all new federal regulations, pending review. In February, he issued another executive order that all new regulations must be accompanied by a cost-benefit analysis before being imposed. Under Reagan, a number of industries were deregulated, including cable television, energy, and banking.

Banking deregulation had begun under Carter with the enactment of the Depository Institutions Deregulation and Monetary Control Act of 1980. Further deregulation was continued into the Reagan administration in the Garn–St. Germain Depository Institutions Act of 1982. Backed by Federal Reserve Chairman Paul Volcker, these acts deregulated the savings and loan industry while tightening federal control over the banking industry. One of the unforeseen consequences of this policy was the collapse in the late 1980s of many savings and loans owing to over-expansion and, in some cases, fraudulent loans. While these consequences could not have been foreseen at the time, the deregulation of the savings and loan industry was a necessary compromise to tighten federal control over the entire banking industry to ensure more efficient monetary policy.[12]

Reagan also cut staffing of regulatory agencies in his attempt to downsize government. He ordered staff cuts in the Consumer Product Safety Commission, the Occupational Safety and Health Administration (OSHA), and the Environmental Protection Agency (EPA). These attacks on regulatory agencies occasionally backfired. For example, mismanagement of the EPA enabled career civil servants to join forces with Democrats in Congress to force the removal of the EPA chief Anne Burford.

Reagan's trouble with the EPA was indicative of a larger problem the president faced throughout his two terms in office: a well-entrenched and formidable federal bureaucracy.[13] To protect themselves from the Reagan White House and the Office of Management and Budget (OMB), federal agencies turned to their allies in Congress and public-interest organizations to fight retrenchment or termination. In this way, Reagan was faced with a war on two fronts: against liberals in Congress and against institutionalized liberalism within the administrative state.

The liberal administrative state had been created during the New Deal and expanded during the Great Society. Under Johnson's Great Society, new entitlement programs such as Medicare were established and existing agencies were reformed to involve citizen groups in the decision-making process. The result was not an expansion of participatory democracy but participatory opportunities for a small circle of public lobbyists. For example, the Federal Trade Commission Improvement Act of 1975 authorized the agency to pay attorneys, expert witnesses, and other public representatives to be involved in rule-making proceedings, thereby providing public funding for consumer advocates supportive of ambitious pro-consumer policies.[14] Statutes written during these decades conferred statutory rights in employment, consumer and environmental protection, welfare, health, and occupational safety. These statutes strengthened the power of federal agencies to make administrative law and invited the federal judiciary to become the final arbiter in the process. The focus of the courts in reviewing administrative law thus changed from preventing unauthorized intrusion of government on private autonomy to arbitrating competing interests. This change in the role of the federal judiciary and the way judges saw themselves only intensified the already charged partisan debate over the courts.

Opposition to the Reagan administration's conservative agenda was especially pronounced in the Environmental Protection Agency, the Department of Health and Human Services, and the Department of Education. Under Terrell H. Bell, Reagan's moderate secretary of education, conservatives were not able to redirect the policies of the department— let alone dismantle it as Reagan had proposed during the presidential campaign. Bell outflanked Reagan when his newly created National Commission on Excellence in Education released the report *A Nation at Risk* (1983), which showed declining academic standards and performance in American schools. This report placed education on Reagan's agenda as the election of 1984 approached. It saved the department from dismantlement and set off a chain of events that eventually led to the call for national academic standards a decade later, a proposal that infuriated many conservatives because of its liberal bias and push for further federalization of education.[15] Even conservative appointments proved disappointing. After a series of mishaps and scandals rocked the Department of the Interior under the leadership of James Watt, many political observers saw Reagan's appointment of Watt as a mistake. Reagan's travails reveal the inherent limitations of political transformation in a democratic regime.

President Reagan faced fewer restraints in conducting foreign policy, but even in this area he found that Congress was intent on restricting presidential powers following the Vietnam War. As a longtime anti-Communist, Reagan was eager to pursue an aggressive foreign policy that challenged the Soviets in strategic weapons and confronted them on their involvement in Asia, Africa, and Latin America. Speaking before the National Association of Evangelicals in Orlando, Florida, on March 8, 1983, Reagan urged his audience to "speak out against those who would place the United States in a position of military and moral inferiority . . . I urge you to beware of the temptation of pride—the temptation of blithely declaring yourselves above it all and [labeling] both sides equally at fault, to ignore the facts of history and the aggressive impulses of an evil empire, to simply call the arms race a giant misunderstanding and thereby remove yourself from the struggle between right and wrong and good and evil." In this speech—soon tagged "the evil empire speech" by the press—Reagan spoke out against a nuclear freeze that would limit further development of nuclear weapons by the United States and the Soviet Union. Such a freeze, he argued, would reward the Soviet Union for its "enormous and unparalleled military build-up," while preventing the "essential and long overdue modernization of United States and allied defenses and would leave our aging forces increasingly vulnerable."[16] Reagan called for an arms buildup in the United States, but he supported serious negotiations with the Soviet Union to achieve substantial, and verifiable, reductions in nuclear arms.

These two positions—militant engagement with the Soviet Union and arms reduction—were not inconsistent; they were central to a conservative foreign policy that had been articulated since the 1950s: peace through strength. This refrain had become the rallying cry among conservatives in opposition to Nixon's détente policies with the Soviet Union and the SALT II talks during the Ford and Carter administrations. Before the election, Reagan had sat on the Committee on the Present Danger's board of directors. This group rejected the strategy of détente and dismissed the view that the American and Soviet systems were converging ideologically and economically. From this perspective, arms control treaties with the Soviet Union would fail unless arms reductions could be verified. Without verifiable arms control reductions, the arms race would continue to escalate; meanwhile, the United States would engage in direct and violent conflict through surrogates—Muslims in Afghanistan, the Solidarity movement in Poland, anti-Communist resistance in Africa, and the Contras in Nicaragua. To counterbalance the Soviet threat, the United States would need to deploy missiles in Europe and engage in economic warfare and technological sabotage.[17] The Cold War was war in every sense except that armies did not face each other directly across the battlefield and nuclear missiles were not exchanged.

For the Left, this strategy was ill-conceived, dangerous, and frightening. The fear of war intensified: One of the most watched television programs of the decade was *The Day After,* a melodramatic movie that aired on ABC in November 1983. This Sunday night movie drew an audience of 100 million viewers, including Ronald Reagan.

Faced with a massive "nuclear freeze" movement in the United States and Europe, and continuous criticism from the mainstream media, Reagan showed exceptional tenacity in pursuing a hardline strategy. Central to this strategy was a massive defense buildup under Defense Secretary Caspar Weinberger. Defense spending had declined by 20 percent (adjusted for inflation) in the 1970s, but under Reagan the Pentagon's annual budget doubled from $158 to $304 billion. The administration spent $2.7 trillion for defense in the next eight years. Under Reagan, conventional military strength was increased and strategic capability enhanced through new Trident missile submarines and additional ICBMs.

This strategy of peace through strength was evident in the administration's deployment of new intermediate-range ballistic missiles in Europe as a means of countering Soviet placement of SS-20s in Eastern Europe in 1977. European leaders, especially German Chancellor Helmut Schmidt, warned that the Soviet missiles created an imbalance that made Europe vulnerable to nuclear blackmail. NATO leaders agreed with this assessment and proposed deploying new Pershing II intermediate-range ballistic missiles and ground-launched cruise missiles in West Germany, Britain, and Italy, with further deployments to be made in Belgium and the Netherlands. Reagan accepted this commitment, but proposed what was called the "zero option": The United States would agree not to deploy any missiles in Europe in exchange for the dismantling of all intermediate-range ballistic missiles by the Soviet Union. Reagan's proposal brought the Soviets to the table in Geneva for negotiations on intermediate-range missiles.

While negotiators met, peace demonstrators gathered at huge rallies to call for a "nuclear freeze"—a complete halt of the production of new weapons on both sides. Demonstrators condemned the U.S.–Soviet arms race, but they directed most of their criticism at the Reagan administration. In the fall of 1982, an estimated 750,000 marchers turned out in New York's Central Park to hear George F. Kennan, Madeleine Albright, and former CIA head William Colby endorse the freeze. They were joined by Hollywood celebrities Ed Asner, Martin Sheen, and Harry Belafonte, as well as rock singers Bruce Springsteen, Jackson Browne, and Bonnie Raitt.[18] Although it unlikely that this movement influenced American or Soviet policy, it did create concern within the Reagan administration that peace demonstrations would encourage the Soviet Union to break off negotiations.

In 1983 Reagan's call for the Strategic Defense Initiative (SDI), an anti–missile-defense system based in outer space, drew widespread protest from peace activists, newspaper columnists, and other opponents who believed that the president was taking the United States one step closer to nuclear war with the Soviet Union. The Reagan proposal rejected the longstanding nuclear strategy of the McNamara years, known as Mutual Assured Destruction (MAD). This strategy assumed that neither side would launch nuclear weapons if its opponent could withstand a massive first attack and then retaliate with a strike of its own. Nixon's 1972 ABM Treaty forbidding the development of new anti–ballistic missile defense systems was based on this premise. The system that Reagan proposed would provide a defense against a first strike, which undermined the concept of mutual assured destruction.

Critics of the ABM Treaty believed that the Soviets had already developed anti–ballistic missile defense systems. Reagan, for his part, rejected MAD. He wanted serious and verifiable arms reductions. He compared MAD to "two westerners standing in a saloon aiming their weapons at each other's heads—permanently."[19] His call for an effective anti–ballistic missile system was supported by the physicist Edward Teller and retired Lt. General Daniel O. Graham, a close associate of the presidential adviser Richard Pipes and head of a defense advocacy group. They were joined by Reagan's science adviser, Jay Keyworth. When announced, the Strategic Defense Initiative caused an uproar among liberals, who claimed that it was an untested and most likely ineffective system that would cost billions of dollars. Longtime Democratic foreign policy advisers like George Ball, George F. Kennan, and Clark Clifford condemned the SDI as a foolish and unworkable system that also had the potential to heighten Soviet anxieties. Later it was revealed that the Soviets were actually engaged in their own, similar program and had deployed, in violation of the ABM Treaty, a radar system in Krasnoyarsk in the interior of the Soviet Union to track incoming missiles.[20]

Conflicts arose within the Reagan administration over the SDI proposal. Secretary of Defense Caspar Weinberger, after some hesitation, signed on to the proposal, but the new secretary of state, George Shultz, opposed SDI on the grounds that it was technically infeasible and violated the ABM Treaty. Reagan refused to back down. SDI received $22 billion in federal support during his presidency and $60 billion by the end of the century. Reagan realized that the development of an effective SDI during his administration was impossible, but he sincerely believed that the completion of such a system would end the threat of nuclear war. SDI reinforced his strategy of engaging the Soviet Union in an arms race that conservatives believed the Russian economy could not sustain.

The Reagan administration waged a war by proxy against the Soviet Union and its allies by aiding resistance groups opposed to Soviet adventurism.[21] In what became known as the Reagan Doctrine, the administration sought to roll back pro-Soviet Communist governments around the globe. One of its most prominent endeavors was support of the anti-Soviet Polish labor movement Solidarity. Through cooperation with American unions led by the AFL-CIO head Lane Kirkland, the Vatican under Pope John Paul II, and European trade unions, the United States smuggled fax machines, printing presses, telephones, cameras, photocopiers, and computers into Poland. The administration bolstered the movement by continuing economic sanctions against Poland into 1987, when negotiations opened between the Communist government and Solidarity leaders led by the charismatic Lech Walesa.

The Reagan administration also sought to aid "freedom fighters" in Central America, Southeast Asia, Africa, and Central Asia. Many of these efforts were extensions of policies that had been initiated under the Carter administration. In Afghanistan, CIA experts provided training and weapons to Islamic forces opposed to the Soviet invasion of 1979. Financial aid from the United States and Saudi Arabia (transmitted through China) supplied the Islamic guerrillas—the mujahidin—with weapons. With strong bipartisan support from Congress, Reagan doubled aid to the Afghan resistance in 1984, providing wire-guided antitank missiles and the handheld Stinger surface-to-air missiles which proved deadly against Soviet air power. This was the largest covert operation in American history. It resulted in the Soviet withdrawal from Afghanistan in 1989.

The administration's strategy of war by proxy was apparent in U.S. support of opposition to the radical pro-Cuban Sandinista government in Nicaragua." The Carter administration initially sided with the Sandinista rebels against the corrupt dictatorship of Anastasio Somoza Debayle, who was overthrown in July 1979. Carter quickly withdrew support as it became clear that the new revolutionary Sandinista government aligned itself with Castro's Cuba and began to export revolution to neighboring El Salvador. When the Sandinista government canceled elections, introduced thousands of Cuban advisers into the country, and signed trade and defense treaties with the Soviet Union, the Carter administration suspended aid to Nicaragua and launched a covert campaign to undermine the revolutionary government.

The Reagan administration extended this effort by directing support and training to opponents of the Sandinista regime, the Contras. CIA-backed operations in Nicaragua were less successful. When a CIA-backed operation to mine the bay of Managua sank a Soviet freighter in 1983, a firestorm of protest broke out in the United States. Although the mines were designed to cause only minimal damage, the incident turned many U.S. senators, including Daniel Moynihan, against the administration's Central American policy. Even the one-time standard-bearer of conservatism, Barry Goldwater, became a foe of the administration's support of the Contras.

The backlash against the Reagan-backed covert war led Congress to pass legislation on October 11, 1983, prohibiting the U.S. government from providing funds or military aid to the Contras for the purpose of overthrowing the Nicaraguan government. The measure, known as the Boland amendment, was sponsored by the Democratic representative Edward Boland of Massachusetts. It was attached to the 1983 fiscal year defense appropriation bill and was renewed each year through fiscal 1986. In hindsight, Reagan would have been better off vetoing the Boland amendment, even though it was attached to an omnibus bill, and taking on congressional opposition directly by going public with his case. Instead, the administration sought to circumvent the amendment by using the National Security Council to supervise covert aid to the Contras. Overseen by National Security Advisers Robert McFarlane and John Poindexter, and directed by U.S. Marine Lt. Colonel Oliver L. North, the operation successfully raised private and foreign funds for the Contras. Although the Saudis provided most of the funds for this covert operation, financial support was also provided by private American citizens drawn to the anti-Communist cause of undermining the Sandinista government.

Reagan waged his proxy war in Nicaragua without deploying U.S. troops, but he was not opposed to using direct force in other situations. In 1982 he ordered 1,500 troops into Beirut to help restore peace after the Israeli invasion of southern Lebanon. Following a terrorist attack on the morning of October 23, 1983, on a Marine compound that killed 241 American servicemen, Reagan quietly withdrew the remaining Marines from Lebanon. Shortly after this withdrawal, which would only encourage more attacks by Islamic militants, Reagan ordered U.S. Marines to help overthrow a pro-Castro Marxist dictator on the tiny Caribbean island of Grenada. The Marines quickly overran the island and captured several hundred Cuban military advisers who appeared to have been rapidly constructing a Soviet air base. The United States installed a friendly government and withdrew. Both Congress and the Organization of American States condemned the invasion, but public opinion polls and the conservative movement showed wide support for Reagan's successful actions in Grenada.

Reagan Protects His Base and Democrats Flounder

Reagan's strong anti-Communist policy, combined with his conservative economic program of tax cuts, allowed the president to keep his conservative base in line, even when the administration failed to win passage of antiabortion and school prayer bills. In Reagan's first year, five major pieces of antiabortion legislation were introduced, including the Garn amendment; the Grassley amendment; the Helms amendment; a human life statute; and the Hatch human life federalism amendment. These proposals revealed both the strength and the divisions within the antiabortion movement.[23] The Helms amendment held the greatest appeal for the grassroots antiabortion movement. It described human life as beginning at conception and offered protection to the human fetus as a person with rights that were protected by the Fourteenth Amendment. Called the "paramount" amendment, it declared that "the paramount right to life is vested in each human being from the moment of fertilization without regard to age, health, or condition of dependency."

Senator Orrin Hatch (R-Utah) offered an alternative amendment that would return abortion policy to state legislatures. Hatch's proposal won the support of the National Conference of Catholic Bishops, but it divided antiabortion forces. Senator Mark Hatfield (R-Oregon), an antiabortion liberal, attempted to reconcile divisions within the movement by proposing a permanent ban on federal funds for abortion unless the life of the mother was endangered, but this qualification proved repellent to both sides—ironically, unifying them in their opposition to Hatfield.

At the same time, Helms and his allies proposed voluntary school prayer legislation that became tied to a debt limit bill, to the chagrin of some conservatives who were more worried about national debt than about cultural issues. As pro-abortion senators rallied to defeat these measures, the Senate became deadlocked when Senator Robert Packwood (R-Oregon) launched a filibuster. In early September, Reagan directly intervened by urging Senate Majority Leader Howard Baker (R-Tennessee) to vote for cloture of the debate and call for a vote on Helms's bill. Reagan's intervention was in large part a response to grassroots activists who called on him to provide leadership in shepherding legislation through Congress. Morton Blackwell, an administration official serving as a liaison to the conservative movement, warned that "we are at a critical moment in the relationship between the President and prolife activists . . . If the President fails to take specific steps to obtain cloture in the Senate on Packwood's filibuster, that failure will be read as a betrayal."[24]

Realizing the importance of the antiabortion constituency to the Republican party, Reagan sent an open letter to the National Right to Life Committee endorsing their cause. He privately sent confidential letters to leading Republicans urging them to vote for cloture against Packwood's filibuster. White House officials launched an aggressive lobbying effort to garner support for the Helms bill. They coordinated their efforts with pro-life organizations to apply pressure to senators. Many activists believed they were going to win. Shortly before the cloture vote came to the floor, White House staff began calling senators to get their vote. These efforts were of no avail, leading Hatch to withdraw his constitutional amendment. Another vote for cloture followed, but it too failed, 50–44, ten votes short of the three-fifths required. A motion to table Helms's amendment passed 47–46, thus ending any further efforts to overturn *Roe v. Wade* in the immediate future.[25]

The fight over the Helms and Hatch amendments created a furor. For the next two decades the antiabortion and pro-abortion forces were locked in an angry struggle that spilled into political campaigns at all levels of government, into court appointments, and into welfare, educational, and health legislation. The debate appeared irreconcilable and never-ending. Both amendments would have returned debate to the states, Helms for ratification and Hatch for ratification and legislation. This turn to the states would have further democratized the debate, but the end result is unclear. It is difficult to imagine states like California, New York, Massachusetts, or New Jersey voting to ban abortion.

After the defeat of these amendments, Reagan attacked abortion and family planning in other areas.[26] He ordered restrictions placed on federal programs supporting abortion at home and overseas, and he sought to appoint conservative judges to the federal bench and the Supreme Court with the expectation that abortion law might be changed, even though he had not applied a litmus test to his appointments. For these reasons, social conservatives stuck with Reagan throughout his eight years in the presidency.

Reagan disclaimed the use of an "ideological litmus test" in appointing more than three hundred judges to the federal courts during his two terms in office. Consequently, his appointments to the Supreme Court were mixed in conservative eyes. When he nominated Sandra Day O'Connor to the Court in 1981, antiabortion groups rallied in opposition. As a state representative in Arizona in the early 1970s, O'Connor had signed a statement calling for population control in the United States. The statement had been drafted by Richard Lamm, an up-and-coming star in Colorado politics at the time and a well-known proponent of population control. To head off a grassroots backlash against the nomination, administrative official Morton Blackwell was assigned to meet with leaders of the antiabortion and pro-family movements. Opposition to O'Connor grew when it was revealed that she had clashed with Dr. Carolyn Gerster, a Phoenix physician and former president of the National Right to Life Committee. In response, Reagan circulated a letter to the grassroots promoting the O'Connor nomination on the basis of her legal and judicial expertise.[27] In the end, conservatives were reluctant to oppose Ronald Reagan publicly.

Reagan carefully cultivated antiabortion activists to make sure they did not abandon him on other issues. Concerned that he might be accused of placing social issues on the back burner, he told an audience at the Conservative Political Action Conference in March 1981: "We [the administration] do not have a social agenda, a separate economic agenda, and a separate foreign agenda. We have one agenda." To emphasize this point, he added, "Just as we seek to put our financial house in order and rebuild our nation's defenses, so too we seek to protect the unborn, to end the manipulation of schoolchildren by utopian planners, and permit the acknowledgment of a Supreme Being in our classrooms just as we allow such acknowledgments in other public institutions."[28]

To further reassure social conservatives, in 1984 Reagan issued a strong antiabortion statement that was published as *Abortion and the Conscience of the Nation*. He continued to meet with antiabortion activists to discuss ways to redirect federal policy on abortion, family planning, and world population control. His appointment of Dr. C. Everett Koop, an evangelical Christian, as surgeon general was a signal to the antiabortion movement that Reagan was on their side. Others with strong antiabortion credentials also received appointments to the administration, including Gary Bauer, Morton Blackwell, and Dee Jepsen in the Public Liaison Office, Michael Uhlmann in the Department of Justice, and Marjory Mecklenburg in the Office of Adolescent Pregnancy Program. Reagan's appointments to head the Department of Health and Human Services, Richard Schweiker, Margaret Heckler, and Otis R. Bowen, were publicly antiabortion. Under Bowen a "gag rule" was issued that banned funding to organizations that performed or counseled abortion—a ruling clearly targeting Planned Parenthood. Funding for domestic and international family-planning programs was drastically curtailed under the Reagan administration.

Reagan's political skills were on further display in 1982, when conservatives attacked him for retreating on some aspects of his tax cuts after the economy went into a recession and interest rates began to skyrocket. Reagan's approval rating began to fall precipitously, and the administration came under pressure to increase taxes. Leading Republicans in Congress, including Robert Dole and Pete Domenici in the Senate, joined by the ranking Republican on the House Ways and Means Committee, Barber Conable (R-New York), called for increased taxes to compensate for the loss of revenues. These Republicans were concerned about balancing the budget and did not buy into the "supply-side" economic program, which assumed that low tax rates would increase government revenue. In the Senate, Dole crafted a tax bill to increase revenues. He pushed it through the Senate in July 1982 in a session that lasted until three in the morning. He prevailed upon Jesse Helms, representing a tobacco state, to support the bill, which included a tobacco tax increase. To this point Reagan had resisted pressure to hike taxes, but in August 1982 he relented and signed the Tax Equity and Fiscal Responsibility Act, marking one of the largest tax hikes in the nation's history. Much of the increase came by rolling back depreciation breaks that had been enacted previously, while imposing new excise taxes on airports, communication, and tobacco.

A month before Reagan signed the measure, conservatives allied with Richard Viguerie complained about the president's willingness to compromise on conservative issues. These conservatives were already upset with Reagan for having backed away from his nomination of M. E. Bradford, a University of Dallas English professor, to head the National

Endowment for the Humanities (NEH). When Bradford came under attack by the conservative columnist George Will for his meager credentials and his pro-southern views, Reagan withdrew the nomination. Traditional conservatives accused Reagan of taking the easy way out by appointing a neoconservative, the philosophy professor William Bennett, to head the NEH.[29]

The July 1982 issue of Richard Viguerie's *Conservative Digest* attacked Reagan for having raised taxes. Published as an open letter to Reagan, the magazine entreated him, "Seize the moment, Mr. President, and restore the faith of people throughout the world who look with hope and excitement to you."[30] Paul Weyrich, the director of the Committee for the Survival of a Free Congress, joined in the criticism by asking whether President Ronald Reagan himself has "the political will to do so" not to raise taxes.[31] An angry Reagan privately responded to John Lofton, the editor of *Conservative Digest:* "I can't conclude this letter without telling you I believe the July *Conservative Digest* is one of the most dishonest and unfair bits of journalism I have ever seen."[32] Reagan pointed to the large tax cuts still in place under the 1981 legislation and noted that the 1982 tax increases were targeted hikes. Moreover, he let Lofton know that he did not like having his conservative credentials called into question. After Reagan's letter, the *Conservative Digest* did not carry any more articles attacking the president, even though over the next couple of years the administration supported other tax increases. Reform of Social Security in 1983, for example, scheduled increases in payroll taxes and allowed for benefits to be taxed. In 1984, Reagan signed the Deficit Reduction Act, which hiked taxes further, though it affected few people and was accompanied by more than $10 billion in spending cuts.

Meanwhile, Democrats fought a rearguard action through Congress and the federal bureaucracy, but they were unable to wage an effective frontal assault on winning the White House. In the 1982 campaign, Democrats took advantage of a recession caused by the Federal Reserve's anti-inflationary policy under chairman Paul Volcker. As unemployment shot up to 10 percent, Democrats triumphed in the 1982 congressional elections, having raised huge amounts of money from the party faithful and lobbying interests. Tony Coelho (D-California) extracted unprecedented contributions from PACs through sheer political muscle, but congressional Democrats were sincere in their belief that

Reagan's economic program was hurting the poor, creating greater disparities in wealth, and leading toward an unnecessary, and dangerous, confrontation with the Soviet Union. Coelho visited hundreds of PAC offices and explained, "We have every committee chairmanship and every subcommittee chairmanship in the House, and we keep score."[33] His efforts paid off. Democrats gained twenty-six seats in the House.[34] Overall, eighty-one freshmen were elected to Congress, fifty-seven of them Democrats.

The gains the Democrats made in the House in the 1982 elections proved disastrous for liberals in the long run. Their success in these midterm elections allowed them to ignore the fact that a sizeable portion of the electorate had shifted politically to the right. Only a few party operatives seemed to realize that the Democratic party needed to shift back toward the center. While some Democrats in the South campaigned as fiscal conservatives, most of the twenty-three freshmen Democrats from the South and Southwest were liberals openly supportive of social programs that the administration had sought to reduce. As a result, Democrats proclaimed themselves the party of social programs and low deficits. First-year Democrats tapped into low-income constituencies within their districts which provided support for a liberal social agenda. For example, Ronald Coleman in his congressional race in Texas drew heavily from Mexican-American clothing workers for whom he had served as a legal adviser during a protracted strike in El Paso. In Georgia, Lindsay Thomas campaigned on nuclear disarmament, while Robert Tallon, Jr., of South Carolina drew heavily on the politically active black community in his district. Things were different in the Senate, where Republicans came out even. The party ratio remained 54–46 Republican.

Democrats at the national level remained divided over strategy and vision.[35] Party liberals were loyal to Walter Mondale, a clear frontrunner for the presidency, but others within the party believed that New Deal liberalism was a lost cause with the electorate because it smacked of old-time special-interest politics. They believed something new was needed. One major challenge came from what became known as neoliberalism. Neoliberalism drew intellectual strength from a group of authors who warned of America's decline as an economy and a world power. Massachusetts Institute of Technology economist Lester Thurow warned in his book *The Zero-Sum Solution* (1985) that the United States faced imminent financial collapse brought on by inflation and Reagan's economic policies. He urged Democrats to turn to Japanese-style industrial policy in which the government directed investment toward new and innovative industries. Thurow's call for America to emulate the Japanese echoed other liberal authors, including Robert Reich and Chalmers Johnson, who sought policies for industrial recovery. Wall Street financier Felix Rohatyn and the historian Paul Kennedy joined in predicting financial collapse caused by bloated budget deficits and an overextended military.

Three prominent Democratic politicians became associated with neoliberalism: Colorado senator Gary Hart, Massachusetts governor Michael Dukakis, and Massachusetts senator Paul Tsongas. While political rivals, these three men had much in common. They spoke about improving the quality of life of Americans, warned about resource limitations, and called for the United States to adjust to a new technology-based economy. They called for welfare reform, a reduction in military expenditures, and government investment in new cutting-edge industries that would revitalize the economy and expand the employment base. Neoliberals proposed targeted industrial investment by the federal government—a proposal that went well beyond New Deal welfare liberalism, which had sought only to mitigate the ills of industrial displacement.

The Democratic Leadership Council (DLC), established in 1985, represented another Democratic response to the electorate's move to the right. The DLC felt that liberal constituency groups had gained too much influence within the national party and the congressional caucus.[36] In response, the DLC sought to shift the party toward the political center with a program that balanced defense and domestic issues. Such a policy would appeal to middle-class suburban voters while maintaining the traditional base of the party. Led by then Virginia governor Charles Robb and attracting southerners like Senator Al Gore (Tennessee) and Arkansas governor Bill Clinton, the DLC called for arms control while opposing a nuclear freeze; sought better relations with the Soviet Union while taking a tougher stance on Communist expansionism; and advocated economic justice while opposing racial hiring quotas and supporting the death penalty. The DLC spoke about the problems created by rising out-of-wedlock births, welfare dependency, and self-defeating patterns of behavior in the inner city.

Members of the DLC represented a minority voice within the party.

Most Democrats continued to carry the liberal banner either as unreconstructed liberals like Mondale or as neoliberals like Gary Hart and Michael Dukakis, who wanted to recast the language of liberalism in more palatable terms. By ignoring the shifting sentiments of the white working and middle classes, Democrats missed an opportunity to challenge Reagan conservatism on its own turf. Advocacy of fiscal conservatism, a strong national defense, welfare reform, and recognition of moral issues might have enabled Democrats to frame arguments in less heated partisan terms.

As the 1984 presidential election approached, Reagan had effectively cemented support from his right wing. The Democrats entered the election divided, but in the end they nominated Walter F. Mondale, a protégé of Hubert Humphrey and former vice president under Jimmy Carter.[37] Mondale's nomination revealed the continuing power of organized labor within the Democratic party. At the urging of NOW, he chose Representative Geraldine Ferraro (D-New York), a liberal feminist, as his running mate.[38] NOW leaders convinced Mondale that by choosing a woman he could exploit a gender gap evident in Reagan's 1980 vote. As an experienced politician, Mondale knew that NOW's refusal to endorse Carter in 1980 had damaged his chances for reelection. Mondale's nomination, his selection of Ferraro, and his liberal program came under attack by Republicans as the politics of old-style liberalism. Mondale tried to deflect this image by attacking Reagan as anti-poor and anti-minority, but in 1984 such rhetoric sounded tired and desperate.

Reagan's optimism contrasted sharply with Mondale's pessimistic picture of an America in decline. No doubt, the turnaround in the economy strengthened the electorate's perception that Reagan was right: Things were getting better. Reagan's ad campaign, particularly one spot titled "Morning in America," projected an image of a restored America, a nation confident and forward-looking. On Election Day, Reagan swept the Electoral College and the popular vote, receiving 54.4 million votes to win 525 electoral votes. Mondale's anemic popular vote of 37.6 million won him only 13 electoral votes. A small margin of fewer than 4,000 votes gave him Minnesota; otherwise he would have lost his own state along with every other state in the union. The election was a triumph for Reagan's powerful and positive message.

This landslide, however, did not translate into an easy ride for Republicans in Congress.[39] They picked up only 14 seats in the House, to bring their total to 182 seats compared with the Democrats' 253. These gains failed to make up for the losses in 1982. Entering the election, Republican strategists had believed that they could pick up 22 to 25 seats. The good news for Reagan was that conservative Democrats picked up states in the South. In the Senate, Republicans lost 2 seats, reducing their majority to 53–47. Political observers noted that many Democrats disassociated themselves from the national Mondale-Ferraro ticket, but the election did not reveal party realignment.

The most exciting news for the Republicans came with the reelection of Republican Jesse Helms in North Carolina against Democratic governor James B. Hunt, Jr. The campaign was the most expensive in Senate history—$22 million—and vicious. Following his election to the Senate in 1972, Helms had forged a conservative network. He had joined with U.S. Senator James Buckley (R-New York), the brother of William F. Buckley, Jr., and Senator Carl Curtis (R-Nebraska) in forming the Republican Steering Committee, a group of conservative senators. At the same time he formed the National Congressional Club with the help of Richard Viguerie to help pay off his campaign debt. He gradually enlarged this organization to support other conservative candidates. Through the National Congressional Club, he also established corporate entities including foundations and think tanks to challenge the liberal establishment. Included among these organizations were the Institute of American Relations, the Center for a Free Society, the Institute on Money and Inflation, and the American Family Institute.

Through his Congressional Club, Helms emerged as a major force in conservative politics. For example, in 1979, the Congressional Club and other Helms-controlled organizations contributed more than $250,000 to the political campaigns of Steven Symms (R-Idaho), Senator Gordon Humphrey (R-New Hampshire), and Representative Larry McDonald (D-Georgia).[40] In the Senate, Helms stood as a leader of conservative opposition to SALT II—urging the United States to "try a SALT-free diet"—and a major critic of the new Sandinista government in Nicaragua. He spoke in favor of pro-family positions, opposed abortion and the ERA, and supported school prayer.[41]

Helms was a major supporter of Reagan in his 1976 bid against Ford. In 1975 Helms had even explored the possibility of a third-party challenge by Reagan against Ford, but Reagan decided to make this fight within the GOP itself. When Reagan won in 1980, however, Helms showed an independent streak that often placed him to the right of the president. He opposed Reagan's call for cigarette labeling; he filibustered against the extension of the 1965 Voting Rights Act; and only after immense pressure exerted by the administration would he support the controversial $99 billion tax-increase bill that came before the Senate in 1982. He came out against declaring the birthday of Martin Luther King, Jr., a national holiday.

As the 1984 Senate campaign opened, Hunt sought to portray Helms as a lone ranger who stood to the right of Reagan. Hunt portrayed himself, meanwhile, as a reasonable conservative who favored increased defense spending, deployment of the MX missile, development of the B-1 and Stealth bombers, and who opposed a nuclear freeze. He was pro-business and supported voluntary school prayer. Both sides rallied their supporters nationwide. Jerry Falwell, head of the Moral Majority based in Lynchburg, Virginia, flew to North Carolina on behalf of Helms to help register one hundred fifty thousand new religious voters through a drive coordinated by fundamentalist churches. The conservative religious activist Reverend Coy Privette sold the North Carolina Baptist State Convention's computerized mailing list to Helms. In turn, Hunt invited the civil rights leader Jesse Jackson to the state for a voter registration drive aimed at African-American voters. When Helms supporters attacked Jesse Jackson's involvement, Hunt accused Helms of appealing to fear on the part of white voters, while the Helms campaign replied, "Who's the racist? the guy out trying to register black voters so they can elect him to the Senate or the guy who's just saying what's going on?"[42]

In the frenzied final days of the campaign, rhetoric on both sides became venomous. Helms's supporters claimed that Hunt had accepted funds from gay activists. Hunt's campaign sought to link Helms to "a tight network of radical rightwing groups" that included Jerry Falwell, Texas oil billionaire Nelson Bunker Hunt, Salvadoran right-wing leader Roberto D'Aubuisson, and Korean evangelist Reverend Sun Myung Moon. In the end, Hunt faced two insurmountable problems: Ronald Reagan and Walter Mondale. Hunt's portrayal of Helms as an extremist within his own party was defused when Reagan came to North Carolina to campaign on behalf of Helms. By contrast, Hunt found it difficult to disassociate himself from the Mondale-Ferraro ticket. Helms took advantage of this vulnerability when he declared in the second and final debate: "Mr. Hunt is a Mondale liberal and ashamed of it. And I'm a Reagan conservative and proud of it."[43]

Reagan carried North Carolina by 62 percent, and Helms won the state with 52 percent of the vote. In addition, the GOP won the Tar Heel governorship, several additional congressional seats, and legislative and county courthouse positions. The Democratic erosion in North Carolina was repeated throughout the South, but Helms's victory in particular was excruciatingly painful for liberals. Exit polls showed that born-again Christians split 60 to 40 percent for Helms, but voters who considered themselves conservative voted three to one for him. Helms credited the registration of thousands of new voters by fundamentalist churches as critical to his victory. Falwell had registered many of these voters, but fundamentalist pastors and churches had also conducted independent registration drives. This was yet another indication of the power of evangelical and fundamentalist churches in the shaping of Republican politics in the South and throughout the nation.[44] At the same time, the close contest indicated a Democratic strategy for attacking conservative Republicans like Helms. Hunt was a liberal, but in his campaign he moved to the right, calling for a strong national defense and a balanced budget. He identified himself as a Christian. At the same time, he did not back away from his strong position on civil rights.

Hunt's defeat disappointed his liberal supporters, who were further discouraged by conservative victories in other states. In Texas, the conservative congressman Phil Gramm won a decisive victory for Republican John Tower's seat, capturing 59 percent of the vote. Furthermore, Texas Republicans won ten of the twenty-seven House seats, a remarkable feat given that only a decade before they had counted their GOP representatives on one hand. Dick Armey, a Republican newcomer, overwhelmed the incumbent Democrat Tom Vandergriff in Fort Worth's 26th District. Republican Joe Barton won in the 6th District, a seat that was vacated by Phil Gramm, who had won the seat in a special election after switching to the Republican party in 1983. In New Hampshire, the conservative Republican Bob Smith garnered 59 percent of the vote to win a second term in the Senate. Democrats had hoped for an upset in Mississippi, but Thad Cochran easily won reelection with 61 percent of the vote.

These 1984 victories were important for extending Republican power in the South, but the GOP's failure to win more seats on the coattails of a presidential landslide indicated that a political realignment had not occurred. Only a few within the Democratic party sensed disarray in their own ranks. One of them was Virginia's Charles Robb, who declared, "There's a feeling that our party has become not a party of the whole but simply a collection of special interests that are narrower than the national interest."[45]

Reagan's Second Term: Squandered Victory

In 1983, the American economy began one of the longest economic booms in its history. Yet even with prosperity the federal government continued to face rising budget deficits, the result of escalated defense spending, built-in spending increases for Social Security and Medicare, tax cuts, and congressional failure to reduce discretionary social spending. Republicans, worried about a potential voter backlash over the deficits, pushed through the Balanced Budget and Emergency Deficit Control Act (1985). Included in the bill was an amendment proposed by Senators Phil Gramm (R-Texas) and Warren Rudman (R-New Hampshire) that set a national debt ceiling and created a mechanism for the comptroller general to implement budget cuts. The bill, which was signed by Ronald Reagan shortly before Christmas 1985, looked good on paper but allowed Congress to adjust deficit ceilings to suit its ends. In any case, the Supreme Court ruled in the summer of 1986 that the law violated the separation of powers by requiring an executive branch agency, the comptroller general, to undertake budget cuts—the so-called line-item veto. Budget cuts were the responsibility of Congress, not the executive branch.

Although deficits plagued the administration throughout Reagan's second term, the president accomplished what many insiders thought impossible—income tax reform. He did so by working with reform minded Democrats in Congress. Tax reform legislation had been proposed by presidential hopefuls Representative Richard Gephardt (D-Missouri) and Senator Bill Bradley (D-New Jersey), who were eager to show a different Democratic party face to middle-class voters. From Reagan's perspective, the mammoth tax code regulations were a reflection of bloated government, wasteful bureaucracy, and spendthrift politicians. Reagan understood that to change that situation he needed to work with Democrats. He would also need to confront lobbyists, corporations, and interest groups that benefited from preferential credits, deductions, exemptions, and subsidies. To that end, Secretary of the Treasury Donald Regan, before he became chief of staff, oversaw the development of a plan to simplify the tax code. The plan was based on legislation proposed by Gephardt and Bradley. President Reagan introduced the plan in his State of the Union address in January 1984.

The legislation came before Congress in 1986 and gained the support of the House Ways and Means Committee chairman, Dan Rostenkowski (D-Illinois), and the Senate Finance Committee chairman, Bob Packwood (R-Oregon). Rostenkowski was critical in bringing Democrats into line; without his support, the Democratic-controlled House would never have voted in favor of the bill. Reagan signed the Tax Reform Act in August 1986. The measure reduced the number of tax brackets, dropped the top marginal rate to 28 percent, removed millions of low-income people from the tax rolls by raising the personal exemption level, increased corporate taxes, and eliminated many loopholes for corporations and interest groups. This reform measure stimulated investment in new technology, brought greater equity to the tax structure, and simplified the code.[46] Although Democrats were instrumental in getting the bill enacted, many within the party were reluctant to associate with a low-tax strategy because it undermined party rhetoric that tax cuts benefited the rich.

Tax reform became part of the Reagan legacy, but the administration will probably be best remembered for ending the Cold War. In his second term, Reagan and Soviet Premier Mikhail Gorbachev achieved substantial disarmament.[47] After undertaking a massive arms buildup, Reagan announced in January 1984 that reducing the risk of war, especially nuclear war, was the number one priority of his administration.[48] This announcement set the stage for a series of critical bilateral summit meetings in Geneva in November 1985; Reykjavik, Iceland, in October 1986; Washington, D.C., in December 1987; and Moscow in May 1988. In these meetings Reagan and Gorbachev reached agreements that changed the course of history. The Intermediate Nuclear Forces Treaty, signed in December 1987, was the first agreement to eliminate an entire class of existing nuclear weapons. Discussions between the two world leaders set the stage for the signing of the START I Treaty, which dramatically reduced America's strategic arsenal by 25 percent and the Soviet

Union's by 35 percent. The following year, President George H. W. Bush and Gorbachev's successor, Boris Yeltsin, signed the START II Treaty, which reduced nuclear arsenals by another 50 percent and abolished land-based Multiple Independently Targeted Reentry Vehicles (MIRVs).

Furthermore, by encouraging Gorbachev's reform policies within the Soviet Union, Reagan played a role in the eventual dismantling of the Soviet empire in Eastern Europe. In the summer of 1989, Poland installed a non-Communist government. The revolution in Poland was followed by the tearing down of the Berlin Wall and the collapse of the hardline Communist regime in East Germany. As the year 1989 drew to a close, Communist regimes collapsed in nearly every Soviet bloc country except Albania. Gorbachev's leadership was critical, but Reagan's role was also essential to this change; it would not have occurred without him. The world appeared to be a much safer place when Reagan left office in 1988, though Islamic terrorism was a problem that had become apparent in a series of attacks on American troops and kidnappings of American officials. The administration's response was that it would not negotiate with terrorists, but this claim was belied by what became known as the Iran-Contra affair.

The Iran-Contra scandal grew out of the administration's determination to pursue a strong anti-Communist policy in Central America despite opposition from Congress.[49] The events that emerged revealed an administration seeking to use the powers of the White House to circumvent liberal opposition in Congress, as well as the State Department bureaucracy. This Byzantine affair began with a series of missteps that escalated into a political disaster. Intent on overthrowing a Nicaraguan government that was pro-Soviet, pro-Castro, and determined to export revolution to its neighbor El Salvador, William Casey, the director of the CIA, instructed National Security Council staff member Lieutenant Colonel Oliver North to contact Robert Owen, a Washington-based lobbyist, to solicit funds and assistance for the Contras. Private efforts to support the Contras charged Major General Richard Secord, a recently retired Air Force officer, and retired General John Singlaub, with coordinating weapons drops to the anti-Sandinista Contras. General Singlaub worked through the recently revitalized United States Council on World Freedom, which was affiliated with the World Anti-Communist League (WACL). WACL had been involved in supporting anti-Communist resistance in Angola, Mozambique, Ethiopia, Cambodia, Vietnam, and Afghanistan.

The administration developed a complex plan, headed by North, to supply the Contras through profits earned by selling missiles to anti-American Iranians and pro-American Saudi Arabians. North later claimed the missiles were sold to Iran to persuade pro-Iranian radical groups to release American hostages who were held in Lebanon. This plan was in direct contradiction to Reagan's declared policy of not negotiating with terrorists. Moreover, the use of public funds to supply arms to the Contras was in violation of the Boland amendment, though conservatives argued that the funds came from private sources and from the Israelis. The details of this bizarre plan were revealed to the public on November 25, 1986, when President Reagan and Attorney General Edwin Meese announced that the supplying of arms to the Contras and the trading of arms with the Iranians were connected.

A joint House-Senate investigative committee met in the summer of 1987 to investigate the Iran-Contra affair. Testimony extended over 250 hours on national television and was reminiscent of the Watergate hearings in its charges of illegality, circumvention of Congress, and abuse of White House powers. When Lieutenant Colonel North appeared before the committee in full-dress uniform defending his position, conservatives across the country rallied to his cause. Many of Reagan's opponents sought to implicate the president directly in the scandal, which could have been a cause for impeachment, but no smoking gun was found. A joint House-Senate committee report roundly criticized the administration and an independent prosecutor continued the investigation through 1992. In late 1992, President Bush pardoned key Reagan officials implicated in the affair, including Secretary of Defense Caspar Weinberger.

The Iran-Contra scandal damaged the Reagan administration and the conservative cause by bogging down White House officials in defending the president against charges that he had abused his powers by trying to circumvent explicit legislation found in the Boland amendment. Many blamed President Reagan's chief of staff, Donald Regan, for not putting a brake on the project in the first place and then not responding quickly to the controversy when it broke. He was asked to tender his resignation, as was National Security Advisor Admiral John Poindexter.

In trying to move past Iran-Contra, defense hawks formed the Coalition for America at Risk to support the administration's anti-Communist policies. This pro-administration group included such organizations as the American Security Council, the American Conservative Union, and Concerned Women for America; individual members included Secretary of Education William Bennett, Budget Director James Miller, and former White House communications director Patrick Buchanan. Still, not all conservatives were happy with the drift of the administration, either in its second-term replacements (for example, the moderate Republican Howard Baker replaced Donald Regan as chief of staff) or in Reagan's acceptance of arms control with the Soviet Union.[50]

Iran-Contra opened an opportunity for the Left to attack the Reagan administration and its anti-Communist policies. Congressional Democrats retreated from a full attack on the administration when polls showed that Americans overwhelmingly rallied to North's defense when he appeared before Congress. Democrats found themselves unable to link Reagan directly to knowledge of the arms-for-hostages and transfer of funds to the Contras. As establishment Democrats moderated their attacks, left-wing fringe groups gained headlines—which had the effect of associating the fringe Left with the Democratic party. Most notable in this regard was a $24 million suit brought by the pacifist Christic Institute in May 1986 against a group of Contra leaders, former U.S. military leaders, and government agencies, accusing them of participating in political assassinations, terrorism, gun-running, and drug smuggling. In June 1988 Federal District Judge James King dismissed the Christic suit as groundless, and in February 1989 he awarded $1 million to the defendants in attorney fees and court costs, declaring that the suit was based on "unsubstantiated rumor and speculation."[51]

The Christic Institute's accusations were wild, but the press nonetheless gave considerable attention to the suit. Moreover, many of the accusations were presented in a PBS *Frontline* documentary in the spring of 1989 that drew heavily from the book *Out of Control: The Story of the Reagan Administration's Secret War in Nicaragua, the Illegal Arms Pipeline, and the Contra Drug Connection,* written by the Christic Institute founder, Daniel Sheehan, and Leslie Cockburn.[52] More temperate liberals refused to accept these claims, and watchdog groups such as the Political Research Associates dismissed Sheehan and Cockburn as promoting a classic conspiracy theory. Unfortunately for the Democratic party, it was easy for Republicans to tar mainstream liberal Democrats with the antics of the fringe Left.

Nonetheless, the Reagan White House had to divert political capital and energy to protecting the administration from this scandal. One of the major casualties of Iran-Contra was Robert Bork, whom Reagan nominated to the Supreme Court in July 1987 following the resignation of Justice Lewis Powell. Conservatives welcomed Bork's nomination. He was a first-rate scholar, a former Yale Law School professor who espoused a legal doctrine of originalism (interpreting law according to the intent of the Framers) and a strict interpretation of the constitution. Bork had shown loyalty when he defended the legality of Nixon's firing of Archibald Cox during the Watergate crisis—the so-called Saturday Night Massacre. He was married to a devout Catholic who was well known in pro-life circles. Most Republicans believed that Bork would win confirmation, despite his conservative views.

Democrats understood that a Bork confirmation would be another step forward in the conservative takeover of the Court. Only the summer before, Associate Justice William Rehnquist had become Chief Justice following Warren Burger's retirement. To fill Rehnquist's seat Reagan nominated the conservative Antonin Scalia. As soon as Bork's nomination was announced, opponents mobilized to prevent confirmation. People for the American Way, a group organized by the television producer Norman Lear, launched a $2 million campaign to defeat Bork. The underlying issue dividing the sides was abortion, but liberals attacked Bork for his writings on civil rights, in which he had questioned several Court decisions. Bork was derided as bigoted, racist, and reactionary.

While Bork's opponents undertook a well-organized campaign to defeat the nomination, the White House did little to rally its troops. The new chief of staff, Howard Baker, was not a strong supporter of Bork, so he did little to organize political support to undermine the anti-Bork campaign. Bork's testimony before the Senate Judiciary Committee appeared dry and pedantic, but the real problem lay with a White House in trouble after the Iran-Contra scandal. The Senate Judiciary Committee voted against the confirmation in early October, and the nomination was rejected by the full Senate on October 23, 1987, in a fifty-eight to forty-two vote. Reagan nominated Judge Douglas Ginsberg, but Ginsberg withdrew after it was revealed that he had smoked marijuana as a professor at Harvard Law School. The administration then nominated and the Senate confirmed Anthony Kennedy, who proved to be mostly a disappointment for conservatives.

The mischaracterization of Bork's views poisoned the political atmosphere. Partisan passions flared in the House in Reagan's second term under Speaker of the House Jim Wright (D-Texas), who had replaced

Tip O'Neill when he retired after the 1986 election. Wright had a reputation as a wheeler-dealer before he stepped into the speaker's seat. He had only been in office a short time when a young Republican Representative from Georgia, Newt Gingrich, charged that Wright had taken a sweetheart deal on a privately published book by a political supporter that provided him with a 55 percent royalty fee (rather than the normal 5 to 15 percent). Gingrich organized a group of other conservatives to make Wright into a symbol of ethical problems in the House. Under pressure from Gingrich and his group, the House Ethics Committee launched an investigation into the matter. Shortly after the conclusion of the investigation, newspapers revealed that Wright's right-hand man, Tony Coelho (D-California), had been involved in a questionable junk-bond deal, leading to his resignation from the House on Memorial Day 1989. Under immense public pressure, Wright was forced to resign his seat in late May 1989. He was replaced by Thomas Foley (D-Washington). Once the dust had settled, it was clear that the House had become a cauldron of bubbling partisan animosities.

Partisan rhetoric found expression in Democrats' accusations that the Reagan administration represented class politics at its worst. Reagan's critics charged that his policies had created economic disaster, accelerated America's deindustrialization, and cut a hole in the welfare safety net protecting displaced workers and the inner-city poor. Reagan was accused of shrinking the middle class and creating a nation of haves and have-nots. Critics contended that his tax cuts for corporations and the wealthy and his cuts in social welfare programs amounted to a war against the poor.[53] Newspapers, nightly network news, movies, and television programs shone a spotlight on homelessness in America, arguing that federal cutbacks in welfare and housing programs as well as alcohol and drug rehabilitation programs had created millions of homeless in America. Moreover, the face of homelessness had changed: the homeless were no longer just down-and-out single men but fathers and mothers and their children who were discovered living in their cars, unsafe residential hotels, or Salvation Army centers. Democrats blamed the crisis on the budgetary austerity and heartless social policy instituted by Reagan conservatives.

Stories of the homeless abounded in newspapers and popular magazines. From 1981 to 1988, the *New York Times* carried 1,585 articles on the homeless, reaching a peak in 1988, when 303 articles on the subject appeared. Another 289 articles appeared in magazines in this same period.[54] From the nightly news to television movies, the homeless problem filled the airwaves. The Center for Media and Public Affairs reported that from November 1986 through 1989, ABC, CBS, and NBC evening newscasts devoted 103 television stories lasting 3 hours and 31 minutes to the homeless in America.[55] Television movies such as *Home Sweet Homeless* (1988) and *No Place Like Home* (1989) showed that anyone might become homeless. The Hollywood entertainment lawyer and television producer Ken Kragen introduced millions of Americans to the plight of the homeless, raising huge sums of money when he organized "Hands across America," in which 5 million Americans held hands across the continent for 15 minutes to show that the homeless did not stand alone. Books, too, abounded on the homeless problem. Jonathan Kozol's *Rachel and Her Children: Homeless Families in America* reached the *New York Times* best-seller list.[56] Welfare cuts, homelessness, and Reagan's America became synonymous for many of Reagan's critic in the 1980s.

In the 1970s, welfare programs such as Aid to Families with Dependent Children (AFDC) had come under criticism. Charles Murray's *Losing Ground: American Social Policy, 1950–1980* (1984), a libertarian critique of the welfare state, became a best seller. Other experts eventually reached similar conclusions concerning the unintended effects of welfare dependency. In the early 1990s, Christopher Jencks, one of the nation's most brilliant and independent-minded social scientists, wrote two books, *Rethinking Social Policy* (1992) and *The Homeless* (1994), that examined with scalpel precision problems related to the breakdown of the family, drug and alcohol dependency, and sexual mores among America's poor. His contention that there were fewer than a million homeless in America drew especially strong criticism from activists who claimed that he had underestimated the numbers of the "hidden" homeless. Jencks argued that homelessness was due to a complex set of social problems, a misplaced emphasis on individual autonomy by liberals, and cutbacks in mental health facilities by conservatives—as well as misconceived social policies that allowed drug and alcohol addicts to indulge their habits.[57]

Contrary to this pessimistic assessment of the Reagan years by critics in the 1980s, later, more sophisticated research revealed that real incomes rose nearly twice as fast and consumption increased as much as one-third faster than original projections made during the Reagan years.[58] Evidence showed that the middle class was not shrinking at all. Moreover, the proportion of Americans in the upper-income groups grew by almost 5 percent. Put another way, people on the whole moved up during the Reagan years, though the number of people at the very bottom also increased. Declining interest rates encouraged Americans to go on a massive shopping spree, buying new appliances like microwave ovens, so that by the end of the decade two out of every three homes had one. More Americans ate out than ever before, dining on a rich variety of ethnic and gourmet foods. They shopped at new, trendy stores such as The Gap, The Limited, and Banana Republic and discount stores such as Circuit City, Home Depot, and Wal-Mart. They went to shopping malls, which increased in number during the decade from twenty-two thousand to thirty-six thousand. Similarly, lower mortgage rates led Americans to buy new homes that were larger and better equipped than what they had known.[59] Although Americans as a whole became more prosperous, there was nonetheless a widening gap between the very rich and the very poor that allowed critics to accuse the Reagan administration of benefiting only the rich.

The portrait of Reagan as a distant, removed president was also projected into the policy debate over Human Immunodeficiency Virus (HIV) and Acquired Immune Deficiency Syndrome (AIDS). Although the origin of HIV/AIDS remains controversial, the disease was first identified in the United States shortly after Reagan came into office. The disease quickly reached epidemic proportions, primarily among gay men and drug users. It found its way into the medical blood supply, infecting those in need of blood transfusions. The full extent of its spread became known to public health officials in the San Francisco area when large numbers of homosexuals began dying from opportunistic diseases that attacked the deficient immune systems of their victims. Initially, gay activists denied that homosexuals were especially vulnerable to HIV/AIDS, but as the mortality rate escalated, homosexuals called for federal intervention for research, treatment, and care for those infected with the disease.

Alarmed by the spread of the disease, public health officials at the local, state, and federal levels launched intensive research and public education efforts. Activists claimed, however, that more needed to be done and accused the Reagan administration of not committing federal research money to a national epidemic in order to avoid alienating the Christian Right. The Christian Right's suggestion that HIV/AIDS was God's infliction for unnatural and sinful behavior outraged gay activists. They were agitated further when the conservative columnist Patrick Buchanan wrote that "nature is exacting an awful retribution" for a sexual revolution that had "begun to devour its children."[60] Critics who felt that the Reagan administration was avoiding the AIDS epidemic noted that in 1981–1982 the Centers for Disease Control spent more on research into Legionnaire's Disease than on AIDS research.

The Reagan administration treated the HIV/AIDS issue as a public health concern. There is no archival evidence that the White House sought to exploit the epidemic to benefit an antigay agenda aimed at appeasing the Religious Right.[61] Although Reagan did not speak out about AIDS until 1985, Secretary of Health and Human Resources Margaret Heckler called the public's attention to the epidemic in 1983. In a public address to the U.S. Mayors Conference in June, she reported that her department had budgeted $26.5 million on research into the disease for that year, including a transfer of $12 million from other health areas. Moreover, she reported that Reagan had requested from Congress the authority to transfer these funds. The mayor of San Francisco, Dianne Feinstein, chairman of a Conference of Mayors study group, declared that Heckler's remarks showed that the Reagan administration was "fully committed to putting all available resources" behind the fight to conquer AIDS.[62]

Heckler's speech drew immediate criticism from Howard Phillips of the Conservative Caucus. Phillips accused the administration of capitulating to gay activists. To head off a conservative backlash against its HIV/AIDS policy, the White House arranged a meeting between Phillips and others from the Conservative Caucus and administration officials, including Faith Ryan Whittlesey and Morton Blackwell, who served as official White House liaison with conservative groups. At the meeting, Phillips asserted that the public had not been told enough about AIDS, specifically that sexual promiscuity was the major cause for spreading the disease. He wanted the administration to come out and publicly condemn homosexuality as a moral wrong and link it to the AIDS outbreak. Although other representatives of the Conservative Caucus did not join Phillips in this request, they did urge the administration to consider ordering the closure of bathhouses as a health menace, just as public health officials had closed public pools during the polio epidemic. Phillips also recommended that federal policy require all blood donors to fill out forms detailing their sexual habits.[63]

The Reagan administration did not act on these recommendations. Reagan officials noted that the American Blood Commission and the American Association of Blood Banks believed that a written questionnaire would do no more to prevent false replies concerning HIV/AIDS symptoms among donors than current practices that relied on predonation verbal interviews. Phillips was not placated by the meeting. In late August 1983, he wrote to Secretary Heckler to inform her that he was "shocked at the extent of your pandering to win votes from the homosexual community even at the risk of jeopardizing the health of the public at large." He advised, "A little less research and a little more quarantine might discourage homosexuals from further infecting themselves and polluting millions of innocent victims." Noted for his bluntness, Phillips added that "homosexuality may be very fashionable in Washington, D.C. and in the corridors of HHS, but most Americans recognize it to be a pattern of behavior which the government should actively discourage rather than seemingly condone and endorse."[64] Phillips enclosed an undated publication from Phyllis Schlafly's Eagle Forum titled "The ERA–Gay Rights Connection" that warned that the "goal of 'gay rights' legislation is not merely to assure the right of consenting adults to exercise their sexual preferences in private. They want public recognition that homosexuality/lesbianism is a socially acceptable lifestyle. They want the rights of husbands and wives."[65]

The Religious Right differed from the Reagan administration in how to handle the AIDS epidemic. Administration policymakers saw AIDS as a health problem and did not want to treat it publicly as a moral problem. The Religious Right, as evidenced in Phillips's remarks, saw the epidemic as a problem of moral misbehavior. They believed that gay and feminist activists were engaged in a campaign, conducted on multiple fronts, to change tradition and law to provide homosexuals with preferential rights including marriage rights, partner benefits, and employment preferences. Religious conservatives urged a political campaign to counter these demands.

Whatever Ronald Reagan personally believed about homosexuality, he had opposed Proposition 6 on the California ballot in 1978 calling for the dismissal of state-employed teachers who openly promoted homosexuality. Although his biographer Edmund Morris quoted Reagan as pondering, "Maybe the Lord brought down this plague," the Reagan administration expanded AIDS research.[66] Indeed, on September 17, 1985, Ronald Reagan announced that the federal government had targeted a half billion dollars for research on AIDS. In his State of the Union address on February 6, 1986, he announced that the AIDS fight was being given the highest priority within the administration.[67] Conservative defenders of Reagan later claimed that the federal government under Reagan spent an estimated $5.7 billion on AIDS.[68]

Whatever complaints some conservatives had of Reagan in office, by the time he left the presidency he had become an icon for conservatives. He had shown that a conservative could win the White House running as a conservative. He had changed the political landscape and political conversation. Yet Democrats had thwarted a conservative revolution. Reagan's success was further circumscribed by the administration's inability to realign the political parties. Democrats had prevented a radical downsizing of government or an extensive scaling back of entitlement programs. Reagan's promise to balance the budget as president remained unfulfilled, leaving the country with a huge public debt. He blamed this failure on what he described as an alliance composed of "parts of Congress, the media, and special interest groups." He believed that this alliance had prevented him from accomplishing a comprehensive program of domestic reform. He declared, "When I came into office, I found the Presidency a weakened institution. I found a Congress that was trying to transform our government into a quasi-parliamentary system. And I found in Washington a colony—that through an iron triangle—was attempting to rule the Nation . . . But we have not restored constitutional balance, at least not fully, and I believe it must be restored."[69] The next four years would bring the GOP Right no closer to restoring to government what it saw as constitutional balance.

8

Democrats Rebound

Ronald Reagan took conservatives to within sight of the Promised Land, but the march was far from over. For Republicans on the Right the next twelve years were characterized by skirmish, pitched battle, retreat, and indecisive victory. The experience of their opponents was much the same. As the century drew to a close, neither Republicans nor Democrats, the Right or the Left, could claim absolute victory. In the end, the best that could be said for conservatives was that the political battles of the 1990s had tempered and strengthened the Republican Right. Democrats were left divided and leaderless.

Reagan's successor, George H. W. Bush, won the presidency in 1988 against the evanid Michael Dukakis, a progressive governor of Massachusetts. In the campaign Bush ran as a conservative, but once in office he moved to the center. His presidency ultimately marked a setback for conservatives. His defeat for reelection in 1992 revealed that a successful Republican candidate needed to mobilize the conservative base. This base was larger than Robertson's Christian Coalition or any single conservative organization. Simply to receive Robertson's endorsement, as Bush had in 1992, was not enough to win an election; a successful candidate would need to win over all conservative voters. For a Republican candidate to ignore this conservative base or take these voters for granted was a fatal mistake. This was a lesson George H. W. Bush was taught in 1992, when Bill Clinton, the governor of Arkansas, ran a centrist campaign to win the White House.

Republicans learned this lesson well. In 1994, led by Representative Newt Gingrich (R-Georgia), they mobilized their base to gain control of Congress for the first time since 1946. The Republican takeover of Congress eventually pushed President Clinton to accept welfare reform and a balanced budget. Although in his first two years in office President Clinton appeared to capitulate to the left wing of his party, once he realized that his reelection for a second term was at stake, he shifted course to distance himself from the Left.

Clinton won elections in 1992 and 1996 running as a New Democrat who sounded at times more conservative than his rivals. This turn to centrism came after the Democratic party had suffered defeats running liberals in 1984 (Mondale) and 1988 (Dukakis). The apparent political lesson offered was that Democrats could win the White House by presenting themselves as centrists. This was an easy lesson to learn and a difficult one to carry out even if taken to heart. Winning the Democratic nomination as a centrist in primaries dominated by Democratic activists and interest groups was a formidable task that called for the political dexterity of someone like Clinton. Even with his great political abilities, though, Clinton was unable to win a majority in the popular vote in 1992 or 1996. By itself the liberal base of the party was not large enough to win the presidency, and the larger conservative vote—about 35 percent of the electorate, compared with the 22 percent identified as liberal—was in the hands of the Republicans. Neither the conservative base of the Republican party nor the liberal base of the Democratic party appeared large enough to elect their candidates outright, so the fight was over the center-moderate voters and independent voters. Republicans, because of their larger base, had a jump on Democrats. They had a further advantage in that moderate voters tended to be more conservative-moderate than liberal-moderate.

Given this political configuration, the Clinton strategy made sense. In the 1990s, Clinton showed Democrats how to win the presidency. Bush showed his party how to lose the White House. These were the lessons of history, and whichever party best learned them held the future in its hands.

Bush Wins an Election Helped by Reagan's Popularity

Reagan passed the mantle of the presidency to George H. W. Bush.[1] Bush knew that to win the nomination he needed to allay conservatives' suspicions that he was not really loyal to the Reagan cause. He needed to appeal to groups such as the National Rifle Association (NRA), the Christian Coalition, the network of right-wing radio hosts led by Rush Limbaugh, and a constellation of think tanks and activist interest groups that had sprung up across America.[2] Bush claimed to be a Texan, but many conservatives continued to see him as a representative of the elitist eastern wing of the Republican party—those internationalist, big government, "me-too" Republicans.

To counter these concerns, Bush undertook an extensive campaign to convince conservatives that he was one of them. He declared himself pro-life; he emphasized his Christian faith; and he affirmed his loyalty to Reagan's agenda. He won the endorsement of the Reverend Jerry Falwell, founder of the Moral Majority. He spoke before conservative groups throughout the country declaring himself a social, economic, and political conservative. His work paid off: Bush entered the Republican primaries as a front-runner ahead of primary challenger Robert Dole, the U.S. senator from Kansas, and the television evangelist Pat Robertson, whom few gave any chance of success. Some conservatives endorsed Representative Jack Kemp (R-New York), but Kemp's propensity to lecture audiences on esoteric economic theory failed to ignite enthusiasm. Pierre "Pete" Du Pont, the governor of Delaware, found that even his eastern-educated rival, George H. W. Bush, came across as more a man of the people than he was. (Bush pointedly referred to Du Pont as "Pierre" during debates.) General Alexander Haig, while displaying a sharp sense of humor about himself, remained a trace element in the Iowa caucuses—an unexplained presence barely registering on the charts.

Bush was stunned when Dole won the Iowa primary and Pat Robertson came in second. Bush responded in New Hampshire with a well-organized and well-financed campaign. He had courted the hardcore conservative Nackey Loeb, the publisher of the *Manchester Union Leader.* The support of the state's governor, John Sununu, provided additional firepower. Bush donned a down jacket, drove an eighteen-wheeler around Cuzzin Ritchie's Truck Stop, and had coffee with the locals. No longer was he a patrician with a devotion to public service and a résumé to prove it: Bush was reconfigured into a "man of the people." His instincts were not to go negative, but his campaign staff, especially Roger Ailes and Lee Atwater, convinced him to go on the attack. The Bush campaign began identifying Dole as a Washington, D.C., millionaire. Dole was accused of wanting to raise income taxes and cut Social Security benefits. Bush insisted that Dole take the pledge of "no new taxes" and renounce his call for "painful solutions" to the budget deficits. The campaign was aimed at New Hampshire Republicans, one of the most fervent antitax constituencies in the Western world.[3] In the end, Bush swept the state, winning 38 percent to Dole's 28 percent. Other challengers—Jack Kemp, Pete du Pont, Pat Robertson, and Al Haig—barely registered on the scale. Dole left in a foul mood. On the night of the primary, he lashed out at Bush on national television, challenging him to "stop lying about my record." Bush, for his part, replied, "Thank you, New Hampshire."

Dole refused to concede defeat, even though his campaign was poorly organized and he faced a rival who had Reagan's support. Dole thought he might have a chance on the newly instituted Super Tuesday, March 8, when sixteen Republican primaries would be held, many of them in the South. He hoped to convince southerners that Bush was not really a conservative and therefore not a rightful heir to the Reagan crown. Dole did pick up some important conservative endorsements, including Barry Goldwater, Jeane Kirkpatrick, and Senator Strom Thurmond (R-South Carolina), but their support did not help. Dole was crushed on March 8. Typical was South Carolina, where Bush won 49 percent to Dole's 21 percent. Bush's endorsement by Jerry Falwell and Pat Roberson had certainly helped. Their support revealed that the Moral Majority and the Christian Coalition had moved closer to the GOP establishment and relinquished their claim as an independent faction within the Republican party. For his part, Bush played up the religious angle by telling crowds that he accepted Jesus Christ as his personal Savior.[4] Analysis showed that Bush won the evangelical and fundamentalist Christian votes, as well as the military vote. Those voters were leery of Dole's position on abortion and did not accept his accusations that Bush was a "wimp" on defense. Overall, Bush won 57 percent of all votes cast on Super Tuesday and won every contested state. When Dole lost Illinois a week later, it was all over. Bush went on to win the Republican nomination.

Meanwhile, the Democrats became embroiled in a heated campaign among Senator Gary Hart (D-Colorado), Congressman Richard Gephardt (D-Missouri), Senator Al Gore (D-Tennessee), Senator Paul Simon (D-Illinois), the civil rights activist Jesse Jackson, and Massachusetts Governor Michael Dukakis (D-Massachusetts). The race came down to Michael Dukakis and Jesse Jackson. When Jackson won Michigan with 53 percent of the vote in late March, mainstream Democrats rallied to Dukakis's cause and gave him the nomination.[5]

Nonetheless, many Democrats worried that Dukakis, a Massachusetts liberal, was a weak candidate. Although he claimed to have turned Massachusetts from a declining industrial state to a high-tech growth state, it was not clear what role he had played in this transformation. During the campaign he showed an instinct to go for the jugular—pushing Senator Joseph Biden (D-Delaware) out of the race with charges that he had plagiarized a speech from a British Laborite politician and running negative ads against the "flip-flops" of Richard Gephardt. But on the campaign trail Dukakis was self-righteous, moralistic, and thin-skinned. He fired his campaign manager, John Sasso, and replaced him with Harvard Law School professor Susan Estrich. Later, he had to bring Sasso back into the campaign. Dukakis's problems ran deeper than staffing, however. Early in the primaries he told the Sunday news program *Meet the Press* that he would not oppose a Soviet "client" state in Latin America provided that the Soviet Union did not introduce nuclear weapons into the region. The Gore campaign pounced on these issues. Gore challenged Dukakis to defend his law-and-order record when he brought up a case involving a convicted felon, Willie Horton, who had brutally raped and tortured an innocent couple after being released on a Massachusetts furlough program supported by Dukakis. The Horton story had appeared in the mass-circulation monthly *Reader's Digest* and would be exploited by the Republicans in the general campaign.

Despite his vulnerabilities, Dukakis entered the general election campaign ahead in the polls as Bush's popular image remained faint and unimpressive. Bush's momentum going into the Republican Convention slowed further when he selected Senator Dan Quayle (R-Indiana) as his running mate. Quayle was seen by political insiders as a weak choice, and many observers suggested that Bush chose him because he feared he might pale alongside a stronger running mate. The selection revived the "wimp" issue that had plagued Bush during the primaries—and, in fact, extended back to his 1980 presidential bid. Quayle, it might be noted, had gained a reputation as a good campaigner by defeating Birch Bayh for the Senate in 1980 and then easily winning reelection against what at the time appeared to be a formidable female candidate. Concerned with the alleged "gender gap" within the Republican party, Bush selected the tall, youthful, and good-looking Quayle as a means of overcoming this problem. The media compared Quayle unfavorably with Dukakis's selection, the more experienced senator from Texas, Lloyd Bentsen.

The Republican Convention in New Orleans outlined the general themes for the rest of the campaign. On the positive side, Bush declared his loyalty to Reaganomics. Mimicking a line from a Clint Eastwood movie, Bush declared, "Read my lips: No new taxes." The line became unforgettable—unfortunately for Bush. In the speech Bush outlined what he thought were his opponent's negatives: Dukakis was a liberal afraid to use the "L-word"; he was soft on crime, allowing convicted criminals out of jail to commit more crimes; he had vetoed the bill requiring public school teachers to lead students in the Pledge of Allegiance in Massachusetts schools; and finally, Dukakis claimed too much for the Massachusetts miracle.

Conservatives were eager for Bush to go on the offensive, and they continued to worry about his fidelity to conservatism. Richard Viguerie declared that "voters want a decisive leader who is in touch with the people and who has an idea of where he wants to take the country."[6] Conservatives, Viguerie maintained, had elected Reagan, but they were not obligated to turn out for Bush. The editors of *National Review* echoed these sentiments by maintaining that the Bush campaign seemed to be running away from Reagan, as if he were an embarrassment. Later it was disclosed that when Bush's speechwriter Peggy Noonan inserted language denouncing abortion and moral decline into a speech drafted for the Texas Republican Convention, Bush deleted the section out of concern that it was "too extreme."[7] Bush wanted to win the conservative vote, but he had the instincts of a moderate. Yet he was a moderate who could play rough.

At the suggestion of Lee Atwater and James Pinkerton, Bush decided to single out the Willie Horton issue. Horton was an African-American man who had been convicted of first-degree murder for the brutal slaying and dismemberment of a seventeen-year-old gas-station attendant during an armed robbery on October 26, 1974, in Lawrence, Massachusetts. Sentenced to life in prison, he was given an unguarded forty-eight-hour furlough under a program set up initially by a Republican governor. Horton failed to return after the two-day leave. In April 1987, he broke into the home of twenty-eight-year-old Clifford Barnes in Oxon Hill, Maryland. He tortured Barnes for seven hours, then when Barnes's fiancée returned home from a wedding party, Horton raped her over a four-hour period. Horton was arrested and returned to prison. Dukakis came under attack but blocked legislation and a referendum to ban furloughs for first-degree murderers. Finally, he relented and agreed to legislation banning furloughs for convicted murderers. These events were covered in more than two hundred articles by two reporters for the Lawrence *Eagle-Tribune.*

The Bush campaign hit hard on this issue with a television spot called "Revolving Door." Filmed in black and white, the spot showed a procession of men in prison outfits passing through a gate. The voice-over reported that Dukakis had vetoed the death penalty and given furloughs to first-degree murderers as well as convicted kidnappers and rapists. Neither Horton's name nor his race was mentioned, and his photo was not seen in the spot because, as the producer explained, "we knew we would be hit with racism."[8]

The spot began appearing on October 5. From September 21 through October 4, however, another television spot had appeared showing Horton's mug shot. The spot, "Weekend Passes," was produced by the National Security Political Action Committee and its affiliate Americans for Bush. The group had been organized by Floyd Brown, a right-wing activist in Washington, D.C. Campaign finance reforms enacted by Congress following the Watergate scandals placed few limits on groups or individuals not affiliated with an official campaign. As a result, independent groups like Americans for Bush could produce independent spots.[9] Conservatives said the ad was about law and order and denied racist intent. Dukakis supporters claimed that the spots combined a fear of violent crime and black criminals into a racist appeal to voters. The Bush campaign distanced itself from the television spot and ordered Brown to change the name of his group, drop the word "Bush" from his organization's name, and declare that his group was not affiliated in any way with the Bush campaign.

Dukakis fell behind in the polls and simply could not land a knockout punch. By the end of the third debate between the two candidates, Bush had opened up a seventeen-point lead. On election night, Dukakis conceded defeat early. Bush-Quayle won 53.4 percent of the popular vote and forty states. Although Dukakis was soundly defeated, his 46 percent share of the popular vote was the highest of any Democratic candidate in the previous twenty years, with the exception of Jimmy Carter.[10] Still, voter turnout was the lowest of any election since 1924.

Bush was the first candidate since Richard Nixon to win the White House while his party lost seats in Congress. In the Senate, Democrats restored their 55–45 majority, coming within four seats of their pre-Reagan numbers in the Senate. The only bright signs were that two Republicans won hotly contested new seats: House Minority Whip Trent Lott of Mississippi and Representative Connie Mack in Florida. Bush's success in Mississippi and Florida provided the margin of victory for these two candidates. In the House, only six of the 408 incumbents running for re-election lost—four Republicans and two Democrats. As a result, Democrats held an 85-seat margin when Bush entered the White House.[11]

Bush Discards Reaganism and Loses

Without Reagan's support, Bush would not have won election to the White House. Yet once in office, Bush quickly discarded the Reagan imprimatur. Only a third of those working for Bush had previously worked for Reagan. Martin Anderson later complained to Bush's sympathetic biographer, Herbert Parmet, that a close look at Bush's appointments would reveal "a very systematic purge that went into effect of anyone with any association with the Reagan-Nixon-Goldwater wing of the party."[12] Relations between Bush and Dan Quayle remained tense as well because the White House believed that the vice president, prompted by his aide William Kristol, persistently undermined the Bush agenda in order to appeal to the right wing.

All presidents demand loyalty within their administrations and within their parties. Bush's purge revealed more than a demand for personal loyalty, however. He revealed that he was uncomfortable with the Reagan wing of the party and the Reagan ideology. He called for a "kinder, gentler" America, as if to contrast himself with the mean years of the Reagan era. He spoke instead about addressing the homeless problem in America and declared himself to be an education president.[13] Using a phrase coined by the speechwriter Peggy Noonan, Bush called for "a thousand points of light" to shine through community groups and individuals volunteering to help their neighbors. These were noble sentiments, but by distancing himself from Reagan, he signaled a belief that the Republican base lay in the center of the political spectrum and not on the right. The dilemma he confronted was how to hang on to his conservative base while moving to the political center.

Although he appointed conservative Jack Kemp to head Housing and Urban Development and the pro-life advocate Dr. Louis W. Sullivan to head Health and Human Services, Bush's other appointments showed his preference for long-time Bush loyalists and moderates. These appointments drew complaints from conservatives, but it was John Frohnmayer's appointment to head the National Endowment for the Arts (NEA) that became a lightning rod for the Right. Unable to wage a head-on attack against a Republican president, the GOP Right was reduced to fighting skirmishes against federal art policy, hardly a core issue. Still, the controversy made for good fundraising opportunities for conservative organizations unhappy with the general direction of the Bush administration.

Frohnmayer's appointment had been promoted by Mark Hatfield, the liberal Republican senator from Oregon. Frohnmayer arrived amid a battle over NEA funding. Controversy erupted in full force when Reverend Donald Wildmon, head of the American Family Association, called a press conference to denounce the NEA's funding of an exhibit that included "Piss Christ," a photo by Andres Serrano of a crucifix submerged in urine. The American Family Association had been founded in 1988 as a reincarnation of the eleven-year-old National Federation for Decency. Wildmon's protest led Senators Jesse Helms (R-North Carolina) and Alfonse D'Amato (R-New York), as well as thirty-six other senators, to denounce the NEA's inclusion of Serrano's photography in the exhibit. Shortly thereafter, in the spring of 1989, the director of the Corcoran Gallery in Washington, D.C., decided to cancel "The Perfect Moment," an exhibit of Robert Mapplethorpe's homoerotic photographs. The reason given for this cancellation was that the director feared the loss of federal funds—some of which would have been used indirectly for the exhibition. Mapplethorpe was a gay activist who believed that his art should reflect his aesthetics and politics. When the exhibit was cancelled, gay activists and cultural libertarians attacked the decision as repressive. The Christian Right, including the American Family Association, the Coalition on Revival (founded in 1987), and Pat Robertson's 700 Club, mobilized their constituents against spending taxpayers' money on art exhibits that they considered sacrilegious.

Not all critics of the NEA were religious. For example, the editors of *The New Criterion,* a leading conservative intellectual journal, joined the call for the NEA to uphold traditional aesthetic values. Established in 1982, the *New Criterion* sought to bring a conservative voice into the arts debate. The editors of the *New Criterion* said they were not anti-modernist, but they were opposed to cultural relativism and subjectivism in postmodernist contemporary art. Under the editorship of Hilton Kramer, and supported by the conservative John Olin Foundation, the *New Criterion* articulated a conservative aesthetic critique of post-modern art. Kramer had served as the art critic for the *Nation* from 1958 to 1961, and he was the art news editor of the *New York Times* from 1965 until 1982. Although often associated with the neoconservative strain of social and political ideas that emerged in the late 1970s, Kramer and his colleagues at the *New Criterion* offered eloquent, if sometimes hyperbolic, criticisms of meretricious postmodern ideology.[14]

Facing such critics, Frohnmayer sought to steer a delicate course by implementing policies that might appeal to congressional critics, while not alienating the art community. He began by canceling NEA grants to four recipients, including one to the lesbian performance artist Holly Hughes. This led to quick and heated attacks by liberals and the art community. Tensions were not eased when Frohnmayer initiated a policy of requiring NEA recipients to sign a pledge that they would not violate *Miller v. California* (1973), a Supreme Court decision that defined obscenity as material that violated "community standards," appealed to the prurient interest, and lacked serious literary or artistic merit.

Yet many conservatives believed that Frohnmayer had not been forceful enough in imposing new NEA standards. They accused him of reversing course at a press conference when he defended his decision to allow Endowment funding of the gay film *Poison*. Frohnmayer won the support of two Republican liberals on the NEA Council, Roy Goodman and Jocelyn Levi Strauss. Moreover, Frohnmayer announced that the Bush administration would not seek content restrictions on federal arts grants. As a result, for the next two and half years, the NEA under Frohnmayer was under continuous attack from congressional conservatives led by Representative Dana Rohrabacher (R-California) and Representative Mel Hancock (R-Missouri) in the House, and Jesse Helms (R-North Carolina) in the Senate. Stronger voices were heard outside of government. One of the more militant lobbying groups was Taxpayers for Accountability, a coalition composed of Phyllis Schlafly's Eagle Forum, Beverly LaHaye's Concerned Women for America, and Pat Robertson's 700 Club. The group called for the complete elimination of the

NEA and federal funding for art. John Frohnmayer resigned two years after taking office.[15]

Although Bush privately grumbled about conservatives' lack of support for his initiatives—complaints that grew in intensity with the passage of time—the administration appeared to do little to appease the conservative wing of the party. Bush's chief of staff, John Sununu, and Richard Darman, director of the Office of Management, displayed particular disregard for the right-wing base of the party. For example, Sununu expanded the role of Reagan's Liaison Office in the White House—initially established to maintain contact with conservatives—into an outreach program for all interest groups. Staff working with conservatives was reduced to a single individual. Sununu and Darman established reputations as being especially arrogant. Conservatives began to exchange stories of who in a given week had received the biggest insult from Sununu. John Podhoretz, who worked in the White House at the time, said a joke circulated among the White House staff that captured their arrogance: "Sununu thinks he's Jupiter and Darman thinks he's Saturn, and they treat us like Uranus."[16]

This arrogance led to a serious miscalculation when Bush nominated the former U.S. senator from Texas John Tower to become secretary of defense. Sununu and congressional pointman Fred McClure convinced Bush that they could get Tower confirmed, even though ugly rumors were already circulating about Tower's excessive drinking and womanizing. Many conservatives rallied to Tower's cause, but not all. Paul Weyrich and some other religious conservatives found Tower's behavior unacceptable in high office. In the end, Tower's nomination failed to win approval from the Senate Armed Services Committee, headed by the respected Sam Nunn (D-Georgia), and then was defeated by the Senate on March 9, 1989, in a fifty-three to forty-seven vote. Dick Cheney, former chief of staff for President Ford and minority whip for the new Congress, resigned his Wyoming seat to become the new secretary of defense.

The Tower defeat added another coal to the fires of partisanship in Congress, even while Bush tried to pursue a centrist policy. Partisan fervor was further heightened when conservative mavericks in the House led by Newt Gingrich (R-Georgia) forced the resignation of Representative Tony Coelho (D-California) and House Speaker Jim Wright (D-Texas) owing to ethics violations. Democrats were embittered by the loss of two of their leaders. "There's an evil wind blowing in the halls of Congress today," declared Texas Democrat Jack Brooks, which is "reminiscent of the Spanish Inquisition. We've replaced comity and compassion with hatred and malice."[17] Thomas Foley (D-Washington) became speaker of the sharply divided House.

Facing a conservative insurgency in the House, and fearful that his base might desert him, Bush took a strong stance against the Supreme Court's decision in *Texas v. Johnson* (1989), which overturned forty-eight state laws that banned the desecration of the American flag. He called for a constitutional amendment to protect the flag, but it failed to receive the necessary votes in the Senate.[18] In addition, the Bush administration tacked to the right on the abortion issue when his solicitor general filed an amicus brief before the Supreme Court that successfully exempted states from having to use their facilities or employees to perform abortions. These positions appealed to Bush's conservative base, but on other issues the president remained in the center. He lacked the political skills to satisfy his right wing while appealing to the general electorate. Too often Bush appeared to be zig-zagging without political conviction.

He called for the renewal of the Clean Air Act enacted under Nixon's administration, and he went against the National Rifle Association by supporting the ban on AK-47 assault rifles. He also supported, contrary to his espousal of government deregulation, the Americans with Disabilities Act, which extended civil rights to people with disabilities, including those suffering from AIDS. Some conservative groups took these stances as tell-tale signs that Bush was a centrist. Yet many conservatives continued to reserve judgment, even after Bush vetoed legislation passed by the Democratic-controlled Congress that would have penalized China following the Tiananmen Square massacre, in which protesting students were gunned down by government forces in Communist Beijing. In addition, Bush waived a congressional ban on Export-Import Bank loans to American firms doing business with China and allowed the sale of sophisticated communications satellites to Beijing, making it clear that business came first.[19]

Although Bush's support among conservatives was shaky, his popularity among the general public remained high. He had taken a strong stand in Panama, ousting the dictator and drug lord Manuel Noriega in October 1989. Shortly afterward, on November 9, 1989, the Berlin Wall, the symbol of Soviet control in Eastern Europe, was dismantled, further enhancing Bush's reputation as a skilled international leader. When Iraq, under the brutal dictatorship of Saddam Hussein, invaded Kuwait in August 1990, Bush received the support of the United Nations Security Council and a Democratic-controlled Congress to launch a massive, multinational military campaign to drive Iraqi troops out of Kuwait. Shortly after the successful conclusion of the Gulf War, Bush signed a treaty with Soviet leader Mikhail Gorbachev to reduce existing arsenals of ballistic missiles. By the end of the year, the Soviet Union had dissolved.[20]

Without doubt, Bush saw himself ushering in a new century in American foreign policy. He liked to tell businessmen visiting the White House that the administration stood for two things: free trade and low taxes. But congressional Democrats knocked the second leg of Bush's program out from under the administration in the 1991 fiscal year budget. When Bush came into office, he was left with the Reagan legacy of a $2.7 trillion national debt. Meanwhile, budget deficits continued to skyrocket. American exports were down and consumer debt precipitously high. Bush wanted to reduce federal spending, but his 1990 budget projected a new deficit of more than $91 billion, only slightly lower than Reagan's deficit. Adding to the weight of deficits was the collapse of the savings and loan industry as a result of overexpansion, shoddy lending practices, and financial manipulation. Bush responded by signing the Financial Institutions Reform, Recovery, and Enforcement Act. To make matters worse, the press revealed that Bush's own son, Neil Bush, was involved in a shady savings and loan.

In this atmosphere of runaway deficits and the savings and loan scandal, Democratic leadership was adamant in its demand that taxes be raised. After eight years of Reagan—and nearly eight years of what they considered compromise politics under their leaders—Democrats were not in the mood to negotiate, nor did Bush have the political will to force a show-down with Congress. Congressional Democrats led by Senator George Mitchell insisted that the administration raise taxes, and Darman and Sununu agreed. Bush hesitated. He had famously pledged not to do so. The Democrats successfully pressured him by allowing a partial shutdown of government when the new fiscal year began on October 1 without a budget. Bush reneged on his pledge not to raise taxes. In late October the Omnibus Budget Reconciliation Act of 1990 won approval in Congress. The marginal tax rate on the wealthy rose from 28 to 31 percent, while taxes on lower-income groups were reduced. In signing the legislation, Bush was convinced that a budget deal with the Democrats was the statesmanlike thing to do. In addition, his political advisers believed that he could overcome any political setbacks caused by tax hikes. Finally, Bush took Democrats at their word that spending would be reduced—a promise that went unfulfilled.

The agreement to raise taxes proved fatal to the administration. During budget negotiations, Bush's closest conservative adviser, Lee Atwater, died of brain cancer. He might have advised Bush against a budget deal that raised taxes. To make matters worse, the administration backed down from its opposition to the Kennedy-Hawkins civil rights bill, which the Bush administration had earlier described as a quota bill. Bush's wishy-washiness on such issues led many conservatives to conclude that the president was as much an enemy as any Democrat.[21] Ed Rollins, co-chair of the National Republican Congressional Committee, denounced the budget deal as a "disaster" and told Republican congressional candidates to campaign against it. Vice President Dan Quayle told the press that Bush's reversal had sent the Republicans' single most important issue—tax cuts—down the drain. Conservatives asked whether Bush had lied in his convention speech or simply had not understood the political situation and acted against what they considered the nation's interests.[22]

Bush was personally hurt by the Right's criticism of him. During the budget negotiations he confided in his diary that "Newt [Gingrich]—can do nothing but criticize. We've got one hell of a problem." A short time later, Bush lamented, "Why they [sic] can't be more supportive—but the right wing is giving me a lot of fits."[23] With the approach of midterm elections, many Republican candidates disassociated themselves from the administration. So serious was Bush's violation of his campaign promise that only a quarter of Republican members in the House and the Senate backed the budget deal when it came before them. Bush's handling of the budget earned him wrath from the GOP Right, disdain from the Democrats, and bewilderment from the general public.

At this point, the administration seemed eager to avoid any public controversy. This was evident in the summer of 1991, when Bush nominated New Hampshire federal judge David Souter to replace William J. Brennan, a liberal, on the Supreme Court. Souter won the support of both Sununu and the former U.S. senator from New Hampshire Warren Rudman. Souter had served as assistant to Rudman when he was state attorney general, and Souter later became attorney general, but he did not leave much of a paper trail. Souter easily won confirmation by the Senate.

Once Souter was seated on the Supreme Court, his liberal decisions convinced conservatives that they had once again been tricked by the Bush administration. In *Planned Parenthood of Southeastern Pennsylvania v. Casey* (1992), Souter joined Sandra Day O'Connor and Anthony Kennedy in a plurality decision upholding the power of states to regulate abortion procedures provided that this did not place an "undue burden" on the woman having the abortion. The *Casey* decision reaffirmed *Roe v. Wade* (1973). Conservatives were further disheartened when Souter was the swing vote in *Lee v. Weisman* (1992), which banned public prayer at high school graduations.

By 1992 polls revealed a public ill at ease with the president's handling of domestic affairs. This sentiment was reinforced by a recession that had led to increased unemployment, particularly among white-collar workers. Bush did not allay fears when he initially dismissed talk of a recession. He had been assured by Richard Darman that the economy was in an upswing. At the same time, Bush promised further economic growth through the North American Free Trade Agreement (NAFTA), which had been set in motion in 1987 when the United States entered into a free trade agreement with Canada. In December 1992 Bush and Canadian Prime Minister Brian Mulroney were joined by Mexican President Carlos Salinas in signing the agreement. In an election year, however, the Democratic-controlled Congress refused to approve NAFTA, arguing that it would export American jobs south of the border, allow exploitation of Mexican workers, and create environmental disaster along American borders. Conservatives were divided on the issue of free trade, with business groups led by the *Wall Street Journal* supporting it, while other conservatives denounced the agreement as working against the national interest for the benefit of globally minded corporations.

Bush sought to rally conservatives when he nominated Clarence Thomas to fill the Supreme Court seat of retiring Justice Thurgood Marshall. The selection of Thomas looked ideal. An African American, Thomas had grown up in poverty in Georgia, raised by his grandfather. He entered the seminary, intent on becoming a priest, but after encountering racism he abandoned his pursuit of the priesthood. He graduated with honors from Holy Cross and was admitted to Yale Law School. After receiving his degree, Thomas went to work for the Republican Missouri state attorney general John Danforth, who was later elected to the U.S. Senate in 1976. After a brief stint as a lawyer for Monsanto Company, Thomas became Danforth's legislative aide in the Senate. In the Reagan administration, Thomas became the assistant secretary for civil rights in the Department of Education and then head of the Equal Employment Opportunity Commission (EEOC), where he made dramatic policy changes, including ending numeric goals for employers and class-action suits that relied solely on statistical evidence.

Thomas performed well under grueling questioning before the Senate Judiciary Committee, maintaining that he had not formulated a legal position on abortion. His nomination seemed certain until Anita Hill, a law professor, came forward at the last minute to charge Thomas with sexual harassment dating back to when she had worked for him at the EEOC. The Bush White House was not prepared for the controversy that erupted. The Left and the Right called out their troops to battle over the nomination. In the televised hearings, the nation became captivated by the drama as pro and con witnesses testified. Finally, Thomas seized his own defense. He accused the Democrats of fueling the stereotype of black males and conducting a legalized lynching. He was narrowly confirmed in a fifty-two to forty-eight vote along partisan lines, with eleven Democratic senators supporting his confirmation. On October 23, 1991, Thomas joined the Court.[24] His nomination was a victory for Bush and a major step in fulfilling the longtime demand of conservatives to retake the Court. Once again, however, Bush seemed incapable of getting credit from conservatives for his achievement.

The nation was further polarized when a riot broke out in South Central Los Angeles following the acquittal of white police officers charged with the beating of an African-American man, Rodney King, that was captured on a home video camera. Television networks showed the film of the beating, thus stoking the flames of minority resentment and rage against police brutality. Bush lamely blamed the riot on the failed liberal policies of the 1960s, and then he instructed the Department of Justice to bring civil rights charges against the acquitted officers involved in the beating of King. Whatever legal justification Bush had for bringing new charges against these officers for a second trial, his actions alienated the Right. Conservatives criticized his use of federal power in local affairs and what they considered double jeopardy in trying the officers twice for the same offense. This defense of the police made it appear to liberals that conservatives were insensitive to African Americans' outrage over police brutality.

As Bush entered the Republican primaries in 1992, he faced a challenge from the newspaper columnist and television commentator Patrick Buchanan, who sought to capture both conservative and general discontent with Bush. Buchanan called for an "America first" policy—echoing the prewar isolationist Right—that promised to restore American sovereignty through trade protectionism, a nationalist foreign policy, enforcement of national borders against illegal entry, and immigration restriction.

Buchanan, a former newspaper reporter and speechwriter for Nixon, gained national visibility as a commentator on CNN's *Crossfire,* from which he took a leave of absence in order to challenge Bush for the Republican nomination. He concentrated his fire in New Hampshire and won 34 percent of the vote, nearly upsetting the incumbent Bush. Energized by the near-upset, the under-financed and under-staffed campaign (the campaign manager was Buchanan's sister) for a time seemed to present a real challenge to Bush. Buchanan did not win the nomination, but he received three million votes, 25 percent of all the Republican votes cast during the GOP primaries, severely damaging Bush.

The Democratic primaries were equally fierce. In the end, Bill Clinton, the governor of Arkansas, emerged the victor. Clinton proved to be politically skillful and ideologically ambidextrous. He presented himself as a candidate who transcended the rancorous partisan debate that had afflicted the nation for the last two decades. He claimed that liberal entitlement programs had gone too far. What was needed was a balance between rights and responsibilities, government obligation and individual self-respect. He called for the creation of a national community based on a "New Covenant." He called for welfare reform, middle-class tax cuts, and more police on the street. To ensure that he was not portrayed as a Dukakis-like candidate weak on crime, Clinton flew back to Arkansas in the middle of the New Hampshire primary to oversee the execution of a man convicted of murder.

Clinton's own bid for the nomination had nearly collapsed when news reports came out that he had an extramarital affair with a woman in Arkansas. There was talk of other women as well. The campaign was saved when Clinton and his wife, Hillary, appeared on the CBS show *60 Minutes,* where Bill confessed that he had "caused pain in my marriage."

Quoting a popular song by the country and western singer Tammy Wynette, Hillary said that she was no "Tammy Wynette standing by my man," but rather a woman devoted to Bill Clinton and their marriage. Their performance succeeded. After winning the New York primary, the nomination was Clinton's. At the Democratic Convention, Clinton selected U.S. Senator Albert Gore, Jr., as his running mate, known at the time as a moderate Democrat who had voted in favor of the Gulf War. The Clinton-Gore team projected an image of dynamic, responsible leadership, compared with what they portrayed as Bush's lackluster, elitist presidency.

Into this political fray came Texas billionaire H. Ross Perot, running as a third-party candidate. He entered the 1992 race for president in the spring, dropped out that summer, and then reentered in September. In a self-financed campaign, Perot attacked the Bush administration as corrupt, elitist, and unresponsive to the people. He promised to fix the problems in Washington by setting term limits, balancing the budget, and returning government to the people.

At the Republican Convention, held in the Houston Astrodome, Bush was determined to regain his support among the grassroots Right by celebrating traditional family values blended with old-time Republican laissez-faire principles. Bush invited Patrick Buchanan to speak to the convention, and Buchanan made the most of it, though it turned out it was to be his last performance at a Republican Convention. In his speech, Buchanan declared that America was engaged in a cultural war between those who believed in traditional values and those who offered relativism and nihilism. He portrayed political battle in terms of absolutes. "Clinton and Clinton," Buchanan declared, referring to the Democratic nominee and his wife, "would impose on America—abortion on demand, a litmus test for the Supreme Court, homosexual rights, discrimination against religious schools, women in combat . . ."[25]

Evangelical Christians received Buchanan's speech as welcome words for what they perceived as a nation in moral decline. Evangelicals had continued to grow in importance to the GOP. In 1972 approximately 6 percent of Republicans considered themselves evangelical; by 1992 that figure had risen to nearly 18 percent. Moreover, it was estimated that 10 percent of all delegates at the convention identified themselves as evangelicals.[26] By offering Buchanan an honored place at the podium, Bush sought to reestablish his base with social conservatives after nearly four years of trying to distance himself from this wing of the party. Bush's standing in public opinion polls rose sharply after Buchanan's speech, but the relentless drumbeat by those opposed to the notion of a cultural war turned the speech into a negative for the campaign.

More significant, however, was the perceived downturn in the economy. In reality the economy had begun to move forward in the summer of 1992, showing a 3.5 percent growth rate, but the public's perception lagged behind actual economic performance. Taking advantage of this perception, the Clinton campaign hammered away at the economic issue. Clinton claimed that Democrats were equipped to handle the new computerized economy whereas Bush was out of touch with the average American. Throughout the campaign, Clinton and Gore insisted that they represented a new kind of Democrat. Under Democratic National Committee Chair Ron Brown, who took the post in 1989, the party shifted to a more pragmatic agenda, while downplaying positions associated with the Far Left. This new image was largely credited to the Democratic Leadership Council (DLC), which had been formed after the disastrous campaign of Walter F. Mondale in 1984. The DLC wanted to move the Democratic party back to the center through a pro-growth, pro-defense, and anticrime agenda. The policy analysts William A. Galston and Elaine Kamarck at the DLC's Progressive Policy Institute showed that for the Democrats to regain the White House they needed to convince the public that they supported a strong national defense, upheld law and order, and reflected mainstream moral values. Clinton pursued the DLC strategy and agenda, which had great appeal to voters.

Bush fought back, but it was an uphill battle. While he appeared to close the gap in the polls, he found that Clinton was able to deflect the cultural and social issues that Bush had used to tarnish Dukakis in 1988. Clinton also had an empathetic and telegenic style that weighed heavily against Bush. Conservatives believed that the media—major metropolitan newspapers and network news programs—contributed to a portrait of Bush as out of touch with the average American. The general sense on the Right was that if Bush walked on water to cross the Hudson River, the media would have reported it as "Bush walks on polluted water caused by his policies." In the end, Bush might have won if Perot had not been in the race. But Perot was in the race. On Election Day, Clinton won 357 electoral votes to Bush's 168. The popular vote revealed how deeply Perot had cut into Bush: the Texas billionaire took 19 percent of the popular vote, Bush 38 percent, and Clinton a plurality with 43 percent. Clinton won three million more votes than Dukakis had received in 1988, but Dukakis received three percentage points more of the popular vote, 46 percent. Comparisons between George H. W. Bush and William Howard Taft, who succeeded the highly popular Theodore Roosevelt only to lose reelection in a three-way race, became inevitable. Much like Taft earlier, Bush was perceived by the insurgents in his party as an opponent of reform. Representative Tom DeLay (R-Texas) later said that many conservatives in Congress feared Bush's reelection in 1992 because it would mean "another four years of misery."[27]

Clinton carried 32 states in the most sweeping triumph for any Democrat since Lyndon Johnson in 1964. By assuming the banner of change, Clinton won the self-described independents and moderates. He ran nearly even among white voters; won among the best-educated (college and higher) and the least-educated (less than high school) voters; and overwhelmed Bush among the under-30 and over-60 voters. Surprisingly, while the Clinton-Gore ticket embodied the values and rhetoric of the baby-boomer generation, they split the 30-to-59-year-old vote. They won heavily among African-American voters (84 percent), which helped take larger cities and the South. Single women went heavily for Clinton-Gore, 53 percent to 31 percent.

Democrats trumpeted the success of female candidates, labeling the election the "Year of the Woman." Especially noteworthy was the election of the first African-American woman to the Senate, Carol Moseley-Braun (D-Illinois). She was joined by the Democrats Barbara Boxer and Dianne Feinstein from California and Patty Murray, the self-styled "mom in tennis shoes," from Washington state. The best news for Senate conservatives was that Lauch Faircloth, with the support of Jesse Helms's Congressional Club, defeated incumbent Terry Sanford (D-North Carolina). In the House, the bright spot for conservatives was the reelection of House Minority Whip Newt Gingrich, who overcame a tough primary and close general election.[28]

The Clinton-Gore victory was a success for the DLC's strategy of winning the moderate-independent vote. Clinton and Gore won 54 percent of the liberal-independent vote to Bush's 17 percent and Perot's 30 percent; and they won 43 percent of the moderate-independent vote (compared with Bush's 28 percent and Perot's 30 percent). The Perot vote took votes mostly away from Bush and therefore helped the Clinton-

Gore ticket. The key to the Democratic victory lay in winning moderate and independent voters, while keeping the left base of the Democratic party together. This lesson pointed the way for the Democratic party to reestablish itself as a majority party, but it was not an easy lesson to put into practice.

Travails of the First Term

Conservatives saw in Clinton everything they despised: a baby-boomer who had protested the war in Vietnam, appeared to be antimilitary, and was pro-abortion even though he declared that abortion should be made "safe, legal and rare."[29] Conservatives believed he was a prevaricator, a closet liberal, and that his wife was a radical feminist. Of course, many of these characteristics—the draft avoidance, the language of caring, flexible politics, and feminist spouses—were found among baby-boomer conservatives as well. Nonetheless, conservatives began attacking Clinton as corrupt even before he entered office. As the editor of *National Review,* Rich Lowry, later admitted, conservatives in the post-Watergate era used scandal as an "excuse not to engage in frank political and ideological argument."[30]

As president-elect, Clinton provided conservatives with an opportunity to attack him when he proposed to fulfill his quiet campaign promise to lift the ban on homosexuals in the military and later when he proposed a national health-care program. During the campaign, Clinton had promised to reverse military policy that banned gays in the military. The grassroots Right took this issue as proof that Clinton was dangerous and launched a massive attack on his administration. Clinton's case was damaged when the head of the Joint Chiefs of Staff, General Colin Powell, and the influential Democratic chair of the Senate Armed Services Committee, San Nunn (D-Georgia), pressured the president into delaying the executive order for six months while a compromise was worked out. In the end, the Pentagon issued a new compromise policy of "don't ask, don't tell." The policy prohibited public homosexuality in the military, but commanding officers were not allowed to ask military personnel about their private sexual preferences. The policy did not appease gay activists, the top brass in the Pentagon, or the many conservatives who demanded expulsion of gays from the military.

In the White House, Clinton showed a marked propensity to avoid tough decisions, leaving cabinet members, advisers, and congressional Democrats frustrated.[31] Doubts were raised about his leadership qualities during the intense partisan fight in the spring and summer of 1993 over the administration's proposed budget. Clinton's $16 billion stimulus package came under severe attack by Republicans, who saw it as tax-and-spend liberalism. In April 1993, Republicans supported a filibuster that killed the stimulus package. Finally, after months of warfare, Clinton won a narrow victory by pushing through a modified budgetary plan. Although opposed by Republicans, he prodded Congress into accepting deficit reduction through higher taxes on the wealthy and corporations, a new energy tax, a tax credit for the working poor, and cuts in the military budget.

In February 1993 Clinton presented to Congress a legislative agenda that retreated from his campaign promise for a New Covenant which balanced the obligations of the government with the responsibilities of its citizens. Instead, he proposed an agenda that appeared to capitulate to liberal interest groups and Democratic members of Congress. He called for health care, job training, and a college loan program. In addition, he proposed an expansion of the earned-income tax credit, unpaid family and medical leave legislation, increased funding for police and crime prevention, and a modest national youth-service program that involved young people in community-service work. This legislative program was by no means radical, but it drew criticism from the left wing of the Democratic party for not being bold enough. Conservatives attacked it as more evidence that Clinton was a big-government liberal.

In the fall of 1993, Clinton threw his support behind the North American Free Trade Agreement. NAFTA was opposed by organized labor, an important constituency within the Democratic party. The free trade agreement was passed with the backing of the Republican congressional leadership and received support from the majority of Republicans in the House and the Senate. A majority of Democrats, including the House majority leader and majority whip, opposed it.[32] Any hopes that Clinton was returning to his centrist campaign roots were quickly dispelled when, in a speech before Congress on September 23, 1993, he unveiled his plan for a national health-care program. Holding up a red, white, and blue "health security card," Clinton promised a guaranteed universal health-care program that would contain rampantly escalating health-care costs. Devised by his wife, Hillary Rodham Clinton, who had headed a health-care task force, the plan was astoundingly complex, requiring a huge expansion of the federal bureaucracy. The legislative bill ran 1,342 pages long. The program mandated that all employers provide health insurance coverage to their employees through highly regulated Health Maintenance Organizations (HMOs). Oversight boards at the local, state, and national level would regulate these HMOs, as well as the price of medical procedures and drugs.

At first it appeared that Clinton's comprehensive plan might win political support in Congress. Democrats came out strongly in favor of the proposal, and even the Republican Senate minority leader Robert Dole told the press that he was willing to cooperate with the administration on the proposal. The bill enraged grassroots conservatives, however. Organized opposition came from the American Conservative Union, conservative and libertarian think tanks, activist groups, and the insurance industry. Through an extensive television advertising campaign that focused on a middle-class couple, "Harry and Louise," a coalition of health insurance companies and health-care providers raised questions about the bureaucratic nature of the proposal.[33] The end came on September 26, 1994, when Senate Majority Leader George Mitchell (D-Maine) announced that the plan was dead. In her memoir *Living History,* published after she left the White House, Hillary Clinton described her opponents, writing, "I had not seen faces like that since the segregation battles of the 1960s." They were "militia supporters, tax protesters, clinic blockaders."[34]

The health-care reform bill placed Clinton on the political defensive. Meanwhile, he found himself ensnared by three distinct scandals that the right wing refused to drop: a sexual harassment suit from the former Arkansas state worker Paula Corbin Jones, a land development deal called Whitewater, and allegations that Hillary Clinton had benefited from insider commodity trading. Whitewater was a complicated financial fraud case involving both Clintons, improper loans issued through an Arkansas savings and loan, federal monies, and abuse of political power at the state level. The case led Clinton's attorney general to appoint an independent counsel, an investigation taken over by the conservative Republican Kenneth Starr, a former federal appeals judge .

Conservatives jumped on these scandals in their direct mail fundraising efforts, while conservative newspapers and magazines appeared to relish each new revelation of alleged wrongdoing. The *American Specta-*

tor took special delight in reporting on accusations by a group of Arkansas state troopers who claimed to have procured women for Clinton and arranged numerous sexual rendezvous for him. The magazine commissioned David Brock, a young, overly ambitious reporter, to go to Arkansas to dig up more dirt on the Clintons. (Brock later claimed that he falsified many of his reports at the encouragement of the editors at *American Spectator.*)[35] Behind the scenes, high-powered conservative attorneys provided pro-bono legal advice to Jones's lawyers in the hope of bringing Clinton down. It nearly worked.

The Jones suit dragged on for years. In early 1994, Clinton's most immediate problems appeared to be not with the Right but with the Democratic leadership on Capitol Hill.[36] Clinton was in open combat with the Democratic Left, which was heavily represented in Congress, largely through gerrymandered safe districts. These Democrats were eager to push policies that expanded reproductive (abortion) rights, affirmative action, and social programs. Clinton seemed intimidated by Democratic leaders in Congress and was unwilling to confront them with his own agenda.

Republican Insurgents

With the Clinton administration on the defensive, the Right rebounded and set its eyes on gaining control of Congress. The unlikely leader of the insurgents was Newt Gingrich, a former Rockefeller Republican elected to represent Georgia's 6th District. He had run twice before for this seat, in 1974 and 1976, before winning election in 1978, the first of eleven terms. Gingrich was fascinated with new technology and its effect on politics. He took advantage of the introduction of C-SPAN television in Congress when each evening he and other fellow conservatives began delivering speeches before an empty House attacking Democratic policy. Speaker Tip O'Neill was so angered by this strategy that he ordered C-SPAN cameras to pan the empty House. Nonetheless, thousands of viewers began tuning in to watch Gingrich and other conservatives attack the Democrats. Once again, Republicans were taking advantage of the new media in their offensive against the Democrats. C-SPAN could hardly be called "alternative media," but it served that purpose for Gingrich.[37]

The young Turks who gradually gathered around Gingrich dreamed of a conservative Republican takeover of the House. Planning for this upheaval began in the early 1980s, with the formation of the Conservative Opportunity Society (COS). Over time, Gingrich attracted a new breed of activist Republican legislators, including Vin Weber of Minnesota, Robert Walker of Pennsylvania, Bob Kasten of Wisconsin, Daniel Lungren of California, Judd Gregg of New Hampshire, Dan Coats of Indiana, Duncan Hunter of California, and Connie Mack of Florida. Dick Armey, a former university economics professor, provided the tactics (and the restraint) that enabled the revolt to succeed. The COS was greeted with hostility by the House Republican leadership. Robert Michel (R-Illinois) told younger members to stay away from the group because of what he considered its right-wing radicalism. Bob Dole was particularly upset with the group for opposing his 1985 budget-reduction plan, which would have frozen cost-of-living increases for Social Security benefits. Nonetheless, other Republican leaders including former HUD secretary Jack Kemp, U.S. Senator Trent Lott (R-Mississippi), and Ford White House chief-of-staff Dick Cheney privately encouraged the group.

Public support for Congress had weakened considerably by the time Gingrich began his campaign. A series of scandals in the House had furthered the public perception that Congress under the Democrats was corrupt. This perception of immorality in Congress was reinforced when reports surfaced that some members of Congress had systematically floated large overdrafts at the House bank. At the same time, Gingrich developed a close alliance with the new Republican national chairman, Haley Barbour, a Mississippi conservative who envisioned making the GOP into a majority party. Although Barbour's only experience as a candidate had been when he ran for the Senate in 1982, he had worked in Republican politics his entire career, from the Nixon campaign in 1968 and the John B. Connally presidential campaign in 1980 to the Reagan White House and later the Bush campaign in 1988. Barbour joined Gingrich in a program to recruit and train a cadre of conservative Republican candidates for state and national office. To further this program, Gingrich and Barbour launched the National Empowerment Television network to broadcast the new Republican agenda. The endeavor was financed by the Amway Corporation, a door-to-door home products company, through a donation of $2.5 million. Gingrich took charge of GOPAC, a political action committee that dispensed funds to young conservatives seeking election.

Gingrich also took advantage of a new format developed by conservatives—talk radio. The king of conservative talk radio was a Missouri-born college dropout with the sharp wit of a natural entertainer, Rush Limbaugh. In 1984, Limbaugh moved to Sacramento, California, to host a radio talk show that featured him and call-in guests. The show hit pay dirt when it became nationally syndicated in the summer of 1988. Beginning with only fifty-eight stations, his audience soared to six hundred stations with twenty million weekly listeners who tuned in to *The Rush Limbaugh Show*. There they would hear "Rush" refer to feminists as "feminazis," liberals as "pinheads," and his own followers as "dittoheads"—a mocking reference to those who accused Rush's fans of being "unthinking" robots. His listeners were largely white, middle-to-upper class, ideologically conservative Republicans.

The success of Limbaugh's show spawned other national radio programs, producing a cadre of conservative talk-show celebrities. AM radio was transformed as stations broadcast local talk-show hosts, often even more conservative than Limbaugh. The proliferation of these programs was made possible by the Federal Communications Commission's repeal of the Fairness Doctrine, which had required equal air time for differing positions. The end of the Fairness Doctrine allowed talk radio to blossom. Conservatives took advantage of radio to invite listeners to vent their complaints against what they perceived as the liberal media—network news, national news magazines, and newspapers. Conservative talk radio tapped into a large, pent-up need in grassroots America to complain about the liberal establishment. Talk radio was also just plain entertaining even for regular listeners with no conservative ax to grind.

Conservative talk radio encouraged a constant barrage of anti-Clinton rhetoric. At times the steady drumbeat against the administration imparted a feeling among Clinton staff that "they" were out to get them. And they were right: Conservatives really were on the offensive. Talk radio treated politics as blood sport. The mobilization of the Republican base was further aided by Pat Robertson's Christian Coalition, which distributed 33 million voter guides, and the National Rifle Association, which contributed $3.4 million to its targeted campaigns. Much of this campaign effort emphasized the importance of cultural and social issues.

While conservatives at the grassroots were fanning the flames of revolt, conservatives in the House maneuvered to take the reins of Republican leadership. The first step had been taken when Richard Cheney (R-Wyoming), who had won office after serving the Ford White House, left the House in 1990 to join the first Bush administration as secretary of defense. Cheney had supported the conservative revolt, but his resignation from Congress opened vacancies in the GOP House leadership. Gingrich immediately declared his candidacy for Republican whip. In a skillfully organized campaign managed by Vin Weber, Gingrich won the support of two key moderates, Steve Gunderson of Wisconsin and Nancy Johnson of Connecticut, both of whom had reached the conclusion that if the Republicans were to gain majority status, moderates and conservatives needed to join forces. At the same time, Jerry Lewis, a moderate from California, decided not to challenge Gingrich, even though Edward Rollins from the National Republican Congressional Committee urged him to do so. The final race pitted Gingrich against the Illinois Republican Ed Madigan. Madigan drew support from some conservatives, including Tom DeLay of Texas, who entertained ambitions of his own.

When Gingrich won, DeLay contritely declared his support for the new whip's agenda. With Gingrich's support growing in the House, Bob Michel announced that he would leave Congress in 1994. Gingrich had become the heir-apparent to Michel. To consolidate his power in the House, Gingrich removed Jerry Lewis of California as chair of the Republican Conference and installed Dick Armey in this key position. Securing party leadership in the House might have satisfied men and women of lesser vision. The conservative insurgents wanted more, however. They sought complete control of the House.

The final weapon in the battle for control of Congress came in the form of a clever election proclamation signed by 337 Republican candidates for the House, the "Contract with America." The ten-point legislative program was promoted as a covenant with the voters—a promise to introduce ten specific pieces of legislation if Republicans became a majority party in the House.[38] The Contract with America had evolved out of extensive polling and focus-group interviews which revealed that voters wanted "accountability" in government. The contract called for welfare reform, anticrime measures, a line-item veto, regulatory reform, and tax reduction. In addition, hot-button issues such as abortion, pornography, and school prayer were not included in the plan in order to avoid the charge that Republicans represented only the Religious Right. Although the exclusion of social issues upset social conservatives like Paul Weyrich, this program gave Republicans the offensive. As the 1994 midterm elections approached, Republicans were on the march, energized by their victory over the Clinton health-care plan.

Democrats, for their part, appeared severely divided on how best to meet the threat.[39] Meanwhile, some Republicans believed that they could nationalize the midterm elections. Conventional wisdom held that all congressional elections were local elections and not national referendums. This wisdom proved wrong. On Election Day, Republicans captured both houses of Congress with a 230–204 majority in the House and eight new Senate seats. The insurgency was aided by reapportionment and an unusually high number of Democratic retirements in 1994. Although the GOP did not control the White House, it had become the majority party.

The key to the Republican victory came in winning the South. By the time Reagan left the presidency the majority of southern voters already identified themselves as Republicans. The 1994 election completed this transformation. Republicans took 119 southern legislative seats and seized the Florida Senate and the North and South Carolina lower assemblies. In addition, Republicans gained control of the majority of southern governorships.[40] The Republican takeover of the South came at a time when the region was undergoing important demographic and economic change. In the 1990s, the South averaged 19 percent population growth, much higher than the national average. By 2000, more than 84 million people, a third of the nation, lived in the 11 former Confederate states. Moreover, much of this growth occurred in the suburbs, where standard Republican issues such as low taxes, low union support, strong family values, and a strong national defense had strong appeal.[41]

The leadership in the House reflected this political shift to the South. New Republican leaders included Speaker Gingrich of Georgia, Majority Leader Dick Armey of Texas, and Majority Whip Tom DeLay of Texas. They represented the new suburban South from cities including Atlanta, Dallas, and Houston. For Democrats, the loss of key leaders including Speaker Thomas Foley (D-Washington), Chairman of the House

Ways and Means Committee Dan Rostenkowski (D-Illinois), New York Governor Mario Cuomo, and Texas Governor Ann Richards, who lost to George W. Bush, the son of the former president, was devastating.

When Congress convened in January 1995, the Contract with America became the focus of the Republican agenda for the next 100 days. Bills were introduced on crime, congressional term limits, welfare reform, a balanced budget, Social Security, defense, illegal drugs, and taxation. The House passed the "Taking Back Our Streets Act," which placed a limit on the number of appeals that a convicted murderer could make to the federal courts and instituted mandatory sentencing for drug-related offenses. In addition, a tax-reduction bill was passed. The House managed to pass all but two pieces of Republican legislation, a term-limit bill and a space-based missile-defense bill, but the conservatives' program met resistance in the Senate.[42] Two pieces of legislation were eventually signed into law, one applying federal employment law to Congress and the other prohibiting unfunded federal mandates. The perception among the public was that Republicans had not lived up to their promises. The failure to enact legislation outlined in the Contract with America raised questions as to Gingrich's leadership, which was not helped by his sometimes arrogant demeanor on television and his unwillingness to temper his remarks before the press.

The Republican insurgence caught the Clinton administration by surprise. The election results left Clinton shocked, angry, and depressed. He turned to Dick Morris, a Republican consultant who had advised him on his political comeback in Arkansas after he had lost his bid for reelection as governor in 1980. With Morris's advice he won reelection in 1982. Morris was not popular among Clinton's other advisers, George Stephanopoulos, James Carville, and Chief of Staff Leon Panetta, but he was a brilliant strategist. He told Clinton that he needed to swing to the right, preempt the Republican program as his own, and distance himself from the left wing of his party, which was well represented among House Democrats. This strategy called for Clinton to accept welfare reform, using the language of moral values and emphasizing fiscal conservatism, without undertaking draconian cuts in the budget. In his third State of the Union message to Congress in January 1996, Clinton took up many of the themes of the Republican agenda while presenting himself as a defender of middle-class entitlements.

Welfare reform was an especially difficult issue for a Democratic president. For nearly a half century, Democrats had identified themselves as protectors of the poor, which often came down to defending welfare. Although the Clinton administration had previously turned to welfare reform following the failure of national health care, the president faced an intransigent Democratic House leadership that was tied ideologically and politically to the New Deal welfare system. House leaders Thomas Foley (D-Washington) and Richard Gephardt (D-Missouri) feared that welfare reform might divide the Democratic caucus. On the other side, Democratic Leadership Council leader Al From urged Clinton to push forward on welfare reform. Fearing the political costs, Clinton continued to waver on the issue. By the summer of 1994, welfare reform had begun to languish in the White House because Clinton refused to endorse a reform bill. The issue was then taken up by the new Republican majority led by Representative Jim Talent (R-Missouri), who used his expertise on the intricacies of welfare in drafting new legislation.[43] When reform legislation passed the Senate by a vote of eighty-seven to twelve, Senate Majority Leader Robert Dole declared that welfare was not just being fixed; "we're revolutionizing it."[44]

Signed into law by Clinton on August 22, 1996, the Personal Responsibility Act barred teenage mothers under the age of eighteen from receiving welfare aid, food stamps, or public housing. Although liberal opponents of the measure, including Senator Daniel Moynihan (D-New York), warned that it would lead to tens of thousands of homeless people, the Personal Responsibility Act proved successful in reducing welfare rolls and encouraging job training and employment programs that provided many poor people with an opportunity to reenter the workplace. Nevertheless, many on the Left felt betrayed by the Clinton administration. The journalist Christopher Hitchens expressed these sentiments when he wrote that Clinton "will be remembered as the man who used the rhetoric of the New Democrat to undo the New Deal."[45]

For all the complaints from his left-wing critics, Clinton claimed welfare reform as his own, much to his political advantage. Morris's strategy was working. Clinton waited for an opportunity to hobble House Republicans, and his chance came when Gingrich overplayed his hand in 1996 during the budget negotiations. Gingrich was convinced that the American public was behind him in wanting a balanced budget. When a constitutional amendment to balance the budget failed, Gingrich placed even higher priority on the issue, promising to balance the budget in seven years. Working with John Kasich (R-Ohio), the chairman of the House Budget Committee, who had emerged as the budget guru of the Republican insurgents, Gingrich produced a budget in early 1995 that called for more than $1 trillion in spending cuts through the elimination of more than 280 programs, including the Departments of Energy, Education, and Commerce. The budget plan also called for a $228 billion, or 50 percent, reduction in the projected rate of growth. After heated debate, the budget narrowly passed the House in a partisan vote of 238–219.

Clinton attacked the Republican budget as harmful to the interests of the poor and the elderly. In late 1995, after reaching loggerheads with the White House, Republicans accepted a budget reconciliation bill that passed both houses in mid-November 1995. Funds were approved to get the government up and running. Gingrich was certain that the president had no choice but to sign the bill, but Clinton surprised him and refused to sign. Gingrich decided to up the stakes and force a showdown by again holding up appropriations to keep government running. The White House responded with a well-orchestrated campaign that warned of cuts in Social Security and Medicare benefit payments.

This strategy had worked for Democrats against President George H. W. Bush, so Gingrich believed that it would work for Republicans. Clinton, too, feared that the plan might work for his opponents, but Morris told him to hang tough in negotiations and not back down. Morris proved correct. Gingrich's ploy backfired and the public blamed House Republicans for the government shutdown. When Congress reconvened after the New Year, Senator Robert Dole told Gingrich that enough was enough. Dole resented a lot of things about Gingrich, including his earlier tag of Dole as the "tax-collector for the welfare state." Dole was eager to be seen as a statesman able to reconcile differences. A year earlier, in April 1995, he had slyly backtracked on tax hikes by signing an antitax pledge with the conservative Grover Norquist of Americans for Tax Reform as a witness. With an obvious eye on the GOP Republican nomination in 1996, Dole stepped forward to end the impasse. By April 1996, the budget fight was over and Clinton emerged as the political winner.

The victory looked like a turning point in the Clinton presidency. Clinton had successfully painted the House Republicans as extremists while positioning himself as a centrist. His reelection to a second term appeared certain. Clinton's success presented an opportunity for the Democratic party to vanquish the GOP Right, and with it much of the Republican party.

Clinton Wins a Historic Second Term, Only to Be Impeached

By 1996, Clinton had regained his political momentum. While his approval rating among the general public hovered around 40 percent, only two years before he had stood on the precipice of defeat. His carefully calculated strategy to distance himself from the Democratic Left in Congress and House Republicans had succeeded. He had moved to the center by claiming welfare reform as his own, outmaneuvering Gingrich on the budget, painting Republicans as obstructionists, and declaring that "the era of big government is over." At the same time, he spoke against right-wing extremism, called for an investigation into the burning of black churches in the South, and urged cooperation between the parties. He had seized the political center, which left little room for a Republican challenger.

Then again, Republicans did not offer much of a candidate when they nominated U.S. Senator Robert Dole to head their ticket. Dole had run as a vice-presidential candidate with Gerald Ford in 1976 and had sought the Republican nomination in 1980 and 1988. He was a genuine war hero, having been wounded during the Second World War when a German artillery shell left his right arm and hand disabled. He worked his way up through the ranks of the Republican party to win election to the U.S. Senate in 1968. In the Senate he gained a reputation as a deal-maker. In winning the 1996 nomination, Dole successfully fought off a challenge from the GOP Right, which had rallied around the candidacy of Pat Buchanan, who surprisingly won the New Hampshire primary. To counter the threat from the Right, Dole won the endorsement of the evangelist Pat Robertson, whose Christian Coalition proved important in winning the southern primaries for Dole. After winning the nomination, he picked the conservative Jack Kemp as his running mate, but Dole's centrist strategy was evident at the convention. After failing to change the antiabortion plank in the Republican platform, he declared in his acceptance speech that "the Republican party is broad and inclusive. It represents many streams of opinion and many points of view." It was a powerful statement to convention delegates, 31 percent of whom considered themselves "born-again Christians" (compared with only 13 percent of delegates to the Democratic National Convention).[46] Nearly all the speeches at the convention were delivered by moderate or liberal Republicans. Newt Gingrich, Pat Buchanan, and Pat Robertson were all denied prime-time slots.

Whether Republicans would have done better running to the right is arguable; there is no doubt, however, that Dole was an especially weak candidate. If the Clinton-Dole contest had been a prize-fight, it would have been stopped midway as an unfair match: Dole's campaign bordered on embarrassing, leading the *Congressional Quarterly Almanac* to conclude afterward that many voters had dismissed Dole as "too old and inarticulate for the television age."[47] Dole won only 41 percent of the vote. In fairness, Bush had won only 40 percent of the vote, but both were a far cry from Reagan's 60 percent in 1984. Clinton increased his popular vote from 41 percent in 1992 to 49.2 percent in 1996, still not a majority. With this thin plurality, Clinton was the first Democrat since Franklin D. Roosevelt to win reelection to a second term. Clinton won the East, the West, and the southern border states, as well as Louisiana and Florida. It was a solid victory, but Clinton still had not won a majority of the popular vote.

Clinton wanted, above all else, to establish a legacy as a great president, but he encountered limited opportunities to put his signature on history. He entered his second term with the promise to balance the federal budget by 2002. He had made this promise when he ran in 1992, but he had been unwilling to undertake the budget cuts necessary to fulfill it. A vibrant economy, however, allowed him to present a balanced-budget proposal for the 1998 fiscal year, and then to announce near the end of the year that the government was running a surplus. While much of this success should be attributed to economic growth and Republican political pressure, Clinton as president received the credit during this time of prosperity.

Yet in the middle of this success, the administration became bogged down defending itself from charges of campaign misconduct and personal scandal involving the president himself. A harbinger of the problems that hobbled Clinton in his second term had become evident before the election. His campaigns slumped near the end, when a plethora of stories began to appear about Democratic party improprieties. One fundraiser, Charlie Trie, was later convicted of illegal fundraising. More devastating were allegations of illegal contributions to the campaign by James Riady, an Indonesian businessman who headed a powerful Asian investment house, the Lippo Group. Much of Riady's fundraising for Clinton appears to have been conducted by John Huang, a Commerce Department employee and Democratic fundraiser with close ties to Clinton. In 1996 Huang raised $1.6 million. There was strong evidence that Riady and Huang had connections with Chinese military intelligence. Maria Hsia, a Democratic fundraiser, arranged for an appearance of Al Gore at a Buddhist temple in California. While Gore denied knowing it was a fundraiser, Hsia was convicted in 2000 by a federal jury in Washington, D.C., on five felony counts of making more than $100,000 in illegal contributions.[48]

More difficulties arose over the sexual harassment suit filed by Paula Jones, a suit that many people believed was going nowhere. Things changed dramatically on May 27, 1997, however, when the Supreme Court unanimously denied Clinton's request to delay the Jones lawsuit until he left office. In hindsight, Clinton should then have sought a settlement with Jones and the case would have been quickly forgotten. At the same time, he delayed turning over Whitewater material subpoenaed by the independent counsel Kenneth Starr. At this point, Starr had not been given the charge to expand his investigation to determine whether Clinton had encouraged the White House intern Monica Lewinsky to lie under oath in the Jones suit. Attorneys representing Jones alleged that Clinton had engaged in a sexual relationship with Lewinsky, thereby showing a pattern of behavior. Starr was not interested in the charges of sexual harassment; he was investigating allegations of obstruction of justice. On January 16, a grand jury was given authority to investigate charges of perjury by Clinton. The next day, in pretrial testimony before the deposition, Clinton denied engaging in sexual relations with Lewinsky. Much of his testimony was presented as narrow legal definitions of what was meant by sexual relations. In the following weeks, Clinton continued to deny to the press, cabinet members, White House staff, members of Congress, and his family that he had been involved with Lewinsky.

In a Byzantine series of events, Starr found indisputable evidence from DNA testing of one of Lewinsky's dresses that Clinton had misled the American public. On August 17, 1998, an angry and contrite Clinton admitted that he had engaged in an "inappropriate" relationship with Lewinsky, but he strongly denied that he had done anything illegal. Grassroots conservatives, as well as hardcore Republicans in Congress, immediately called for Clinton to resign or be impeached. Meanwhile, the Democratic Left rallied to Clinton, declaring his involvement with Lewinsky inappropriate but a personal matter and not a political one.[49]

In early September, Starr delivered his report on the Lewinsky affair to the House of Representatives. Although Starr did not expect the report to be made public, he concluded that Clinton's actions "may constitute grounds for impeachment." Some members of Congress called for censure of the president, but the Republican Right thought that censure would let Clinton off the hook. A national debate erupted that further stirred partisan acrimony. Polls showed that the vast majority of the public felt that Clinton should not be impeached. Meanwhile, charges emerged that leaders in the House were not without their own sins: It was revealed that Henry Hyde (R-Illinois), a leading voice of the anti-abortion Right, had engaged in a lengthy adulterous affair when he was younger, and that J. C. Watts, an African-American conservative Republican from Oklahoma, had fathered a child out of wedlock. Earlier, in January 1997, scandal had reached Gingrich, who was reprimanded by the House for violations that included giving the Ethics Committee false information and using tax-exempt donations for political purposes. He was fined $300,000.

Conservatives hoped that a weakened Clinton presidency might rally the American public to the Republican cause in the midterm elections of 1998. Pursuing this strategy, Republicans decided to make impeachment a campaign issue and tighten their grip on Congress. Their plan backfired. The overwhelming majority of the American public opposed impeachment. Contrary to Republicans' expectations, as well as the predictions of most pundits, Republicans lost four seats in Congress, retaining a bare majority in both Houses. Many blamed Gingrich for the loss. Shortly after the election, Gingrich announced that he was resigning as speaker and giving up his seat in Congress. It was later revealed that he had been carrying on an extramarital affair. House Republicans selected Bob Livingston (R-Louisiana), a committed conservative, to take Gingrich's seat. A short time later Livingston resigned amid charges that he, too, had committed adultery. It seemed that marital infidelity was not a partisan affair.

The 1998 midterm elections set Republicans back politically, but House Republicans moved forward on impeachment. In December a severely divided House approved two articles of impeachment that charged the president with perjury and obstruction of justice. The trial began in the Senate the following month. Opponents of impeachment admitted that Clinton had disgraced the office and betrayed his supporters, friends, and family, but they argued that his personal transgressions should not be punished by impeachment as described in the Constitution. In the end, the Senate voted against removing Clinton from office. The ordeal had consumed the nation, and it clearly had a profound effect on Clinton's second term.

The 1990s left George H. W. Bush, Bill Clinton, and Newt Gingrich with tarnished images. For whatever success George Bush might have enjoyed in foreign policy, he left office as a president who had squandered the Reagan legacy and betrayed his campaign pledge not to raise taxes. Bill Clinton displayed great political adroitness in winning reelection, but the lesson that should have been taken from his victory was not easily learned in a party dominated by its left wing. Personal scandal weakened Clinton's presidency, but his larger failure was his inability to convince his entire party to move to the political center in a way that Tony Blair, the leader of the Labour party, had done in England. Gingrich's reputation was also damaged by personal sexual scandal; moreover, his arrogance was turned against him time and again—in his negotiations over the budget, in the impeachment crisis, and in the election of 1996. His single most important accomplishment remained his successful mobilization of the party's base to give the GOP a majority in Congress. It was a lesson that Republicans would take with them into the 2000 presidential election.

9

Americans Divided

George W. Bush's election to the White House in 2000 completed a political struggle that conservatives had begun a half century earlier. Less than a year after the election, on September 11, 2001, the United States was attacked by Islamic terrorists who flew hijacked commercial airliners into the World Trade Center in New York City and the Pentagon in Washington, D.C., killing more than three thousand people. The attack transformed American politics. National security reemerged as a major issue for the first time since the end of the Cold War. Bush's leadership during this crisis strengthened him politically in his first six years in office, enabling Republicans to retain control of Congress for the first time since 1946.

In the process, Bush put his own stamp on conservatism. His proclamation of himself as a "compassionate conservative" during the 2000 election was more than campaign rhetoric. Through this identity Bush sought to combine traditional conservative principles of individual responsibility, free enterprise, low taxes, and resistance to government spending with an acceptance of the important role that government had come to play in American life. He sought to use activist government for conservative ends by allowing faith-based charitable organizations to provide social services to the poor; by making public schools more accountable by linking federal aid to national standards; and by expanding federal health insurance for prescription drugs to the elderly. He believed that the federal government could help promote moral values, regulate abortion, and encourage individual responsibility. At the same time, he called for reform of Social Security through limited privatization. Bush's compassionate conservatism reflected his religious faith as a born-again Christian who believed in the responsibility to be "thy brother's keeper."[1] The Bush vision of government was far from what the first generation of postwar conservatives—Hayek, Rand, or Buckley—had called for when they sought to overturn the New Deal liberal order.

Under Bush's leadership, the GOP strengthened party organization by mobilizing the grassroots. Unlike his predecessor, Bill Clinton, who downplayed party identification and his association with congressional Democrats, Bush emphasized party identity, his own conservatism, and his commitment to a Republican Congress. Bush's efforts at party building led to an unprecedented string of Republican electoral victories at the state, congressional, and national levels in 2002 and 2004. At the same time, Bush attempted to reconfigure the liberal welfare state by directing federal funds to the nonprofit sector, which included faith-based organizations and local community groups, to provide social services and health and education programs. In advancing this ideological and partisan agenda, Bush intended to circumscribe the "iron triangle" alliance of congressional Democrats, federal bureaucrats, and public-interest groups which had thwarted the Reagan Revolution. In addition, he sought to transform the federal judiciary by appointing conservatives to the courts. This multiple attack on the liberal regime intensified an already highly partisan political environment.

Military intervention in Afghanistan and Iraq sharpened partisan feelings between the two parties and among the electorate. Bush's decision to invade Iraq and to involve the United States in what turned out to be an ongoing war placed the entire Republican party on the line politically. America's involvement in Iraq and Afghanistan (along with a series of political scandals in the administration) jeopardized the gains made by Republicans in Bush's first term. Under Bush, the GOP had become a majority party. The question remained, however, whether the Republican triumph could be sustained in an electorate severely divided.

The Election of 2000

Both Democrats and Republicans understood going into the election that it would be close. The key for both parties lay in winning sixteen battleground states that could go either Republican or Democratic. Bush strategists believed that to win they had to get their large party base to the polls. Democrats realized they needed to mobilize their base while also reaching out to new voters. Clinton had won election in 1992 with only 43 percent of the popular vote; he had then gone on to win reelection in 1996 against a weak Republican candidate with less than 50 percent of the popular vote. In winning both elections, the Clinton-Gore ticket took key swing states including Arkansas, Kentucky, Missouri, Tennessee, Louisiana, and Florida.

George W. Bush, Texas governor and son of the former president, won the Republican party nomination in 2000 after declaring himself a compassionate conservative. This label tapped into rhetoric used by Republican presidential hopefuls who had sought the nomination in the past. Jack Kemp, a presidential candidate in 1988, described himself as a "conservative with a bleeding heart," and even the hardcore conservative Patrick Buchanan declared himself in favor of "conservatism of the heart." Bush's compassionate conservatism showed a similar impulse to temper hard-edged conservative ideology based on laissez-faire economics and Manichean morality, but it also reflected an understanding of where the American electorate stood ideologically.

According to one survey conducted in 2000, 80 percent of all Republicans polled considered themselves "conservatives," compared with half of all independents and 40 percent of all Democrats.[2] Yet when asked about the "most important problems" facing the country, respondents to the University of Michigan National Election Studies survey listed education, social welfare, and medical care. Twelve percent listed morality. Republicans were much more concerned than Democrats about what they saw as moral decay in the nation. On the abortion issue, the electorate divided into 56 percent pro-choice and 44 percent antiabortion, revealing that the public accepted a woman's right to choose. Fifty-nine percent of Democrats described themselves as pro-choice, while 53 percent of Republicans were antiabortion. The majority of Americans wanted increased funding for education, but roughly two-thirds of Republicans favored school vouchers, as did half of all Democrats. Issues such as defense, foreign affairs, and immigration were not high on the voters' minds in the 2000 election. Surprisingly, trust in government had risen in the Clinton-Gore years, though overall it was lower than it had been in the 1960s, the early 1970s, or even 1984.[3]

This ideological configuration explains much about the Bush strategy during the campaign. Bush declared himself to be an "education candidate" and spoke about returning integrity to government and to the nation. He ran as a caring conservative who did not believe in "big government" or the failed liberal programs of the past—but he did not dismiss government as the problem. In this way, he differed from Reagan in his 1980 campaign.

A booming economy should have favored Bush's rival, Albert Gore, Jr. In 1992, the Clinton-Gore ticket had made the faltering economy their number one issue. By 2000, the United States economy had experienced an extended period of prosperity, and the federal deficit that had mushroomed under the Reagan-Bush administration had been transformed into a surplus.[4] During the campaign, however, Gore failed to capitalize on the prosperous economy because he was reluctant to link himself too closely with the Clinton administration and the Lewinsky scandal. Gore was eager to portray himself as an independent actor and a candidate concerned with moral values. In his acceptance speech at the Democratic National Convention, he declared, "There's something else at stake in this election that's even more important than economic progress. Simply put, it's our values." Gore went on to declare that family values meant "putting Social Security and Medicare in an iron-clad lockbox where politicians can't touch."[5]

Although the issues of Medicare and middle-class tax cuts appealed to Democratic voters, post-election surveys showed that neither a tax cut nor Social Security–Medicare was significant in determining how Americans voted. Education was an important issue, however, and Gore campaigned on the need to increase federal spending on schools. In this respect, the two candidates were in agreement. The difference between them concerned school vouchers: Gore was opposed to them and Bush supported them. Bush's position reflected general public sentiment on this issue. In a close contest in which every vote counted, the education issue helped Bush.

The issue of national defense also benefited Bush, though both candidates promised to increase defense spending. Gore's selection of U.S. Senator Joseph Lieberman (D-Connecticut) as his running mate signaled his support of a powerful American military. Lieberman was a strong supporter of the U.S. pro-Israel foreign policy and antiterrorism. At the convention, Gore recalled that he had been one of the few U.S. senators to vote in favor of military intervention in the first Gulf War. He promised to make sure that the nation's armed forces continued to be the "best equipped, best trained, and best led in the entire world." He warned that the nation faced new threats from terrorism and new kinds of weapons of mass destruction. Yet in the end, voters viewed Bush as stronger on national defense.

The larger problem for Gore in an evenly divided electorate in which the majority of voters identified themselves as conservative or moderate was that he was seen as a liberal. Gore reinforced this perception at the convention and on the campaign trail with his attacks on "big tobacco, big oil, big polluters, the pharmaceutical companies, the HMOs." Gore was eager to activate his party base and to expand the electorate by turning out minorities and single women to the polls. He proclaimed himself a "fighter for the people" against special interests. He declared that in his presidency he would honor "the ideal of equality by standing up for civil rights and defending affirmative action." He called for expanding child-care and after-school programs. He pledged to protect and defend a woman's right to choose an abortion, noting that "the last thing this country needs is a Supreme Court that overturns *Roe v. Wade.*"

Gore was fiery and often eloquent on the campaign trail. Yet Bush was perceived by the electorate as standing closer to their values. Gore's support for hate-crime legislation, gun control, abortion, and women's rights won the Democratic candidate the women's vote, 54 percent to 43 percent, but these issues overall were not strong enough to win an election. Bush's compassionate conservatism clearly benefited him on Election Day, though the election proved to be the closest in American history. Gore won the popular vote 48.4 percent to 47.8 percent but lost the Electoral College 271 to 266 votes. Gore lost every southern and border state that the Clinton-Gore team had carried in 1996, including Gore's home state of Tennessee.

A change of 537 votes in Florida would have resulted in Gore's election. The difference in the vote was only 0.00045 percent after three recounts. In the end, the election came down to a legal battle over ballots in Florida. In a 5–4 decision in *Bush v. Gore* (2000), the Supreme Court ruled that Bush had won Florida, letting the original count stand and overturning two Florida state supreme court rulings that had ordered more recounts of the ballots. Written by Justice Anthony Kennedy and joined without reservation only by Justice Sandra Day O'Connor, *Bush v. Gore* articulated a novel and strained equal-protection analysis. Both conservative and liberal legal scholars found reasons, albeit different ones, to criticize the majority decision. Conservatives, however, were more supportive of Chief Justice Rehnquist's concurrence, joined by Justices Scalia and Thomas. Rehnquist maintained that the state court had violated article II, section 1, of the Constitution by invading the authority of the state legislature to set election standards and procedures.[6] The intervention of the Supreme Court became a rallying cry for Democrats, who claimed that Bush had won the election by judicial fiat. Bush became the "president-select." For the next four years, Democrats spoke about the illegitimate presidency of George W. Bush and the stolen election of 2000.

Although Bush lost the popular vote, he extended his support among conservative Christians. The Bush coalition was in large part an alliance among white Christians, led by observant evangelical Protestants and Roman Catholics. Bush won 63 percent of the vote among those who attended church services more than weekly, 57 percent among those who attended weekly, 46 percent among those who attended monthly, 42 percent among people who seldom went to church, and 32 percent among those who never went.[7] In doing so, he strengthened an important core of the Republican coalition. Data collected by the University of Akron Survey Research Center in 2000 showed that of the total vote, self-declared Protestants made up 55 percent and Roman Catholics 22 percent. Of these, the "more observant" evangelical Protestants went 84 percent for Bush; Bob Dole in 1996 had received only 70 percent of this group's support. "More observant" Roman Catholics went 57 percent for Bush and only 43 percent for Gore. Secular voters went overwhelmingly for Gore (65 percent), about the same as they had for Clinton in 1996.[8] In short, regular church attendance correlated with voting for Bush.

The Bush campaign effectively targeted conservative Christian organizations as a means of mobilizing the Christian vote. These groups were actively engaged in the mass distribution of voter guides, pamphlets, and placing radio advertisements, and they were a familiar presence on talk radio programs. Although Pat Robertson's Christian Coalition had waned in influence, other evangelical Christian organizations were important in getting out the vote among their constituencies. Religious social networks made direct contact with voters, which proved even more effective than voter guides and pastoral commentary. In addition, these religious networks served as important sources for recruitment to other conservative groups. Perceiving themselves as embattled by secular forces, conservative Christians felt compelled to become involved politically in order to stop America from descending into moral poverty. The Bush campaign stuck deeper roots into this Christian base than had any previous Republican presidential campaign, even though the Democratic party tried to use its economic program to compete for the Protestant evangelical vote.[9]

The Texas political consultant Karl Rove, who had worked for Bush's father at the Republican National Committee in the 1970s, masterminded the Republican coalition. Rove had begun his career working for the College Republicans to help organize campus support for Senator Ralph Smith (Illinois), a conservative who had been appointed to take Everett Dirksen's seat after his death. Vietnam antiwar protest had turned Illinois college campuses into hostile environments for Republicans, but Rove revealed himself to be a master organizer. He tied College Republicans to the conservative Young Americans for Freedom. He also showed a wicked ability for political tricks; at one point he distributed leaflets at a rock concert and a soup kitchen announcing, "Free beer, free food, girls, and a good time for nothing," for a headquarters opening for Alan Dixon, a Democrat who was running for state treasurer. Hundreds of Chicago's most dissolute people appeared at the opening, disrupting the gala. Although the election of 1970 proved to be a disaster for Republican candidates in Illinois, largely as a result of a new income tax enacted by the Republican governor, Rove won the respect of Washington insiders, including George H. W. Bush.

In the 1980s, Rove moved to Texas, where he built the most powerful Republican consulting firm in the state. He aligned himself with George W. Bush's political career. In 1994, Bush challenged Ann Richards, the Democratic incumbent governor. Rove brought into the campaign Karen Hughes, a Texas Republican operative, and Vance McMahan, a lawyer and policy guru. The campaign to defeat Richards began when Kay Bailey Hutchison won a special election in 1993 to take Senator Phil Gramm's seat after he resigned to run for president. Hutchison defeated Richards's hand-picked candidate. In 1994, Bush went head-to-head against Richards, who had gained national attention for a line in her keynote speech at the Democratic National Convention: "Poor George. He can't help it—he was born with a silver foot in his mouth." The Bush campaign focused on substantive issues like education, juvenile crime, and welfare reform. Nevertheless, nasty rumors circulated during the campaign that Richards had appointed a disproportionate number of lesbians to government positions in the state. Democrats blamed Rove for starting these rumors, but there was no evidence to back the charge. At the same time, rumors circulated among Democrats that Bush was a hothead who would snap under pressure. This was Texas politics at its worst. But on Election Day Bush swept East Texas, a conservative Democratic stronghold. Bush had taken his first step toward the presidency. He had campaigned on education and welfare-reform issues, and he had mobilized evangelical Christian voters in the state. The gubernatorial race would be the model for his presidential campaign six years later.[10]

The Day the World Changed

In his victory speech on December 13, following the Supreme Court's decision in *Bush v. Gore,* Bush promised to serve as a leader of "one nation" and not "one party." After eight years of political conflict during the Clinton presidency, few insiders believed that this was the end of partisan warfare in Washington, D.C. Indeed, Democratic leaders declared that Bush lacked a public mandate for his program, while activists in the party insisted that his presidency was illegitimate. Although Republicans maintained a slight majority in both houses of Congress, when U.S. Senator James Jeffords of Vermont left the Republican party to declare himself an independent in May 2001, the Senate became deadlocked. For conservatives, Bush's greatest accomplishment was his success in pushing through an 11-year, $1.35 trillion tax-cut bill that reduced the top income rate to 35 percent. Republicans claimed that this measure benefited lower- and middle-income Americans by refunding $300 million.

Throughout the campaign, Bush continued to speak of the need to reform the nation's education system. Unlike Reagan and his conservative allies, Bush proposed expanding the role of the Department of Education by linking federal aid to state benchmarks of adequate yearly progress in public education. Having barely won election, Bush became convinced that he needed the influential Senator Ted Kennedy (D-Massachusetts), a nearly mythic foe of conservatives, on board for any education bill to pass. At an inauguration day luncheon, Senator Alan Simpson (R-Wyoming) brought Kennedy up to Bush and said, "He [Kennedy] is an ornery S.O.B., but you can do business with him." Two days later Bush met with senior members of the House and Senate education committees in the Oval Office. He told the group that he was "strongly committed to seeing the neediest children get the benefits of these reforms." Moreover, he was prepared to "take on the forces in Congress and among the governors who just wanted to spread the money around."[11]

Joined by Senator Judd Gregg (R-New Hampshire) and Representatives John A. Boehner (R-Ohio) and George Miller (D-California), the Bush White House drafted new legislation to reform the education system. What emerged was a proposal to greatly extend the federal government's role in the system. The proposal called for increased funding to states and direct targeting of funds for poor-performance students and struggling schools. The measure also required schools to track performance through annual tests from grades three through eight. In addition, states would set their own performance standards that would be assessed in biennial reports.

The initiative drew criticism from the education establishment represented by the National Education Association and other interest groups, as well as conservative groups that opposed the increased power of the federal government through the Education Department, which Reagan had targeted for elimination. African-American and Latino leaders expressed concern that testing would stigmatize these ethnic groups. Within the House, approximately thirty to sixty conservative Republicans stood against the president's bill. They were especially upset that the bill did not include a voucher program. On the other side, many liberals, including Senator Paul Wellstone (D-Minnesota), raised issues about the quality of the required tests. In the spring of 2001, the Senate and the House had passed their own bills, but efforts to reconcile the two bogged down in committee.[12]

On September 11, Bush was in a Florida classroom trying to build public support for the initiative when he received word that Islamist terrorists had flown planes into the World Trade Center in New York and the Pentagon, outside of Washington, D.C. The attacks were the most destructive foreign assaults on American soil in modern times. Shocked by the devastation that cost nearly three thousand lives and billions of dollars in economic loss, Americans united in the immediate aftermath of 9/11. Appearing before a joint session of Congress on September 20, Bush outlined the nation's retaliatory response against those who launched the attack and against global terrorism. More than three-quarters of the nation saw the address. Bush's approval rating shot up to 90 percent.

Following the attacks, Bush was eager to carry the war to the terrorists. The administration viewed Afghanistan as the center of terrorist activity. The country was under the control of a fanatical sect of Muslims, the Taliban, that provided a refuge for Osama bin Laden, head of the international terrorist group al Qaeda, which had planned the 9/11 attacks. In a carefully crafted diplomatic strategy, Bush demanded that the Taliban government turn over Bin Laden. In pursuing this strategy, Bush pushed the American military to develop plans for rapid action. Within the administration there was little dissent to Bush's course of action, with the notable exception of Deputy Defense Secretary Paul Wolfowitz, who feared that American troops might become mired in a land war in mountain fighting in Afghanistan. Instead, he proposed an attack on Iraq, which he felt was a brittle, oppressive regime about ready to collapse. He believed that Iraq's leader, Saddam Hussein, was probably involved in the 9/11 attacks.[13] Vice President Dick Cheney, Secretary of Defense Donald Rumsfeld, and Secretary of State Colin Powell initially opposed action on Iraq.

On October 7, 2001, the United States, Britain, and other European allies launched an invasion against the Taliban regime. Joined by Afghan rebels from the north, the Western allies quickly defeated the Taliban government. The democratic elections that followed brought a pro-Western government into power. The quick results misled the Bush administration into thinking that an invasion of Iraq would lead to similar results.

While terrorism absorbed Americans' attention, the administration found new momentum in pushing its agenda before a Congress bent on showing the nation that it was united. Taking advantage of this sentiment, Bush persuaded Congress to pass his education bill. Signed in January 2002, the "No Child Left Behind Act" marked a triumph of bipartisanship and promised to transform public education in America. The cornerstone of the act was standardized testing, but conservatives were quick to point out that Bush had backed away from vouchers and greater spending flexibility for states. In addition, the act boosted the education budget by billions. Chester E. Finn, Jr., a conservative educational policy specialist, called the act a "political win" for Bush and an opportunity to elevate the achievement of American students, especially the poorest among them. He also noted that the bill, which was more than twelve hundred pages, imposed many mandates on the states and the school systems receiving federal monies.[14]

Once implemented, however, the No Child Left Behind Act drew heavy criticism from all sides. The Left complained that classroom instruction was geared to testing and not critical thinking, and that not enough money was being spent on resources like tutoring; conservatives noted the hundreds and hundreds of regulations issued by the Department of Education and the astronomical costs the act imposed; state governors protested that the federal government did not appropriate sufficient funds to carry out the act's provisions; and many parents complained that the tests were no good when their Johnnies and Sallies performed poorly on them. These complaints (and there were many more) spoke to the difficulty of reforming American education. What is especially striking about the bill, and foretold much about the Bush White House, is that conservative activists and policy experts appeared to play a small role in its drafting. Bush wanted educational reform, and he brought conservative Republican legislators such as Senator Judd Gregg (R-New Hampshire) and Representative John Boehner (R-Ohio) early into the process. Bush was eager to show that he was bipartisan, but he also wanted to enact legislation. To do this, he needed the support of Ted Kennedy and Representative George Miller (D-California), well known for his liberal politics in the House. In the end, Bush got some of what he wanted, educational testing and accountability, but at the cost of extending federal involvement in education, spending more money, and further bureaucratizing the system.

2002: A Cautious Mandate

Bush's forceful response to 9/11 changed perceptions of him from a weak partisan president to a strong leader willing to defend American democracy against militant foreign enemies. Polls before the September 11 attack marked Bush as an even more polarizing figure than Clinton had been during his presidency.[15] A year after the attack, Bush's popularity rating stood at an unprecedented 60 points. Bush sought to reinforce this image of presidential leadership by pushing his domestic agenda, even as he declared war on terrorism. Immediately after 9/11, he began promoting market-based prescription drug coverage for seniors, a supply-focused energy policy, an overhaul of pension laws, and regulatory relief for business. Bush also called for a homeland security bill, permanent tax rate cuts, and confirmation for his judicial nominees. The midterm election of 2002 expressed a general perception of Bush as a "can-do" president.

Bush believed that Republicans needed to retake control of the Senate after Jeffords's defection if his administration was to move forward on his domestic and foreign policy agenda. A deadlocked Congress might be fatal to his chances of reelection. Realizing the importance of the midterm election, Bush's key strategist, Karl Rove, began recruiting candidates to run for Congress in 2002. In the process, Rove and Bush showed the pragmatic side of their politics by selecting and backing candidates they deemed electable. This meant, at times, turning their backs on more conservative candidates, much to the irritation of right-wing activists. Bush was willing to make some sacrifices to win larger conservative goals.

Bush's fundraising ability rivaled Reagan's. Thanks to his efforts, by the time of the election the Republican National Committee had a six-fold advantage in available funds over the Democratic National Committee, $30 million to $5 million. Bush also took to the campaign trail to support Republican candidates, making 108 campaign visits on behalf of 26 House candidates and 20 Senate candidates. In the final days of the campaign, he traveled 10,000 miles across 15 states to stump for Republican candidates. In this whirlwind tour, Bush sought to nationalize the election by talking about the war on terror and the need for a new Department of Homeland Security.[16] He attacked Democratic senators who opposed the new department. He put his presidency on the line for the Republican party.

Bush combined these efforts with a strategy to mobilize the base of the GOP. Bush and Rove believed that the Democrats had out-organized the Republicans "on the ground" in 2000 in turning out the vote. As a result, Bush worked with the Republican National Committee to strengthen the party and its voter-turnout operation. Their strategy differed from that of the Democratic party, which relied on outside partisan groups like organized labor to mobilize voters. The Republican National Committee's 72-Hour Task Force devised a national effort to get voters to the polls.[17] These efforts proved successful: Overall the turnout in

2002 was higher than it had been in the 1998 midterm elections, with more than 39 percent of the eligible voters going to the polls in 2002. Yet even with the slightly higher turnout, which usually rewards Democrats, the Democratic vote fell by 1.3 percent, while the Republicans increased their vote by about a half a percentage point. In close elections, such margins prove critical. Former Christian Coalition strategist Ralph Reed, the chairman of the Georgia Republican party, noted that parties "still win elections now as a century ago: friend to friend."[18]

Republicans had the advantage for two additional reasons: redistricting and incumbency. Republican redistricting efforts had provided a more favorable terrain for the GOP. What's more, the political environment benefited incumbents. In the 34 Senate races in 2002, only 4 incumbents lost their seats. The power of incumbency was even more striking in the House, where just 4 of the 390 incumbents running for reelection lost their seats. Before the election, Democrats believed that their strongest chances for gains lay in 7 Republican-held seats, but all were in states that Bush had carried in 2000. On the other hand, Republicans found their best chances for gains in 6 seats, 4 of them in states that Bush had also carried over Gore.

The final results showed how close the margins of victory could be. Republicans gained two seats in the Senate and increased their majority in the House of Representatives. For the first time since Franklin Roosevelt, a president saw his party gain in both houses of Congress in a midterm election. As a consequence, the midterm election of 2002 belied what had become a cliché in political circles: that the American electorate preferred divided government. The election enhanced Bush's reputation as a party leader. His efforts for specific candidates appeared to benefit them on Election Day.

The Republican victory occurred with a shift in only a few seats. As the journalist David Nather observed in the *Congressional Quarterly* regarding the 2002 election, "It [2002] was not a tidal wave that swept Republicans into majorities in the House and Senate," but it did not have to be because a few seats were sufficient to return control of Congress to the GOP.[19] The Republican strategy had targeted key seats in the Senate and the House, and often the margins of victory proved slight. In Missouri, Republican challenger Jim Talent defeated incumbent Democratic U.S. Senator Jean Carnahan by one percentage point. In the campaign Talent mobilized the conservative rural vote, while conceding the state's largest city, St. Louis. In Minnesota, Norm Coleman beat former vice president Walter F. Mondale, who had entered the race following the death of Paul Wellstone in a plane crash, by a mere two points. Coleman was helped when the Wellstone family, joined by liberal Democrats, turned Wellstone's memorial service into a vituperative attack on the Republicans.

In a closely divided electorate, campaigning was fierce. In Georgia, Representative Saxby Chambliss challenged the Democratic incumbent Max Cleland, a triple-amputee Vietnam War veteran. Chambliss attacked Cleland as being soft on defense and too liberal for the state. At the same time, the GOP undertook an intensive registration campaign that targeted 50,000 Hispanics in the state. In the final week of the campaign, Ralph Reed, the Republican state chairman, orchestrated a telephone campaign that reached 170,000 voters on specific issues. Volunteers knocked on thousands of doors in Republican neighborhoods. The results devastated the Democrats. Republicans took the governor's mansion and defeated the state house speaker and the Senate Majority Leader. The sweep was impressive. It was further evidence of Democratic party erosion in the South owing to issues such as national defense that favored Republicans.

The Republican takeover of Congress further solidified the position of the GOP Right within Congress. The Bush strategy called for the mobilization of grassroots conservatives as the key to Republican success. The national Republican party and the administration threw their support behind candidates who endorsed the Bush program. In some cases, this meant supporting less conservative candidates within the party, but on the whole, Republicans elected to Congress were to the right on the political spectrum. By contrast, Democrats elected to Congress tended to be on the left politically. This resulted in increased ideological homogeneity within each party, completing a pattern that had begun in the 1980s.

War in Iraq and the 2004 Election

The war in Iraq set the context for the 2004 presidential election and helped Bush defeat his Democratic challenger, Senator John Kerry (D-

Massachusetts). Senate Majority Leader Trent Lott told the press after the election, "You cannot ignore the fact that America did change on 9/11."[20]

The impending intervention in Iraq had served as the backdrop for the midterm elections of 2002. Following the election, the Bush administration thought that toppling the regime of Saddam Hussein would send a message to neighboring Syria and Iran to stop supporting terrorist groups like Hezbollah, the well-organized faction in Lebanon that had gained popular support for its attacks on Israel and its aid to Palestinian refugees living in Lebanon. In addition, American intelligence indicated that Iraq was rapidly developing weapons of mass destruction (WMDs). More immediately, Saddam Hussein continued his cat-and-mouse game with U.N. inspectors over access to Iraq's weapons program, which was required by the terms of the 1991 cease-fire. The Bush administration feared that Saddam was building weapons of mass destruction that could be used by terrorists in chemical and biological attacks on the United States. Bush viewed Saddam Hussein's regime as a threat to Middle Eastern stability, a thorn in the Israeli-Palestinian conflict, and a potential source of terrorist funding. The administration also was eager—critics later claimed overly eager—to argue that Saddam Hussein was attempting to acquire materials to develop nuclear weapons. The administration's strongest case for intervention was that Saddam Hussein had continued to flout U.N. sanctions and refused U.N. inspection of his country's weapons program.

Saddam Hussein's reluctance to allow inspectors into Iraq convinced the Bush administration that the regime was continuing to develop weapons of mass destruction. In December 2000 the Central Intelligence Agency and other intelligence groups had produced a report titled "Iraq: Steadily Pursuing WMD Capabilities." The report estimated that Iraq had stockpiled one hundred tons of mustard gas and Sarin nerve agents. Later, other CIA intelligence reports raised suspicions of a link between Iraq and al Qaeda. The administration appears to have given little consideration to the view that Hussein was bluffing in order to compensate for the shoddiness of Iraq's army.

Bush and a group of neoconservative hawks in the administration, including Paul Wolfowitz, wanted to take military action against Iraq. Secretary of State Colin Powell urged the administration to win U.N. approval and international support before launching an invasion unilaterally. When the administration failed to receive a second U.N. approval, largely because of opposition from France, Germany, and Russia, Bush decided to forgo international action. On October 10, 2002, the House of Representatives voted 296–133 to authorize the president to use military force against Iraq. The following day, the Senate, including the presidential hopeful Senator John Kerry (D-Massachusetts), supported the measure 77–23. Kerry later insisted that he voted not for war but for diplomacy backed by the threat of American military intervention.

On March 20, 2003, the United States, joined by the United Kingdom and representative forces from twenty other nations, launched an invasion of Iraq. The Hussein government fell quickly, but American military forces found themselves ill prepared for an insurgency by Sunni Moslems and an incipient sectarian civil war. Secretary of Defense Donald Rumsfeld insisted at the outset of the invasion that American forces be limited in size, even though some military planners projected that more than 380,000 troops would be needed to occupy Iraq following the invasion. Rumsfeld and others within the administration believed that following the liberation of Iraq, a coalition of Iraqis would take the reins of power, including policing activities. Moreover, the Bush administration thought that support for rebuilding Iraq would come from the international community, including the United Nations. After a lighting-fast drive into Baghdad, the Saddam Hussein regime fell. Anxious to gain international and political support for the American presence in Iraq, Bush declared on May 1, 2003, under a banner reading "Mission Accomplished," that major combat operations in Iraq had ended. Bush's premature proclamation was aimed at reassuring the international community, but it was also good for political consumption at home as the 2004 presidential race opened.

After a closely contested primary race, the Democratic party nominated a Vietnam War veteran and U.S. senator from Massachusetts, John Kerry, to challenge Bush in 2004. Kerry had won the nomination after a grueling primary campaign against eight other candidates. By December 2003, former Vermont governor Howard Dean had emerged as the front-runner in the polls and in fundraising. Dean had utilized the Internet to build a grassroots campaign that tapped into anti–Iraq War sentiment within the Democratic party. Kerry's well-organized campaign in the Iowa caucuses in January won him 38 percent of the delegates, while U.S. Senator John Edwards from North Carolina, a newcomer to national politics, came in a close second. Dean took a distant third with only 18 percent of the vote. Kerry's success in Iowa was followed later that month by a win in the New Hampshire primary. After Dean dropped out, the battle came down to Kerry and Edwards. Kerry did not sew up the nomination until he decisively won Super Tuesday in March, when Edwards did not carry a single state. In July, shortly before the Democratic National Convention, Kerry named Edwards as his running mate. Most observers believed that the election would be a close one, coming down to sixteen battleground states, including Edwards's home state of North Carolina.

The Kerry-Edwards campaign wanted to adopt the theme "Stronger at home, respected in the world." The Democratic candidates were eager to focus on domestic issues, while contending that the Iraq War was a distraction from the War on Terror. In his acceptance speech to the Democratic National Convention, Kerry declared that "here at home, wages are falling, health-care costs are rising, and our great middle class is shrinking." He agreed that "we are a nation at war: a global war on terror against an enemy unlike we've ever known before." Kerry wanted to appeal to voters as an officer who had fought in Vietnam and could provide the military leadership necessary for a nation at war. He introduced himself to the convention by referring to his military background: "I'm John Kerry, and I'm reporting for duty."[21] Unfortunately for Kerry, his opponents remembered his antiwar activism following his service in Vietnam.

A group calling itself "Swift Boat Veterans for Truth" launched a negative advertising campaign against Kerry that highlighted his antiwar activities. The group was headed by the Houston attorney John O'Neill, a former commander of Swift Boat PCF 94 during the Vietnam War. O'Neill had debated Kerry on national television in 1971. The group included sixteen of the twenty-three officers who had served with Kerry off the coast of Vietnam. The Swift Boat group challenged Kerry's military record in Vietnam, claiming that the senator had exaggerated his combat duty and had unfairly received a Silver Star. These claims appeared in O'Neill's and Jerome Corsi's book *Unfit for Command: Swift Boat Veterans Speak Out against John Kerry,* which quickly became a best seller after its release in August 2004. The group produced four hard-hitting advertisements that attacked Kerry's actions in Vietnam and his subsequent activities in an antiwar veterans' group. Kerry responded by defending his war record and filing a formal complaint with the Federal Election Committee charging that the Swift Boat Veterans group was being illegally coordinated with Republicans and the Bush-Cheney campaign. The charges, however, threw the Kerry-Edwards campaign off stride.

Meanwhile, Bush and Cheney launched an extensive television campaign that aired more than forty-nine thousand negative ads attacking Kerry as a "flip-flop" candidate who could not be trusted. The Kerry campaign responded with sixteen thousand negative television ads of its own. Kerry remained on the defensive throughout the campaign. Bush, for his part, was challenged on September 8, when Dan Rather reported on the CBS news program *60 Minutes Wednesday* that recently discovered evidence revealed that undue political influence had been exerted to secure a spot for George W. Bush in the Texas Air National Guard in 1972 and 1973. Questions were immediately raised about the authenticity of the documents, which forensic experts characterized as forgeries. An investigation disclosed that the CBS News producer Mary Mapes had obtained the documents from Lieutenant Colonel Bill Burkett, a former officer in the Texas Air National Guard who had made similar unsubstantiated claims in the past. Republicans claimed media bias on the part of Dan Rather and CBS News. The way this episode was turned against the established media illustrated the effectiveness of the Bush-Cheney campaign and the inability of the Kerry-Edwards campaign to handle itself under attack.

These negative attacks arguably did not change many voters' minds; rather, they merely confirmed images held by partisan supporters. In the end, the election came down to which side was better organized to turn out its supporters. In this regard, the Bush-Cheney campaign had the advantage. In 2004, the Republican candidates sought to replicate their 2000 victory by energizing the conservative base rather than swing voters. After stepping into the White House, Bush had worked to strengthen the Republican party and expand its base. By the time of the election, he had attracted more than one million new donors to the GOP. (Reagan had attracted 852,595 first-time donors when he was president.) The Bush-Cheney ticket in 2004 constructed a multiple-level campaign organization that was operated from headquarters in Arlington, Virginia. Paid regional and state coordinators conducted grassroots operations that concentrated on battleground states. More than a million individuals volunteered to work on the campaign at the county, city, and precinct levels. The national headquarters set volunteer-recruitment goals and oversaw campaign events and voter-registration drives, while state campaign officials held volunteers accountable for meeting their targets. The Bush-Cheney campaign was a well-coordinated and tightly disciplined party operation. The Democratic party campaign, meanwhile, also worked at the grassroots level, but it relied heavily on auxiliary groups to conduct much of its voter-turnout work at the grassroots. As a result, Democrats' efforts were not as well coordinated as their opponents'.

The Republican National Committee had increased party rolls by registering 3.4 million voters between 2002 and 2004.[22] The Bush campaign was determined to get its supporters to the polls. The 2002 congressional campaign showed the success of the "72 Hour Task Force" in mobilizing Republican voters. Campaign strategy, crafted by Karl Rove and his deputy Ken Mehlman, focused especially on what they called "values voters," including white evangelical Christians as well as anti–gun control, antitax, and land-rights activists.[23] This mobilization of Bush's conservative base was critical in winning the election. Even as late as two days before Election Day, Bush's bid appeared shaky. To rally his base, Bush began to press moral issues such as abortion and the need to restore traditional values. He was convinced that by doing so he could tap a reservoir of four million Christian voters who had not gone to the polls in 2000. The Bush strategy called for mobilizing evangelical and fundamentalist Protestants and increasing GOP support among Roman Catholics, who made up 27 percent of the electorate.

In 2000, Bush had won 47 percent of the Catholic vote; in 2004 he won 52 percent. Thousands of campaign workers were sent to Catholic churches to win support for the president. Catholic support in states like Ohio and Florida proved critical. In Ohio, Bush won 55 percent of the Catholic vote to Kerry's 43 percent. The turnaround in the Catholic vote was stunning. Leonard Leo, a Catholic adviser to the Bush-Cheney campaign, noted, "In 2004, you have a Catholic running on a Democratic ticket, and he garners less Catholic support than the President, who is a Methodist."[24] Among born-again and evangelical Christians, who made up 23 percent of the vote in 2004, 78 percent voted for Bush and his support of the "right-to-life" position and marriage for heterosexuals only.

Although some observers later disputed the importance of so-called moral issues in winning the election for Bush, exit polls at the time showed that a plurality of voters (22 percent) named "moral values" as their top priority, and that the majority of voters who were concerned about this issue voted for Bush.[25] (Those voters who placed terrorism as their top issue still broke for Bush over Kerry by about a four-to-one margin.) Bush's ascertainment of the importance of moral issues proved correct. He received 9 million more votes than he had in 2000, winning over 62 million votes with a margin of 3.3 million votes, or 3 percent of the electorate. This gave George W. Bush 286 Electoral College votes to Kerry's 252. The election was decidedly close and came down to the final vote in Ohio, which was not decided until the next day.

Republicans maintained control of the Senate and the House, thanks in large part to Bush's willingness to campaign for other Republican candidates. This strategy contrasted sharply with Richard Nixon's victory in 1972 and Bill Clinton's policy of triangulation in 1996. In the Senate, the Republicans picked up four seats, bolstering their previous 51–48 majority. In the House, Republicans extended their majority by four seats to 231–201. This was the first time since January 1933 that the GOP had held the House for 12 straight years. Falling to the Republican onslaught was Senate Minority Leader Tom Daschle (D-South Dakota), who had successfully stalled much of Bush's first-term legislation.

Most people on both sides of the political spectrum agreed that John Kerry hurt the Democrats. As David Boaz, the executive vice president of the libertarian Cato Institute, declared, "Were it not for the relative unattractiveness of Kerry and his old-fashioned liberal agenda, Bush would have lost."[26] Boaz had a vested interest in downplaying the importance of social issues to Bush's victory, but surveys supported his claims in this regard: A surprising 60 percent of voters in the 2004 election said they favored some legal recognition of same-sex couples. Twenty-five percent said they favored marriage rights, while 35 percent favored "civil unions." On the other hand, 37 percent told pollsters that same-sex couples should not be granted any form of legal recognition. These polling numbers suggest that the exact difference between same-sex marriage and same-sex civil unions was probably unclear in most voters' minds, but it also indicated general divisions within the electorate.[27]

It is debatable whether Bush's strategy of mobilizing Christian voters and pushing moral issues might have backfired with a stronger Democratic candidate. Whatever the case, Democrats were not able to mobilize their voters by playing on the fears of a Christian Right takeover of government. Moreover, in some states, social issues such as a ban on gay marriages appeared to favor Republicans. Eleven states had initiatives banning gay marriage, a powerful incentive for social conservatives to turn up at the polls. In all eleven of these states, the initiatives passed by large margins. Republicans seized upon the gay-marriage ban after Massachusetts state judges ruled in November 2003 that gay marriage was protected by the state's constitution and ordered state legislators to begin issuing licenses to gay couples. The Massachusetts decision immediately drew fire from conservative and traditional religious groups, which pushed for statewide initiatives. Gay rights organizations found themselves on the defensive. Matt Foreman, representing the National Gay and Lesbian Task Force, declared that "fundamental human rights should never be put up for a popular vote. We'll win some states and we'll lose some states."[28] His prediction proved overly optimistic. On Election Day, gay rights did not win a single state.

Social issues like the ban on gay marriage trumped economic issues in midwestern states. For example, Bush carried Ohio, which had lost 232,000 jobs since the beginning of his presidency. Phil Burress, the president of the Cincinnati-based Citizens for Community Values and an antipornography crusader, mobilized voters to enact a ban against civil unions. In the 1990s, Burress had spent much of his time fighting strip clubs and X-rated bookstores. He saw the issue of civil unions and gay marriage as an even greater threat to traditional family values. Even before the Massachusetts Supreme Court ruling, Burress had begun laying the groundwork for a church-based conservative movement. In January 1996, he helped organize a national meeting of Christian conservatives to combat same-sex marriage. In the fall of 1996, these activists had persuaded Congress and President Clinton to enact legislation defining marriage as a union between a man and a woman. Thirty state legislatures followed suit by enacting similar legislation.

The Ohio measure was the broadest of the eleven initiatives passed because it barred any legal status for "relationships of unmarried individuals that intends to approximate the design, qualities, significance, or effect of marriage." In pushing the initiative, Burress tapped into a groundswell of anger over the Massachusetts ruling. The Ohio initiative took on a life of its own as church-backed groups and volunteers circulated petitions to make the measure a ballot question. Burress's organization gathered 575,000 signatures to place the measure on the ballot. The initiative movement faced major opposition from most of the state's Republican establishment, including Governor Bob Taft, Attorney General Jim Petro, and Senators George V. Voinovich and Mike DeWine. Burress denounced these Republicans as "enablers" of a homosexual agenda that sought to have homosexuality taught in schools as equal to heterosexuality. Rumor was that Bush and the White House opposed the amendment as well, fearing a liberal backlash. Nonetheless, the initiative passed on Election Day and appeared to draw equal support from men and women, blacks and whites.[29]

The success of these initiatives displayed the power of the Christian pro-family movement at the state level. In the Ohio election, evangelical Christians accounted for 25 percent of the state's vote. This wing of the party sought a broader agenda that included prohibiting abortions, banning pornography, supporting school vouchers, and lowering taxes. With many members who were evangelical Christians and orthodox Roman Catholics and Mormons, pro-family groups also called for community and church-backed efforts to eliminate poverty and to provide housing and support for the poor.[30] This religious faction of the GOP represented only one force within the party. Nevertheless, in 2004 it flexed its muscle and helped give Republicans control of government. Social conservatives pointed to a poignant fact: In every state in which a marriage amendment was placed on the ballot in 2004, with the single exception of Utah, the amendment received a larger vote than Bush received.

BUSH's remaking of the Republican party was a major achievement. By strengthening party organization at the national and state levels, Bush had enabled the GOP to harness grassroots activism to win control of Congress and the White House. Partisanship within the electorate had been on the rise since the 1980s, and Bush tapped into this sentiment to mobilize voters. The result was a high voter turnout in the midterm elections of 2002 and the presidential election in 2004.

As president, Bush sought to reconfigure relations among the White House, Congress, and the federal bureaucracy. Ronald Reagan had complained that an "iron triangle" of liberals in Congress, federal bureaucrats concerned with protecting their agencies, and public-interest lobbies interested in promoting progressive causes had subverted his agenda of reducing federal spending and downsizing government. Bush attempted to counter this iron triangle by getting Republicans elected to Congress and creating new public-interest groups through his faith-based initiatives. Through these initiatives, church and "value-oriented" organizations became eligible for federal funds to provide social services and develop other programs at the state and community levels. This strategy reflected Bush's own belief that private nonprofit organizations could provide more effective programs for drug and alcohol rehabilitation, child care, family planning, youth and parenting education, health care and elder care, and other community needs. In this respect, Bush accepted the important role of the federal government in the modern welfare state, but he sought to transform the liberal welfare state into a conservative welfare state.

While postwar conservative critics of modern liberalism had called for the dismantling of the welfare state, Bush Republicans were unable and unwilling to restrain the growth of the administrative state.[31] Instead, Bush calculated the negative costs of calling for a complete dismantling of the welfare state, as Goldwater had done in his 1964 campaign, while acknowledging the important role religious organizations played through their social service and community programs. Bush's compassionate conservatism gave a place to these faith-based and "value-oriented" organizations in the modern welfare state. His was an incremental conservatism.[32]

Bush's program led some conservatives to accuse his administration of compromising traditional conservative antistatist principles for political gain. Broadsides appeared complaining that Bush was an "impostor" who had turned his back on free-market economics, the heart of Reaganism, and that the Republican party had become "crapulent and corrupt."[33] Some conservatives and libertarians decried Bush's "big government" Republicanism, which included the federalization of education through the No Child Left Behind Act and drug prescriptions for the elderly. Bush's response to the possibility of terrorist attacks led to the expansion of government through the establishment of a cabinet-level Department of Homeland Security as well as his war in Iraq. The criticism from the Right was reminiscent of the kinds of complaints directed at Reagan for betraying principle. Still, in his first term in office Bush showed a remarkable ability to mobilize the grassroots and to maintain his hold on the Republican party. Ideological conservatives remained an independent voice within the party and would break ranks with the administration on a series of issues in Bush's second term.

From the moment Bush won reelection in 2004, both Democrats and Republicans expected a cataclysmic Senate showdown over court nominations.[34] The battle for the Supreme Court began when Justice Sandra Day O'Connor announced her retirement the following July. Bush nominated John G. Roberts, Jr., a conservative appellate lawyer and federal appeals court judge, to fill her seat. When Chief Justice William H. Rehnquist died on September 3, 2005, Bush nominated Roberts to succeed him as chief justice. The soft-spoken, articulate Roberts won confirmation seventy-eight to twenty-two. The fifty-year-old Roberts became the youngest chief justice since John Marshall to sit on the Court.

With few exceptions, conservatives saw the Roberts nomination as a success for their cause. Bush's next appointment left them stunned. On October 3, 2005, the day the Supreme Court began its new term, Bush nominated Harriet Miers, a sixty-year-old Texas lawyer, White House counsel, and born-again Christian, as his choice to fill Sandra Day O'Connor's seat. Miers had never served as a judge, and her background in law consisted of having been the first female head of a large Dallas law firm and president of the Texas Bar Association. Editor of the *Weekly Standard* William Kristol expressed a common conservative sentiment when he declared that he was "disappointed, depressed, and demoralized." Bush defended his choice by telling the press, "I picked the best person I could find." Most conservatives believed he had not looked very far if Miers was the best he could find.[35] It did not help that Senate Minority Leader Harry Reid (D-Nevada) came out in favor of Miers.

Under heavy pressure from the Right, Bush withdrew Miers's nomination in late October. Shortly afterward, he nominated Samuel A. Alito, Jr., a fifteen-year judge on the Third Circuit Court of Appeals. In doing so, Bush gave conservatives what they wanted.[36] In a mostly party-line vote, the Senate confirmed Alito's nomination, fifty-eight to forty-two. Bush appeared to have shifted the Court to the right, thereby fulfilling the expectations of many conservatives who had voted for him. Yet even in its triumph with Alito, the GOP became a party sharply divided over issues of immigration, budget deficits, the war, and even the future of the party. These divisions were aggravated by Bush's plummeting approval ratings.

Still, George W. Bush left an indelible mark on conservatism and the Republican party. In this respect, he reflected the ascendance of conservatism in the last half century of American politics. This turn in American politics coincided with, and encouraged, a loss of confidence in New Deal and Great Society liberalism within large segments of the electorate. This is not to say that progressive ideology was dead or that the Democratic party would remain a minority party. Rather, this is to argue that the Republican party had become the voice of conservatism and that this voice appealed to the large segment of the electorate that was center-right on social and moral issues.

In their success, conservative Republicans challenged a New Deal political order that had emerged in response to an economic crisis brought about by a world depression. In responding to this crisis, the New Deal built on a modern liberal tradition developed in the late nineteenth century to remedy some of the most flagrant ills apparent in an industrial and urban society. This modern liberal response called for the expansion of government powers to regulate the economy, protect workers, and provide minimal security for the disadvantaged. The New Deal political order was built on an industrial society with a unionized workforce and an urbanized electorate. Democrats hammered into place a political coalition of blue-collar workers in the urban North and traditional Democrats in the South.

This was an uneasy coalition. Although southern Democrats accepted with considerable hesitation much of the New Deal welfare program and were essential to the New Deal coalition, they were obsessive in their defense of racial segregation and feared federal intrusion into state affairs. As a consequence, they presented an obstacle within the party to the full expansion of the New Deal liberal agenda. In addition, southern Democrats remained fiercely anti-Communist, pro-military, and, at heart, antiliberal. This presented the Democratic party with an uneasy alliance of African-American and white, largely Catholic, voters in the North, and white voters in the South.

This political coalition proved unstable in the postindustrial economy that emerged in the postwar years. This economy was characterized by a large service sector based on few industrial workers and a sizable white-collar workforce, high technology, and global competition. Urban decay created large pockets of poverty, especially among inner-city blacks. This led to outbreaks of urban rioting, crime, and racial tension. The newly created suburbs offered middle-class whites and blacks new opportunities for improved housing closer to employment, better schools for their children, and safer environments for their families. As suburbs flourished, urban ills and enclaves of poverty became less visible and more cut off from local community concerns.

At first the GOP Right was unable to take full advantage of this changing environment, though conservatives found growing strength in the Sunbelt states. After easily defeating the conservative Barry Goldwater in 1964, President Johnson pushed the liberal agenda through his Great Society. His administration accomplished a great deal, including the enactment of Medicare. Under his leadership, the rate of poverty fell by half. A black civil rights movement pushed for legislation to end racial discrimination and to guarantee equal opportunity. The Johnson administration fulfilled this promise with the enactment of the Civil Rights Act of 1964. This legislation marked the high point in modern liberalism, but soon urban riots, campus protest, and the war in Vietnam would lead many voters to become disenchanted with the administration.

By the close of the 1960s, a social and cultural crisis was evident in American politics. This crisis coincided with the deterioration of the traditional two-parent family and a decline in traditional religious values. Fear of social disorder was intensified by the emergence of a feminist movement against an allegedly oppressive patriarchal society. Abortion and gay rights emerged as critical demands of this liberation movement. At the same time, traditional cultural and religious values, as well as established institutions, came under attack by an array of critics who called for new expressions of liberation. Many on the Left welcomed these changes, whereas conservatives saw them as radical and destabilizing. Republicans were able to tap into the large new constituency of culturally conservative voters who were angry about the excision of religion from public life and what they considered the assault on their cultural values. Rallying around demands for low taxes, smaller government, a strong national defense, and traditional cultural values, conservatives won control of the Republican party.

The transformation of the GOP into a party of the Right intensified partisanship in an already polarized political environment. Some observers of the American political scene argued that this polarization was evident only in the nation's political elites and members of Congress. They pointed to the surprisingly slight differences on policy issues between

281

Republican and Democratic voters. Even on the divisive issue of abortion, it was noted, most voters shared common ground, specifically, the belief that abortion should be legal under certain circumstances. Only 30 percent of Democrats thought abortion should always be legal, and fewer than 30 percent of Republicans thought it should be illegal under any circumstances. On most other issues, there was even less of a division among voters.[37] Yet as political scientist James Q. Wilson maintains, there is much evidence to show that polarized opinions among elites foster division in the general electorate. He observes, "On central issues of the times, liberals and Democrats are more opposed to conservatives and Republicans today than they were three decades earlier. This reflects a profound change in attitudes, and not simply the tidying up of party affiliation."[38]

The war in Iraq and the growing number of American soldiers killed or wounded in the conflict increased polarization between the parties and in the electorate, continuing a trend that had begun in the 1980s under Reagan. In this heightened partisan environment both political parties employed rhetoric to mobilize their bases. Presidential campaigns were filled with charges of moral turpitude, falsification of military records, and dirty tricks. Partisan groups operating outside official campaigns employed especially negative attacks against the personal character of their opponents. Such negative tactics fueled partisan emotions and created more acrimony and further polarization.[39]

Nonetheless, partisanship increased voter participation. Contrary to the predictions of many political observers, the division between the parties did not lead to an apathetic electorate. Nor was there a decline in ideology among voters, as predicted. In fact, large numbers of American voters readily identified themselves as conservatives or liberals. The largest segment of voters described themselves as moderates, but the majority of them fell on the conservative-moderate side of the spectrum. Partisanship was most pronounced among the political elites and was seen in the sharp divisions in Congress, which political scientists Thomas Mann and Norman Ornstein described as "tribal politics."[40] Intense partisanship spilled into the general electorate, represented in the bases of both parties, Democratic and Republican. Partisan divisions were reinforced by conservative talk radio, liberal and conservative blogs, and special-interest groups organized to promote causes around such issues as abortion, same-sex marriage, education, and the war in Iraq. Divisions over core issues of the day made political compromise difficult and led to deadlock in Washington. This stalemate led, as it had in the late nineteenth century, to calls for reforms such as congressional redistricting and the addition of at-large congressional seats to make government more cohesive and less divisive.

Although voter turnout increased in the late twentieth and early twenty-first centuries, many Americans indicated great distrust in government, politicians, and public officials. This erosion of confidence reversed public attitudes expressed in the 1950s, when confidence in government and public officials had been high. Public opinion surveys first showed a decline in public trust in government beginning with the war in Vietnam and the Watergate scandal. In the first years of the Clinton administration, it appeared that the public's confidence in government was being restored, but this trend did not last long. A Council for Excellence in Government poll conducted by Peter Hart and Robert Teeter in late May and early June 1999 showed that 34 percent of the public felt "fairly disconnected" from the federal government and another 29 percent felt "very disconnected." In this survey, 38 percent of Americans blamed "special interests" for what was wrong with government, while 29 percent held "the media" responsible, and another 24 percent held elected officials responsible. This trend continued into the 2000 election. For example, in early July 2000 a Gallup poll found that 49 percent of Americans believed that "quite a few" people running government were crooked, and that 70 percent of Americans believed that government was being run by "a few big interests looking out for themselves." Even after the terrorist attacks of September 2001, public confidence in government remained low: A Harris poll conducted from January 16 to January 21, 2002, showed that only 50 percent of Americans had significant confidence in the White House (compared with 21 percent a year earlier), and only 22 percent had confidence in Congress (compared with 18 percent a year earlier).[41]

The war in Iraq intensified distrust in government. The failure to discover weapons of mass destruction in Iraq following American military intervention—one of the reasons President Bush gave for toppling the regime of Saddam Hussein—seems to have led large numbers of Americans to believe that the U.S. government was directly involved in the 9/11 terrorist attacks. As Lee Hamilton, the vice chairman of the National Commission on Terrorist Attacks ("the 9/11 Commission"), observed, "A lot of people I've encountered believe the U.S. government was involved. Many say that the government planned the whole thing." He added that there was no evidence for this belief, but conspiracy theories abounded. A survey by Scripps Howard News Service and Ohio University reported widespread resentment toward and alienation from the national government. The survey reported that nearly a third of Americans suspected that the federal government—the Bush administration—had assisted the 9/11 terrorists or had taken no action in preventing the attacks so that the United States could justify going to war in the Middle East. The poll found that young adults under the age of twenty-five were most likely to give "some credence" to the notion of U.S. government involvement in 9/11.[42]

These beliefs, presuming the survey was accurate, indicated that Republican control of government could not be sustained in Bush's second term. Political scandals involving Republicans at the national and state level further alienated large numbers of voters who were dismayed by revelations of bribery, illegal campaign contributions, and sexual impropriety on the part of some high-ranking congressional and state Republicans. Most damaging to the Bush presidency and the Republican party was the war in Iraq. Although Bush had effectively used the war in the 2002 and 2004 elections, the continuing loss of American lives and nightly reports of carnage resulting from Sunni and Shi'ite sectarian conflict pushed Bush's approval ratings down into the mid-to-high 30s. Opposition to the war was most pronounced on the Left and in the Democratic party, and led to the Republican loss of Congress in 2006.

Division within Republican and conservative ranks also became apparent. The *American Conservative,* a magazine founded in 2002 under the editorship of the former *New York Post* editor Scott McConnell, emerged as the most critical voice of conservative opposition to the Iraq War. The magazine expressed the views of Patrick Buchanan and the nationalist wing of the conservative movement. Although Buchanan endorsed Bush in 2004, he had been especially adamant in his criticism of the war. He was joined by other conservatives. For example, the Swarthmore College political scientist James Kurth predicted American failure in Iraq similar to what the United States had experienced in Vietnam in the 1970s. Furthermore, he predicted that the failure in Iraq would "discredit similar U.S. efforts elsewhere," resulting in other countries' dismissing "any U.S. proclamations and promotions of democratization as just another preposterous, feckless, and tiresome American conceit."[43] Similar criticism was raised by Andrew J. Bacevich, a historian at Boston University, who concluded that "bringing democracy to the Arab world is akin to making bricks without straw—a trick best left to others."[44] At the core of this criticism was deep opposition to the concept of nation building.

These authors were not alone in their criticism of the war. Brent Scowcroft, the elder Bush's national security adviser, was an early critic of the conflict. As the sectarian fighting in Iraq grew, other conservatives began to express opposition to continued American involvement in the war. After much hesitation, William F. Buckley, Jr., concluded that democratization of Iraq was impossible. He was joined by the influential columnist George Will, who wrote that the belief that democracy could be brought to Iraq was an illusion. The neoconservative David Frum called for the partition of Iraq into ethnic regions.[45]

In his military intervention in Iraq, Bush placed his presidency and the Republican party on the line. Nonetheless, his administration left an indelible imprint on conservatism and the GOP. The Bush presidency marked the culmination of a fifty-year campaign to transform the GOP into a majority party and a voice of conservatism. The result was far from what the founders of the conservative movement had envisioned when they called for overturning the New Deal welfare state. The postwar infusion of European thought deepened the Right's criticism of modern-day liberalism and excited followers with a new awareness of the American republican tradition. These early founders of conservatism espoused the virtues of unfettered capitalism, individualism, and small government. They warned of the threat that Soviet Communism posed to the United States and the West. Conservatism was then a negligible force, marginalized, politically powerless, and restricted to a small band of intellectuals often given to internecine argument, esoteric and idiosyncratic to outsiders. Joined by a grassroots anti-Communist movement, these conservatives seemed unlikely to achieve electoral success.

The defining moment in the conservative movement came with the Republican nomination of Barry Goldwater in 1964. Goldwater's nomination gave rise to a boisterous, self-confident conservatism, but the ascendance of the GOP Right would prove uneven. The fragile state of the Right was evident at any number of turning points in which the course of American political history might have been different. Marginalized after Goldwater's defeat, conservatives turned to Richard Nixon in 1968, only to feel betrayed once Nixon entered office. The Watergate scandals and Nixon's resignation left the Republican party and the conservative faction within the party demoralized.

Their fortunes were revived in the 1970s by emerging social issues and the mobilization of evangelical Christians, traditionalist Catholics, and Mormons. The GOP Right took advantage of a population shift to the Sunbelt states and the desertion of whites from the Democratic party. The transformation of the South, once a Democratic stronghold, into a Republican region had been gradual. Republicans appealed to the new suburban voter by calling for low taxes, a stronger military, and family values. In the process, the Republican party in the South became the party of middle-class and upper-income whites, while the southern Democratic party represented lower-income whites and blacks. Winning the South proved critical to Ronald Reagan's election in 1980 and later the Republican takeover of Congress in 1994. Still, it is worth remembering that the Republican triumph—control of Congress and the presidency— did not occur until the 2000 elections.

George W. Bush's election in 2000 marked the triumph of the conservative ascendancy. The New Deal political coalition had finally been defeated, but the Bush presidency revealed the enduring strength of the liberal welfare state that had been created under Franklin Roosevelt and expanded under Lyndon Johnson. Bush sought to challenge the liberal order by building and strengthening a disciplined Republican party and by reconfiguring (albeit unsuccessfully) the welfare state to impart new power to faith-based public-interest groups. He introduced proposals to bring minimal privatization to Social Security and new measures to allow greater choice in Medicare. These proposals fell on deaf ears or had little impact, and as a consequence the liberal welfare state endured, a lasting legacy of New Deal liberalism.

The conservative ascendancy revealed the gap between ideological ideal and policy achievement in a political system carefully designed to ensure restraint and avoid radical change. American politics in the twenty-first century, however, seemed far from restrained. In a highly partisan, polarized environment neither political party was given to easy compromise. Although this caused rightful consternation, we must remember that debate within a democracy often proves shrill, contention rancorous, and conflict seemingly irreconcilable; yet such is the vibrancy of a mature democracy. Discord illustrates the strength of the democratic process, even while it has a disquieting effect on society.

Notes
Acknowledgments
Index

Notes

Introduction

1. John T. Flynn, *The Decline of the American Republic and How to Rebuild It* (New York, 1955), pp. 5–6 (original italics).

1. European Intellectuals and Conservative Firebrands

1. Indeed, the most thorough and intellectually formed critique of the New Deal was found not on the Right but on the Left, in the columnist Walter Lippmann's book *The Good Society* (1937), which accused the New Deal of betraying the principles of the Founding Fathers and their inherent distrust of centralized government. Insight into Lippmann's book is provided by the historian Gary Dean Best in "Introduction to the Transaction Edition," Walter Lippmann, *The Good Society* (New Brunswick, N.J., 2005), pp. xxiii–xlvii. For an important discussion of Lippmann, see Ted V. McAllister, *Revolt against Modernity: Leo Strauss, Eric Voeglin, and the Search for a Postliberal Order* (Lawrence, Kans., 1996).

2. For insight into Elizabeth Dilling and other right-wing cranks in the prewar Right, see June Melby Benowitz, *Days of Discontent: American Women and Right-Wing Politics, 1933–1945* (DeKalb, Ill., 2002); Glen Jeansonne, *Women of the Far Right: The Mothers' Movement and World War II* (Chicago, 1996); and Leo Ribuffo, *The Old Christian Right: The Protestant Far Right from the Great Depression to the Cold War* (Philadelphia, 1933).

3. Ronald Reagan, "Remarks at Conservative Political Action Conference," March 1, 1985, Presidential Papers of Ronald Reagan.

4. For Mencken, see Terry Teachout, *The Skeptic: A Life of H. L. Mencken* (New York, 2002).

5. Quoted in J. David Hoeveler, Jr., *The New Humanism: A Critique of Modern America, 1900–1940* (Charlottesville, Va., 1977), p. 18. This distrust of mass democracy is found in Irving Babbitt, *Democracy and Leadership* (Boston, 1924).

6. Of special value in understanding the New Humanist movement is Russell Kirk, "Foreword," Irving Babbitt, *Democracy and Leadership* (Boston, 1924, reprint, Indianapolis, 1978), pp. 11–22.

7. Nock was especially influential among a later generation of conservatives and libertarians through his books, including *Memoirs of a Superfluous Man* (New York, 1943), *Our Enemy, the State* (New York, 1935), and, to a lesser degree, *Theory of Education in the United States* (New York, 1932). On Nock, see Robert Crunden, *The Mind and Art of Albert Jay Nock* (Chicago, 1964). Ralph Adams Cram exerted less of an influence on later generations of conservatives, but his eloquent writings merit attention for their understanding of prewar conservatism. It is worth noting that the leading publisher of conservative books, Henry Regnery, republished both Babbitt and Nock. Russell Kirk speaks of Babbitt's influence on him in his Foreword to the 1978 edition of *Democracy and Leadership*, issued by the Liberty Fund.

8. Ralph Adams Cram, a High Church Anglican and Anglophile, gained fame as one of the nation's best architects. Cram led the Gothic revival in American architecture at the turn of the twentieth century. He designed many of the buildings at Cornell University, the University of Richmond, Wheaton College in Massachusetts, and Princeton University, including Campbell Hall, the Graduate College, the University Chapel, and McCormick Hall. He also designed Christ Church in Hyde Park, New York, the Cathedral of Saint John the Divine in New York, and St. Thomas in New York City. His aesthetic values reflected his love of the Middle Ages and his loathing of industrialism and democracy. In his writings, he denounced egalitarian democracy and called for the recovery of medieval values in the United States. He believed that the roots of decay were found in industrialism, which had led to mass democracy, class warfare, and the collectivist state. Ralph Adams Cram, *The End of Democracy* (Boston, 1937). Cram is discussed by J. David Hoeveler, Jr., "The American Review," in Ronald Lora and William Henry Longton, eds., *The Conservative Press in Twentieth-Century America* (Westport, Conn., 1999), pp. 240–242.

9. Twelve Southerners, *I'll Take My Stand: The South and the Agrarian Tradition* (Baton Rouge, 1977, original 1930). Alexander Karanikas, *Tillers of a Myth: The Southern Agrarians as Social and Literary Critics* (Madison, Wis., 1966); and Grant Webster, *The Republic of Letters: A History of Postwar American Literary Opinion* (Baltimore, 1979), pp. 66–67, 74–76, 139–141; and John J. Langdale III, "Superfluous Southerners: Cultural Conservatism and the South, 1920–1990" (Ph.D. diss., University of Florida, 2006).

10. John Crowe Ransom, "Happy Farmers," *American Review* (October 1933), p. 529, quoted in Hoeveler, "American Review," p. 238.

11. This sentiment found its most eloquent expression in José Ortega y Gasset's *Revolt of the Masses,* published in 1932. Although Ortega y Gasset was not a con-

servative per se, he found enthusiastic reception in American conservative circles. For example, Richard Weaver, author of *Ideas Have Consequences* (1948), acknowledged the great influence that Ortega y Gasset's philosophy had on his 1946 doctoral dissertation on the Confederate South.

12. For an informative account of Flynn's turn against the New Deal, see John E. Moser, *Right Turn: John T. Flynn and the Tradition of American Liberalism* (New York, 2005).

13. José Ortega Y Gasset, *The Revolt of the Masses* (New York, 1932), p. 11.

14. Utley and Lindbergh are quoted in Justus D. Doenecke, *Storm on the Horizon: The Challenge to American Intervention, 1939–1941* (Lantham, Maryland, 2000), pp. 213 and 218–219; Also, Doenecke, *Not to the Swift: The Old Isolationists in the Cold War* (Lewisberg, Pa., 1979).

15. William Henry Chamberlain, *The Confessions of an Individualist* (New York, 1940).

16. This discussion of New Deal liberalism relies on Sidney M. Milkis, *Political Parties and Constitutional Government: Remaking American Democracy* (Baltimore, 1999), pp. 72–102.

17. The importance of Hayek's book *The Road to Serfdom* is discussed in Paul Gottfried and Thomas Fleming, *The Conservative Movement* (Boston, 1988), pp. 1–14; and George H. Nash, *The Conservative Intellectual Movement in America since 1945* (New York, 1976).

18. Alan Ebenstein, *Friedrich Hayek: A Biography* (Chicago, 2001), pp. 115–146. For an engaging intellectual biography, see Bruce Caldwell, *Hayek's Challenge: An Intellectual Biography of Friedrich Hayek* (Chicago, 2003). Not all libertarians considered Hayek a libertarian. See Brian Doherty, *Radicals for Capitalism: A Freewheeling History of the Modern American Libertarian Movement* (New York, 2007).

19. Ebenstein, *Friedrich Hayek: A Biography*, pp. 122–124.

20. Friedrich Hayek, *The Road to Serfdom* (London, 1944), pp. 27 and 13, quoted in Ebenstein, *Friedrich Hayek: A Biography*, p. 124.

21. Quoted in Ebenstein, *Friedrich Hayek: A Biography*, p. 134.

22. Ibid.

23. Ibid., p. 45.

24. Quoted in Nash, *The Conservative Intellectual Movement*, p. 27. Nash describes the formation of the society in greater detail on pp. 26–27.

25. Nash, *The Conservative Intellectual Movement*, p. 284.

26. "Aaron Director, Founder of the Field of Law and Economics," University of Chicago News Office, September 12, 2004: www.news.uchicago.edu/ releases/04/ 04/040913.director.shtml; and Ronald H. Coase, "Autobiography," *Les Prix Nobel, The Nobel Prizes 1991*, ed. Tore Frängsmyr (Stockholm, 1992).

27. Nash, *The Conservative Intellectual Movement;* and Jennifer Burns, "Goddess of the Market: Ayn Rand and the American Right, 1930–1980" (Ph.D. dissertation, University of California, Berkeley, 2005).

28. Richard Weaver, *Ideas Have Consequences* (Chicago, 1948); Eric Voegelin,

The New Science of Politics: An Introduction (Chicago, 1952) and *Order and History* (Baton Rouge, 1956); and Leo Strauss, *The City and the Man* (Chicago, 1964). For insight into the history of the conservative tradition, see Samuel Francis, *Beautiful Losers: Essays on the Failure of American Conservatism* (Columbia, Mo., 1993). A discussion of these intellectuals can be found in J. David Hoeveler, Jr., *Watch on the Right: Conservative Intellectuals in the Reagan Era* (Madison, Wis., 1991); and Nash, *The Conservative Intellectual Movement.*

29. For a discussion of Strauss's thought on public intellectuals who became associated with neoconservatism in the 1980s, see Chapter 4. There is a rich literature on Strauss's thought, and the best place to begin is with Strauss himself, *Persecution and the Art of Writing* (1952); *The City and Man* (1964); *Liberalism: Ancient and Modern* (1968); and *The Rebirth of Writing* (New York, 1952). This discussion of Strauss is informed by Catherine H. Zuckert and Michael Zuckert, *The Truth about Leo Strauss: Political Philosophy and American Democracy* (Chicago, 2006); Ted V. McAllister, *Revolt against Modernity: Leo Strauss, Eric Voegelin, and the Search for a Postliberal Order* (Lawrence, Kans., 1996); and Thomas L. Pangle, *Leo Strauss: An Introduction to His Thought and Intellectual Influence* (Baltimore, 2006).

30. Regnery Press grew out of a pamphlet series launched by *Human Events,* a conservative magazine founded in 1944. Established by Henry Regnery, whose father had been a founder and financial supporter of the America First Committee, the press gained a reputation for publishing thought-provoking books, including original works and reprints by authors such as T. S. Eliot and Ezra Pound. In 1948, Regnery published William F. Buckley's book *God and Man at Yale.* Other successful books followed, including Elinor Lipper, *Eleven Years in Soviet Prison Camps* (1951), Louis Budenz, *The Techniques of Communism* (1954), and Wilhelm Röpke, *Economics of a Free Society* (1963).

31. Russell Kirk, *The Conservative Mind: From Burke to Eliot* (Chicago, 1953), pp. 7–8. See also Grant Webster, *The Republic of Letters: A History of Postwar American Literary Opinion* (Baltimore, 1979), pp. 66–94.

32. Kirk, *The Conservative Mind,* pp. 6–8.

33. Ibid., pp. 75–80.

34. Ibid., p. 500.

35. "A Proud Name," *Wall Street Journal,* April 29, 1955, reprinted in Peter Viereck, *Conservatism: From John Adams to Churchill* (Princeton, N.J., 1956).

36. For a succinct discussion of the magazine, see Robert Muccigrosso, "The American Mercury, 1924–1980," in Lora and Longton, eds., *The Conservative Press in Twentieth-Century America,* pp. 243–253.

37. Charles H. Hamilton, "Freeman, 1950–," in Lora and Longton, eds., *The Conservative Press in Twentieth-Century America,* p. 322.

38. Lee Edwards, *Educating for Liberty: The First Half-Century of the Intercollegiate Studies Institute* (Washington, D.C., 2004).

39. Founded in 1944, *Human Events* grew out of the noninterventionist, anti–New Deal Right. Its founding editors were Frank C. Hanighen, author of the antiwar exposé *The Merchants of Death* (1934), and Felix Morley, a former editor at the

Washington Post and past president of Haverford College. *Human Events* had reached a circulation of only 10,000 in 1954, before Hanighen and Morley resigned to be replaced by Allan H. Ryskind. Under the new management and its new editor, Thomas S. Winter, the newspaper grew to 110,000 readers by 1964. Thomas J. Ferris, "Human Events," in Lora and Longton, eds., *The Conservative Press in Twentieth-Century America,* pp. 449–459.

40. John Judis, *William F. Buckley, Jr., Patron Saint of the Conservatives* (New York, 1988); and Patrick Allitt, *Catholic Intellectuals and Conservative Politics in America, 1950–1985* (Ithaca, N.Y., 1993). Also of interest is Daniel Kelly, *James Burnham and the Struggle for the World: A Life* (Wilmington, Del., 2002).

41. Rusher had been active in the Republican Party since his undergraduate days at Princeton University. While attending law school at Harvard University in 1947, he founded the Young Republican Club, which became the largest political group on campus. He broke with establishment Republicanism, however, when the New York party endorsed Jacob Javits for Congress. Rusher believed that Javits had not explained adequately his earlier association with the Communist Party. After a stint working as special counsel for the Senate Subcommittee on Internal Security, Rusher became the publisher of the *National Review.* William A. Rusher to author, September 6, 2001; December 30, 2004, in author's possession. See also William A. Rusher, *Special Counsel* (New Rochelle, N.Y., 1968), and *The Rise of the Right* (New York, 1984).

42. Jeffrey Hart, *The Making of the American Conservative Mind: National Review and Its Times* (Wilmington, Del., 2005). For a critical assessment of the magazine from another conservative perspective, see Chilton Williamson, Jr., "National Review at 50," *The American Conservative,* December 5, 2005, pp. 21–25.

43. Meyer's conservatism is explored in Kevin J. Smant, *Principles and Heresies: Frank S. Meyer and the Shaping of the American Conservative Movement* (Wilmington, Del., 2002); and Nash, *The Conservative Intellectual Movement,* pp. 174–181. For a critique of fusionism, see Paul Gottfried, *The Search for Historical Meaning: Hegel and the Postwar American Right* (DeKalb, Ill., 1986).

44. Frank S. Meyer, "Collectivism Rebaptized," *The Freeman* (July 1955), pp. 559–562. Meyer's criticisms of Kirk are detailed in Nash, *The Conservative Intellectual Movement,* pp. 159–163.

45. Russell Kirk, "Mill's 'On Liberty' Reconsidered," *National Review,* January 25, 1956, pp. 23–24.

46. Frank S. Meyer, "In Defense of John Stuart Mill," *National Review,* March 28, 1956, pp. 23–24.

47. For Meyer's views on McCarthy, see "McCarthy's Unforfeited Word," *National Review,* June 14, 1958, p. 548; and "The Meaning of McCarthy," *National Review,* June 14, 1958, p. 565. Also, for an excellent discussion of Meyer's views on McCarthyism, see Smant, *Principles and Heresies,* p. 45. I would like to thank Gregory Schneider for directing me to these sources.

48. Ronald Hamowy, "*National Review:* Criticism," *New Individualist Review* (November 1961), pp. 3–7.

49. William F. Buckley, Jr., "Three Drafts of an Answer to Mr. Hamowy," *The New Individualist Review* (November 1961), pp. 7–10.

50. For a full discussion of conservatism and black civil rights, see Chapter 2.

51. An engaging discussion of the Communist spy cases is found in John Haynes and Harvey Klehr, *Early Cold War Spies: The Espionage Trials That Shaped American Politics* (New York, 2006).

52. FBI logs of the wiretap on Thomas Corcoran are in Case Philip Jacob Jaffe, et al., File 100–2673601516, May 28, 1950, quoted in Herbert Romerstein and Eric Breindel, *The Venona Secrets: Exposing Soviet Espionage and America's Traitors* (Washington, D.C., 2000), 167–168.

53. Information drawn from Bentley interviews became known in Fr. John F. Cronin, *The Problem of American Communism in 1945: Facts and Recommendations* (Baltimore, 1945), based on secret information given to him by J. Edgar Hoover, director of the FBI.

54. Romerstein and Breindel, *The Venona Secrets,* 143–190; and Harvey Klehr and John Earl Haynes, *The Secret World of American Communism* (New Haven, 1995), pp. 309–313. Of importance is Elizabeth Bentley's autobiography, *Out of Bondage* (New York, 1988). This reissue includes an extensive afterword by Hayden Peake, which rebutted attacks on Bentley's testimony, especially those found in David Caute, *The Great Fear: The Anti-Communist Purge under Truman and Eisenhower* (New York, 1978); and Richard Gid Powers, *Not without Honor: The History of American Anticommunism* (New York, 1995), pp. 195–197.

55. Gouzenko's information also helped the United States break some 2,200 Soviet coded-cables gathered by an intelligence project called Venona. Although not released to the general public until 1995, Venona confirmed the extent of Soviet penetration into the U.S. government. John Earl Haynes, *Red Scare or Red Menace? American Communism and Anti-Communism in the Cold War Era* (Chicago, 1996), pp. 50–63.

56. For the Rosenberg case see Ronald Radosh and Joyce Milton, *The Rosenberg File: A Search for the Truth* (New York, 1983). For an attempt to exonerate the Rosenbergs, see Walter and Miriam Schneir, *Invitation to an Inquest: A New Look at the Rosenberg-Sobell Case* (New York, 1973).

57. Romerstein and Breindel, *The Venona Secrets,* pp. 40–53.

58. Sam Tanenhaus captures Chambers's personality in his definitive book *Whittaker Chambers: A Biography* (New York, 1997).

59. These documents, called the "pumpkin papers" because Chambers had hidden them in a hollowed-out pumpkin on his Maryland farm, included four sheets of paper in Hiss's handwriting; sixty-five typewritten State Department documents; four sheets in Harry Dexter White's handwriting, and four microfilm rolls of State Department and Navy Department documents from 1938.

60. Quoted in M. J. Heale, *American Anti-Communism: Combating the Enemy Within, 1830–1970* (Baltimore, 1990), p. 148. The following discussion of anti-Communism in the period relies on Heale's tightly written study.

61. Studies of the McCarthy years are numerous, but a good entry into this period and literature about it are found in David Oshinsky, *A Conspiracy so Immense: The World of Joe McCarthy* (New York, 1983); Arthur Herman, *Joseph McCarthy: Re-examining the Life and Legacy of America's Most Hated Senator* (New York, 2000). Although Herman's book received generally unfavorable reviews from all sides, it contains a wealth of information not found in other accounts of McCarthy.

62. Historical evidence reveals that the North Korean invasion was approved by Josef Stalin. See John Gaddis, *We Now Know: Rethinking the Cold War* (New York, 1997).

63. Congressional criticism of McCarthy certainly did not mean opposition to investigating Communist infiltration into government. Indeed, he was censured not for any of his anti-Communist allegations but for obstructing a Senate investigation of him. For example, Senator John McClellan (D-Arkansas), who led Democratic opposition to McCarthy in the Committee on Government Operations and later replaced McCarthy as chair of the committee, remained staunchly anti-Communist and continued to argue that the Communist Party should be outlawed. For an excellent discussion of the role of television in the Army-McCarthy hearings, see Thomas Doherty, *Cold War, Cool Medium: Television, McCarthyism, and American Culture* (New York, 2003), pp. 189–214.

64. Gallup polls revealed an intriguing breakdown of viewers of the Army-McCarthy hearings. Thirty-eight percent of those asked believed that Secretary Stevens and his legal counsel, John Adams, used improper means in trying to stop Senator McCarthy from investigating the Army, while 32 percent did not, and 30 percent 30 had no opinion. When those who followed the hearings were asked who impressed them the most, the poll reported Joseph McCarthy, 16 percent; Joseph Welch, 15 percent; Robert Stevens, 12 percent; Roy Cohn, 7 percent; Ray Jenkins, 7 percent; others or no opinion, 43 percent. Those viewed most unfavorably were McCarthy, 31 percent; Cohn, 12 percent; Stevens, 7 percent; Welch, 6 percent; Jenkins, 1 percent; others or no opinion, 43 percent. George H. Gallup, *The Gallup Poll, Public Opinion 1935–1971* vol. 2 (New York, 1971), p. 1247.

65. The examples of popular anti-Communism are drawn from Powers, *Not without Honor*, pp. 229–233 and 245–255.

66. Phyllis Schlafly, "Notes of Speech, Robert Welch, August 14–15, 1959," Subject Files Pre-1972 (12 pages); Robert Welch, *The Blue Book of the John Birch Society* (Boston, 1961), pp. 19–20. For more on the John Birch Society, see Chapter 2.

67. "Is This Tomorrow? American under Communism," Catechical Educational Guild Society (1947).

68. Dr. Fred Schwarz, *Beating the Unbeatable Foe* (Washington, D.C., 1996).

69. "Billy James Hargis, 79, Pastor and Anti-Communist Crusader, Dies," *New York Times,* December 9, 2004.

70. L. Edward Hicks, *"Sometimes in the Wrong, but Never in Doubt": George S. Benson and the Education of the New Religious Right* (Knoxville, Tenn., 1994).

71. This figure is cited in Arnold Forster and Benjamin R. Epstein, *Danger on the*

Right: The Attitudes, Personnel, and Influence of the Radical Right and Extreme Conservatives (New York, 1964), p. 60. See also pp. 47–60 for a general discussion of Schwarz.

72. Herbert Philbrick to Jack H. Such, March 14, 1960, Box 3, Herbert Philbrick Papers, Library of Congress.

73. Major George Racey Jordan, *From Major Jordan Diaries* (New York, 1952).

74. Robert Welch to Fred Schwarz, September 6, 1960, and Fred Schwarz to Robert Welch, September 19, 1960, Box 173, Herbert Philbrick Papers.

75. The Truman administration was troubled by the Communist issue, and Taft Republicans wanted Dewey to attack Democrats on the issue. See Robert J. Donovan, *Conflict and Crisis: The Presidency of Harry S Truman, 1945–48* (New York, 1977), pp. 399 and 411–414. See also Alonzo Hamby, *Man of the People: Harry S Truman* (New York, 1995); Hamby, *The Imperial Years* (New York, 1976), pp. 147–148; James T. Patterson, *Grand Expectations: The United States, 1945–1974* (New York, 1996), pp. 134–164; Patterson, *Mr. Republican: A Biography of Robert A. Taft* (Boston, 1972), pp. 407–472.

76. Quoted in Donovan, *Conflict and Crisis,* p. 399.

77. W. A. Stubblefield to Editorial Department, May 29, 1952, Robert Taft Papers, Box 410, Library of Congress.

78. Merwin K. Hart to Earl Harding, March 26, 1954, Box 62, Manion Papers.

2. Triumph and Travail in 1964

1. This phrase is found in a letter drafted by William Scranton aides circulated before the 1964 convention. See Theodore White, *The Making of the President—1964* (New York, 1964).

2. T. Coleman Andrews, commissioner of the Internal Revenue Service under Eisenhower, made a losing third-party effort in 1956 under the states' rights banner. Edgar C. Bundy to Phyllis Schlafly, July 19, 1955, Abraham Lincoln Folder, Subject Files, Eagle Forum Archives; Herbert Philbrick to Mr. Panzieri, October 19, 1963, Box 5, Herbert Philbrick Papers.

3. Rusher reached the conclusion that the Republican Party did not have any principles at all when the New York Republican State Committee nominated Jacob Javits for U.S. senator, "even though the great majority of those present knew of his undenied and unrepentant associations with the Communists." Bill Rusher to Bill Buckley, October 10, 1960, Box 121, William A. Rusher Papers; Thomas J. Anderson, "Straight Talk," speech before the Free Electors Meeting, Jackson, Mississippi, June 17, 1963, Subject Files, Communism, Eagle Forum Archives.

4. Robert E. Wood to Clarence Manion, April 13, 1959, Box 70, Clarence Manion Papers, Chicago Historical Society.

5. For correspondence regarding *The Independent Citizen,* see Clarence Manion to Senator Brookhard, February 12, 1929; Clarence Manion to Hon. Gifford Pinchot, February 12, 1929; Clarence Manion to Nicholas Murray Butler, February 18, 1929; Clarence Manion to Hon. James A. Reed, February 18, 1929, and Febru-

ary 25, 1929; and Clarence Manion to Herman Gessner, February 25, 1929, Box 1, Clarence Manion Papers. Also see Clarence Manion, *Lessons in Liberty: A Study of American Government* (South Bend, Ind., 1939); and *The Education of an American* (South Bend, Ind., 1939).

6. An excellent discussion of Manion at Notre Dame is found in Robert E. Burns, *Being Catholic, Being American: The Notre Dame Story, 1934–1952*, vol. 2 (Notre Dame, Ind., 2000), pp. 428–436. For Manion's involvement in the America First Committee, see George B. Baldwin to Clarence Manion, August 6, 1941; Robert E. Wood to Clarence Manion (telegram), September 12, 1941; Clarence Manion to General Robert E. Wood, September 15, 1941; Mrs. Walker Everett to Clarence Manion, September 22, 1941; Clarence Manion to Hon. Hamilton Fish, September 22, 1941; Robert E. Wood to Clarence Manion, September 22, 1941; Douglas Stuart, Jr., to Clarence Manion, October 16, 1941; and Clarence Manion to Robert A. Taft, October 21, 1941, Box 1, Clarence Manion Papers.

7. Included in the group were General Bonner Fellers representing the conservative group For America; the publisher and rancher Hubbard Russell; New York lawyer George Montgomery; South Carolina Republican committeeman and textile manufacturer Roger Milliken; L. L. Smith of the Kohler Company of Wisconsin; Brent Bozell, Jr.; Texas activist and historian Evetts Haley; Robert Welch, founder of the newly organized John Birch Society; and Illinois attorney Fred Schlafly.

8. Goldwater felt that his Jewish name was a handicap, and that he was unqualified for the job of president because he had only one year of college. He was convinced that the race within the GOP was between Nixon and Rockefeller and only a miracle could "draw lightning his way." Minutes, Conference on Goldwater, May 15, 1959, Box 69, Clarence Manion Papers.

9. Manion to William F. Buckley, Jr., September 28, 1959, Box 62, Clarence Manion Papers. Finding a southern Democrat willing to run for president led to a series of bizarre discussions within the Manion camp, whose members at times sounded like boys forming a secret club and deciding who was going to be inducted. Within the small Manion circle, names were bandied about as possible candidates. J. Bracken Lee suggested a William Jenner–Strom Thurmond ticket. Manion replied that "personally, nothing would please me more than a Jenner-Thurmond ticket, but I believe it would be hazardous to start naming names at this time." J. Bracken Lee to Pat Manion, March 16, 1959; Manion to Lee, March 25, 1959, Box 69, Clarence Manion Papers.

10. Manion was not alone in having doubts about placing Faubus on a third-party ticket. Texas conservative Evetts Haley had met with Faubus in Little Rock, and afterward he ran the idea past some of his "friends in the Midwest" who told him that such a run would be a disaster for the Republican Right. Haley's friends warned him that the press would shoot him to pieces and "financial support would be difficult to find." Frank Hanighen, editor of *Human Events*, wrote to Manion that there was profound discouragement in the South over a revolt in the Democratic Party and that Faubus had little support in the South. For one thing, the business community in Arkansas was "anti-Faubus" and "blamed him for the fact that Ar-

kansas lost the momentum it once had for getting new industries." Jim Johnson to Dean Clarence Manion, March 24, 1954, Box 69; and Frank C. Hanighen to Clarence Manion, Box 70, Clarence Manion Papers. See also J. Evetts Haley to Hugh Grant, A. G. Heinsohn, R. A. Kilpatrick, Box 70, Clarence Manion Papers.

11. Working through William Jennings Bryan Dorn, a former congressman, Manion discussed the possibility of Hollings's declaring himself for president. To boost Hollings's candidacy, a group of southern congressmen circulated a Hollings-for-President petition. Dorn added to the momentum by trumpeting a call for conservatives to launch "an offensive to gain control of both the Democratic and Republican national parties and defeat the liberal elements in each party." William Jennings Bryan Dorn to Manion, October 28, 1959; Manion to Hon. William Jennings Bryan Dorn, October 22, 1959, Box 70, Clarence Manion Papers.

12. Manion wrote to one supporter that "nobody is more ardently devoted to the prospect of a new party than I am. It is simply a matter of ways and means. Unfortunately, the ways and means cannot be disclosed at this time or at Courtney's meeting without destroying our effectiveness." Clarence Manion to Hon. J. Bracken Lee, September 21, 1959; Dan Smoot to Hubbard S. Russell, October 13, 1959; and Frank E. Holman to William H. MacFarland, October 15, 1959, Box 70, Clarence Manion Papers.

13. Stuart G. Thompson withdrew from the Manion committee because of Welch's involvement in the group. He sent Manion a copy of a letter he had received from the former American Bar Association president Frank Holman, who complained that Welch's book was "full of much intemperate things and language." Stuart G. Thompson to Manion, September 14, 1959; Frank Holman to Stuart Thompson, September 16, 1959; Stuart Thompson to Clarence Manion, September 17, 1959, Box 70, Clarence Manion Papers; Eugene Pulliam to Clarence Manion, June 1, 1959; Frank Brophy to Pat Manion, June 1, 1959, Box 69, Clarence Manion Papers.

14. Clarence Manion, "Confidential Draft Memorandum, Barry Goldwater for President" (n.d. 1959), Box 70, Clarence Manion Papers. Manion wrote to one conservative activist that he was "disturbed and angry about Goldwater's continuous praise for Nixon." Clarence Manion to Hubbard Russell, December 4, 1959; James I. Wick to Clarence Manion, December 2, 1959, Box 70, Clarence Manion Papers.

15. Clarence Manion to William F. Buckley, Jr., September 28, 1959; Clarence Manion to Roger Milliken, January 29, 1960, Box 62; and Clarence Manion to Frank Brophy, July 28, 1959, Box 70, Clarence Manion Papers.

16. Barry Goldwater, *The Conscience of a Conservative* (New York, 1961), pp. 14–15, 91.

17. Ibid. pp. 25–31.

18. "Civil Rights Act of 1957," *Congressional Record-Senate*, 103:6 (Washington, D.C., 1957), p. 3716.

19. Quoted in Earl Mazo, *Richard Nixon: A Political and Personal Portrait* (New York, 1959), p. 292. See also Dean J. Kotlowski, *Nixon's Civil Rights: Politics, Principle, and Policy* (Cambridge, Mass., 2002). The following account of the 1960 con-

vention draws on many sources, including newspaper clippings found in Subject Files: Goldwater, Eagle Forum Archives, as well as many excellent secondary accounts of the convention, including Theodore White, *The Making of the President, 1960* (New York, 1961); Rick Perlstein, *Before the Storm: Barry Goldwater and the Unmaking of the American Consensus* (New York, 2001); Robert Alan Goldberg, *Barry Goldwater* (New Haven, 1995); Lee Edwards, *Goldwater: The Man Who Made a Revolution* (Washington, D.C., 1995); Michael Kramer and Sam Roberts, *"I Never Wanted to Be Vice-President of Anything!" An Investigative Biography of Nelson Rockefeller* (New York, 1976).

20. Kramer and Roberts, *"I Never Wanted to Be Vice-President of Anything!,"* p. 227.

21. This discussion of the "Fifth Avenue Compact" and the convention fight relies heavily on Kramer and Roberts, *"I Never Wanted to Be Vice-President of Anything,"* pp. 230–242; and Rick Perlstein, *Before the Storm,* pp. 76–99.

22. Proceedings of the 27th Republican National Convention, 1960, p. 291. Also see Goldberg, *Barry Goldwater,* a superb biography.

23. William Rorabaugh captures the optimism and tensions of the early 1960s in *Kennedy and the Promise of the Sixties* (New York, 2002).

24. Tom Anderson, "Straight Talk," Speech to Free Electors Meeting, Jackson, Mississippi, June 17, 1963, in Subject Files, Communism, Eagle Forum.

25. *Fail-Safe* was exciting, although overly didactic. As the terrible climax nears, Russian Premier Nikita Khrushchev, speaking with the American president, laments, "We have worked ourselves into a position of suspicion and hatred so great that the only way out is to proceed with what you suggest [the destruction of New York]." An American military officer adds, "Who needs more muscle now? Neither side . . . The thing of piling bombs on bombs and missiles on missiles when we both have a capacity to overkill after surviving a first strike is just silly." Eugene Burdick and Harvey Wheeler, *Fail-Safe* (New York, 1962), pp. 8, 147, 258, 263. Also see Sidney Hook, *The Fail-Safe Fallacy* (New York, 1963); Allen Winkler, *Life under a Cloud: Anxiety about the Atom* (New York, 1993).

26. In his memoirs Khrushchev recalled of his days in Ukraine and Byelorussia, "I won't hide it, this was a happy time for me . . . At the same time we were still conducting arrests. It was our view that these arrests served to strengthen the Soviet state and clear the road for the building of socialism on Marxist-Leninist principles." Quoted in William Taubman, *Khrushchev: The Man and His Era* (New York, 2002), p. 139; also see pp. 114–146.

27. "Proof Positive," *National Review,* May 18, 1965, p. 47.

28. For example, see Phyllis Schlafly, "Statement Made to the Platform Committee of the Republican National Convention, July 21, 1960," Schlafly, President, Illinois Federation of Republican Women, Box 1960, Personal Papers of Phyllis Schlafly, Eagle Forum Education Center, Clayton, Missouri.

29. Tad Szulc, *Fidel: A Critical Portrait* (New York, 2000 edition), p. 541. See also Christopher Andrew and Vasili Mitrokhin, *The World Was Going Our Way: The KGB and the Battle for the Third World* (New York, 2005), pp. 27–58.

30. Nathaniel Weyl, *Red Star over Cuba: The Russian Assault on the Western Hemisphere* (New York, 1960); William F. Buckley, Jr., "Herbert Matthews and Fidel Castro: I Got My Job through the *New York Times*," in *Rumbles Left and Right: A Book about Troublesome People and Ideas* (New York, 1963), pp. 60–70.

31. Szulc, *Fidel*, pp. 548–549. Discussion of the consequences of the Bay of Pigs failure for subsequent Kennedy foreign policy can be found in B. Bruce-Briggs, *The Shield of Faith: A Chronicle of Strategic Defense from Zeppelins to Star Wars* (New York, 1988), pp. 161–165. See also Gregg Herken, *Cardinal Choices: Presidential Science Advising from the Atomic Bomb to SDI* (Stanford, Calif., 2000); Marc Trachtenberg, *History and Strategy* (Princeton, N.J., 1991); Glenn Seaborg, *Kennedy, Khrushchev, and the Test Ban* (Berkeley, Calif., 1981).

32. The Committee to Defend Cuba was a broad-based conservative group that included people like the liberal anti-Communist Sidney Hook, the physicist Edward Teller, the foreign policy expert Robert Strausz-Hupe, and others. The Committee for the Monroe Doctrine called for the protection of the Western Hemisphere from Soviet intrusion. For a perspective on grassroots organizing efforts among student and anti-Communist groups in Boston see Charles A. Steele to Herbert Philbrick, June 16, 1963, Box 5, Herbert Philbrick Papers.

33. Manion Forum, "We Should Blot Out Communism in Cuba This Week," March 12, 1961, Cuba, Subject Files, Communism, Eagle Forum Archives.

34. Fred Schwarz, "The Meaning of Cultural Exchanges," March 11, 1959, Box 1959, Phyllis Schlafly Personal Papers.

35. Most Birchers were fervent anti-Communists who had no difficulty distinguishing the educational mission about the real Communist threat from Welch's personal views. Still, the society attracted its share of people who were given to thinking that dark forces were at work behind the scenes in America. JBS correspondence is full of wild accusations such as that anti-Communist Herbert Romerstein was a Trotskyite or that Communists in the federal government were involved in a plot to fluoridate public water supplies. On Romerstein, see Michael Schuler to Herb Philbrick, April 13, 1960, Box 3; and George B. Stallings to Herb Philbrick, November 23, 1959; Free Enterprise, "All America Must Know How Reds Work in Our Government," Box 3, Herbert Philbrick Papers.

By 1967, the John Birch Society was republishing John Robison's anti-Masonic *Illuminati, Proofs of a Conspiracy against Religions and Governments of Europe* (1798). In issuing the book, the publishers declared that if clever conspirators could use so fine a group as the Masons, then "we must open our minds to consider what infinite possibilities are available to them in our present day society. Their main habitat these days seems to be the great subsidized universities, tax-free foundations, mass media communications systems, government bureaus . . . and a myriad of private organizations such as the Council on Foreign Relations."

36. Clare Boothe Luce to William F. Buckley, Jr., October 30, 1961, Box 220, Clare Boothe Luce Papers, Library of Congress.

37. To JBS members, becoming fully educated about Communism and other threats to America was a gravely serious occupation. Gerald Schomp, a JBS coordi-

nator in South Florida in the 1960s, captured his frustration about the lack of political activity in the JBS agenda when he wrote in his memoir, "The worst part of my coordinator's job was sitting through a Birch film every night and looking like I was enjoying every minute of it . . . The rest of the old Birch hands were either lucky or devious. They found various nooks and crannies where they could secretly snooze, or retreated into the kitchen on the pretense of slaving over the inevitable cookies and coffee served after the second reel." Even when he got close to political activity, he found frustration. On one occasion in speaking to a Dade County community group on "supporting the local police," he had to contend with a policeman who interrupted his talk by declaring, "The police department is as crooked as the tailpipe on a Cadillac. You should not support it at all." The interruption ruined his evening. "I almost forgot to sell my books that night," he recalled. Gerald Schomp, *Birchism Was My Business* (New York, 1970), pp. 46–62.

Welch's retraction is found in Gordan Hall, "Birch Society Head Now Says Ike Was No Communist . . . Only," *Boston Globe,* March 24, 1963, p. 33.

38. John Birch Society, *The Blue Book of the John Birch Society* (Belmont, Mass., 1961), pp. 12–21.

39. A good example of the Left's attitude toward the Birchers can be found in Arnold Forster and Benjamin R. Epstein, *Danger on the Right* (New York, 1964), p. 11.

40. William F. Buckley, Jr., "The Question of Robert Welch," *National Review,* February 13, 1962, p. 87; and "Goldwater and the John Birch Society," *National Review,* November 19, 1963, p. 430. See also Robert Welch to Fred Schwarz, September 6, 1960, and Fred Schwarz to Robert Welch, September 19, 1960, Box 173, Herbert Philbrick Papers.

For example, Herbert Philbrick, the most popular lecturer on the anti-Communist circuit in the 1950s, wrote a secret memorandum to the FBI in which he described "the cloak and dagger" atmosphere of a Welch seminar he attended in August 1959. Philbrick was shocked by Welch's "constant emphasis of 'treason' on the part of our present national leaders, including President Eisenhower." He warned that if the Birchers reached a membership of a million or more and fell into the "wrong hands" they "would have a rather highly explosive force." Philbrick became an active supporter of the JBS in public and a member-at-large of the society. See Herb Philbrick to Frank Willette, May 28, 1959, Box 129; Philbrick to Robert Welch, August 4, 1959; Welch to Philbrick, August 6, 1959; Philbrick to Welch, August 10, 1959; Welch to Philbrick, September 14, 1959; Philbrick to Welch, December 31, 1959, Box 173. Also see Frank E. Holman to Stuart Thompson, September 16, 1959; Stuart G. Thompson to Clarence Manion, Box 70, Clarence Manion Papers. For Welch's reaction to Buckley's attack, see Robert Welch to Members of Our Council, December 14, 1962, Box 61, Clarence Manion Papers.

41. Author unknown (Charles Lichenstein?), Confidential Memorandum, March 1964, Box 155, William A. Rusher Papers, Library of Congress.

42. Young Americans for Freedom, "Sharon Statement," September 11, 1960.

43. For the history of YAF, see Gregory L. Schneider, *Cadres for Conservatism:*

Young Americans for Freedom and the Rise of the Contemporary Right (New York, 1999); and John A. Andrews, *The Other Side of the Sixties: The Rise of Conservative Politics* (New Brunswick, N.J., 1997). For a comparison of young conservatives and young leftist radicals, see Rebecca E. Klatch, *A Generation Divided: The New Left, the New Right, and the 1960s* (Berkeley, Calif., 1999). Also, for young conservatives see Niels Bjerre-Poulsen, *Right Face: Organizing the American Conservative Movement, 1945–65* (Copenhagen, 2002), pp. 163–184.

44. "New Drive against the Anti-Communist Program," *Hearing before the Subcommittee to Investigate the Administration of the Internal Security Act and Other Internal Security Laws,* July 11, 1961, Eighty-seventh Congress, 1st Session (Washington, D.C., 1961), pp. 26–29.

45. "Right-Wing Officers Worrying Pentagon," *New York Times,* June 18, 1961, p. 1.

46. J. W. Fulbright to John F. Kennedy, June 28, 1961, Box 277, National Security Files, Papers of President John F. Kennedy, John F. Kennedy Library; Strom Thurmond, "Military Anti-Communist Seminars and Statements," *Congressional Record,* July 20, 1961, 87th Congress, 107:128; Monday, July 31, 1961, 107:129; August 2, 1961, 107:131; August 3, 1961, 107:138; August 15, 1961, 107:104; August 25, 1961, 107:15989–997; 15998–16003.

47. Willard Edwards, "Censors Cut Speeches of 79 High Officers," *Chicago Tribune,* January 26, 1962, p. 1; "The Right to Know Our Enemy," *Strom Thurmond Reports to the People,* July 1961.

48. C. V. Clifton to John F. Kennedy, August 9, 1961, Box 277, National Security Files, Papers of President Kennedy. The Fulbright Papers are full of letters protesting the memorandum and the Walker Affair. In particular see Box 28, William Fulbright Collection, University of Arkansas Archives.

49. "What Price Glory," *Dan Smoot Report,* August 28, 1961, pp. 1–8; "Complete Disarmament of American People Now Planned Through the U.N.," *The Manion Forum,* January 7, 1962, pp. 1–4; "Strategic Consequences of the Fulbright Memorandum," *Washington Report,* October 11, 1961, pp. 1–8. See also "Inquiry on Muzzling," *America's Future,* January 19, 1962, pp. 1–3; and Hannah Marie Haug, "The Fulbright Memorandum," *American Mercury* (November 1961), pp. 17–25.

50. "Text of Walker's Statement to Senate Panel and Request to Resign from Army," *New York Times,* November 3, 1961, p. 22; Edwin A. Walker, "The American Eagle Is Not a Dead Duck," Press Release, February 9, 1962, Muzzling the Military Folder, Subject Files, Eagle Forum Archives.

51. "General Edwin Walker, 83, Is Dead; Promoted Rightist Causes in 60s," *New York Times,* November 2, 1993, p. B10.

52. Robert Welch to Members of Our Council, October 8, 1962, Box 61, Clarence Manion Papers.

53. Walker was arrested on four federal charges for having incited a riot at Oxford, Mississippi, in October 1962. Under Robert Kennedy's orders, Walker was transported to the federal mental prison in Springfield, Missouri, where he was held for observation without consultation of his lawyers. He was charged with four

counts of insurrection and seditious conspiracy, but a federal grand jury failed to indict him. Walker sued newspapers across the country for libel in charging him with having incited the riot. Fred Schlafly, working through an organization he had been instrumental in creating, Defenders of American Liberties, participated in filing libel suits. Walker won a total of $23 million in libel damages, including an $800,000 jury award in Fort Worth against the Associated Press. A Louisiana jury awarded Walker another $3 million in damages in another libel suit. On June 12, 1967, the Supreme Court ruled 9–0 to overturn the Associated Press award, stating that public figures were the same as public officials and therefore the media deserved protection for mistakes made without malice.

Walker also came into public light when Lee Harvey Oswald attempted to assassinate him using the same rifle that later was used in the Kennedy assassination. This provided fodder for conspiracy theorists on both the left and the right, although the best evidence is that Oswald acted alone in both cases and sought to assassinate Walker because of his anti-Cuban statements. On June 23, 1976, Walker was again in the news when he was arrested on a charge of public lewdness at a restroom in a Dallas park for allegedly making sexual advances to an undercover officer. In 1982, the army restored Walker's pension rights as a major general. He died on November 2, 1992.

54. John A. Andrew, *The Other Side of the Sixties: Young Americans for Freedom and the Rise of Conservative Politics* (New Brunswick, N.J., 1997); and Andrew, *Power to Destroy: The Political Use of the IRS from Kennedy to Nixon* (Chicago, 2002). See also Perlstein, *Before the Storm*, p. 151.

55. John F. Kennedy, Speech before Democratic Party Dinner, Los Angeles, November 18, 1961, *Public Papers of the Presidents of the United States: John F. Kennedy* (Washington, D.C., 1962), pp. 733–736; Tom Wicker, "Kennedy Asserts Far Right Groups Provoke Disunity," *New York Times,* November 19, 1961, p. 1.

56. Quoted in Jonathan M. Schoenwald, *A Time for Choosing: The Rise of American Conservatism* (New York, 2001), pp. 96–97.

57. Quoted in ibid., p. 97.

58. Alan Barth, "Report on the 'Rampageous Right,'" *New York Times Magazine,* November 26, 1961, pp. 1–4; T. George Harris, "The Rampant Right Invades the GOP," *Look,* July 16, 1963, p. 14.

59. "The New Right: Populist Revolt or Moral Panic," introductory essay in Francis G. Couvares, Martha Saxton, Gerald N. Grob, and George Athan Billias, eds., *Interpretations of American History: Patterns and Perspectives* (New York, 2000, seventh edition), pp. 392–405.

60. Daniel Bell, "The Dispossessed," in *The Radical Right* (Garden City, N.Y.), p. 14.

61. Ibid., pp. 17–45.

62. An excellent discussion of this literature is found in Richard Gid Powers, *Not without Honor: The History of American Anti-Communism* (New York, 1995; reprinted New Haven, 1999), pp. 273–318. Also see Lisa McGerr, *Suburban Warriors: The Origins of the New Right* (Princeton, N.J., 2000), pp. 9–10.

In his etiological study of the Right in *The Strange Tactics of Extremism* (New

York, 1964), Harry Allen Overstreet diagnosed right-wing thinking as a mental disease. The titles of such books told their readers what to expect; for example: *Challenges to Democracy: Consensus and Extremism in American Politics* (Austin, Tex., 1965), by Murray Havens; *The American Ultras: The Extreme Right and the Military Industrial Complex* (New York, 1962), by Irwin Suall; and *The Christian Fright Peddlers* (New York, 1964), by Brooks Walker. *St. Louis Post-Dispatch* reporter Richard Dudman offered an exposé of the Right in *Men of the Far Right* (1962). Other books of this period include Mark Sherwin, *The Extremists* (New York, 1963); and Donald Janson, *The Far Right* (New York, 1963).

63. Fred J. Cook, "The Ultras: Aims, Affiliations and Finances of the Radical Right," *The Nation*, June 23, 1962, pp. 565–595.

64. For Welch's reaction to the *Post* article, see Robert Welch to Members of Our Council, December 14, 1962, Box 61, Clarence Manion Papers.

65. Phyllis Schlafly, "Notes of Speech, Robert Welch," August 14–15, 1959, John Birch Society Folder, Subject Files, Eagle Forum Archives, Clayton, Missouri.

66. Oliver's expulsion is discussed in "A Birch Society Founder Quits: Pressure by Welch Is Reported," *New York Times*, August 16, 1966 (copy), Box 173, Herbert Philbrick Papers; on DePugh, see Robert Welch to Mrs. W. B. McMillan, July 13, 1964, Box 61, Clarence Manion Papers. Of particular importance on the relationship between the Citizens' Council and the John Birch Society is Neil R. McMillen, *The Citizens' Council: Organized Resistance to the Second Reconstruction, 1954–65* (Urbana, Ill., 1971), pp. 189–204, especially pp. 200–201; and James Graham Cook, *The Segregationists* (New York, 1962), pp. 77, 80–81, 263–265.

67. Much of the discussion of Communist infiltration into the civil rights movement is found in pamphlets, a good deal of it produced by the Citizens' Council, but not all of it. For example, see Zygmund Dobbs, with a foreword by Archibald B. Roosevelt, *Red Intrigue and Race Turmoil* (New York, 1958); Herbert Ravenel Sass, *Mixed Schools and Mixed Blood* (Greenwood, Miss., 1958); Reverend G. T. Gillespie, *A Christian View on Segregation* (Greenwood, Miss., 1954); Mississippi State Junior Chamber of Commerce, *Oxford: A Warning for Americans* (Jackson, Miss., 1962); Lloyd Wright and John Satterfied, *Blueprint for Total Federal Regimentation: Analysis of the Civil Rights Act of 1963* (Washington, D.C., 1963); and The Fact Finder, *Will Negroes Give Their Votes to the Communists?* (Chicago, 1965).

68. Robert D. Novak, *The Agony of the G.O.P.* (New York, 1965), p. 25; Kramer and Roberts, *"I Never Wanted to Be Vice-President of Anything,"*.

69. Names of potential candidates floated in and out of the news—New York Congressman John Lindsay; former vice presidential candidate Henry Cabot Lodge; former American Motors chief and Michigan governor George Romney; and Pennsylvania governor William Scranton.

70. Graham T. Molitor, Position Paper on Communism, August 31, 1963, Graham T. Molitor Papers, Rockefeller Family Archives.

71. Quoted in Kramer and Roberts, *"I Never Wanted to Be Vice-President of Anything,"* pp. 274–276.

72. "Go West, Young Man," *National Review,* July 16, 1963, pp. 11–12.

73. Barry Goldwater, Diary Entry, March 18, 1977, Box 8/3 Personal and Political Series III, Barry Goldwater Papers, Arizona State University Archives.

74. Barry Goldwater to Dean Burch, January 21, 1963; Dean Burch to Barry Goldwater, January 14, 1963, Box 8/3, Personal and Political Series III, Goldwater Papers. There are several excellent studies on Goldwater in the 1964 election, including Mary C. Brennan, *Turning Right in the Sixties: The Conservative Capture of the GOP* (Chapel Hill, 1995); and Robert Alan Goldberg, *Barry Goldwater,* (New Haven, 1995). Also informative are Perlstein, *Before the Storm;* and Lee Edwards, *Goldwater: The Man Who Made a Revolution* (Washington, D.C., 1995); J. William Middendorf, *A Glorious Disaster: Barry Goldwater's Presidential Campaign and the Origins of the Conservative Movement* (New York, 2006).

75. *None Dare Call It Treason* encapsulated in 254 pages the extensive corpus of grassroots anti-Communist views.

76. Phyllis Schlafly, *A Choice Not an Echo* (Alton, Ill., 1964, third edition), p. 6.

77. For a full description of this book and its distribution, see Donald T. Critchlow, *Phyllis Schlafly and Grassroots Conservatism: A Woman's Crusade* (Princeton, N.J., 2005).

78. The following discussion of the Republican Party and the 1964 primary campaign draws heavily on John Howard Kessel, *The Goldwater Coalition: Republican Strategies in 1964* (Indianapolis, 1968), pp. 25–28.

79. Ibid., p. 60.

80. A useful study on California conservatism is Kurt Schuparra, *Triumph of the Right: The Rise of the California Conservative Movement, 1945–1966* (Armonk, N.Y., 1998).

81. One confidential memorandum reported that "fortunately or unfortunately, the Birchers are contributing a substantial portion of our workers and some of our leaders in important areas . . . the Society does, in fact, harbor some of the soundest conservatives and some of the wildest extremists." Author unknown, Memorandum, March 1964, Box 173, William A. Rusher Papers.

82. Quoted in Kessel, *The Goldwater Coalition,* pp. 103–104.

83. Perlstein, *Before the Storm,* p. 366.

84. Schorr's CBS report is quoted in ibid., p. 375.

85. This description of press reaction and the convention is drawn from Goldberg, *Barry Goldwater,* pp. 108–209, especially p. 201.

86. "More Voices of Moderation," *National Review,* October 6, 1964, p. 854.

87. An excellent discussion of the 1964 platform and the fight over it is found in Goldberg, *Barry Goldwater,* pp. 202–204.

88. Quoted in ibid., p. 204.

89. "Mr. Goldwater," *Congressional Record-Senate,* 110:II (Washington, D.C., 1964), p. 14319.

90. The six Republicans opposed to cloture were John Tower (Texas); Edwin L. Mecham (New Mexico); Milward L. Simpson (Wyoming); Wallace F. Bennett (Utah); Milton B. Young (North Dakota); and Goldwater. Dirksen's role in the Civil

Rights Act, from which this discussion follows, is from Edward L. Schapsmeier and Frederick H. Schapsmeier, *Dirksen of Illinois: Senatorial Statesman* (Urbana, Ill., 1985), pp. 155–163.

91. The House and Senate vote on the Civil Rights Act of 1964 is found in the *Congressional Quarterly Almanac* (Washington, D.C., 1964), 20:636–637 and 696.

92. Quoted in full in Jeffrey Hart, *The Making of the American Conservative Mind: National Review and Its Times* (Wilmington, Del., 2005), p. 103.

93. William F. Buckley, Jr., "The Call to Color Blindness," *National Review,* June 18, 1963, p. 488. Also on race, see "The Race Issue and the Campaign: A Special Report," *National Review,* September 22, 1964, pp. 813–821.

94. Frank S. Meyer, "The Negro Revolution," *National Review,* June 18, 1963, p. 496.

95. Schapsmeier and Schapsmeier, *Dirksen of Illinois,* pp. 162–163.

96. Interview, Charles Lichenstein with author, Washington, D.C., August 12, 2001.

97. This description of the 1964 election relies on Goldberg, *Barry Goldwater,* pp. 233–235, especially p. 233.

3. Trust and Betrayal in the Nixon Years

1. Jonathan Schoenwald, *A Time for Choosing: The Rise of Modern American Conservatism* (New York, 2001), views the conservative movement as bounding forward in the late 1960s, after having expelled "the extremists" in the ranks of the GOP.

2. Quotations are from "Only 725 days Left," *Time,* November 20, 1964, p. 1.

3. Karl Hess, *In a Cause That Will Triumph* (Garden City, N.Y., 1967), p. 135. Quoted in Philip A. Klinkner, *The Losing Parties: Out-Party National Committees, 1956–1993* (New Haven, 1994), p. 74.. See also pp. 71–83.

4. Klinkner, *The Losing Parties,* pp. 64–66.

5. Edward L. Schapsmeier and Frederick H. Schapsmeier, *Dirksen of Illinois: Senatorial Statesman* (Urbana, Ill., 1985), p. 169.

6. Klinkner, *The Losing Parties,* p. 66.

7. Bliss's charges of extremism in the GOP were specifically directed toward members of the John Birch Society, but many on the Republican right saw the attack as aimed at them. Ray Bliss, "Statement of Extremism by Republican National Chairman Ray C. Bliss," November 5, 1965, National Federation of Republican Women (NFRW) Files, Eagle Forum Office Files.

8. William Rusher, *The Plot to Steal the GOP* (New York, 1967).

9. Phyllis Schlafly to Iris F. Maloney, July 11, 1967; and Phyllis Schlafly to Ray Bliss, June 6, 1967; "Mrs. Schlafly Assails Bliss, Calls His Office Un-Neutral," *St. Louis Post-Dispatch,* June 8, 1967, Box 1, NFRW Files, Personal Papers of Phyllis Schlafly.

10. Factional struggles within the GOP occurred between moderates and conservatives, as well as among conservatives. Some right-wing conservatives such as Mike

Djordjevich, a California activist, accused William F. Buckley, Jr., Clifton White, and William Rusher of forming a clique to control the Young Republicans. See Mike Djordjevich to Glenn Campbell, August 15, 1965; Djordjevich to William F. Buckley, Jr., July 7, 1965; Djordjevich to Willis Carto, June 7, 1965; Djordjevich to William A. Rusher, June 7, 1967; NFRW Files, Personal Papers of Phyllis Schlafly.

11. For an inside look at the purge, see C. Montgomery Johnson Papers, Special Collections, University of Washington, Boxes 26 and 27.

12. Surveys on racial attitudes, including racial riots, are examined in Rita James Simon, *Public Opinion in America, 1936–1970* (Chicago, 1974), pp. 55–75, especially pp. 71–72.

13. James T. Patterson, *Grand Expectations: The United States, 1945–1974* (New York, 1996), pp. 662–663.

14. Michael W. Flamm, *Law and Order: Street Crime, Civil Unrest, and the Crisis of Liberalism in the 1960s* (New York, 2005), pp. 83–84.

15. Conservative support for America's involvement in Vietnam is succinctly articulated in a pamphlet published by Gonzaga University Rev. Daniel Lyons, S.J., "The Future of Vietnam" (Spokane, Washington, 1965); and the widely distributed book by Suzanne Labin, *Vietnam: An Eye-Witness Account* (Springfield, Va, 1964).

16. "This Week," *National Review,* July 13, 1965, p. 577.

17. For a typical account of this revisionist view of Vietnam among conservatives, see George F. Will, "The U.S. Had the Vietnam War Won in 1967," *The Wanderer,* May 21, 1981, p. 5.

18. For a discussion of how conservatives employed the law-and-order issue—and the failure of liberals to respond to this issue—see Flamm, *Law and Order.*

19. In 1970, Schmitz ran as a Republican in a special election to fill the vacancy caused by the death of Representative James B. Utt.

20. Dan T. Carter, *The Politics of Rage: George Wallace, the Origins of New Conservatism, and the Transformation of American Politics* (Baton Rouge, 1995); and Earl Black and Merle Black, *The Rise of Southern Republicans* (Cambridge, Mass., 2003). For a contrary view, see Joseph Aistrup, *The Southern Strategy Revisited: Republican Top-Down Advance in the South* (Lexington, Ky., 1995).

21. Black and Black, *The Rise of Southern Republicans.*

22. The Right's antipathy toward Romney is found in Antoni E. Golan, *Romney: Behind the Image* (Arlington, Va., 1967). M. Stanton Evans's introduction provides a good insight into how Romney was viewed by conservatives.

23. The potential for party realignment was openly discussed by Kevin Phillips in *The Emerging Republican Majority* (1969) and Ben Wattenberg in *The Real Majority* (1970). Nixon's strategy for creating a Republican majority is traced in Robert Mason, *Richard Nixon and the Quest for a New Majority* (Chapel Hill, 2005). Mason contends that this strategy entailed seeking a conservative majority.

24. William Rusher to Michael Djordjevich, January 7, 1969, Box 26, William Rusher papers.

25. Quoted in William F. Buckley, "Is Nixon One of Us?," *Inveighing We Will Go* (New York, 1972), p. 68.

26. For an excellent study of Nixon's early career that provides great insight into the man and his politics, see Mark Gellman, *The Contender: Richard Nixon, the Congressional Years, 1946–1952* (New York, 1999).

27. Nixon appointed Patrick Buchanan, a conservative editorial writer for the *St. Louis Globe-Democrat,* as a speech writer, and he appointed the former YAF activist Howard Phillips as head of the Office of Economic Opportunity. Joan Hoff, *Nixon Reconsidered* (New York, 1994); Stephen Ambrose, *Nixon* (New York, 1987); and Herbert S. Parmet, *Richard Nixon and His America* (New York, 1990).

28. "Answer Please, Mr. Nixon," *National Review,* March 8, 1966, p. 196; "Nixon and the 'Buckleyites,'" *National Review,* April 5, 1966, p. 294; and "Mr. Nixon's Reply," *National Review,* April 5, 1966, p. 304. See also William A. Rusher, "The Long Detour," *Claremont Review of Books* (Summer 2005), V:5, pp. 32–35; and Robert Mason, *Richard Nixon and the Quest for a New Majority* (Chapel Hill, 2005).

29. Michael Barone, *Our Country: The Shaping of America* (New York, 1990), pp. 457–459.

30. Quoted in Theodore White, *Breach of Faith: The Fall of Richard Nixon* (New York, 1975), p. 163.

31. Vincent J. Burke and Vee Burke, *Nixon's Good Deed: Welfare Reform* (New York, 1974); Kenneth M. Bowler, *The Nixon Guaranteed Income Proposal: Substance and Process in Policy Change* (Cambridge, 1974); and Daniel P. Moynihan, *The Politics of a Guaranteed Income: The Nixon Administration and the Family Assistance Plan* (New York, 1973). See also Hoff, *Nixon Reconsidered.*

32. For an excellent discussion of middle-class benefits and Nixon's willingness to expand universal coverage of social benefits while cutting programs for the poor, see Neil Gilbert, *Capitalism and the Welfare State* (New Haven, 1994).

33. Quoted in William D. Snider, *Helms and Hunt: The North Carolina Senate Race, 1984* (Chapel Hill, 1985), p. 18.

34. The Right took immediate advantage of this tragedy. The John Birch Society's press, Western Islands, published Zad Rust, *Teddy Bare* (Belmont, Mass., 1971). In 1988, Leo Damore, *Senatorial Privilege* (New York, 1988), appeared. For a political perspective on Chappaquiddick, see Barone, *Our Country,* p. 467.

35. David A. Noebel, "Communism, Hypnotism, and the Beatles" (Tulsa, Okla., 1965), pp. 1, 25.

36. See the haunting biography of Timothy Leary, the drug guru of the 1960s, whom many, including liberals, saw as little more than a drug addict: Robert Greenfield, *Timothy Leary: A Biography* (New York, 2006).

37. Charles Reich, *The Greening of America* (New York, 1976), p. 468, quoted in Barone, *Our Country,* p. 468.

38. Flamm, *Law and Order,* p. 257, n. 8.

39. See David Holloway, *The Soviet Union and the Arms Race* (New Haven, 1983), pp. 45–93.

40. Clarence Manion to Eugene Lyons, April 19, 1971, Clarence Manion Papers,

Box 46, Chicago Historical Society. For the Nixon administration's relations with mainland China, see Jim Mann, *About Face: A History of America's Curious Relationship with China from Nixon to Clinton* (New York, 1999).

41. Buckley, "Is Nixon One of Us?," p. 77.

42. Rep. John M. Ashbrook, "How the U.S. Lost Military Superiority," *Congressional Record*, February 1, 1972 (reprint), American Security Council (1972).

43. Donald T. Critchlow, *Phyllis Schlafly and Grassroots Conservatism: A Woman's Crusade* (Princeton, 2005), pp. 208–209.

44. "Ashbrook Tells UROC He Won't Back Nixon," *San Francisco Examiner*, August 27, 1972, p. 3, Box 26, William Rusher Papers.

45. Byron R. Shafer, *The Quiet Revolution: The Struggles for the Democratic Party and the Shaping of Post-Reform Politics* (New York, 1983).

46. John Andrews III, *Power to Destroy: The Political Uses of IRS from Kennedy to Nixon* (Chicago, 2002); and Carter, *The Politics of Rage.*

47. Quoted in "Nixon's Landslide Victory Fails to Produce Republican Congress," *Congressional Quarterly*, XXVIII (1972), p. 1012. My description of the 1972 election relies heavily on this article.

48. Snider, *Helms and Hunt*, p. 9.

49. For insight into congressional thinking at the time, see J. Brian Smith, *John J. Rhodes: Man of the House* (Phoenix, Ariz., 2006), pp. 3, 104.

50. John J. Rhodes, *I Was There* (New York, 1995); and J. Brian Smith, *John J. Rhodes: Man of the House* (Phoenix, Ariz., 2005).

51. Smith, *John J. Rhodes*, p. 88. After Ford's confirmation, a Democrat won the special election to fill Ford's seat in Grand Rapids, Michigan, the first time a Democrat had won this seat since 1910.

52. Barone, *Our Country*, pp. 525–534.

53. Donald T. Critchlow, "When Conservatives Become Revolutionaries: Conservatism in Congress," in Julian E. Zelizer, ed., *The American Congress: The Building of Democracy* (New York, 2004), pp. 703–731.

54. William Rusher to William F. Buckley, Jr., February 19, 1973, and February 21, 1973, William Rusher to William Buckley, March 13, 1975, Box 121, William Rusher Papers.

55. Howard Phillips, "Conservatives Should Help Remove Nixon" (press release), July 30, 1974, Box 71, William Rusher Papers.

4. The Power of Ideas and Institutions

1. See John B. Judis, *Grand Illusions: Critics and Champions of the American Century* (New York, 1992), p. 143. For Trotsky's views concerning the revolutionary process, see *The History of the Russian Revolution*, trans. Max Eastman (New York, 1932).

2. For the emergence of conservative think tanks see Donald T. Critchlow, "Think Tanks, Antistatism, and Democracy: The Nonpartisan Ideal and Policy Re-

search in the United States, 1913–1987," in Mary Furner and Michael J. Lacy, eds., *The State and Social Investigation in Britain and the United States* (Cambridge, England, 1993), pp. 279–322; James Allen Smith, *The Idea Brokers: Think Tanks and the Rise of the New Policy Elite* (New York, 1991); and Lee Edwards, *The Power of Ideas: The Heritage Foundation at Twenty-five Years* (Ottawa, Ill., 1997).

3. An excellent study of this transformation is Byron Shafer, *Quiet Revolution: The Struggle for the Democratic Party* (New York, 1983).

4. Theodore White, *The Making of the President, 1972* (New York, 1973), p. 180; quoted in Geoffrey Layman, *The Great Divide: Religious and Cultural Conflict in American Party History* (New York, 2001), pp. 40–50, especially p. 41.

5. This discussion of the importance of religion and culture in American politics relies on Layman, *The Great Divide.*

6. Layman, *The Great Divide,* p. 341. For an argument concerning the declining influence of the Religious Right on the American electorate, see Clyde Wilcox, "Wither the Christian Right? The Elections and Beyond," *The Election of the Century and What It Tells Us about the Future of American Politics,* ed. Stephen J. Wayne and Clyde Wilcox (Armonk, N.Y., 2002), pp. 107–124.

7. Layman, *The Great Divide,* pp. x, 10, 17, 19, 35, 101, 127, 326–341.

8. He later recalled, after meeting the enlisted commoners in his regiment, many of whom came from Cicero, Illinois (the home of Al Capone): "I said to myself, 'I can't build socialism with these people. They'll probably take it over and make a racket out of it.'" Irving Kristol, "Second Thoughts: A Generational Perspective," *Second Thoughts: Former Radicals Look Back at the Sixties,* ed. Peter Collier and David Horowitz (Lanham, Md., 1989), p. 184. Also quoted in Gary Dorrien, *The Newconservative Mind: Politics, Culture, and the War of Ideology* (Philadelphia, 1993), p. 71. The discussion of Kristol's experience in revolutionary socialist politics is drawn from Dorrien, as well as from Kristol's essays found in *NeoConservatism: The Autobiography of an Idea* (New York, 1985).

9. Irving Kristol, "Civil Liberties 1952—A Study in Confusion," *Commentary* (March 1952).

10. Mark Gerson, *The Neoconservative Vision: From the Cold War to the Culture Wars* (Lanham, Md., 1996), pp. 62–65.

11. A useful summary of Strauss's ideas is found in John P. East, *The American Conservative Movement: The Philosophical Founders* (Washington, D.C., 1986), pp. 143–174.

12. Kristol, "An Autobiographical Memoir," *Neoconservatism,* pp. 3–51, quotation p. 24.

13. Ibid., pp. 28–29.

14. An insightful discussion of the career of *Commentary* is found in George H. Nash, "Joining the Ranks: Commentary and American Conservatism," *Commentary in American Life,* ed. Murray Friedman (Philadelphia, 2005).

15. Norman Podhoretz, *Making It* (New York, 1967). For an extremely useful synopsis of the history of *Commentary,* see George H. Nash, "Joining the Ranks:

Commentary and American Conservatism," *Commentary in American Life,* ed. Murray Friedman (Philadelphia, 2005), pp. 151–216.

16. Norman Podhoretz, "The Language of Life," *Commentary* (October 1953), pp. 380–382; and Podhoretz, "William Faulkner and the Problem of War," *Commentary* (September 1954), in *Doings and Undoings: The Fifties and after in American Writing* (New York, 1964), pp. 13–24. See also Dorrien, *The Neoconservative Mind,* pp. 133–206.

17. Norman Podhoretz, "My Negro Problem—And Ours," *Commentary* (February 1963), republished in Podhoretz, *Doings and Undoings.* This discussion of Podhoretz relies on his autobiographical writings, including *Breaking Ranks: A Political Memoir* (New York, 1979); *Making It;* and *Ex-Friends* (New York, 1999); as well as Dorrien, *The Neoconservative Mind,* pp. 133–207; and J. David Hoeveler, Jr., *Watch on the Right: Conservative Intellectuals in the Reagan Era* (Madison, Wis., 1991), pp. 9–12.

18. Quoted in Dorrien, *The Neoconservative Mind,* p. 157.

19. This issue of authenticity is raised in Hoeveler, *Watch on the Right,* pp. 10–11.

20. Jeane J. Kirkpatrick, "The Revolt of the Masses," *Commentary* (February 1973), pp. 58–72, quoted in Hoeveler, *Watch on the Right,* pp. 152–176, especially p. 157.

21. The world of Jewish intellectuals in these early years is discussed by Alexander Bloom, *Prodigal Sons: The New York Intellectuals and Their World* (New York, 1986), which emphasizes the social ascendance of Jews in modern America; and Alan Wald, *Intellectuals: The Rise and Decline of the Anti-Stalinist Left from the 1930s to 1980s* (New York, 1987), which is prolix and overly polemical from a Marxist perspective.

22. This discussion of neoconservatism relies on Dorrien, *The Neo-Conservative Mind;* Mark Gerson, *The New Conservative Vision: From the Cold War to the Cultural Wars* (Lanham, Md., 1996); Peter Steinfels, *Neo-Conservatism: The Men Who Are Changing America's Politics* (New York, 1979). See also John Ehrman, *The Rise of Neoconservatism: Intellectuals and Foreign Affairs, 1945–1994* (New Haven, 1995).

23. Kristol, "An Autobiographical Memoir," p. 31.

24. There is a sizeable polemical literature on the Right against the neoconservatives. Representative of this literature is Paul Gottfried and Thomas Fleming, *The Conservative Movement* (Boston, 1988); Samuel Francis, *Beautiful Losers: Essays on the Failure of Conservatism* (Columbia, Mo., 1993); Joseph Scotchie, ed., *The Paleoconservatives: New Voices of the Old Right* (New Brunswick, 1999); and Patrick Buchanan, *Where the Right Went Wrong: How Neoconservatives Subverted the Reagan Revolution and Hijacked the Bush Presidency* (N.Y., 2004).

25. Irving Kristol, "Memoirs of a 'Cold Warrior,'" *Neoconservatism: The Autobiography of an Idea* (New York, 1995), p. 465; Irving Kristol, *Two Cheers for Capitalism* (New York, 1978).

26. The language used is derived from Owen Bradley, *A Modern Maistre: The Social and Political Thought of Joseph De Maistre* (Lincoln, Neb., 1999), p. 24.

27. This is a point made by Jürgen Habermas, "Neoconservative Cultural Criticism in the United States and West Germany," *The New Conservatism: Cultural Criticism and the Historians' Debate* (Cambridge, Mass., 1989), pp. 22–48, especially pp. 24–29.

28. There is an extensive literature on the emergence of the administrative state. A good start into this literature begins with Stephen Skowronek, *Building a New American State: The Expansion of National Administrative Capacities* (New York, 1982); and Sidney M. Milkis, *Political Parties and Constitutional Government: Remaking American Democracy* (Baltimore, 1999). Also useful is Ronald J. Pestritto, "Woodrow Wilson, the Organic State, and American Republicanism," in Bryan-Paul Frost and Jeffrey Sikkenga, eds., *History of American Political Thought* (Lanham, Md., 2003), pp. 549–568; and John Marini and Ken Masugi, eds., *The Progressive Revolution in Politics and Political Science* (Lanham, Md., 2005).

29. Trustees included conservatives such as economic journalist Henry Hazlitt, legal scholar Roscoe Pound, and dean of the Harvard Business School Charles C. Abbott.

30. Nick Thimmesch, "The Right Kind of Think Tank at the Right Time," *Human Events* October 7, 1978, pp. 12–21; Tom Bethell, "The Rewards of Enterprise," *New Republic,* July 16, 1977, pp. 17–19.

31. AEI, *William J. Baroody, Sr. Remembered by Paul McCracken, Robert H. Bork, Irving Kristol, and Michael Novak* (Washington, D.C., 1981).

32. Donald T. Critchlow, "Think Tanks, Antistatism, and Democracy: The Nonpartisan Ideal and Policy Research," in Michael J. Lacey and Mary O. Furner, *The State and Social Investigation in Britain and the United States* (Cambridge, England, 1993), pp. 279–319.

33. Andrew Rich, *Think Tanks, Public Policy, and the Politics of Expertise* (New York, 2004); and Justin Raimondo, *An Enemy of the State: The Life of Murray N. Rothbard* (Amherst, N.Y., 2000).

5. The Accident of History

1. "Politics: 1974 Elections," *Congressional Quarterly,* XXX (1974), pp. 839–864.

2. For the importance of the administrative state, see Sidney Milkis, *Political Parties and Constitutional Government: Remaking American Democracy* (Baltimore, 1999).

3. This description of Ford's career relies on Michael Barone, *Our Country: The Shaping of America from Roosevelt to Reagan* (New York, 1990), pp. 530–541.

4. In hindsight, George H. W. Bush would have made a far less controversial appointment. Herbert Parmet, *George Bush: The Life of a Lone-Star Yankee* (New York, 1977), p. 165. William F. Buckley, Jr., to President Gerald Ford, August 14, 1974, White House Central Files, Box 434, Subject Files, Buckley, Ford Papers.

5. Steven F. Hayward, *The Age of Reagan: The Fall of the Old Liberal Order, 1964–1980* (Roseville, Calif., 2001), p. 398; John Robert Green, *The Presidency of Gerald R. Ford* (Lawrence, Kans., 1995), p. 30; Robert T. Hartman, *Palace Politics: An Inside Account of the Ford Years* (New York, 1980), pp. 233–235.

6. Richard A. Viguerie, *The New Right—We're Ready to Lead* (Falls Church, Va., 1980), p. 60.

7. Howard Phillips, *The New Right at Harvard* (Vienna, Va., 1983), p. 116.

8. Viguerie, *The New Right,* p. 2.

9. The biographical information for Viguerie relies on ibid., pp. 19–81.

10. There is a plethora of studies on the New Right and the Christian Right. Especially useful are Clyde Wilcox, *God's Warriors: The Christian Right in Twentieth-Century America* (Baltimore, 1992); Wilcox, *Onward Christian Soldiers? The Religious Right in American Politics* (Boulder, Colo., 1996); and Steve Bruce, *The Rise and Fall of the New Christian Right: Conservative Protestant Politics in America, 1978–1988* (New York, 1988). Also see Steve Bruce, Peter Kivisto, and William H. Swatos, Jr., eds., *The Rapture of Politics: The Christian Right as the United States Approaches the Year 2000* (New York, 1995); Matthew Moen, *The Christian Right and Congress* (Tuscaloosa, Ala., 1983); Robert Liebman and Rother Wuthnow, eds., *The New Christian Right: Mobilization and Legitimation* (New York, 1991); and David Bromley and Anson Shupe, eds., *New Christian Politics* (Macon, Ga., 1984). For the New Right, see Alan Crawford, *Thunder on the Right: The "New Right" and the Politics of Resentment* (New York, 1980).

11. David E. Kyvig, *Explicit and Authentic Acts: Amending the U.S. Constitution, 1776–1995* (Lawrence, Kan., 1996), pp. 379–385. Also see Philip Hamburger, *Separation of Church and State: A Theologically Liberal, Anti-Catholic, and American Principle* (New York, 2002); and James Hitchcock, *The Supreme Court and Religion in American Life* (Princeton, N.J., 2004).

12. *Strom Thurmond Reports to the People* (November 11, 1963), Education-Prayer folder, J. Evetts Haley Papers (unprocessed), Eagle Forum Archives, St. Louis, Missouri.

13. Thurman Sensing, "We Must Restore Prayer to the Schools in Order to Defeat Communism," *Manion Forum,* May 24, 1964.

14. Adolph Bedsole, *The Supreme Court Decision on Bible Reading and Prayer: America's Black Letter Day* (Grand Rapids, Mich., 1964).

15. Kyvig, *Explicit and Authentic Acts,* p. 282.

16. Quoted in ibid., p. 184.

17. National Committee to Restore Prayer in Schools, *Let Us Pray,* Education-Prayer Folder, J. Evetts Haley (unprocessed), Eagle Forum Archives, Clayton, Missouri.

18. The Roman Catholic view of abortion is articulated by Pope John Paul II, *Evangelium Vitae* (1995). For differences within Protestant churches, see Donald T. Critchlow, *Intended Consequences: Birth Control, Abortion, and the Federal Government in Modern America* (New York, 1999), p. 139.

19. Jo Freeman, *The Politics of Women's Liberation: A Case Study of an*

Emerging Social Movement and Its Relation to the Policy Process (New York, 1975); Sheila M. Rothman, *Woman's Proper Place: A History of Changing Ideals and Practices, 1870 to the Present* (New York, 1978); Leila Rupp and Verta Taylor, *Survival in the Doldrums: The American Women's Rights Movement, 1945 to the 1960s* (New York, 1983).

20. A good study of abortion reform law in Hawaii is Patricia G. Steinhoff and Milton Diamond, *Abortion Politics: The Hawaii Experience* (Honolulu, 1977). A feminist perspective on family planning and abortion is offered by Linda Gordon, *Woman's Body, Woman's Right: Birth Control in America* (New York, 1976). Also useful is Kristin Luker, *Abortion and the Politics of Motherhood* (Berkeley, 1974). The abortion reform movement on the state level before *Roe* is discussed by David Garrow, *Liberty and Sexuality: The Right to Privacy and the Making of Roe v. Wade* (New York, 1994). An abortion reform perspective is found in Lawrence Lader, *Abortion II: Making the Revolution* (Boston, 1973). Other discussions of the politics of abortion can be found in Barbara Hinkson Craig and David M. O'Brien, *Abortion and American Politics* (Clatham, N.J., 1993); Raymond Tatalovich and Byron W. Daynes, *The Politics of Abortion: A Study of Community Conflict in Public Policy* (New York, 1981). For the antiabortion movement, see Keith Cassidy, "The Right to Life Movement," in *The Politics of Abortion and Birth Control in Historical Perspective,* ed. Donald T. Critchlow (University Park, Pa., 1996). Also important is Suzanne Staggenborg, *The Pro-Choice Movement: Organization and Activism in the Abortion Conflict* (New York, 1991). Useful for understanding the abortion debate on the state level is Robert J. Spitzer, *The Right to Life Movement and Third Party Politics* (Westport, Conn., 1987); and Faye D. Ginsburg, *Contested Lives: The Abortion Debate in an American Community* (Berkeley, 1989). Two journalistic accounts are found in Andrew H. Merton, *Enemies of Choice: The Right to Life Movement and Its Threat to Abortion* (Boston, 1981); and Connie Paige, *The Right to Lifers: Who They Are, How They Operate, Where They Get Their Money* (New York, 1983).

21. Craig and O'Brien, *Abortion and American Politics,* pp. 51–58.

22. Merton, *Enemies of Choice,* pp. 43–45.

23. The first permanent state antiabortion group was organized in Virginia; the Illinois Right to Life Committee formed the following year. Minnesota Citizens Concerned for Life, which attracted a membership of ten thousand by 1973, became a model for other state groups. Paige, *The Right to Lifers,* pp. 58–60.

24. In both NARAL and NRLC, the majority of members were women (78 percent and 63 percent, respectively); most were married (55 percent of NARAL's members, compared with 87 percent of NRLC's members); and most were college educated (46 percent of NARAL's members had advanced postgraduate degrees, compared with 32 percent of NRLC's members). What separated these two groups was religious affiliation. The composition of abortion and antiabortion groups is found in Donald Granberg, "The Abortion Activists," *Family Planning Perspectives* 13:4 (July-August 1981), pp. 157–163. On the Catholic role in the abortion issue see Mary T. Hanna, *Catholics and American Politics* (Cambridge, 1979). See also Con-

stance Balide, Barbara Danziger, and Deborah Spitz, "The Abortion Issue: Major Groups, Organizations and Funding Sources," *The Abortion Exerience,* ed. Howard J. Osofsky and Joy D. Osofsky (Hagerstown, Md., 1973), pp. 496–529; Kenneth D. Wald et al., "Evangelical Politics and the Status Issue," *Journal for the Scientific Study of Religon* 28:1 (1989), pp. 1–15.

25. Critchlow, *Intended Consequences,* p. 139.

26. Thomas Littlewood, *The Politics of Population Control* (Notre Dame, Ind., 1977). Also see John H. Kessell, *The Domestic Presidency: Decision-Making in the White House* (North Scituate, Mass., 1975).

27. Dan Carter, *The Politics of Rage: George Wallace, the Origins of New Conservatism, and the Transformation of American Politics* (New York, 1995).

28. Little, *The Politics of Population Control,* pp. 107–132; and Theodore White, *The Making of the President,* New York, 1973), pp. 51–52; 242–244. Nixon's appeals to Catholics were expressed in Richard Nixon, "Statement about Policy on Abortions at Military Base Hospitals in the United States," April 3, 1971, *Public Papers of the Presidents of the United States: Richard M. Nixon, 1971* (Washington, D.C., 1972), p. 500; and "Remarks at the Annual Convention of the National Education Association in Philadelphia, Pennsylvania, April 6, 1972," in *Public Papers of the Presidents of the United States: Richard M. Nixon, 1972* (Washington, D.C., 1974), pp. 243–244. See also "The New York Campaign," *National Journal,* November 28, 1972, pp. 1676–1678; Theodore White, *The Making of the President, 1972* (New York, 1973); and Barone, *Our Country,* pp. 436–453.

29. Federal abortion policy is discussed by Karen O'Connor, *No Neutral Ground? Abortion Politics in an Age of Absolutes* (Boulder, Colo., 1996); and Craig and O'Brien, *Abortion and American Politics.*

30. Joyce Gelb and Marian Lief Palley, "Interest Group Politics: A Comparative Analysis of Federal Decision Making," *Journal of Politics,* 41 (May 1979), pp. 362–392, especially pp. 375–377.

31. Critchlow, *Intended Consequences,* pp. 201–206.

32. Gelb and Palley, "Interest Group Politics." For a history of the federal role in abortion policy, see Critchlow, *Intended Consequences.*

33. There is an extensive literature on the ERA fight. An overview of the debate can be found in David E. Kyvig, *Explicit and Authentic Acts: Amending the U.S. Constitution, 1776–1995* (Lawrence, Kan., 1996); Janet K. Boles, *The Politics of the Equal Rights Amendment: Conflict and the Decision Process* (New York, 1979); Jane J. Mansbridge, *Why We Lost the ERA* (Chicago, 1986); and Donald T. Critchlow, *Phyllis Schlafly and Grassroots Conservatism* (Princeton, N.J., 2005).

34. Dean J. Kotlowski, *Nixon's Civil Rights: Politics, Principle, and Policy* (Cambridge, Mass., 2001), pp. 232–240.

35. Helen Thomas, "Betty Ford Backs ERA," *Columbus Citizen Journal,* September 15, 1974, Ohio ERA Action Folder, ERA Files, Eagle Forum Archives.

36. "First Lady Sticks to Her Guns on ERA," *Los Angeles Times,* February 18, 1975, Ford Folder, ERA Files, Eagle Forum Archives.

37. Winzola McLendon, "Betty Ford Talks about Homemaking," *Good House-*

keeping (August 1976); "Mrs. Ford Phones ERA Passage," *Washington Post*, February 15, 1975, Box 4, Elizabeth O Neill Files, University of Michigan Archives, Ann Arbor, Michigan.

38. Critchlow, *Phyllis Schlafly and Grassroots Conservatism*; Carol Felsenthal, *The Sweetheart of the Silent Majority: The Biography of Phyllis Schlafly* (New York, 1981). For the role of conservative women, see Lisa McGirr, *Suburban Warriors: The Origins of the New American Right* (Princeton, N.J., 2000). Also see Rebecca Klatch, *Women of the New Right* (Philadelphia, 1987); Sara Diamond, *Road to Dominion: Right-Wing Movements and Political Power in the United States* (New York, 1995); and Elinor Burkett, *The Right Women: A Journey through the Hearts of Conservative America* (New York, 1998).

The tradition of women as moral reformers is found in an extensive literature on the subject. Especially useful are Jane Dehart, "Gender on the Right: Meanings behind the Existential Scream," *Gender and History*, 3 (Autumn 1991); Zillah R. Eisenstein, "The Sexual Politics of the New Right," *Feminist Theory*, 7 (Spring 1982); Kathleen M. Blee, *Women of the Klan: Racism and Gender in the 1920s* (Berkeley, 1991); and Leonard J. Moore, *Citizen Klansmen: The Ku Klux Klan in Indiana, 1921–1928* (Chapel Hill, 1991).

39. "What's Wrong with 'Equal Rights' for Women?" *The Phyllis Schlafly Report* (February 1972), and "The Fraud Called the Equal Rights Amendment," *The Phyllis Schlafly Report* (May 1972). See also Paul Freund, "The Equal Rights Amendment is Not the Way," *Harvard Civil Rights–Civil Liberties Law Review* (March 1971).

40. Carol Mueller and Thomas Dimieri, "The Structure of Belief Systems among Contending ERA Activists," *Social Forces* (March 1982), p. 665.

41. Mansbridge, *Why We Lost the ERA*, pp. 135–138 and 173–178.

42. Ruth Rosen, *The World Split Open: How the Modern Women's Movement Changed America* (New York, 2000); Carol G. Heilbrun, *The Education of a Woman: The Life of Gloria Steinem* (New York, 1995); and Daniel Horowitz, *Betty Friedan and the Making of the Feminine Mystique: The American Left, the Cold War, and Modern America* (Amherst, 1998).

43. Kent L. Tedin et al., "Social Background and Political Differences between Pro- and Anti-ERA Activists," *American Politics Quarterly*, 5:3 (July 1977), pp. 395–404; Mueller and Dimieri, "The Structure of Belief Systems," pp. 657–676.

44. The view that women's groups had failed to connect with "homemakers" is found in Bonnie Cowan to Jane Wells (national coordinator of ERAmerica), March 19, 1976, ERAmerica, Box 1, Library of Congress, Washington, D.C.

45. In 1978 Congress extended the ERA deadline another three years, but to no avail. The ERA campaign ultimately failed, and the ERA died on June 30, 1982.

46. This discussion of Ford's foreign policy relies on Hayward, *The Age of Reagan*, pp. 395–446; and Guenter Lewy, *America in Vietnam* (New York, 1978).

47. Jean-Louis Margolin, "Cambodia: The Country of Disconcerting Crimes," *Black Book of Communism: Crimes, Terror, Repression* (Cambridge, Mass., 1999), pp. 588–611.

48. David Holloway, *The Soviet Union and the Arms Race* (New Haven, 1983), pp. 58–59 and pp. 45–99.

49. Hayward, *The Age of Reagan*, p. 424.

50. Patrick Glynn, *Closing Pandora's Box: Arms Races, Arms Control, and the History of the Cold War* (New York, 1999), pp. 269–270.

51. Quoted in Hayward, *The Age of Reagan*, p. 437.

52. Richard Cheney, Memo, November 13, 1975, Box 1, Richard Cheney Papers, Gerald Ford Presidential Library, Ann Arbor, Michigan.

53. Foster Chanock, "Key Issues Difference," June 1976, Box 1, Foster Chanock Papers, Gerald Ford Presidential Library.

54. John Ehrman, *The Rise of Neoconservatism: Intellectuals and Foreign Affairs, 1945–1994* (New Haven, 1995), pp. 63–97.

55. The following discussion of the 1976 election relies on Hayward, *The Age of Reagan;* and Craig Shirley, *Reagan's Revolution: The Untold Story of the Campaign That Started It All* (New York, 2005). Also useful for this discussion are Elizabeth Drew, *American Journal: The Events of 1976* (New York, 1976); and Jules Witcover, *Marathon: The Pursuit of the Presidency* (New York, 1977).

56. William Rusher to William Loeb, May 27, 1975, Box 53, William Rusher Papers, Library of Congress, Washington, D.C.

57. Mickey Edwards to Ronald Reagan, March 22, 1975, Ronald Reagan Correspondence, 1975–1979, Ronald Reagan Series (unprocessed), J. Evetts Haley Papers, Eagle Forum Archives, Clayton, Missouri.

58. Both Reston and Osborne are quoted in Hayward, *The Age of Reagan*, p. 455.

59. Barry Goldwater to Efrem Zimbalist, Jr., June 29, 1976, Ronald Reagan Series (unprocessed), Rosalind Kress Haley Collection, Eagle Forum Archives, Clayton, Missouri.

60. Efrem Zimbalist, Jr., to Barry Goldwater, July 15, 1976, Ronald Reagan Series, Rosalind Kress Haley Collection.

61. Quoted in Hayward, *The Age of Reagan*, p. 469.

62. Ibid., pp. 473–477.

63. Quoted in Steven Hayward, *The Age of Reagan*, p. 476.

64. Critchlow, *Phyllis Schlafly and Grassroots Conservatism*, p. 242.

65. Critchlow, *Intended Consequences*, pp. 202–203.

66. Quoted in Hayward, *The Age of Reagan*, p. 503.

6. Forward to the Promised Land

1. See http://uselectionatlas.org.

2. The story is recounted in John Mickethwait and Adrian Woolridge, *The Right Nation: Conservative Power in America* (New York, 2004), p. 83; and James Morone, *Hellfire Nation: The Politics of Sin in American History* (New Haven, 2003).

3. Gary M. Fink, *Prelude to the Presidency: The Political Character and Legislative Leadership Style of Governor Jimmy Carter* (Westport, Conn., 1980), pp. 23–43.

4. For a critical assessment of Carter at the time of his presidency, see Victor Lasky, *Jimmy Carter: The Man and the Myth* (New York, 1979).

5. Quoted in ibid., p. 15. For a sympathetic account of Carter after his presidency, see Douglas Brinkley, *The Unfinished Presidency: Jimmy Carter's Journey to the Nobel Peace Prize* (New York, 1999). Also see Burton I. Kaufman, *The Presidency of James Earl Carter, Jr.* (Lawrence, Kan., 1993).

6. Quoted in Michael Barone, *Our Country: The Shaping of America from Roosevelt to Reagan* (New York, 1990).

7. Godfrey Hodgson, *The Gentleman from New York: Daniel Moynihan* (New York, 2000).

8. Jimmy Carter, *Keeping Faith: Memoirs of a President* (New York, 1982), p. 80; quoted in Sidney M. Milkis, *Political Parties and Constitutional Government: Remaking American Democracy* (Baltimore, 1999), p. 133. Also see Erwin Hargrove, *Jimmy Carter as President: Leadership and the Politics of the Public Good* (Baton Rouge, 1988).

9. Paul H. Nitze, *From Hiroshima to Glasnost: At the Center of Decision, a Memoir* (New York, 1989), pp. 338–341.

10. Ibid., pp. 343–344.

11. Ibid., p. 355.

12. For an informed and judicious assessment of the Carter presidency and the women's movement, see Susan Hartmann, "Feminism and Public Policy," *The Carter Presidency: Policy Choices in the Post–New Deal Era* (Lawrence, Kan., 1998), pp. 224–243. This discussion of the Carter administration draws on Hartmann's essay.

13. For divisions in the Carter administration, see Clark R. Mollenhoff, *The President Who Failed: Carter Out of Control* (New York, 1980), pp. 162–164; Joseph Califano, *Governing America: An Insider's Report from the White House and the Cabinet* (New York, 1981).

14. Carolyn Cole, "Bella Abzug, a Dedicated Activist," *Waterloo Courier,* September 17, 1978; Leslie Bennetts, "The New Bella Abzug: She's Down, but Not Out," *Chicago Tribune,* December 10, 1978; "Bella: An Old Fashioned Woman Removes Her Political Kid Gloves for ERA," *Everett Herald,* March 24, 1978.

15. "Women Exerting a Lot of Energy Says Judy Carter," *Atlanta Journal,* February 22, 1978; Marguerite Sullivan, "Judy Carter on the Campaign Trail for ERA," *Herald News,* November 9, 1977.

16. Paul Scott, "White House's ERA Problem," *The Washington New Intelligence Syndicate,* June 27, 1979; White House, "President's Advisory Committee for Women, Monday, May 14, 1979," *Weekly Compilation of Presidential Documents,* vol. 5:19, pp. 789–843; Jack Germond and Jules Witcover, "Battle for ERA May Be Finished," *Newark Star Ledger,* December 9, 1978.

17. For a view that Carter was not consistent in his support of women, see Emily

Walker Cook, "Women White House Advisers in the Carter Administration: Presidential Stalwarts or Feminist Advocates?" (Ph.D. diss., Vanderbilt University, 1995); and Mary Frances Berry, *Why ERA Failed: Politics, Women's Rights, and the Amending Process of the Constitution* (Bloomington, Ind., 1986).

18. "Carter Signs Extension of ERA," *Chicago Tribune,* October 21, 1979, Carter Folder, ERA Files, East Forum Archives.

19. Nadine Brozan, "Smeal and Goldsmith Fight for Leadership of NOW," *New York Times,* June 8, 1985, p. A13; and "NOW Delegates Cheer Call for Unity amid Leadership Struggle," *The Dallas Morning News,* July 21, 1988, p. 4A.

20. John Leonard, "Books of the Times," *New York Times,* October 30, 1981.

21. "The New Congress: A Small Step to the Right," *Congressional Quarterly Almanac* (1978), pp. 3B–20B. The following discussion of the 1978 elections draws from this report, as well as from Barone, *Our Country,* pp. 576–577.

22. Figures are cited in Robert Kuttner, *Revolt of the Haves: Tax Rebellions and Hard Times* (New York, 1980), p. 55.

23. Ibid., p. 69. For an argument that the Jarvis-Gann initiative, and other tax-reduction initiatives, were manipulated by elite political organizations, see Daniel A. Smith, *Tax Crusades and the Politics of Direct Democracy* (London, 1998), especially pp. 8–9, 30–33.

24. Kuttner, *Revolt of the Haves,* pp. 276–277.

25. Robert S. Allen, "Panama Faces Internal Turmoil," *Human Events,* August 21, 1971, p. 6.

26. Norman Podhoretz, "The Present Danger," *Commentary* (March, 1980), p. 33, quoted in Gary Dorrien, *The Neoconservative Mind: Politics, Culture, and the War of Ideology* (Philadelphia, 1993), p. 167.

27. Nitze, *From Hiroshima to Glasnost,* pp. 351–353; and Patrick Glynn, *Closing Pandora's Box: Arms Races, Arms Control, and the History of the Cold War* (New York, 1992), pp. 268–272.

28. Quoted in John Ehrman, *The Rise of Neo-Conservatism: Intellectuals and Foreign Affairs, 1945–1994* (New Haven, 1995), p. 112; and Stephan Halper and Jonathan Clarke, *America Alone: The Neo-Conservatives and the Global Order* (New York, 2005).

29. Limitations of SALT II are described by Nitze, *From Hiroshima to Glasnost,* p. 362.

30. Glynn, *Closing Pandora's Box,* pp. 287–289.

31. Andrew E. Busch, *Reagan's Victory: The Presidential Election of 1980 and the Rise of the Right* (Lawrence, Kan., 2005).

32. Barone, *Our Country,* pp. 586–588.

33. Ibid., p. 587.

34. David Farber, *Taken Hostage: The Iran Hostage Crisis and America's First Encounter with Radical Islam* (Princeton, 2006); and Mark Bowden, *Guests of the Ayatollah: The First Battle in America's War with Militant Islam* (New York, 2006).

35. Jeff Greenfield, *The Real Campaign: How the Media Missed the Story of the 1980 Campaign* (New York, 1982), p. 39.

36. Quoted in Lou Cannon, *President Reagan: The Role of a Lifetime* (New York, 1991), p. 46. This discussion of the 1980 campaign draws from Cannon's full-length biography of Reagan.

37. Greenfield, *The Real Campaign*.

38. Ibid., p. 196.

39. Quoted in ibid., p. 159. Greenfield offers an insightful analysis of the platform and the party's shift to the ideological right.

40. Quotations and concepts for this discussion of the Republican Party platform are drawn from Hayward, *The Age of Reagan*, pp. 674–675. Also see Harvey C. Mansfield, Jr., *American's Constitutional Soul* (Baltimore, 1991).

41. See Greenfield, *The Real Campaign*, p. 172.

42. Quotations from Reagan's speech are found in ibid., pp. 172–175.

43. Matthew C. Moen, "From Revolution to Evolution: The Changing Nature of the Christian Right," *Sociology of Religion* (1994), pp. 345–357. There is a huge literature on the Christian Right. Useful are Clyde Wilcox, *God's Warriors: The Christian Right in Twentieth-Century America* (Baltimore, 1991); Matthew Moen, *The Transformation of the Christian Right* (Tuscaloosa, Ala., 1992); Kenneth Wald, *Religion and Politics in the United States* (New York, 2nd ed., 1992); and Ted Jelen, *The Political Mobilization of Religious Beliefs* (Boulder, Colo., 1991);

44. Moen, "From Revolution to Evolution," p. 349.

45. Howell Raines, "Reagan Backs Evangelicals in Their Political Activities," *New York Times,* August 23, 1980, p. B9, quoted in L. Edward Hicks, *"Sometimes in the Wrong, but Never in Doubt": George S. Benson and the Education of the New Religious Right* (Knoxville, Tennessee, 1994), p. ix.

46. Quotations from Reagan, Harris, Young, and Coretta Scott King are found in Hayward, *The Age of Reagan*, pp. 695–697.

47. Quotations from *National Review* and Reagan's quip on economic recovery are found in Hayward, *The Age of Reagan*, pp. 683 and 685, respectively. Hayward provides a concise summary of these gaffes on pp. 677–699.

48. Hayward, *The Age of Reagan*, pp. 683–690.

49. "Reagan Buries Carter in a Landslide," *Congressional Record Almanac,* XXXVI (1980), pp. 3B–7B. The following discussion of the 1980 election relies on this analysis.

50. This argument is spelled out in great quantitative detail in Byron E. Shafer and Richard Johnston, *The End of Southern Exceptionalism: Class, Race, and Partisan Change in the Postwar South* (Cambridge, Mass., 2006).

51. "GOP Wins Senate Control for First Time in Twenty-eight Years," *Congressional Quarterly Almanac* (1980), pp. 7B–13B. Polling data also suggested that voters felt the need for a change.

7. The Reagan Decade

1. Ronald Reagan, "Remarks at the American Conservative Union," March 8, 1985, *Ronald Reagan Papers, 1985*.

2. Sidney M. Milkis and Jesse H. Rhodes, "George W. Bush, the Republican Party, and the 'New' American Party System" (unpublished paper).

3. For overviews of the Reagan presidency, see Christopher M. Gray, "Ronald W. Reagan," *Encyclopedia of American History*, vol. 10, ed. Gary Nash and Donald T. Critchlow (New York, 2003), pp. 258–261; W. Elliot Brownlee and Hugh Davis Graham, eds., *The Reagan Presidency: Pragmatic Conservatism and Its Legacies* (Lawrence, Kan., 2004); Larry Berman, ed., *Looking Back on the Reagan Presidency* (Baltimore, 1990); John Hogan, *The Reagan Years* (Manchester, England, 1990); Stephen Skowronek, *The Politics Presidents Make: Leadership from John Adams to George Bush* (Cambridge, 1993); and Dick M. Carpenter, "Ronald Reagan and the Redefinition of the 'Education President,'" *Texas Education Review* (Winter, 2003–2004), www.Texaseducationreview.com.

4. This point is made by the political historian Sidney Milkis in *Political Parties and Constitutional Government* (Baltimore, 1999), p. 135. Milkis's views of the administrative state inform much of this chapter.

5. Although some historians characterize Reagan as shallow and unreflective, recent archival evidence shows him to be a highly principled and confident thinker who eloquently recorded his views in handwritten letters and a daily diary. Robert M. Collins, *Transforming America: Politics and Culture in the Reagan Years* (New York, 2007). Especially useful is Kiron Skinner, Annelise Anderson, and Martin Anderson, eds., *Reagan in His Own Hand* (New York, 2001), and *Reagan: A Life in Letters* (New York, 2003). For a contrary view, see Lewis L. Gould, *The Modern American Presidency* (Lawrence, 2003), pp. 191–192.

6. Ronald Reagan to Clymer L. Wright, Jr., May 18, 1982, *Reagan: A Life in Letters*, ed. Skinner, Anderson, and Anderson (New York, 2003), p. 555.

7. For the Baker appointment, see Lou Cannon, *President Reagan: The Role of a Lifetime* (New York, 2001), pp. 47–49. Archival records at the Reagan Presidential Library in Simi, California, offer the best insight into the efficiency of the administration, but participants in the Reagan administration have left a useful record for historians. See Peggy Noonan, *What I Saw at the Revolution: A Political Life in the Reagan Era* (New York, 1990); Michael Deaver, *Behind the Scenes* (New York, 1987); Richard Darman, *Who's in Control? Polar Politics and the Sensible Center* (New York, 1987); David Stockman, *The Triumph of Politics: How the Reagan Revolution Failed* (New York, 1986); Donald Regan, *For the Record: From Wall Street to Washington* (New York, 1988); and Martin Anderson, *Revolution* (Palo Alto, 1990).

8. Thomas W. Evans, *The Education of Ronald Reagan: The General Electric Years and the Untold Story of His Conversion to Conservatism* (New York, 2007).

9. Ronald Reagan, "Inaugural Address of Ronald Reagan, January 20, 1981," *Presidential Papers of Ronald Reagan* (Washington, D.C., 1982), quoted in Milkis, *Political Parties and Constitutional Government*, p. 142.

10. This discussion of Reagan's legislative record draws from John Ehrman, *The Eighties: America in the Age of Reagan* (New Haven, 2005).

11. Milkis, *Political Parties and Constitutional Government*, p. 149.

12. A popular account of the savings and loan crisis is found in Martin Mayer,

The Greatest-Ever Bank Robbery: The Collapse of the Savings and Loan Industry (New York, 1990). More useful is Jonathan E. Gray, *Financial Deregulation and the Savings and Loan Crisis* (New York, 1988).

13. This discussion of Reagan and the administrative state draws heavily on Milkis, *Political Parties and Constitutional Government,* pp. 103–137.

14. Ibid., p. 125.

15. M. R. Berube, *American Presidents and Education* (New York, 1991); Maris Vinovsis, "*A Nation at Risk* and the 'Crisis' in Education in the Mid-1980s," in *The Road to Charlottesville: The 1989 Education Summit* (Washington, D.C., 1999); and Gareth Davies, *See Government Grow: Education Policy from Johnson to Reagan* (Lawrence, Kans., 2007).

16. Ronald Reagan, "Remarks at the Annual Convention of the National Association of Evangelicals in Orlando, Florida," March 8, 1983, *Presidential Papers of Ronald Reagan* (Washington, D.C., 1983).

17. A highly informative synthesis of Reagan's defense policies is found in Collins, *Transforming America.* Also see Peter Schweizer, *Reagan's War: The Epic Story of His Forty-Year Struggle and Final Triumph over Communism* (New York, 2002); also useful are Robert M. Gates, *The Ultimate Insider's Story of Five Presidents and How They Won the Cold War* (New York, 1996); and Peter W. Rodman, *More Precious Than Peace: The Cold War and the Struggle for the Third World* (New York, 1994). Critical accounts of Reagan can be found in Derek Leebaert, *The Fifty-Year Wound: The True Price of America's Cold War Victory* (New York, 1990); and Frances FitzGerald, *Way out There in the Blue: Reagan, Star Wars, and the End of the Cold War* (New York, 2000).

18. Adam M. Garfinkle, *The Politics of the Nuclear Freeze* (Philadelphia, 1984).

19. Ronald Reagan, *An American Life* (New York, 1990). Also see Donald R. Baucom, *The Origins of SDI, 1944–1983* (Lawrence, Kan., 1992); and Edward Teller, *Memoirs: A Twentieth-Century Journey in Science and Politics* (Cambridge, 2001).

20. Angelo Cordevilla, *Informing Statecraft: Intelligence for a New Century* (New York, 1992).

21. An excellent study of Reagan's anti-Communist policies in developing nations is found in Rodman, *More Precious Than Peace.*

22. A considerable literature about United States involvement in Nicaragua has developed. A useful study is Robert Kagan, *A Twilight Struggle: Power and Nicaragua, 1977–1990* (New York, 1966). Opposition to United States policy is discussed by Christian Smith, *Resisting Reagan: The United States Central American Peace Movement* (Chicago, 1996).

23. See Edward Keynes, *The Court vs. Congress: Prayer, Busing and Abortion* (Durham, N.C., 1989); and Donald T. Critchlow, "Mobilizing Women: The 'Social' Issues," in W. Elliot Brownlee and Hugh Davis Graham, eds., *The Reagan Presidency: Pragmatic Conservatism and Its Legacies* (Lawrence, Kan., 2003), pp. 293–326.

24. Morton C. Blackwell to Elizabeth Dole, August 20, 1982, Abortion Files, Box

1, Elizabeth Dole Papers, Ronald Reagan Library, quoted in Critchlow, "Mobilizing Women," p. 303.

25. For a discussion of the politics of the pro-life amendments, see Critchlow, "Mobilizing Women."

26. Tanya Melich, *The Republican War against Women: An Insider's Report from behind the Lines* (New York, 1998); Karen O'Connor, *No Neutral Ground? Abortion Politics in an Age of Absolutes* (Boulder, Colo., 1996).

27. See Donald T. Critchlow, *Intended Consequences: Birth Control, Abortion, and the Federal Government* (New York, 1999).

28. Ronald Reagan, "Conservative Political Action Conference: Remarks at Conference Dinner," March 20, 1981, *Administration of Ronald Reagan, 1981* (Washington, D.C., 1981), pp. 327–328.

29. Paul Gottfried and Thomas Fleming, *The Conservative Movement* (New York, 1992), pp. 71–72. Also see Stephen J. Tonsor, "Why I Too Am Not a Neoconservative," and "Introduction," in Gregory L. Schneider, ed., *Equality, Decadence, and Modernity* (Wilmington, Del., 2005), pp. 231–238 and pp. xvi–xvii.

30. Richard A. Viguerie, "An Open Letter to President Reagan," *Conservative Digest* (July 1982), pp. 46–47.

31. Paul Weyrich, "The White House, the Elections, the Right," *Conservative Digest* (July 1982), p. 45.

32. Ronald Reagan to John Lofton, July 30, 1982; Draft, July 30, 1982, Presidential Handwritten File, Series II, Presidential Records, Box 3, Folder 46, Ronald Reagan Papers, Reagan Library. The author would like to thank Robert Collins for bringing this letter to his attention.

33. Quoted in Michael Barone, *Our Country: The Shaping of America from Roosevelt to Reagan* (New York, 1980), p. 625.

34. An excellent summary of the 1982 election is found in "Lasting Election Effects Likely in House," *Congressional Quarterly Almanac* (Washington, D.C., 1982), pp. 3B–13B.

35. An astute discussion of this dilemma and various responses to the problem is found in Dan Balz and Ronald Brownstein, *Storming the Gates: Protest Politics and the Republican Revival* (New York, 1996), pp. 65–71.

36. Milkis, *Political Parties and Constitutional Government*, p. 157.

37. For the 1984 election, see Elizabeth Drew, *Campaign Journal: The Political Events, 1983–84* (New York, 1984); Jack N. Germond and Jules Witcover, *Wake Us When It's Over: Presidential Politics of 1984* (New York, 1985); and Jane Mayer and Doyle McManus, *Landslide: The Unmaking of the President, 1984–1988* (Boston, 1988).

38. Steven Gillion, *The Democrats' Dilemma: Walter Mondale and the Liberal Legacy* (New York, 1992); and Ronald Radosh, *Divided They Fell: The Demise of the Democratic Party, 1964–1996* (New York, 1992).

39. For congressional elections, see "Democrats Have Net Gain of Two Senate Seats" and "GOP Disappointed with Gains in the Houses," *Congressional Quarterly Almanac* (1984), pp. 7B–15B.

40. The material on Helms is drawn from William D. Snider, *Helms and Hunt: The North Carolina Senate Race, 1984* (Chapel Hill, 1984). See also Ernest Ferguson, *Hard Right: The Rise of Jesse Helms* (New York, 1986).

41. Quoted in Snider, *Helms and Hunt,* p. 61.

42. Ibid., p. 97.

43. Ibid., pp. 179, 199, 173.

44. Ibid., pp. 201–211.

45. One of the great disappointments in the House elections in 1984, and one that sparked anger among Republicans that would stick in their craw for many years, was the seating of Democratic incumbent Frank McCloskey in Indiana's 8th District over the certified winner, Republican Richard D. McIntyre. The Democratic-controlled Congress accepted McCloskey's claim that he had won the seat in a recount. Many Republicans were angered by what they considered a raw power grab on the part of the Democrats. This loss was especially bitter because Daniel B. Crane, a conservative Republican, lost his seat in Illinois's 19th District, after being censured in a sex scandal involving a female congressional page. William D. Snider, *Helms and Hunt,* p. 210.

46. An excellent account of tax reform under Reagan is Jeffrey Birnbaum and Alan Murray, *Showdown at Gucci Gulch: Lawmakers, Lobbyists, and the Unlikely Triumph of Tax Reform* (New York, 1987); and also Ehrman, *The Eighties,* pp. 133–136; and Collins, *Transforming America,* pp. 71–80.

47. Given Reagan's heated rhetoric in his first term, his second-term focus on arms reduction led some conservatives at the time, and later some historians, to perceive a radical shift in his foreign policy approach in his second term. For example, see Beth A. Fischer, "Reagan and the Soviets: Winning the Cold War?" in Brownlee and Hugh Graham, *The Reagan Presidency.* Also see Derek Leebaert, *The Fifty-Year Wound: The True Price of America's Cold War Victory* (Boston, 2002). For the argument that Reagan pursued a consistent policy in his presidency, see Schweizer, *Reagan's War.* Especially useful on Reagan's foreign policy is Gates, *From the Shadows.*

48. Quoted in Robert M. Collins, "Transforming America" (manuscript), pp. 460–461.

49. For an understanding of Iran-Contra in a larger context, see Milkis, *Political Parties and Constitutional Government,* pp. 148–149. For a defense of Reagan's policies, see Rodman, *More Precious Than Peace;* and for a critical view, see Theodore Draper, *A Very Thin Line: The Iran-Contra Affair* (New York, 1991).

50. Hugh Sidey, "The Establishment Steps In," *Time,* March 23, 1987, p. 26.

51. Chip Berlet, "Populist Party, LaRouchian, and Other Neo-Fascist Overtures to Progressives, and Why They Must Be Rejected," Political Research Associates website, www.publiceye.org.

52. Leslie Cockburn, *Out of Control: The Story of the Reagan Administration's Secret War in Nicaragua, the Illegal Arms Pipeline, and the Contra Drug Connection* (New York, 1987).

53. For example, see Barbara Ehrenreich, "Is the Middle Class Doomed?" *New York Times Magazine,* September 7, 1986.

54. These figures are derived from the *New York Times Index* and the *Readers Guide to Periodical Literature* from 1981 through 1988. Specifically, the number of articles on the homeless in the *New York Times* is 1981: 60; 1982: 97; 1983: 96; 1984: 157; 1985: 234; 1986: 291; 1987: 347; and 1988: 303. The number of magazine articles is 1981: 4; 1982: 15; 1983: 24; 1984: 35; 1985: 33; 1986: 53; 1987: 60; and 1988: 65.

55. Center for Media and Public Affairs, "The Visible Poor: Media Coverage of the Homeless, 1986–1989," *Media Monitor* (March 1989).

56. Jonathan Kozol, *Rachel and Her Children: Homeless Families in America* (New York, 1987). Most of the stories were heartbreaking, but Hollywood gave the problem a comedic twist in the highly successful 1983 film *Trading Places,* starring Dan Aykroyd and Eddie Murphy. The film told the story of a yuppie, uncaring stockbroker (Dan Aykroyd) who finds himself trading places with a homeless African-American man when two owners of a Wall Street firm test a social theory that anybody can be homeless in America. Of course, the message of the film is that anyone can become homeless in America, and many did in this decade of the super-rich and the very poor.

57. Christopher Jencks, *Rethinking Social Policy: Race, Poverty, and the Underclass* (Cambridge, 1992), and *The Homeless* (Cambridge, 1994).

58. For an analysis of these data, see Ehrman, *The Eighties,* pp. 119–121.

59. These figures are drawn from Ehrman, *The Eighties,* pp. 120–127.

60. Patrick Buchanan, "Nature's Retribution," *Washington Times,* May 29, 1983. In an op-ed piece, William F. Buckley, Jr., suggested that public identification of HIV carriers might be warranted in the future: "Crucial Steps in Combating the AIDS Epidemic: Identify All the Carriers," *New York Times,* March 18, 1986. Activist responses to the AIDS epidemic and the Reagan administration are found in Randy Shilts, *And the Band Played On: Politics, People, and the AIDS Epidemic* (New York, 1983).

61. For a contrary view, see Didi Herman, *The Antigay Agenda: Orthodox Vision and the Christian Right* (Chicago, 1997).

62. William E. Schmidt, "Mrs. Heckler Lists Added AIDS Funds," *New York Times,* June 15, 1983, p. A:18.

63. Judi Buckalew to Faith Ryan Whittlesey, "AIDS Meeting on Tuesday, August 2, 1983," Faith Whittlesey Papers, Box 1, Ronald Reagan Presidential Library.

64. Howard Phillips to Margaret M. Heckler, August 22, 1983, Faith Whittlesey Papers, Box 1, Ronald Reagan Presidential Library.

65. Eagle Forum, "The ERA–Gay Rights Connection" (1979), Faith Whittlesey Papers, Box 1, Ronald Reagan Presidential Library.

66. Edmund Morris, *Dutch: A Memoir of Ronald Reagan* (New York, 1999), p. 457.

67. Ronald Reagan, "The President's News Conference," September 17, 1983, II:1103–1110; "Remarks to Employees of the Department of Health and Human Services," February 5, I:142–143; "Message to the Congress on America's Agenda for the Future," February 6, 1986, I:149–163; "Interview with Eleanor Clift, Jack

Nelson, and Joel Havemann," June 23, 1986, I:825–832; "Message to the Congress on 'A Quest for Excellence,'" January 27, 1987, I:61–79; "Informal Exchange with Reporters in Columbia, Missouri," March 26, 1987, I:283–284; "Remarks Announcing the AIDS Research Patent Rights Agreement between France and the United States," March 31, 1987, I:308–309; "Toasts at the State Dinner for Prime Minister Jacques Chirac of France," March 31, 1987, I:312–314; "Informal Exchange with Reporters," April 1, 1987, I:314–315; "Remarks at a Luncheon for Members of the College of Physicians in Philadelphia, Pennsylvania," April 1, 1987, I:317–321; "Interview with White House Newspaper Correspondents," April 28, 1987, I:424–430; "Statement on the Establishment of a National Commission on AIDS," May 4, 1987, I:463; "Remarks at the American Foundation for AIDS Research Awards Dinner," May 31, 1987, I:584–587; "Message to the Congress Transmitting the Annual Report on International Activities in Science and Technology," June 17, 1987, I:675–678; "Executive Order 12601—Presidential Commission on the Human Immunodeficiency Virus Epidemic," June 24, 1987, I: 717–18; "Executive Order 12603—Presidential Commission on the Human Immunodeficiency Virus Epidemic," July 16, 1987, II:834; "Remarks at a Panel Discussion on AIDS Awareness and Prevention Month, 1987," September 29, 1987, II:1097–1098; "The President's News Conference," October 22, 1987, II:1218–1225; "1988 Legislative and Administrative Message: A Union of Individuals," January 25, 1988, I:91–121; "Statement on the Report of the Presidential Commission on the Human Immunodeficiency Virus Epidemic," June 17, 1988, I:844–845; "Statement to Announce a Human Immunodeficiency Virus Epidemic," August 5, 1988, II: 1027–1030; "Message to the Congress on the Human Immunodeficiency Virus Epidemic Action Plan," August 5, 1988, II:1219–1226; "Proclamation 5892—National AIDS Awareness and Prevention Month, 1988," October 28, 1988, II:1415–1416; "Letter to the Speaker of the House of Representatives and the President of the Senate Transmitting the Fiscal Year 1990 Budget," January 9, 1989, II:1693–1701, *Public Papers of President Ronald Reagan, 1986* (Washington, D.C., 1981–1989).

68. This estimate is based on a Congressional Research Service report: Judith A. Johnson, *AIDS Funding for Federal Government Programs: FY1981–FY1999* (Washington, D.C.: Congressional Research Service, 1996A). Also see Deroy Murdock, "Anti-Gay Gipper," *National Review Online*, December 3, 2003.

69. Ronald Reagan, "Remarks to Administration Officials on Domestic Policy," December 13, 1988, *Papers of President Ronald Reagan* (Washington, D.C., 1989); also quoted in Milkis, *Political Parties and Constitutional Government*, p. 143.

8. Democrats Rebound

1. This section on the 1988 election draws from Herbert S. Parmet, *George Bush: The Life of a Lone Star Yankee* (New York, 1997), pp. 310–356; Jack W. Germond and Jules Witcover, *Whose Broad Stripes and Bright Stars: The Trivial Pursuit of the Presidency, 1988* (New York, 1988); Elizabeth Drew, *Election Journal: Political Events of 1987–1988* (New York, 1989); and Peter Goldman and Tom Mathews, *The Quest for the Presidency, 1988* (New York, 1989).

2. Dan Balz and Ronald Brownstein, *Storming the Gates: Protest Politics and the Republican Revival* (New York, 1996), p. 15.

3. Michael Barone and Grant Ujifusa, *The Almanac of American Politics 1990* (Washington, D.C., 1990), pp. 732–733.

4. Quoted in Drew, *Election Journal,* p. 145.

5. For the Democratic side of the primary see Drew, *Election Journal.*

6. Quoted in Parmet, *George Bush,* p. 341.

7. Ibid., p. 341.

8. Ibid., p. 350.

9. Robert James Bidinotto, "Getting Away with Murder," *Reader's Digest* (July 1988), pp. 1–7. Also see Germond and Witcover, *Whose Broad Stripes and Bright Stars,* pp. 92, 157–163; and Donald T. Critchlow, *Phyllis Schlafly and Grassroots Conservatism* (Princeton, N.J., 2005), pp. 292–295.

10. "Bush Victory Fits 20-Year Presidential Pattern," *Congressional Quarterly Almanac* (1988), 44, pp. 3A–6A.

11. "Democrats Tighten Senate Hold by One Seat," and "St. Germain Out, but Incumbents Still Strong," *Congressional Quarterly* (1988), pp. 8–13 and 14–20.

12. Parmet, *George Bush,* pp. 360–361, quotation p. 361.

13. Ibid., p. 362.

14. Paul Notley, "New Criterion, 1982–," *The Conservative Press in Twentieth-Century America,* ed. Ronald Lora and William Henry Longton (Westport, Conn., 1999), pp. 605–612.

15. John Frohnmeyer, *Leaving Town Alive: Confessions of an Arts Warrior* (New York, 1993); and John Podhoretz, *Hell of a Ride: Backstage at the White House Follies, 1988–1993* (New York, 1993), pp. 168–172.

16. Podhoretz, *Hell of a Ride,* p. 42.

17. Quoted in Dan Balz and Ronald Brownstein, *Storming the Gates of Heaven: Protest Politics and the Republican Revival* (New York, 1996), p. 133.

18. Parmet, *George Bush,* pp. 400–401.

19. For a forceful critique of Bush's foreign policy toward Beijing see James Mann, *About Face: A History of America's Curious Relationship with China from Nixon to Clinton* (New York, 1999).

20. Lawrence Freedman and Efraim Karsh, *The Gulf Conflict, 1990–1991* (Princeton, N.J., 1993); and Aharon Zorea, "George H. W. Bush," *Encyclopedia of American History,* X, ed. Donald T. Critchlow and Gary Nash (New York, 2003), pp. 44–46.

21. Herbert Parmet details the tax agreement in *George Bush,* pp. 375–383.

22. Ibid., pp. 434–435.

23. George H. W. Bush diaries, July 24 and 31, August 11, 1990, Office of George Bush, quoted in Parmet, *George Bush,* pp. 440nn.86, errata? 87, 548.

24. Scott Douglas Gerber, *First Principles: The Jurisprudence of Clarence Thomas* (New York, 1999); and Andrew Peyton Thomas, *Clarence Thomas: A Biography* (New York, 2001).

25. Patrick J. Buchanan, "1992 Republican National Convention Speech," August 17, 1992, www.buchanan.org.

26. Geoffrey Layman, *The Great Divide: Religious and Cultural Conflict in American Party Politics* (New York, 2001), pp. 100–108.

27. Quoted in Balz and Brownstein, *Storming the Gates,* p. 147.

28. "Democrats Reclaim Electoral College," "Women, Minorities Join Senate," and "Wave of Diversity Spared Many Incumbents," *Congressional Quarterly* (1992), pp. 3A–7A, 8A–14A, and 15A–29A, respectively. Also see Drew, *Election Journal.*

29. "Democrats Reclaim Electoral College," p. 6A.

30. Rich Lowry, *Legacy: Paying the Price for the Clinton Years* (Washington, D.C., 2003), p. 124.

31. Ibid., p. 5.

32. Sidney M. Milkis, *Political Parties and Constitutional Government: Remaking American Democracy* (Baltimore, 1999), p. 161.

33. John Micklethwait and Adrian Wooldridge, *The Right Nation: Conservative Power in America* (New York, 2004), pp. 16–17.

34. Quoted in Lowry, *Legacy* (New York, 2003), p. 110; Hillary Clinton, *Living History,* (New York, 2003), pp. 248–249.

35. David Brock, *Blinded by the Right: The Conscience of an Ex-Conservative* (New York, 2002).

36. Clinton's difficulties with Democrats in Congress are detailed in Major Garrett, *The Enduring Revolution: How the Contract with America Continues to Shape the Nation* (New York, 2005); William C. Berman, *From Center to the Edge: The Politics and Policies of the Clinton Presidency* (Lantham, Md., 2001); and Lowry, *Legacy.*

37. In many ways, Gingrich was an unlikely leader in this revolution. Initially, he considered himself a Rockefeller Republican. He was well educated, having received an undergraduate degree from Emory University in 1965 and a master's and doctorate from Tulane University in 1971. Throughout the 1970s he taught environmental studies and history at West Georgia College, where he established a reputation as an outstanding lecturer and local activist in the Republican Party. He gradually moved to the right politically. He was an articulate, ambitious firebrand. Exuberant in his plans for a Republican takeover of the House, Gingrich was often dismissed by the more moderate Republican leadership. He attracted followers among younger Republican members who were tired of the condescending arrogance shown by the Democrats across the aisle, while their Republican elders continued to speak of the need for bipartisanship.

38. In *The Enduring Revolution,* Major Garrett provides an excellent account of the Republican Revolution, though he downplays the importance of Gingrich and places much of the success on other key figures, including Dick Armey, Tom DeLay, Bob Walker, and Bill Paxon. Also important are inside accounts of the Clinton presidency, including David Gergen, *Eyewitness to Power: The Essence of Leadership, Nixon to Clinton* (New York, 2000); Dick Morris, *Behind the Oval Office: Winning the Presidency in the Nineties* (New York, 1997); Robert Reich, *Locked in the Cabinet* (New York, 1997); and George Stephanopoulos, *All Too Human: A Political Ed-*

ucation (New York, 1999). Also useful is Bob Woodward, *The Agenda: Inside the Clinton White House* (New York, 1994).

39. Garrett, *The Enduring Revolution,* p. 90.

40. The importance of the 1994 election is discussed by Milkis, *Political Parties and Constitutional Government,* pp. 163–164.

41. Quoted in Earl Black and Merle Black, *The Rise of Southern Republicanism* (Cambridge, Mass., 2002), p. 7.

42. Garrett, *The Enduring Revolution,* pp. 10–32.

43. There is an extensive literature on welfare reform in the Clinton years, but a good summary of the legislative battle is found in Balz and Brownstein, *Storming the Gates,* pp. 89–91; and Garrett, *Contract with America,* pp. 131–150.

44. Quoted in Balz and Brownstein, *Storming the Gates,* p. 3.

45. Hitchens later broke with the hardline Left over America's military intervention in Iraq following the September 11 attacks. Quoted in Christopher Hitchens, *No One Left to Lie To: The Triangulations of William Jefferson Clinton* (London, 1999), p. 64.

46. Layman, *The Great Divide,* p. 109.

47. "Voters Hand Clinton a Second Term," *Congressional Quarterly Almanac* (1996), 52, pp. 13–18.

48. Although Hsia faced up to five years in prison, U.S. Federal Judge Paul Friedman handed her ninety days of home detention, three years of probation, and a fine of $5,300. This sentence caused a buzz in conservative circles when it was reported by the columnist Michelle Malkin: "The Woman Who Helped Launder Al Gore's Buddhist Temple Money," *Jewish World Review,* February 12, 2002, www.Jewishworldreview.com.

49. The partisan nature of the impeachment is reflected in Peter Baker, *The Breach: Inside the Impeachment and Trial of William Jefferson Clinton* (New York, 2000); Joe Klein, *The Natural: The Misunderstood Presidency of Bill Clinton* (New York, 2002); Sidney Blumenthal, *The Clinton Wars* (New York, 2003); Michael Isikoff, *Uncovering Clinton: A Reporter's Story* (New York, 1999); Joe Conason and Gene Lyons, *The Hunting of the President: The Ten-Year Campaign to Destroy Bill and Hillary Clinton* (New York, 2000); Barbara Olson, *Hell to Pay: The Unfolding Story of Hillary Rodham Clinton* (Washington, D.C., 1999); Edward Timperlake and William C. Triplett II, *Year of the Rat: How Bill Clinton Compromised U.S. Security to Chinese Cash* (Washington, D.C., 1998); and Susan Schmidt and Michael Weissikopf, *Truth at Any Cost: Ken Starr and the Unmaking of Bill Clinton* (New York, 2000). Important in this entire discussion of impeachment is Kenneth Starr, *The Starr Report* (New York, 1998).

9. Americans Divided

1. This chapter's discussion of the Bush presidency is guided by Sidney M. Milkis and Jesse H. Rhodes, "George W. Bush, the Republican Party, and the 'New' American Party System" (unpublished, 2006).

2. Figures cited are from Arthur H. Miller and Thomas F. Klobucar, "The Role of Issues in the 2000 U.S. Presidential Election," *Presidential Studies Quarterly,* 33 (March 2003), pp. 101–123.

3. In this survey, 17 percent of respondents listed education, 16 percent general social welfare, 12 percent medical care, and 12 percent morality. Ibid., pp. 103, 105, 110, and 113.

4. Ibid., pp. 108–109.

5. "U.S. Vice President Al Gore Delivers Acceptance Speech at Democratic National Convention," August 17, 2000, www.cnn.com/Election/2000/conventions/democratic/transcripts/gore. All subsequent quotations from Gore's acceptance speech are from this source.

6. Matthew J. Frank, "Election 2000 Revisited," *Presidential Studies Quarterly,* 33, 1 (March 2003), pp. 238–242. For a conservative perspective on the decision see Richard A. Posner, *Breaking the Deadlock: The 2000 Election, the Constitution, and the Courts* (Princeton, N.J., 2001). Also see Howard Gilman, *The Votes That Counted: How the Court Decided the 2000 Presidential Election* (Chicago, 2001); and Karen Foestel, "Right Sees an End to Its Wait," *Congressional Quarterly Weekly,* December 16, 2000, pp. 2852–2856.

7. John C. Green et al., "Faith in the Vote: Religiosity and the Presidential Election," *The Public Perspective,* 12, 2 (March–April 2001), pp. 33–35; Gertrude Himmelfarb, "Religion in the 2000 Election," *The Public Interest,* 143 (Spring 2001), pp. 20–26.

8. These figures are drawn from Todd Breyfogle, "Some Paradoxes of Religion in the 2000 Presidential Election," *Reviews in Religion and Theology,* 8, 5 (2001), pp. 543–547.

9. Mark D. Regnerus et al., "Voting with the Christian Right: Contextual and Individual Patterns of Electoral Influence," *Social Forces,* 7, 4 (June 1999), pp. 1375–1401. Also see James Guth et al., "Political Activity of Evangelical Clergy in the Election of 2000: A Case Study of Five Denominations," *Journal for the Scientific Study of Religion,* 42, 4 (December 2003), pp. 501–514.

10. A negative, partisan account of Karl Rove and the Bush presidential campaign is found in James Moore and Wayne Slater, *Bush's Brain: How Karl Rove Made George W. Bush President* (Hoboken, N.J., 2003), pp. 129–130.

11. Quoted in David S. Broder, "Long Road to Reform," *Washington Post,* December 17, 2001.

12. This account of the education bill draws heavily from ibid.

13. Bob Woodward, *Bush at War* (New York, 2002), pp. 83–91. Also see Michael R. Gordon and Bernard Trainor, *Cobra II: The Inside Story of the Invasion and Occupation of Iraq* (New York, 2006); James Mann, *The Rise of the Vulcans: The History of Bush's War Cabinet* (New York, 2004).

14. Chester E. Finn, Jr., "Leaving Education Reform Behind," *The Weekly Standard,* January 1, 2002, http://www.weeklystandard.com.

15. Gary C. Jacobson, "Terror, Terrain, and Turnout: Explaining the 2002 Elections," *Political Science Quarterly,* 118, 1 (2003), pp. 1–22. Polling of the Bush presidency is discussed on p. 5.

16. Milkis and Rhodes, "George W. Bush, the Republican Party, and the 'New' American Party System," pp. 24–25.

17. James Carney and John Dickerson, "W. and the 'Boy Genius,'" *Time*, November 11, 2002, pp. 41–45; Howard Fineman, "How Bush Did It," *Newsweek*, November 11, 2002, pp. 29–31.

18. Quoted in Rebecca Adams, "Georgia Republicans Energized by 'Friend to Friend' Campaigns," *Congressional Quarterly Weekly*, November 9, 2002, p. 2892. Turnout is also discussed in great detail by Jacobson, "Terror, Terrain, and Turnout," pp. 15–16.

19. David Nather, "Still-Thin Edge Leaves GOP with Cautious Mandate," *Congressional Quarterly Weekly*, November 9, 2002, pp. 2287–2289. Also see in this special election issue Bob Beneson, "GOP Won Midterm War by Winning Series of Small Battles," p. 2890; Mary Clare Jalonick, "Senate Changes Hands Again," p. 2907; Derek Willis, "Nurturing the GOP Agenda," pp. 2930–2931.

20. Quoted in Nather, "Still-Thin Edge Leaves GOP with a Cautious Mandate," p. 2889.

21. "Text of John Kerry's Acceptance Speech at the Democratic National Convention," *Washington Post*, July 29, 2004, www.washingtonpost.com.

22. These figures are from Milkis and Rhodes, "George W. Bush, the Republican Party, and the 'New' American Party System.".

23. John Micklethwait and Adrian Wooldridge, "Triumph of the Right," *Newark Star Ledger*, November 28, 2004, pp. 1, 4.

24. Quoted in Todd S. Purdum and David D. Kirkpatrick, "Campaign Strategist Is in Position to Consolidate Republican Majority," *New York Times*, November 5, 2004, A19.

25. The importance of moral values in the 2004 election is discussed by David Nather, "Social Conservatives Propel Bush, Republicans to Victory," *Congressional Quarterly Weekly*, November 6, 2004, pp. 2586–2589. See also John C. Green, "Winning Numbers," *The Christian Century*, 121, 24 (November 30, 2004), pp. 8–9. For a contrary point of view, see Adolph Reed, "The 2004 Election in Perspective: The Myth of 'Culture Divide' and the Triumph of Neoliberal Ideology," *American Quarterly*, 57, 1 (2005), pp. 1–15; Gregory L. Giroux, "Effect of 'Moral Values' Voters Exaggerated, Say Analysts," *Congressional Quarterly Weekly*, November 12, 2004, pp. 2688–2689; James Q. Wilson, "Why Did Kerry Lose? (Answer: It Wasn't Values)," *Wall Street Journal*, November 8, 2004; Morris P. Fiorina, *Culture War? The Myth of a Polarized America* (New York, 2005); and Jacob Hacker and Paul Pierson, *Off Center: The Republican Revolution and the Erosion of American Democracy* (New York, 2005).

26. Quoted in Nather, "Social Conservatives Propel Bush, Republicans to Victory," p. 2588. Also see John Cochran, "Religious Right Lays Claim to Big Role in GOP Agenda," *Congressional Quarterly Weekly*, November 13, 2004, pp. 2684–2689.

27. Kate Zernike and John M. Broder, "War? Jobs? No, Character Counted Most to Voters," *New York Times*, November 4, 2004, P1 and P4.

28. The states that approved constitutional amendments banning gay marriage

were Mississippi, Montana, and Oregon, while initiatives banning both gay marriage and civil unions were passed in Arkansas, Utah, Michigan, Ohio, Oklahoma, Kentucky, North Dakota, and, Georgia.

29. James Dao, "Flush with Victory, Grass-Roots Crusade against Same-Sex Marriage Thinks Big," *New York Times,* November 26, 2006, p. 28; Alan Johnson, "State Issue of Constitutional Amendment," *The Columbus Dispatch,* November 2, 2004, p. 1; Alan Johnson, "Gay-Marriage Ban," *The Columbus Dispatch,* October 11, 2004, p. 1; Joe Hallett, "Churches Flexing Political Muscle," *The Columbus Dispatch,* April 11, 2005, p. 1; James Dao, "Movement in the Pews Tries to Jolt Ohio," *New York Times,* March 27, 2005; and Associated Press, "Eleven States Ban Gay Marriage," November 3, 2004.

30. Hallett, "Churches Flexing Political Muscle," p. 1.

31. Michael Uhlmann, "The Right Stuff," *Claremont Review of Books* (Summer 2005), p. 38.

32. The use of "incremental conservatism" is drawn from Daniel Casse, "What Is a Bush Republican?" *Commentary* (March 2006), pp. 39–44.

33. Bruce Bartlett, *Impostor: How George W. Bush Bankrupted America and Betrayed the Reagan Legacy* (New York, 2006); Matthew Continetti, *The K Street Gang: A Rise and Fall of the Republican Machine* (New York, 2006). A defense of Bush from a conservative perspective is offered by Jonah Goldberg, "Living in the Real World," *National Review,* March 22, 2006, pp. 16–18.

34. Isaiah J. Poole, "Two Steps Up, One Step Down," *Congressional Quarterly Weekly,* January 9, 2006, pp. 80–84 and pp. 114–115; and "Legislative Background: Recent Action on Judicial Nominees," *Congressional Digest* (May 2005).

35. Seth Stern and Keith Perine, "Defending Miers on All Sides," *Congressional Weekly,* October 10, 2005, pp. 2720–2722.

36. Keith Perine and Seth Stern, "Bush Quells Dissent with New Pick," *Congressional Quarterly Weekly,* November 7, 2005, pp. 2984–2986.

37. This argument is articulated in Fiorina et al., *Culture War?;* and Hacker and Pierson, *Off Center.*

38. James Q. Wilson, "Response," *Commentary* (May 2006), pp. 6–8.

39. Vituperation was not new in American politics; indeed, the personal assault on character was far more common and nastier in the nineteenth century, even though the use of sexual scandal was less common than it is today. Mark W. Summers, *Rum, Romanism and Rebellion: The Making of a President, 1884* (Chapel Hill, 2000), and *Party Games: Getting, Keeping and Using Power in the Gilded Age* (Chapel Hill, 2003).

40. Thomas Mann and Norman Ornstein, *The Broken Branch: How Congress Is Failing America and How to Get It Back on Track* (New York, 2006).

41. Survey data are found in PollingReport.com. For a more specific account of Americans' distrust in government, see John R. Hibbing and Elizabeth Theiss-Morse, *Congress as Public Enemy: Public Attitudes toward American Political Institutions* (New York, 1995). Also, useful essays on public confidence in government are found in John R. Hibbing and Elizabeth Theiss-Morse, *What Is It about Governance That Americans Dislike?* (New York, 2001).

42. Hamilton quotation and data are found in Thomas Hargrove and Guildo H. Stempel, "Anti-Government Anger Spurs 9/11 Conspiracy Belief," newsPolls.org.

43. James Kurth, "Iraq: Losing the American Way," *American Conservative*, March 15, 2004, reprinted in Gary Rosen, *The Right War? The Conservative Debate on Iraq* (New York, 2005), pp. 36–48, especially p. 47.

44. Andrew J. Bacevich, "A Time for Reckoning," *American Conservative*, July 19, 2004, reprinted in Rosen, *The Right War?* pp. 96–101.

45. This debate in the Right over the Iraq War is summarized in a defense of Bush's foreign policy in Norman Podhoretz, "Is the Bush Doctrine Dead?" *Commentary* (September 2006), pp. 17–31.

Acknowledgments

Allow me to reverse the typical order of acknowledgments by thanking first my wife, Patricia. She read and commented on innumerable drafts of the manuscript. I did not always accept her advice, and if the past tells us anything, this will be to my detriment.

Next I want to thank my editor at Harvard University Press, Joyce Seltzer. Her reputation as one of the finest editors in publishing is well deserved. Her detailed editing of an early draft of the manuscript made for a better book. She was exacting in her comments, judicious in her editing, and engaging to work with.

During the writing of this book, I kept in mind the sentiments Jonathan Swift expressed in the "Tale of the Tub" (1687). He wrote, "By the assistance of some thinking, and much conversation, he had endeavour'd to strip himself of as many prejudices as he could: I say real ones because, under the notion of prejudices, he knew to what dangerous heights some men had proceeded." I learned much from correspondence and conversation from many friends and colleagues. My good friend Paula Baker provided an interpretative framework for the book, insight into the history of the Republican Party, and good advice on a range of other issues. Her spouse, Steve Thomas, a political scientist, directed me to important literature on political philosophy. I learned much from others knowledgeable on American politics and history, including William Rorabaugh, Gregory Schneider, George Nash, John Schlafly, Irving Gellman, Jonathan Bean, Alan Gallay, and John Carroll.

Saint Louis University granted me a leave of absence to accept a fellowship at the Social Philosophy and Policy Center at Bowling Green State University. The center provided a splendid environment for the research and writing that went into producing the final manuscript. Fred Miller, the executive director of the center and an Aristotelian philosopher, offered intellectual stimulation and encouragement. This book owes much to the associate director of the center, Jeffrey Paul, who directed me to key conservative-libertarian debates and the importance of understanding classical liberalism as the foundation of modern American conservatism. But he did more than this. His views informed the direction of the book and changed my thinking on many other intellectual and historical issues.

Two research assistants deserve acknowledgment. Cindy Stachecki undertook research into voting and polling statistics, biographical information, and media reporting of the AIDS epidemic and the homeless issue in the 1980s and 1990s. She brought diligence and skill to this work. Peter Jaworski, a graduate student in philosophy, assisted in research but, more important, carefully proofread and commented on the entire final manuscript. His understanding of libertarian political thought proved invaluable.

This book benefited from the superb copy-editing of Christine Thorsteinsson and my good friend Liza Forshaw.

A special thanks is due Sidney Milkis, a political scientist whose work on American politics and government informs a central theme of this book, the relationship of conservative politics and the national administrative state. He sent me a lengthy essay on the presidency of George W. Bush, which informs the last two chapters of this book. He is a model of collegiality and intellectual grace.

Finally, I want to acknowledge the many archivists who assisted my research. In writing this book, I drew upon previous archival research in presidential libraries and political collections across the country. This research was supplemented by further archival research in the writing of this book. In particular, I want to thank Deborah Pentecost, archivist at the Eagle Forum Library, for granting me access to the recently acquired

Rosalind Kress-Haley Collection, which contained twelve boxes of Ronald Reagan's presidential campaign materials from 1975 through 1980. In addition, Special Collections at the University of Washington arranged for the C. Montgomery Johnson papers to be copied and sent to me.

Thank you all.

Index